SCIENTISTS IN THE QUEST FOR PEACE

A History of the Pugwash Conferences

Participants in the First Pugwash Conference
1. J. Ogawa 2. Chou Pei-Yuan 3. V. P. Pavlichenko 4. S. Tomonaga 5. C. F. Powell
6. A. M. B. Lacassagne 7. A. V. Topchiev 8. A. M. Kuzin 9. E. Rabinowitch 10. G. Brock Chisholm
11. D. V. Skobeltzyn 12. J. S. Foster 13. C. S. Eaton 14. J. Rotblat 15. H. J. Muller
16. H. Thirring 17. L. Szilard 18. W. Selove 19. E. H. S. Burhop 20. M. L. E. Oliphant
21. M. Danysz

SCIENTISTS IN THE QUEST FOR PEACE

A History of the Pugwash Conferences

J. Rotblat

The MIT Press Cambridge, Massachusetts, and London, England

Copyright © 1972 by J. Rotblat

This book was printed on Mohawk Neotext Offset
by The Colonial Press, Inc.
and bound by The Colonial Press, Inc.
in the United States of America.

All rights reserved. No part of this book may be reproduced in any form
or by any means, electronic or mechanical, including photocopying, record-
ing, or by any information storage and retrieval system, without permission
in writing from the publisher.

Library of Congress Cataloging in Publication Data

Rotblat, Joseph, 1908--
  Scientists in the quest for peace.

  1. Pugwash Conference on Science and World Affairs--
History. I. Title.
Q101.P8R62   327'.172   72-6108
ISBN 0-262-18054-5

The Pugwash Conferences on Science and World Affairs

President
Prof. H. Alfvén

Secretary-General
Prof. J. Rotblat

CONTINUING COMMITTEE

Chairman
Prof. Sir Rudolf Peierls

Members
Prof. E. Amaldi
Acad. L. A. Artsimovitch
Acad. A. T. Balevski
Prof. C. Djerassi
Prof. B. T. Feld
Prof. Patricia Lindop
Prof. O. Maaløe
Acad. I. Málek
Dr. H. Marcovich
Acad. M. D. Millionshchikov
Prof. E. Rabinowitch
Acad. I. Supek
Prof. F. G. Torto
Dr. C. Varsavsky

Central Office
9 Great Russell Mansions
60 Great Russell Street
London, WC1B 3BE, England

Contents

Foreword by H. Alfvén   xiii

Preface   xvii

1   THE BIRTH OF PUGWASH   1

1.1   Early Efforts to Convene an International Conference of Scientists   1

1.2   The Russell-Einstein Manifesto   2

1.3   Plans for a Conference in India   2

1.4   Cyrus Eaton Offers Financial Help   3

1.5   The First Conference: Pugwash, July 7-10, 1957   4

1.6   Significance of the First Pugwash Conference   6

1.7   First Meeting of the Continuing Committee   7

1.8   Further Conferences   8

1.9   Pugwash Questionnaire   8

1.10   The Name of the Movement   9

2   THE ORGANIZATION OF PUGWASH   11

2.1   The Continuing Committee   11

2.2   The Executive Committee   12

2.3   Officers   13

2.4   Central Office   14

2.5   Finance   14

2.6   National Pugwash Groups   15

2.7   Organization of Conferences   16

2.8   Participants   17

2.9   Other Members of the Conference   18

Contents   vii

2.10 Symposia   21

2.11 Contact with Other Organizations   22

3   PUGWASH ACTIVITIES   25

3.1   Conferences   25

3.2   Symposia   26

3.3   Study Groups   28

3.4   Regional Conferences   30

3.5   International Activities of National Pugwash Groups   32

3.6   Special Meetings   33

3.7   Other Activities of the Continuing Committee   34

3.8   Publications   36

4   THE PUGWASH CONFERENCES   37

4.1   Second Conference: Lac Beauport, March 31–April 11, 1958, "The Dangers of the Present Situation, and Ways and Means of Diminishing Them"   37

4.2   Third Conference: Kitzbühel and Vienna, September 14–20, 1958, "Dangers of the Atomic Age and what Scientists Can Do About Them"   38

4.3   Fourth Conference: Baden, June 25–July 4, 1959, "Arms Control and World Security"   41

4.4   Fifth Conference: Pugwash, August 24–29, 1959, "Biological and Chemical Warfare"   42

4.5   Sixth Conference: Moscow, November 27–December 5, 1960, "Disarmament and World Security"   44

4.6   Seventh Conference: Stowe, September 5–9, 1961, "International Co-operation in Pure and Applied Science"   47

4.7   Eighth Conference: Stowe, September 11–16, 1961, "Disarmament and World Security"   49

4.8   Ninth Conference: Cambridge, August 25–30, 1962, "Problems of Disarmament and World Security"   51

Contents   viii

4.9   Tenth Conference: London, September 3-7, 1962, "Scientists and
      World Affairs"   52

4.10 Eleventh Conference: Dubrovnik, September 20-25, 1963, "Current
      Problems of Disarmament and World Security"   56

4.11 Twelfth Conference: Udaipur, January 27-February 1, 1964, "Current
      Problems of Disarmament and World Security"   58

4.12 Thirteenth Conference: Karlovy Vary, September 13-19, 1964, "Disarmament and Peaceful Collaboration among Nations"   60

4.13 Fourteenth Conference: Venice, April 11-16, 1965, "International
      Co-operation for Science and Disarmament"   63

4.14 Fifteenth Conference: Addis Ababa, December 29, 1965-January 3,
      1966, "Science in Aid of Developing Countries"   65

4.15 Sixteenth Conference: Sopot, September 11-16, 1966, "Disarmament
      and World Security, Especially in Europe"   67

4.16 Seventeenth Conference: Ronneby, September 3-8, 1967, "Scientists
      and World Affairs"   70

4.17 Eighteenth Conference: Nice, September 11-16, 1968, "Current
      Problems of Peace, Security and Development"   73

4.18 Nineteenth Conference: Sochi, October 22-27, 1969, "World Security,
      Disarmament and Development"   76

4.19 Twentieth Conference: Fontana, September 9-15, 1970, "Peace and
      International Co-operation: A Programme for the Seventies"   78

4.20 Twenty-first Conference: Sinaia, August 26-31, 1971, "Problems of
      World Security, Environment and Development"   81

5   SUMMING UP   85

APPENDICES   135

1 The Russell-Einstein Manifesto   137

2 Statement from the First Pugwash Conference, held in Pugwash, July 7-10, 1957   141

3 Statement from the Second Pugwash Conference, held in Lac Beauport, March 31-April 11, 1958   148

Contents

4 Statement from the Third Pugwash Conference, held in Kitzbühel and Vienna, September 14-20, 1958   151

5 Statement from the Fourth Pugwash Conference, held in Baden, June 25-July 4, 1959   159

6 Statement from the Fifth Pugwash Conference, held in Pugwash, August 24-29, 1959   161

7 Statement from the Sixth Pugwash Conference, held in Moscow, November 27-December 5, 1960   166

8 Statement from the Seventh Pugwash Conference, held in Stowe, September 5-9, 1961   170

9 Statement from the Eighth Pugwash Conference, held in Stowe, September 11-16, 1961   185

10 Bentley Glass. Report on the Ninth Pugwash Conference, held in Cambridge, August 25-30, 1962   188

11 J. Rotblat. The Work of the Pugwash Continuing Committee (Report to the Tenth Pugwash Conference in London)   199

12 Report to the Standing Committee on Future Activities to the Tenth Pugwash Conference in London   206

13 Statement from the Tenth Pugwash Conference, held in London, September 3-7, 1962   209

14 Statement from the Eleventh Pugwash Conference, held in Dubrovnik, September 20-25, 1963   215

15 Statement from the Twelfth Pugwash Conference, held in Udaipur, January 27-February 1, 1964   222

16 Statement from the Continuing Committee on the Thirteenth Pugwash Conference, held in Karlovy Vary, September 13-19, 1964   230

17 Statement from the Continuing Committee on the Fourteenth Pugwash Conference, held in Venice, April 11-16, 1965   236

18 Statement from the Continuing Committee on the Fifteenth Pugwash Conference, held in Addis Ababa, December 29, 1965-January 3, 1966   246

19 Statement from the Continuing Committee on the Sixteenth Pugwash Conference, held in Sopot, September 11-16, 1966   256

20 Statement from the First South-East Asian Regional Pugwash Conference, held in Melbourne, January 23-27, 1967   265

21 Statement by the Continuing Committee on the Non-Proliferation Treaty (May, 1967)   272

22 J. Rotblat. The Work of the Continuing Committee since 1962 (Report to the Seventeenth Pugwash Conference in Ronneby)   275

23 Report of the Standing Committee on Future Activities to the Seventeenth Pugwash Conference in Ronneby   287

24 Statement from the Continuing Committee on the Seventeenth Pugwash Conference, held in Ronneby, September 3-8, 1967   291

25 Statement from the Continuing Committee on the Eighteenth Pugwash Conference, held in Nice, September 11-16, 1968   301

26 Statement from the Continuing Committee on the Nineteenth Pugwash Conference, held in Sochi, October 22-27, 1969   320

27 Statement from the Continuing Committee on the Twentieth Pugwash Conference, held in Fontana, September 9-15, 1970   330

28 Statement from the Continuing Committee on the Twenty-first Pugwash Conference, held in Sinaia, August 26-31, 1971   361

Name Index   377

Subject Index   391

Figures

1. Histogram of number of conferences attended by participants   19

2. Percentages of participants from the physical and social sciences in each of the Pugwash Conferences   19

Tables

1. Changes in the Membership of the Continuing Committee   88

2. National Pugwash Groups   90

3. List of Participants in the 21 Pugwash Conferences held between 1957 and 1971   91

4. Geographical Distribution of Participants   107

5. Attendance at Pugwash Conferences   108

6. Classification of Participants by Profession or Field of Study   109

7. List of Observers and Scientific Staff in the 21 Pugwash Conferences Held between 1957 and 1971   110

8. List of Science Writers in the 18th, 19th and 20th Conferences   115

9. List of Student Participants in the 20th and 21st Conferences   116

10. List of Suggested Topics for Pugwash Symposia Prepared in 1968   118

11. Pugwash Symposia   120

12. List of Participants in the 16 Pugwash Symposia Held between 1968 and 1972   123

13. Participants in Meetings of the Study Group on Biological Warfare   133

Foreword

Pugwash is a union of scientists who are concerned about the relations between science and society. Its purpose is not to promote the interest of scientists, nor to fight for the status of science, to discuss salaries or funds for research. Instead we are alarmed by the fact that science, which for so long was thought to confer nothing but blessings to mankind, today also displays a different aspect. It can be exploited--and is exploited--also for destruction and repression. Something has gone wrong, seriously wrong, either with science, or society, or with the relations between science and society. The most serious problem facing mankind today is how science can be used, not for warfare, but for the welfare of the human race.

The relations between science and society have changed over the centuries. When modern science was born during the Renaissance, its first epoch was a fight for its life against an authoritarian and repressive society. After that fight had been won, science released creative forces leading to the scientific avalanche. The second epoch started in the Age of Enlightenment, in itself partly the result of the application of scientific thinking to society. It resulted in the destruction of the feudal society and added more momentum to the march of science. A third epoch began with the technological application of science, which has done more to change the quality of human life than any other development in the history of mankind.

Thus far science had displayed only a benevolent aspect. But the fourth epoch, which has just begun, is marked by increasing fear of the negative aspects of science which are the product of its very success. The dynamic society caused by science is marked by a large number of exponentially increasing variables. Too many of them are now approaching catastrophic values. The atomic bomb, the population explosion, and the deterioration of the human environment are all the products of science, or rather of the malfunctioning of the relations between science and society. We are facing a serious crisis.

There are many people, including scientists, who call these fears "doomsday prophecies," and claim the dangers are exaggerated. Are not the bombs in the hands of responsible people? Does not the earth abound in waste land ready to absorb the population increase? Is pollution really such a serious problem? Admittedly some of the fears may be exaggerated, but no one who has made any serious study of the arms race and the population explosion can fail to be alarmed. Lack of concern stems either from ignorance or from an attitude of *après nous le déluge*.

Among scientists there also exists a third variant, often termed the "ivory tower" attitude: a scientist should be a scientist and nothing else. His works aim at the increase of knowledge, and knowledge is a good in itself. He should leave to others the task of deciding how to use it. This attitude worked perfectly throughout the whole long era during which science contributed almost exclusively to the progress of mankind. But this is no longer the case.

How are we to tackle this crisis? Some have adopted the defeatist view that our scientific-technological culture carries within itself the seeds of its own destruction. Man rules the earth at present but will soon be extinct, like the dinosaurs who were once masters of the world. Our crazed technology and outmoded political systems are the instruments of our own destruction. Perhaps a few of us can escape and start a new culture if we get away from the Blue Planet in time and form a space colony.

All this may be true, but we must strive instead for other solutions. They do not lie easy to hand. Some think that the development of science and technology should be halted. This "technophobic" view is shortsighted. Science and technology confer such enormous benefits that they must not be halted, but used in a sensible way. We come closer to the truth if we say that it is the rules that govern world politics that must be changed: power politics have now become so dangerous that they must be abolished. The creation of the League of Nations and of the United Nations was inspired by this belief in the need for an effective international authority capable of checking the destructive aspects of unlimited national sovereignty.

Pugwash stems from the same belief. Scientists already constitute an international community, which collaborates very efficiently on an international basis. There is no other field in which people of different countries and of different races work together on important problems as closely and amicably. But so far the joint efforts have been confined essentially to purely scientific matters. A number of scientists, however, have been involved in political consultations as government advisors and special experts, and many of them have been profoundly shocked to observe how the findings of science are applied for the purposes of destruction, repression, and power politics. A widespread fear exists that science and technology have injected too much power into a global political structure which is not equipped to handle it in a responsible manner. A drastic change is called for both in the attitude of scientists and of those responsible for government.

Scientists and technologists are accustomed to look with pride on all the "progress curves" that rise exponentially and think it their agreeable duty to keep them rising or even induce them to rise still faster. But we have now learned that the rise of many of these curves spells disaster, and scientists cannot plead innocence by putting the blame on others and saying: We scientists are simply doing our job, and "others" must take the blame if our findings are used irresponsibly. There are no "others" willing to assume this responsibility.

Many organizations exist to exploit science and technology for the benefit of private companies, military and other organizations, and for the benefit of individual countries. But there are few which aim at using them for the welfare of mankind as a whole.

There are many instances in which new discoveries can bring power and wealth to certain groups, but only at the expense of others. Possibly mankind as a whole is paying the price through a decline in security, the deterioration of human environment, and the widening gap between rich and poor. In cases such as these, who is there to advocate the interests of mankind? Indeed, there are few who are capable of it, since often only a handful of specialists really understand the consequences of new discoveries.

It is the belief of Pugwash that scientists have an important role to play in several of these respects. By meeting and pooling together the knowledge gained from different areas of research and different countries, it becomes possible to clarify, at least in part, the real position and decide what measures should be taken to avoid catastrophe.

But what could scientists really do? The founders of Pugwash believed there was a relatively easy course: simply to tell the truth--in the case of the atomic bomb, the terrible truth that it is so destructive that its use is suicidal. To some extent this has been successful. It is largely thanks to the efforts of the original Pugwash group that most people now realize this, and that this knowledge has so far deterred the politicians and the military men from using atom bombs in the post-war period.

But in an equally important respect it has been unsuccessful: the nuclear arms race continues at a breakneck speed. Hence there remains a problem that is even more serious. Why are world politics running amok, and what can be done about it? The superpowers are spending enormous sums on increasing their "overkill" capacity: each of them is now capable of wiping out more than 100 million people in under one hour, but all this increase in power gives them no increase in security, only greater fear, greater anxiety to arm still more fiercely.

It is not science alone that has gone wrong and needs reforming. It is at least as true of the obsolete pattern of world politics. The leading politicians of the World continue to think like petty tribal chieftains: no glory surpasses that of outwitting and killing your enemy and bringing home his scalp. This attitude is out-of-date. The atomic age has made all hawks dangerous anachronisms. But this has still to be understood by all. At present it is not even understood by all scientists. There are still famous scientists who subscribe to the most infamous of all activities: that of preaching nationalism and hatred in the atomic age.

All this means that Pugwash must continue its work but widen its range. It is necessary to dig deeper into the international problems vital to our survival: can a stable and peaceful world be built, and how is it to be done? This is a problem more difficult, more vital and more challenging than all other scientific problems. Will the scientists be competent to solve it?

This problem, which Pugwash puts to itself--and others--implies first of all the identification of what are the most important factors today. What really goes on in the world today is often different from what we are told by political propaganda. How can we correct for this? And even if we could see clearly and find reasonable solutions for our problems, how would we convince those who rule and those who are ruled that this is what must be done?

The efforts by Pugwash to tackle these problems in the past are described in the present book by Professor Joseph Rotblat, Secretary-General of Pugwash, who has been at the heart of the Pugwash organization from its earliest beginnings, has held it successfully together and helped it grow into what it is today. Pugwash is to a large extent a product of his commitment to a vital cause, his hard work, and his diplomatic skill.

H. Alfvén
April 1972

Preface

Pugwash is an international movement, started in 1957, involving some of the most famous men of learning and aiming to ensure that mankind will not destroy itself. Yet few people, other than its participants, are aware of its existence. The cause of this obscurity lies within the Pugwash Movement itself. Anonymity is the price paid for bringing eminent scientists together and getting them to talk freely and without inhibition on matters which are of deep concern to them but on which they are not necessarily experts. Such talks can be effective, and generate original ideas, only if the participants do not have to worry that what they say may be taken down and published, more likely than not in a distorted fashion. For this reason the meetings are private and the Press not admitted. But if the Press is excluded its members do not write about them, and hence the ignorance of the public about Pugwash.

There are other organizations which debate the same issues in public, in front of a wide audience and in full glare of the mass media. But usually the discussions turn into speeches for the benefit of the audience, and little original thinking takes place; on the whole such gatherings are less conducive to the emergence of new concepts than a true confrontation of minds, with cross-fertilization of ideas, in a small meeting round a table.

This is not meant to decry the value of open meetings. Clearly there is room in the world for all types of activities: for propaganda and for think tanks; to influence public opinion directly and to aim to reach governments; for public debates and for private discussions. Rightly or wrongly, Pugwash has chosen the latter. However, although our meetings are private, Pugwash is not a secret society. On the contrary, we are anxious that the public should know who we are, how we operate, and what we talk about. In view of our aspirations, the public is entitled to have the answers to these questions. This book attempts to provide this information.

In writing this book which, unlike most of the Pugwash publications, is intended for the open market, I decided that it should be a formal history rather than a story, that it should give a chronicle of events, a methodical, factual and unemotional account of the organization and activities of the Pugwash Movement, rather than present impressions, highlight the more dramatic episodes, and throw in anecdotes and reminiscences. The latter method would make the book more amusing and lively, but it would also be subjective and incomplete. There probably is a need for such a story, but I believe that there is even a greater need for a more formal history, as presented here.

In the attempt to give an unbiased and impersonal account, I have probably managed to deprive the characters of all individuality. I may have given the impression that the scientists in the Pugwash Conferences are stereotype intellectuals, always logical and clear-headed but cool and impassive.

This would certainly be the wrong impression. I have been privileged to be closely associated with Pugwash from the very beginning, and this gave me the opportunity to get to know intimately the principal characters in Pugwash and to recognize their individual characteristics and idiosyncrasies. There was Bertrand Russell, who by physical appearance came nearest to the proverbial dry philosopher, but who had an innate kindness and love for human beings; great things were his concern but he never overlooked the little things; he aimed at saving mankind from annihilation, but bothered about the slightest hurt to the individual. There was Cecil Powell, an outstanding physicist and Nobel laureate but also a scholar and connoisseur of the arts and literature, an eloquent speaker and charming raconteur; he had the unique talent for reconciling divergent views. There was Alexander Topchiev, an ardent communist and a hard party-liner, but with a heart of gold and loyal to his friends, by whom he would stand in time of need even if he disagreed with them. There was Leo Szilard, irascible and individualistic because he was always a generation ahead of time with his ideas, but with a wonderful sense of humour.

I have sketched a few leaders of Pugwash who have passed away, but many of these characteristics apply to those who are still alive. They all share a concern for the well-being of man, even though their approaches differ; they make passionate speeches, display emotions, and argue violently, like other human beings. The main difference is that, being scientists, they have learned the value of objectivity and are ready to listen to a reasoned argument and be convinced by it. This is the main reason why Pugwash has made more progress than other groups concerned with the same problems.

This brings me to the last of my apologia. In the book I have described what Pugwash has done but not what it has achieved. The reason is that achievement is often a matter of judgment rather than of fact. In the highly complex problems discussed in Pugwash, where so many diverse factors interact, it is impossible to measure the influence exerted by any single factor. For this reason we cannot determine with scientific precision the effect which Pugwash has had on world security. Another reason is that I have been too closely associated with the Pugwash Movement to give me the necessary perspective. However, other people, who looked at Pugwash from a distance, did express opinions about our achievements. Thus, a very senior American scientist has stated that Pugwash has been an important force in bringing better understanding between East and West in the last decade. U Thant spoke about the careful attention given to Pugwash resolutions at the United Nations and about their influence on decision-making processes by national governments. Some people go further and attribute to Pugwash the few successes achieved so far in disarmament, such as the partial test ban treaty, or the non-proliferation treaty.

It will be some time before the correctness of such specific claims can be assessed, but there is no doubt that Pugwash has stimulated scientists all over the world to think about problems of peace and world security, and encouraged them to engage in full-time research on these problems. I hope that the account in this book of the efforts and strivings of scientists to create more understanding and good will in the world will stimulate many others to follow in their footsteps.

J. Rotblat
London,
May 1972

SCIENTISTS IN THE QUEST FOR PEACE

A History of the Pugwash Conferences

1 THE BIRTH OF PUGWASH

1.1 Early Efforts to Convene International Conferences of Scientists

The advent of the atomic age brought to many scientists the realization that they can and should concern themselves with the fate of mankind. This concern was expressed in various national groups which were formed immediately after World War II; among these were the Federation of American Scientists (FAS) in the United States, and the Atomic Scientists' Association (ASA) in Great Britain. It was also the main motivation for the formation of the World Federation of Scientific Workers (WFSW). In stimulating these activities a very prominent part was played by the *Bulletin of the Atomic Scientists*, whose editor, Eugene Rabinowitch, was one of the first to call and work for the setting up of international discussions; it is largely due to his enthusiasm and devotion that many of the events recorded here have materialized. One example of his untiring efforts was the convening of an informal talk in September 1951 in Chicago, during a conference on nuclear physics attended by scientists from many countries.

The intensification of the arms race, which followed the development of the H-bomb and its first tests, made the need for international co-operation amongst scientists even more urgent. Early in 1954 the Prime Minister of India, Jawaharlal Nehru, called for the setting up of a committee of scientists to explain to the world the effect a nuclear war would have on humanity. This idea was taken up in a correspondence between the FAS and the ASA, and, in July 1954, in direct discussion between Eugene Rabinowitch and Joseph Rotblat (Executive Vice-President of the ASA) and other members of the Council of the ASA. This resulted in the setting up by the ASA of study groups to prepare for an "International Conference on Science and Society."

Up to that stage the talks were mainly within Anglo-American groups. Soviet scientists joined a discussion on these issues at a conference organized not by scientists, but by a group called the Association of Parliamentarians for World Government, with headquarters in London. The organizers of this group asked several scientists, including Alexander Haddow and Rotblat, for help in preparing a programme for their conference. This they did together with Rabinowitch during another of his visits to Europe. The Conference took place in London, August 3-5, 1955. Only some of the participants were scientists; the Soviet group of 4 scientists was led by Alexander Topchiev, a staunch supporter of international co-operation among scientists, who later played a major role in establishing the Pugwash Movement. As well as endorsing the Russell-Einstein Manifesto (section 1.2), the Conference set up three commissions charged with carrying on studies in preparation for another conference. The topics for the three commissions were (1) the assessment of the consequences of nuclear weapons and nuclear power development (with Rotblat as convener); (2) problems of disarmament (convener Peter Hodgson); (3) social responsibility of scientists (convener Jacob Bronowski). However, apart from discussions within the ASA, these commissions never developed into proper study groups and they gradually faded away.

1.2 The Russell-Einstein Manifesto

The initiative for organizing the first international conference of scientists, and thus the credit for starting the Pugwash Movement, goes to Bertrand Russell. With prophetic insight he assessed the dangers inherent in the changed world and arrived very early at the conclusion that scientists had an important part to play in saving the world from disaster. In a speech to the House of Lords on November 28, 1945--only a few months after the Hiroshima bomb--Russell had forecast the tremendous destructive power of the H-bomb and the resulting threat to civilization, and had suggested that a meeting between Western and Soviet scientists might provide the best opening for genuine co-operation and the establishment of a system of international controls.

When, in 1954, the menace of nuclear weapons became as great as he had predicted, Russell decided that the time had come to take action. On December 23 he broadcast over the British radio a talk called "Man's Peril," in which he made a remarkable evaluation of the dangerous situation resulting from the development of nuclear weapons and of the catastrophic consequences which would follow another war. He followed up this broadcast, which made a great impact on public opinion, by drafting the text of a Manifesto intended for signature by scientists from various countries. He was anxious that these scientists should represent different shades of opinion so that the statement would not be regarded as favouring one side. One of the first of the scientists to be approached was Albert Einstein, who signed it two days before his death. It was because of this that the Manifesto became generally known as the Russell-Einstein Appeal. The signatories were mostly Nobel Prize winners. They included Max Born, Percy Bridgman, Leopold Infeld, Frédéric Joliot-Curie, Herman Muller, Linus Pauling, Cecil Powell, Joseph Rotblat and Hideki Yukawa.

The Manifesto, the full text of which is given in Appendix 1, was read by Russell at a Press conference held in London on July 9, 1955. Rotblat, the only other signatory present in London at the time, took the chair. The largest room in Caxton Hall was packed to capacity with representatives of the Press, radio and television from all over the world. It was clear from this, as well as from the tone of the questions which followed the reading of the Manifesto, that the Press realized the far-reaching significance of the statement.

The Press gave the Manifesto excellent coverage, with the result that hundreds of letters and cables, from individuals and groups, came pouring in from many countries, expressing approval and offering help. It was evident that the Manifesto touched a sensitive cord in the minds of the public and scientists; that the idea that scientists should take an active part in world affairs had the approval of public opinion.

1.3 Plans for a Conference in India

Apart from the appeal to abolish war and the warning about the perils to mankind, the Manifesto also called for a conference of scientists to appraise these perils and to discuss means of achieving international understanding. In the preparation of this conference Bertrand Russell asked

for help from Powell, Rotblat and Burhop. Cecil Powell was Chairman of
the Executive Council of the WFSW and a Vice-President of the ASA. Eric
Burhop was an active member of the WFSW and had previously been in touch
with Russell on behalf of Frédéric Joliot-Curie, the President of WFSW.
From the beginning, however, Russell insisted that the proposed conference
must in no way be associated with any established organized body, and that
it must consist of a truly neutral and independent effort. The Pugwash
Conferences have strictly adhered to these principles and throughout the
subsequent years have remained genuinely independent.

The first plan was to convene a conference of scientists in New Delhi, in
January 1957. The venue was chosen because of the talks which Powell had
with Nehru and with Indian scientists during his visit to India early in
1956, and in which he found strong support for such a conference. Letters
of invitation, over the signature of Bertrand Russell on behalf of the
signatories of the Manifesto, went out to a number of scientists in June
1956. However, the Suez crisis in October and November 1956 made it
doubtful whether it would be possible to travel to India, and since the
Conference was to be held in conjunction with the Indian Science Congress
which takes place annually in January, the plan for calling the India
meeting had to be abandoned.

1.4 Cyrus Eaton Offers Financial Help

Among the difficulties encountered when preparing the India Conference,
one of the greatest was the financial aspect. Hospitality in India was
offered by the Indian Science Congress, but funds had still to be found
for travelling expenses for most of the participants. In September 1956,
letters were sent out to a number of wealthy people in various countries
asking for financial support. A few small contributions were received,
but most of those who were approached refused. Among those refusals, however,
there were two which carried a conditional offer of help. Mr. Aristotle
Onassis, the Greek ship owner, offered to pay all expenses for the
Conference if it were held in Monte Carlo; and Mr. Cyrus Eaton, the Cleveland
industrialist, made a similar offer for a conference to be held in
Pugwash, Nova Scotia, Canada. Mr. Eaton was approached because in July
1955, after the publication of the Manifesto, he had sent an enthusiastic
letter to Lord Russell, offering to finance anonymously a meeting of scientists
in Pugwash.

Both these offers had to be declined while it was being planned to hold
the Conference in India, but after the abandonment of this plan Russell
decided that Mr. Eaton's offer should be pursued. There followed an exchange
of letters, as the result of which Mr. Eaton agreed to pay all necessary
travelling expenses of participants and to provide accommodation
and hospitality for a Conference to be held at Pugwash in July 1957. A
small fishing village in Nova Scotia, Pugwash, the birthplace of Cyrus
Eaton, has since 1955 been the venue of meetings of scholars and educators
brought together by Eaton for an opportunity "to relax, exchange views,
sharpen their own thinking and design formulae for us to live in this
brand-new world." It was agreed, however, that the proposed Conference of
scientists would in no way be connected with these other meetings. In his

offer of financial help Eaton made it clear that while the participants would be his guests they would be completely independent; that the preparatory work and organization would be handled by Russell and his colleagues, and that the conduct and proceedings of the Conference would be left entirely for the participants. Under these conditions it was felt that the basic principles laid down for the Conference would be safeguarded.

1.5 The First Conference: Pugwash, July 7-10, 1957

As in the case of the abortive Conference in India, the letters of invitation to the Pugwash Conference were sent out by Lord Russell, who wrote them on behalf of the signatories of the Manifesto. The letter made it clear that the Conference would meet in private, and that the participants would themselves decide whether to issue any public communication at the end. It also expressed the desire of the organizers that the participants, although coming as individuals, without any commitments, should represent different political opinions and the geographical distribution of scientists. Letters were sent to individual scientists from a list compiled according to these principles.

Altogether, 64 letters of invitation were sent out, but only 30 scientists accepted; 8 of these were subsequently unable to come. Many of the refusals were due to previous engagements, a natural enough occurrence among eminent scientists. Some scientists refused because they feared that the Conference might have ulterior motives and be politically biased. Only a small minority expressed open opposition to the idea of such a conference, and claimed that it was not the business of scientists to meddle in such matters. This negative attitude was also encountered at the next few conferences. It took several years, until after the Sixth Conference in Moscow, in 1960, for this attitude to be dispelled.

Of the 22 participants, 15 were physicists, 2 chemists, 4 biologists, and one was a lawyer. It was envisaged from the start that there should be representatives from the biological and social sciences, in addition to those from the physical sciences. This pattern was followed in subsequent conferences, although the predominance of physicists gradually decreased, while the percentage of social scientists has gradually increased (see section 2.8 and Figure 2). The geographical distribution of the participants of the First Conference was as follows: 7 from the United States, 3 each from the Soviet Union and Japan, 2 each from Great Britain and Canada, and one each from Australia, Austria, China, France and Poland. Burhop was also present as a member of the organizing committee. Ruth Adams, Rabinowitch's assistant in editing the *Bulletin of the Atomic Scientists*, helped with the secretarial work. In the absence of Russell, whose age did not permit him to make a long journey, but who sent a stimulating message, Powell presided at the plenary sessions. The meetings were conducted in English and Russian, with Vladimir Pavlichenko, Topchiev's secretary, acting as interpreter.

Although the first formal session of the Conference did not start until the afternoon of July 7, many of the participants arrived earlier and they spent the whole of July 6 on informal talks. Leo Szilard took a leading part in these talks, with his recollections of the first attempts by scientists in the United States to influence the government's policy in relation to the discovery of atomic energy, and the subsequent actions and attitudes of scientists towards the deployment of the first atom bomb. Several of those present at Pugwash had taken an active part in the development of the atom bomb, but for many of the participants these first-hand accounts provided a useful background to the discussions at the Conference.

The programme of the Conference was essentially the same as the one which Haddow, Rabinowitch and Rotblat had prepared for the Parliamentarian Conference in London in 1955. After a general discussion at the first plenary session, the Conference divided into three committees, corresponding to those set up at the 1955 Conference, viz. (1) hazards arising from the use of atomic energy in peace and war; (2) control of nuclear weapons; and (3) the social responsibility of scientists. Most of the work of the Conference was carried out in these committees which met in parallel and sat till very late at night. At the plenary sessions, which met in the mornings or afternoons, there were general discussions on the same topics, usually based on papers presented by participants.

The most progress was made by the first committee, on radiation hazards. At that time little was yet known about the physical and biological processes associated with the testing of nuclear weapons, and the findings of this committee probably comprise the first agreement to be reached between scientists from East and West on the effects of tests. The fact that the topic of discussion for this committee was largely technical in nature no doubt explains the large measure of agreement even on matters of detail. By contrast, the second committee, on the control of nuclear weapons, very quickly came to the conclusion that the problem was too complex and controversial to enable the members to reach agreement on specific proposals in the time available. The committee had, therefore, to be content with outlining the general objectives of disarmament, leaving the working out of a detailed plan to future meetings. This topic became in fact the major item of discussion at subsequent Pugwash Conferences. The third committee, on the social responsibilities of scientists, met with surprising success, considering the divergence of views held by scientists on this subject. The committee summarized its findings in the form of eleven items of common belief; subsequently these became the basis for the Vienna Declaration (see section 4.2).

All three committees prepared reports which were discussed at the plenary sessions on the last day and incorporated in the statement published at the end. The statement, the text of which is enclosed as Appendix 2, was adopted by all present, with the exception of John Foster of Canada and Leo Szilard. The latter, the most stimulating of the participants, was also the most individualistic, and for these reasons he often abstained from conference statements, although substantially helping in their preparation.

1.6 Significance of the First Pugwash Conference

The fact that a long statement, dealing in some detail with the most controversial issues of the day, and setting out the role and responsibility of scientists, was accepted almost unanimously by such a diverse group of scientists, was in itself of great significance. This was probably the first time that a truly international conference, organized by scientists, with participants from East and West, was convened not to discuss specific technical matters, but the social implications of scientific discovery. In the state of political distrust and tension which existed at the time, it seemed an even chance that the Conference might break up in disagreement. Indeed, after the preliminary exchange of views, it appeared that there was a considerable divergence of opinion between scientists from East and West, even on purely technical matters, such as the evaluation of radiation hazards. However, it soon became clear that many of these apparent differences resulted from different ways of looking at the same problem. Since scientists are used to rational discussions and are ready to accept a sound argument and—above all—since they came to the Conference as individuals and not as representatives of governments, it was not long before agreement was reached on many issues. On some issues it was evident that agreement could not be reached without a great deal of further intense study. What the Conference did accomplish in relation to these items was a definition and outlining of areas of divergence. A certain measure of mutual understanding of each other's opinions was also achieved.

The character of the Conference itself helped greatly in this respect. Unlike other conferences whose participants meet only in formal sessions, here all members lived together, ate together, and talked to each other continuously, in small or large groups. The informal talks proved to be of immense value in helping towards a better understanding of each other's views. The generous hospitality of the host, Cyrus Eaton, and the stimulating conversations with the hostess, Mrs. Anne Jones (who later became Mrs. Eaton) all contributed to the setting up of a friendly and congenial atmosphere. This was, of course, facilitated by the fact that many participants had known each other professionally if not personally, and had respect for each other's scientific integrity.

This First Pugwash Conference proved that scientists have a common purpose which can transcend national frontiers without violating basic loyalties. It had shown that, by virtue of their training and their knowledge, scientists are capable of discussing objectively the complex problems which have arisen from the progress of science, with the aim of finding a solution to these problems.

The realization of this unanimity of intent decided the participants to make further efforts in the same direction. For this purpose a Continuing Committee of 5 persons was set up at the end of the Conference, with instructions to organize further conferences of a similar nature. Bertrand Russell, with whom contact had been maintained during the Conference by telephone, was elected Chairman of the Continuing Committee, and the four members, all physicists, were Cecil Powell, Eugene Rabinowitch, Joseph Rotblat and Dmitri Skobeltzyn.

The Continuing Committee

The First Pugwash Conference did make some impact on society, although not as great as had been hoped. Many scientific journals reprinted the statement in full, and its recommendations were adopted by other groups of scientists and lay people in various countries. In the Soviet Union the Academy of Sciences formally endorsed the statement, and there were large meetings of scientists to support it. In China too the statement received much publicity. In the West the reaction was less conspicuous and much slower, but it was evident from subsequent developments that the point of the Conference was taken by many scientists.

1.7 First Meeting of the Continuing Committee

The Continuing Committee met for the first time on December 18-20, 1957, in Joseph Rotblat's office at St. Bartholomew's Hospital Medical College in London, where several of the subsequent committee meetings have also been held. All members of the Committee attended, and Lord Russell took the chair. In addition, Leo Szilard and Carl von Weizsäcker were invited. There were also informal meetings with many British personalities, including J. D. Bernal, P. M. S. Blackett, Alexander Haddow, Kathleen Lonsdale and J. B. Priestley.

This first meeting of the Committee was of great importance, since a decision had to be reached about future activities and, in particular, about the type of conference to be convened. Prior to the meeting, Rabinowitch in the United States and Rotblat in Great Britain had sent a questionnaire to a number of scientists about the type of future meetings they would favour. The majority of those who replied preferred small meetings of two types: (a) meetings to discuss immediate political problems, and primarily directed at influencing governments; and (b) meetings to study the social implications of scientific progress, and aimed at clarifying the thinking of scientists themselves. Some scientists were also in favour of a third type, i.e., larger meetings, to deal with general problems and to issue resolutions directed to the world at large.

After two days of intense discussion the Committee concluded that it wanted to pursue all three of the foregoing aims: to influence governments, to form a channel of communication among scientists, and to educate public opinion. It was clear, however, that it would not be possible to do all these things at the same time, and that a different type of meeting would have to be convened for each purpose. Taking into account the tense political situation, which at that time had greatly deteriorated after the breakdown of the United Nations disarmament talks in London, the Committee decided that there was an urgent need for a small conference to discuss means of averting a political crisis. It was thought that if the Conference were held in private, and that if those invited were informed in advance that it was not intended to issue a public statement, it would be possible to attract scientists who had made a study of these problems, and who were influential with their governments. The urgency of the situation demanded that the Conference be held at the earliest feasible date, i.e., during the Easter period of 1958. Once again, lack of funds compelled the Continuing Committee to seek Eaton's assistance. This came very promptly. In a telephone conversation Eaton agreed to finance the next Conference, on condition that it be held in Canada. Since Pugwash was not a suitable place at that time of the year, another locality had to be chosen. Eaton subsequently recommended Lac Beauport, a small skiing resort, about 10 miles from Quebec.

1.8 Further Conferences

Apart from deciding to convene the Lac Beauport Conference, the Committee also approved plans for another conference to be held in September 1958. It was decided that this should be a larger conference dealing with the social implications of science in general, as well as with the particular problem of averting the dangers of the atomic age. This conference was also to discuss future activities. Taking into account that many scientists were to be present at the Second International Conference on the Peaceful Uses of Atomic Energy in Geneva, it was decided to hold this conference in Austria. In addition to issuing an important document, the Vienna Declaration, which may be considered the tenet of the Pugwash Movement, this Conference decided to enlarge the Continuing Committee and instructed it to convene further conferences (see section 4.2).

Thus started the series of Pugwash Conferences, which by the end of 1971 reached a total of 21. The history of those Conferences is taken up in Chapter 4. Other Pugwash activities are described in Chapter 3.

Although, in the course of the years, the Pugwash Movement became firmly established, there is still no constitution or membership, and very little organization. The Movement gradually evolved, making up its rules and procedures as it went along, and remaining amorphous in its structure. The only link between the various activities is the Continuing Committee, and this body too worked for a time without any well-defined rules, and only gradually adopted some measure of organization. The work of the Continuing Committee and the organization of the activities are described in Chapter 2.

1.9 Pugwash Questionnaire

Although the total number of scientists directly involved in Pugwash activities is still very small (less than 1,000) the Movement has the support of a much larger body of scientists. This was ascertained quite early in the history of Pugwash, in 1959, when a questionnaire was sent out to many scientists, together with the text of the Vienna Declaration.

The questionnaire contained four general questions:

1. Do you agree that scientists have the responsibility to be concerned with the social and political implications of the progress of science?

2. Do you believe that scientists could make a useful contribution toward easing international tension and establishing co-operation among nations?

3. Do you approve of the Vienna Declaration?

4. Do you consider it a proper basis for future international activities of scientists?

Altogether about 35,000 questionnaires were sent out, including 5,000 printed in Russian and mailed by the Soviet Academy of Sciences. The printing and mailing of the English text was done at Mr. Eaton's expense in Cleveland. Among those who replied there was overwhelming support for Pugwash. Between 93 percent and 100 percent of the returns gave affirmative replies to all four questions. The remaining 7 percent were from Western countries, and of these 4 percent were noncommittal and 3 percent answered in the negative.

The questionnaire also asked about the type of activities to be carried out by the Continuing Committee. In this respect there was a slight majority among the Soviet scientists in favour of large open meetings aimed at influencing public opinion, while in the Western countries the majority preferred smaller conferences or study groups to explore specific problems.

The main difference between the returns from East and West was that while from the Soviet Union 83 percent of the questionnaires were returned, from the Western countries only about 20 percent replied. A second poll was then conducted in one Western country, Great Britain. This questionnaire met with a 90 percent response, probably because a stamped addressed return envelope was enclosed! An analysis of these replies has shown that in Western countries about half of the scientists were in favour of the Pugwash Movement, about a quarter were against, and the remaining quarter were indifferent.

It should, however, be remembered that the questionnaire was circulated in 1959, when the Pugwash Conferences were still in their infancy, and little known among the scientific community. Judging from the eager response to invitations to later Pugwash Conferences, it seems probable that if the questionnaire had been set out a few years later it would have resulted in much more positive support.

1.10 The Name of the Movement

Only two of the 21 Pugwash Conferences were held in Pugwash itself. Nevertheless, the name of the Movement remained firmly associated with the village in Nova Scotia, despite the fact that the links with Cyrus Eaton have been disconnected for a long time.

In the first few Pugwash Conferences, Cyrus Eaton was virtually the only financial supporter, and the Pugwash Movement owes him a great debt of gratitude. However, the Committee came to the conclusion that, in order to preserve its independence of aims and action, it must not rely for financial support on any one individual. For this reason, no help has been asked from Mr. Eaton since 1959; the expenses for the subsequent conferences were obtained from various foundations, as well as from a number of individuals. The growing reputation of the Pugwash Movement has made it easier to obtain grants from different institutions, although this was not always sufficient to meet all the needs.

There was also another reason for separating from Cyrus Eaton. That was his increasing involvement in political activities and his public statements, which could be interpreted by some people as representing the views of the Continuing Committee. In fact, the three United States members of the Continuing Committee felt obligated to publish in September 1959 a statement setting out the facts about the relationship between the Pugwash Conferences and Mr. Eaton. They said in it, "Mr. Eaton generously accepted the cost of three out of five conferences held to date, and the organizers and participants owe him gratitude for having been a generous host, without attempting to influence the composition, programme and conclusions of the Conferences. However, as Mr. Eaton has come to play an increasingly active and controversial role in political affairs, the scientists felt that his exclusive support of their conferences may place them in the wrong light," and conclude, "We are sorry that an encouraging co-operation between a generous businessman, eager to assist the scientists of the world in their efforts to prevent the misuse of science for the destruction of mankind, and to further its use for constructive purposes, has been made impossible by his reluctance to keep his support of the scientists' conferences clearly separated from his increasing involvement."

The United States members of the Committee felt that the name Pugwash might give rise to confusion with the other conferences which Cyrus Eaton was convening each year at Pugwash, and they decided that the United States National Group would use the name COSWA (Conferences on Science and World Affairs). They also suggested that the whole Movement should change its name, but the large Conference in London decided that the name Pugwash should be retained (see section 4.9). Despite occasional confusion with the other type of meetings organized by Eaton at his birthplace in Nova Scotia, the name Pugwash is now firmly associated with the Movement, and the term "Pugwashite" has come to denote those attending the Pugwash Conferences or adhering to their spirit.

2 THE ORGANIZATION OF PUGWASH

2.1 The Continuing Committee

The responsibility for organizing the Conferences as well as for other Pugwash activities rests with the Continuing Committee. Over the years, and in parallel with the increasing scope of activities and range of interests, the Committee grew in size; by 1969 it numbered 17 persons plus the two officers: the President and the Secretary-General.

The first enlargement of the original Continuing Committee took place at the Third Conference in Kitzbühel in 1959, when it was decided that in addition to the Chairman, Bertrand Russell, there should be 9 members—three each from the United Kingdom, the United States and the Soviet Union. Following that, elections of the Continuing Committee were held only at the Quinquennial Conferences, in London in 1962 and in Ronneby in 1967. These Quinquennial Conferences differ from the other Pugwash Conferences in that participants in all past Conferences are invited to them, and that decisions about future activities and organization are taken, and officers and members of the Continuing Committee elected. These Conferences may, therefore, be regarded as a kind of General Assembly of the Pugwash Movement. The next Quinquennial Conference is scheduled for September 1972 in Oxford.

At both the London and Ronneby Conferences the serving members were re-elected, but the Continuing Committee was enlarged by the addition of members from other European countries as well as from other continents.

Apart from these elections there have been changes in the Continuing Committee due to retirements and death. The retirements are sometimes occasioned by members taking up official positions; thus, Rolf Björnerstedt and Ignacy Malecki retired from the Committee upon taking up posts with the U.N. and UNESCO, respectively. Some retired due to pressure of other work, and others because they felt that there was a need to bring in fresh blood. The Ronneby Conference recommended that the membership of the Continuing Committee should rotate, so as to enable a larger number of scientists to serve on the Committee, but so far this principle of rotation has not been applied systematically.

When a vacancy occurs in between Quinquennial Conferences it is filled by nominations from the relevant country or region. Thus, the National Pugwash Groups in the Soviet Union or the United Kingdom or the United States submit to the Continuing Committee names for replacements of members from these countries. In the case of Eastern or Western Europe this is done by correspondence between the relevant Pugwash National Groups, or at a meeting of representatives from these countries.

The various changes that have occurred in the membership of the Continuing Committee since 1957 are listed in Table 1; only two of the members elected at the first Pugwash Conference still serve: Eugene Rabinowitch and Joseph Rotblat.

The Continuing Committee normally meets twice a year, for two or three days. One of these meetings is usually held in late summer, just prior to the Annual Conference, and continues after the Conference. The other meeting is held in the spring and sometimes coincides with a Symposium. In the earlier days most of the Committee meetings were held in London, either at Rotblat's office at St. Bartholomew's Hospital Medical College, or at the Ciba Foundation. Altogether, 36 meetings were held by April 1972. The principle was established that if a member of the Continuing Committee is unable to be present, he may appoint another scientist to attend in his place. The Committee also invites, from time to time, other persons to attend meetings for specific purposes.

Most of the time of Committee meetings is taken up with the planning, preparation and organization of Conferences and Symposia. However, the Committee is also involved in various other activities, such as publications, contact with the National Groups, and liaison with other bodies. From time to time the Committee also intervenes privately or publicly in matters of importance to security in general, or to scientists in particular (see section 3.7).

The meetings are presided over by the Chairman of the Committee. During the first ten years Bertrand Russell was Chairman, but this was largely a courtesy title because, due to his age and state of health, he was unable to attend meetings; the last time he chaired a meeting of the Continuing Committee was in August 1962. Usually, Powell presided at the meetings, and in recognition of this fact he was appointed in 1964 Vice-Chairman of the Continuing Committee. At the Ronneby Conference Powell was formally appointed Chairman of the Continuing Committee. He held this office until his death in 1969, and Rudolf Peierls was subsequently appointed as his successor.

It is characteristic of Pugwash that, after its first meeting in 1958, no vote has ever been taken at the meetings of the Continuing Committee. Frequently there are very strong differences of opinion between the members on matters of substance and procedure, but these differences are resolved by argument and the decisions taken are always by general agreement.

2.2 The Executive Committee

The large size of the Continuing Committee made it necessary to have a smaller body which could be convened more easily, and which could take urgent action in between meetings of the Continuing Committee. For this purpose, an Executive Committee was established in 1963, with five members. The first Executive Committee consisted of Bentley Glass, Herbert Marcovich, Cecil Powell, Joseph Rotblat and Dmitri Skobeltzyn. The composition of the present Executive Committee is Bernard Feld, Herbert Marcovich, Mikhail Millionshchikov, Rudolf Peierls and Joseph Rotblat.

The Executive Committee usually conducts its business by letter, cable or telephone, but on occasions there are actual meetings, as for example in Moscow in February 1969 to discuss the agenda for the Sochi Conference. The Executive Committee is empowered to act on behalf of the Continuing

Committee in cases where a quick or urgent action is necessary, as well as to carry out duties delegated to it by the Continuing Committee. All actions of the Executive Committee are reported to the next meeting of the Continuing Committee for approval.

2.3 Officers

2.3.1 President.
The founder of the Movement, Bertrand Russell, was its natural head. Although, due to restriction in travel, he personally attended only two Pugwash Conferences, he was kept informed about everything that happened at the Conferences, and all projected activities were discussed with him. Gradually, however, Russell's interests shifted away from Pugwash to other areas, and his involvement in Pugwash decreased. His last appearance at a Pugwash Conference was in London in 1962.

At the Quinquennial Conference in Ronneby in 1967, when the future organization of Pugwash was discussed, the need was expressed for an active person to be the titular head of Pugwash. Accordingly, the office of President was established. His role was to preside over the Annual Pugwash Conferences and, in addition, between Conferences, to offer his counsel and advice to the members of the Continuing Committee and the Secretary-General, and thereby assist them in the execution of the activities of the Movement.

At Ronneby, Sir John Cockcroft was unanimously elected as President. It was his intention to raise funds and to help in the initiation of other activities for the effective running of the Movement; unfortunately, he died suddenly ten days after his election. The Continuing Committee then invited Lord Florey to become President, but he too died within a few weeks. At that stage, the Committee decided to leave the permanent office of President in abeyance, and to have instead a rotating President, with a term of one year. The intention was that this office be held by a distinguished person in the country where the Conference was to be held in the current year. Francis Perrin was elected President for 1968, Mikhail Millionshchikov for 1969, and Eugene Rabinowitch for 1970. In September 1970, the Continuing Committee decided to revert to the original decision of having a permanent office of President, with a five-year term of office like the members of the Continuing Committee, and invited Hannes Alfvén to become President. Alfvén took up the office of President of Pugwash at the end of the Fontana Conference.

2.3.2 Secretary-General.
The organizational work of Pugwash was from the beginning handled by Joseph Rotblat. In the earlier days there was no office and little secretarial help; all the correspondence and other administrative tasks were carried out by Rotblat and his secretary in their spare time. The letters of invitation to Conferences were initially signed by Bertrand Russell, but when he took up residence in North Wales this became impracticable, and subsequently all the invitations were signed by Rotblat on behalf of the Continuing Committee.

By 1959 it was felt that there was a need to regularize the organizational set-up, and Rotblat was formally appointed Secretary-General of Pugwash.

In this capacity he was responsible for carrying out the decisions of the Continuing Committee and for the day-to-day running of the business of Pugwash. He was greatly helped in this task by Patricia Lindop and, in recognition of this, she was appointed in 1964 Assistant Secretary-General, a post she held until 1970, when she was elected a full member of the Continuing Committee.

The officers and members of the Continuing Committee serve in an entirely honorary capacity, and no fees or salaries are paid to any of them. All the work of Pugwash is handled in their free time, on top of the University or other full-time posts held by them.

2.4 Central Office

In the early days, all the secretarial work was carried out in Joseph Rotblat's office at the Medical College of St. Bartholomew's Hospital. In 1959 the Continuing Committee decided that a Central Office be established in London with suitable secretarial staff and equipment. However, owing to financial stringency, this decision remained on paper only. Until 1968, Rotblat's private residence (at 8, Asmara Road) was the official address of the Pugwash Movement, to the surprise--and dismay--of many Pugwashites from other countries who made pilgrimages to the headquarters of the Pugwash Movement. A full-time secretary was appointed in 1963, but she worked in a room in Rotblat's Department at St. Bartholomew's.

At the Ronneby Conference it was decided "that there be established a full-time office which will be directed by the Secretary-General, and with a full-time Executive Secretary to assist him in carrying out the manifold activities associated with this office." It took another year for the financial aspect to be settled and for this decision to be implemented. In 1968, suitable office accommodation was found at 60, Great Russell Street, opposite the British Museum. Frank Barnaby was appointed full-time Executive Secretary with a staff of two secretaries. Barnaby resigned in 1970 and since then the Central Office has been managed by one full-time secretary.

At one time it was felt that there was a need for a Public Relations Officer, and in 1959 Wayland Young (Lord Kennet) was appointed to this office, which he held until 1962. In subsequent years Press Officers were appointed for the period of a Conference only. In this capacity John Maddox, Gerald Leach, John Davey, Nigel Calder and Howard Lewis acted at various Conferences.

2.5 Finance

The generous help given by Cyrus Eaton during the first two years of the Pugwash Movement was confined to Conference expenditure, and no funds were ever made available by him for the running of the secretariat. For a number of years the Central Office was run on a shoestring, and it was not until the Committee realized that Joseph Rotblat was no longer able to give up so much time from his University duties, that the decision was made to provide a budget for the Central Office. The annual budget agreed upon by the Ronneby Conference was $50,000; this money was to come from contributions from Pugwash Groups in a number of countries. However, this sum was never realized, and the actual budget of the Central Office is currently about $18,000 per annum. It is met mainly by contribution from the American Academy of Arts and Sciences, the Soviet Academy of Sciences, and the British Pugwash Group; from time to time contributions are also made by Pugwash Groups in several other countries. In addition, donations are occasionally made by individuals; in this respect, Mr. William Swartz of Chicago has been outstandingly and consistently generous. The expenditure is mainly for office accommodation and services; secretarial help; postage, telephones and cables; publications (Proceedings and Newsletters); and staff travel to Conferences and Symposia.

The actual expenditure involved in organizing the Conferences and Symposia, including travel of participants, is considerably greater than the above sum, but this is distributed among many countries. Hospitality to participants for the duration of the Conference or Symposium is usually provided by the National Pugwash Group in the host country. Travel expenses are generally met by National Pugwash Groups for their nationals. In some countries, participants can obtain travel assistance from various grant-giving bodies, academies, universities, etc. Travel expenses for participants from some developing countries are sometimes provided by the National Groups in other countries, mainly the United States.

2.6 National Pugwash Groups

For practical reasons Pugwash Conferences are limited to about 100 participants. However, it has never been the intention to confine Pugwash activities to a small group of scientists who are meeting from time to time for private deliberations. On the contrary, the Movement was conceived with the idea of making most scientists conscious of their responsibility and of inducing them to fulfil this responsibility. One way of involving more scientists in Pugwash activities was by setting up National Pugwash Groups. These took different forms. In some countries they were composed mainly of those who had participated in the Pugwash Conferences, and the chief tasks of the Groups were to prepare papers for Conferences and to advise in the selection of their participants; in other countries many other scientists joined, and the activities included holding regular meetings or lectures, organizing study groups, and the issuing of periodicals. By the end of 1971 there were 30 National Pugwash Groups; a list of them is given in Table 2. Each of the Groups has its own form of organization, makes its own rules about membership and decides on its own type of activity. Some of the Groups have a purely nominal existence and their only activity is to nominate participants in Conferences; others are very active and organize Symposia and various other functions.

The most active Pugwash Group in the 1963-1969 period was in Czechoslovakia, where it worked under the auspices of the Czechoslovak Academy of Sciences. It gave the Continuing Committee a standing invitation for Symposia and other Pugwash meetings to be held annually in Marianske Lazne; it produced a film, *To Be or Not To Be*, which depicted the history of the Pugwash Movement up to the Karlovy Vary Conference in 1964; and it published at its own cost the history of Pugwash, *Pugwash--The First Ten Years*, written by Joseph Rotblat in 1967.

Another example of a regular Pugwash activity is the International Summer School organized biennially by the Italian Pugwash Group (see section 3.5).

National Groups from a given geographical area sometimes arrange regional meetings. Thus, between 1959 and 1964, representatives from several European National Groups held a number of meetings in Geneva; scientists from 12 European countries took part in these meetings. The Study Group of European Security (see section 3.3.2) largely took over the work of these meetings.

Regional Conferences are particularly suitable for National Groups in the more remote countries of Asia, Africa and Latin America, which, because of travelling expenses, cannot afford to send many scientists to the international Conferences. An example of this was the Regional Pugwash Conference of scientists in South East Asian countries held in Melbourne in 1967 (see section 3.4).

2.7 Organization of Conferences

The organization and procedure at Pugwash Conferences has evolved gradually, and although no two Conferences have been identical with respect to organization, some general principles are discernible. The first step is a decision about the venue which is made by the Continuing Committee after receiving invitations from National Pugwash Groups to hold an Annual Conference in their country. In reaching such a decision, one of the considerations is that the Conferences should alternate between East and West (and also South) but there is no fixed rule about this. Another condition is a reasonable assurance from the organizers that all participants will be able to obtain visas. Usually, the Conference is sponsored by the senior scientific society in the host country; for example, the United States National Academy of Sciences, the Soviet Academy of Sciences, the Royal Society. This sponsorship may take different forms, and ranges from providing grants to cover the whole cost of the Conference, to moral encouragement. The actual preparatory work is done by an Organizing Committee set up by the Group in the host country. It is the task of this Committee, in consultation with the Central Office, to provide suitable meeting facilities, secretarial staff and equipment, accommodation for participants, domestic transport and the social programme.

At a meeting of the Continuing Committee, to which a representative of the Organizing Committee is invited, decisions are reached about the theme of the Conference and the topics for Working Groups. At a later stage the Continuing Committee approves the programme and detailed timetable of the Conference and appoints the conveners of Working Groups and chairmen of plenary sessions; in this too some sort of balance between countries and disciplines is aimed at. The invitees to the Conference are asked to state their choice of Working Group; they are also informed that papers will be welcome, but submission of these is not a condition of attendance. Participants are asked to send in papers early enough for prior circulation, and those received in the Central Office up to a few weeks before the Conference are edited, reproduced and sent out to all expected to attend. In practice, however, many participants hand in typescripts of papers after arrival at the Conference, and these have to be reproduced quickly and distributed at the beginning of the Conference. During the Conference itself, participants sometimes write short papers, often on topics which have arisen during the course of the discussions, and these papers too are distributed.

English and Russian are the only languages of the Conference, since most participants from the West speak English and most from the East speak Russian. Initially, the papers distributed at the Conferences were issued in both languages; the translation of all documents imposed a very heavy burden both in time and cost. However, it became clear that almost all the participants from the East know some English and, although they may find it difficult to speak or to follow a discussion in English, they can manage to read a paper. For this reason, at the later Conferences all papers, reports and statements were issued in English only. At plenary sessions simultaneous translation is provided from English into Russian and vice versa. The Soviet Group always brings with it several first-rate interpreters. Groups from other countries in the East sometimes also bring interpreters to help during Working Group meetings, which are generally conducted in English.

2.8 Participants

Despite the considerable increase in the number of persons attending Pugwash Conferences, the principles governing participation remain the same as at the first Pugwash Conferences. First, every participant is invited individually and represents nobody but himself. Second, every participant must be a scientist or scholar; these terms are used in a very broad sense, with the result that the participants range from the most eminent scientists of the world to other eminent persons whose association with science is somewhat tenuous. Third, at each conference there must be scientists from East and West (nowadays also from the developing countries), although no attempt is made to achieve an exact numerical balance.

The geographical distribution of the participants in a given Conference is determined by its theme and the topics for Working Groups, while the total number is often limited by the available accommodation, as well as by the general desire to keep the size sufficiently small to ensure that participants may get to know each other quickly. After the Continuing Committee has decided on the number of scientists from each country, the Secretary-General writes to the chairmen or secretaries of the National Pugwash Groups, where such exist, asking them to nominate the scientists from their country. The Committee reserves the right to reject some or all of these nominations and to invite scientists other than those nominated, although in practice this has happened very seldom. Letters of invitation on behalf of the Committee are then sent out by the Secretary-General individually to each person. In countries where there are no National Pugwash Groups, names of persons to be invited are obtained from past participants. Occasionally, letters are sent to Academies of Sciences asking for nominations.

A list of all participants who have attended any of the 21 Pugwash Conferences held up to the present time is given in Table 3; the list is arranged by countries and it gives the serial numbers of the Conference attended by each person. A summary of the geographical distribution of participants is given in Table 4. It will be noted that three out of the 61 countries listed, i.e., the Soviet Union, the United Kingdom and the United States, account for 50 percent of all attendances. On the other hand, the attendance from China amounts to only 0.5 percent; this is due to the fact that Chinese scientists did not attend any Pugwash Conferences after the Sixth in 1960, despite invitations sent to them regularly.

The total attendance in all the 21 Conferences was 1517, but the actual number of persons participating was 620; this gives an average of 2.4 Conferences attended per Pugwashite. Actually, as seen from the histogram in Figure 1, the distribution is highly skewed, with just over half of all Pugwashites having attended only one Conference. Only one person (Joseph Rotblat) has attended all twenty-one Conferences; one other (Eugene Rabinowitch) attended 20 of the Conferences.

Table 5 summarizes the attendances at the individual Conferences. Both the number of participants and the number of countries seem to be growing steadily. The last column shows the percentage of those who attended a given Pugwash Conference for the first time. At each Conference about one-third of the participants are newcomers to Pugwash.

Another classification of interest is by profession or field of study. Table 6 shows the distribution of the participants in all the twenty-one Conferences according to their field of work. It is seen that the physical sciences account for nearly half of all participants. However, there is a definite trend towards increasing the participation from the social sciences. Thus, during the first quinquennium 60 percent were from the physical sciences and 18 percent from the social sciences; for the newcomers in the third quinquennium the corresponding figures were 39 percent and 37 percent. This trend can be seen in more detail in Figure 2, which shows the proportions of physical and social scientists in consecutive Conferences. (The dip in both classes in the Fifth Conference was due to the unusually high proportion of biological scientists at that Conference.) This trend is partly explained by the widening areas of Pugwash interests and partly by the increasing number of scientists who take up such fields as international relations as a full-time occupation.

2.9 Other Members of the Conferences

In addition to participants, Pugwash Conferences are usually attended by other persons; these are classified as observers, scientific staff, guests, science writers and students.

2.9.1 Observers.
Several international organizations, such as the U.N., UNESCO, WHO, FAO, IAEA, SIPRI, which are concerned with the subject matter discussed at Pugwash, have expressed an interest in having their representatives at the Conferences. Usually, one to three persons are nominated by the head of each of these organizations. Generally, these are scientists with some expert knowledge of the subjects under discussion. However, since they come as representatives, they cannot be full participants,

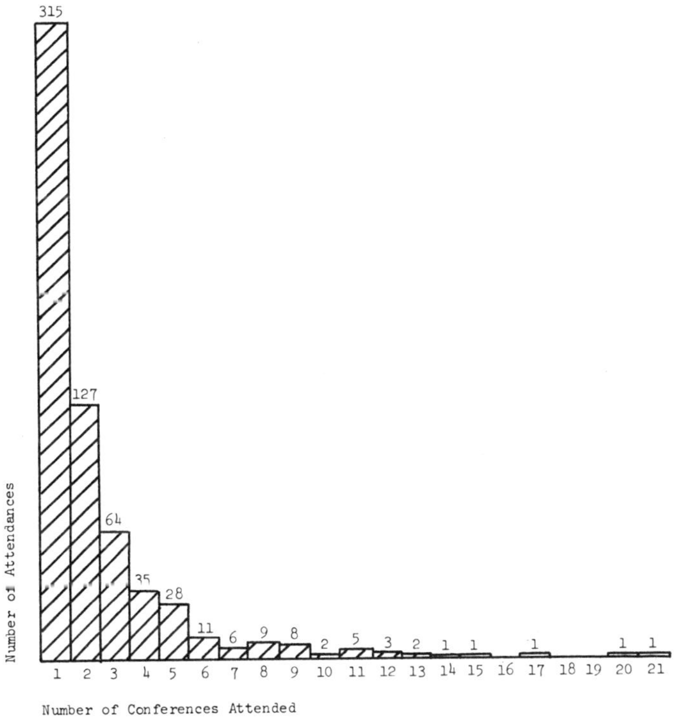

Other Members of the Conferences 19

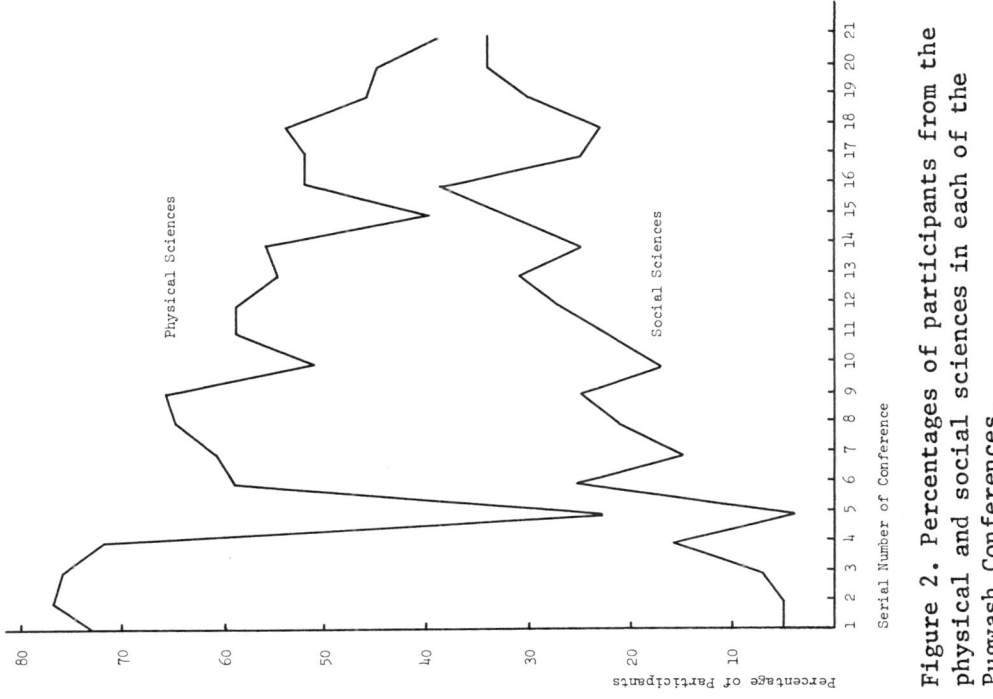

Figure 2. Percentages of participants from the physical and social sciences in each of the Pugwash Conferences.

Figure 1. Histogram of number of conferences attended by participants.

and are therefore classified as observers; in practice this does not make much difference, as observers have the right to take part in the discussions, and since no voting takes place at Pugwash Conferences. The number of official observers at each of the recent Conferences varied from eight to ten.

In the earlier Conferences other, and rather vague, categories of observers were admitted; these included Government officials, such as civil servants in the Foreign Office, or ambassadors, or official scientific advisers to governments, who thus did not fulfil the condition of being uncommitted. Another group of observers were scientists who would otherwise qualify as participants, and who were in a position to contribute usefully to the discussion, but whose inclusion would make the group from a given country unduly large; usually, these were scientists from the host country who were able to come without extra expense. In 1967 the Continuing Committee decided to abolish this category of observer since it was felt that the distinction between them and participants was rather artificial. Nowadays, the host country is allowed to bring in a somewhat larger than normal quota of participants, all of whom have the full status of participants.

2.9.2 Scientific Staff. The earlier Conferences were usually also attended by persons specifically involved in the organization; for example, in the editing of papers. These were usually scientists with sufficient qualifications to participate in their own right, but for the reasons mentioned above they were not listed as participants but as scientific staff. In subsequent Conferences this distinction has also been abolished, and many of those who were earlier listed as scientific staff have subsequently attended as full participants.

A list of persons who attended the Pugwash Conferences as official observers, or as unofficial observers or scientific staff at earlier conferences, is given in Table 7. It will be noted that some of the names in this list are also listed in Table 3; of the 180 persons in Table 7, 130 attended Pugwash as observers or scientific staff only.

2.9.3 Guests. On a few occasions the Continuing Committee has invited as guests persons who have made financial contributions to Pugwash and who have shown a special interest in the Movement. Those invited under this category included Mr. Cyrus Eaton, Mrs. Agnes Meyer, Mr. William Swartz and Mr. James Wise.

2.9.4 Science Writers. In 1967 the Continuing Committee came to the conclusion that a better projection of the Conferences to the scientific community could be obtained if a limited number of science writers were invited to attend the Conferences. The understanding was that they were entitled to write in their journals about the Conference in any way they wished, but with the same restriction as that imposed upon the members of the Conference; namely, not to attribute a specific point of view to a named individual, or in any way that would identify that individual. This experiment was tried out at Nice in 1968 and at Sochi in 1969, with eight science writers on each occasion (Table 8). The results were very satisfying, and these two Conferences received a much larger coverage in the popular scientific press than other Conferences. However, the scheme ran into difficulties at the Fontana Conference in 1970, since the United States Organizing Committee found it difficult to select a few science writers from the very large number available without offending all the others. The scheme has, therefore, been left in abeyance for the time being.

2.9.5 Students. In an attempt to bridge the generation gap and make Pugwash familiar to the younger generation, the Continuing Committee has decided to allow a certain number of students to attend the Conferences. These are mostly post-graduates, who have started on a higher degree course or on a research project. The students come mainly from the host country, but include foreign students who happen to study there. The selection is somewhat haphazard and relies upon participants supplying names of young people working in their university Departments. The students are expected to help the secretariat with various organizational tasks, but otherwise they participate in the plenary sessions and Working Groups; some of the students fully exercised this privilege and took an active part in the discussions in the Working Groups.

This experiment has been tried out on two occasions only, at Fontana in 1970 and Sinaia in 1971 (Table 9), but in view of the satisfactory results it may be continued at future Conferences.

2.10 Symposia

At the Ronneby Conferences it was decided that there should be an additional, regular activity of Pugwash; namely, Symposia (see section 3.2). As distinct from Conferences, the initiative for organizing Symposia is left largely to National Pugwash Groups, although approval for each Symposium must be obtained from the Continuing Committee. As with Conferences, no two Symposia were alike in organization, but a certain general routine has evolved. As a first step, a given National Pugwash Group informs the Continuing Committee that it wishes to organize a Symposium on a certain topic. The topic is taken from a list prepared by the Continuing Committee in 1968 (Table 10), or it can be an entirely new item, or one arising from a previous Symposium or Conference. As the next step, the National Group is asked to submit to the Continuing Committee a detailed agenda, a background paper, and a proposed list of participants. The Continuing Committee scrutinizes the material very carefully and often advises the National Group that more time may be needed to prepare the Symposium; it is reckoned that it takes about a year to prepare a symposium properly. After approval has been given, the organizational work is shared between the National Pugwash Group and the Central Office. The invitations usually go out from the Central Office. Like the Conferences, the Symposia have an international character, but the participants are selected not on a geographical basis but on the basis of expertise in the topic of the Symposium. For this reason National Pugwash Groups in other countries are not generally involved in the nomination of participants. Workers in various international organizations are often included in the

Symposium, and they are listed as participants and not as observers. The host country always provides hospitality for the participants, but not travel expenses.

Table 11 gives a list of the sixteen Symposia which were held up to April 1972, together with some statistical data about the participants. The host country is usually allowed a larger number of participants from its own nationals, and the table shows how much they made use of this privilege. One of the purposes of the Symposia is to bring more scientists into Pugwash, and the success of this is indicated in the last column of the table. Altogether 259 scientists were brought into Pugwash for the first time through the Symposia; 22 of these subsequently participated in Pugwash Conferences. A list of all those who attended any of the sixteen Symposia held so far is given in Table 12. The total number of attendances was 515, spread over 385 participants.

2.11 Contact with Other Organizations

In line with the basic principle of Pugwash that participants attend as individuals and not as representatives of other organizations, it is the policy of Pugwash to exist as an independent body and not to affiliate itself with other organizations, either on a permanent or even on a temporary basis. For this reason the Continuing Committee has always refused to take part with other organizations in joint actions or appeals, even if the action or appeal is in accordance with the aims of Pugwash. Another expression of this principle was the decision not to seek for Pugwash the status of a Non-Governmental Organization in the United Nations, although by virtue of its activities and function Pugwash would be entitled to such a status.

This policy does not prevent Pugwash from maintaining contact with other organizations, but this is usually done on a personal basis by individual Pugwashites rather than by formal arrangements.

An example of such arrangement is the contact with SIPRI (Stockholm International Peace Research Institute). Pugwash has been associated with the project to set up SIPRI from the beginning (see section 4.12). The committee, under the chairmanship of Alva Myrdal, which was set up by the Swedish Government to study the feasibility of establishing a Peace Research Institute, included Hannes Alfvén and Martin Fehrm, who had participated in Pugwash Conferences. During 1964 and 1965 the members of this committee have met members of the Continuing Committee and of National Pugwash Groups in several countries. Projects to be undertaken by the Institute were also discussed at several Pugwash Conferences.

SIPRI came into being in July 1966, and among the 8 members of the Board of Governors, 2 (Ivan Malek and Joseph Rotblat) were intimately connected with Pugwash. Most of the other Board members, as well as of the 24-member Scientific Council, had also attended various Pugwash Conferences. The first Director of SIPRI, Robert Neild, is a Pugwashite, and so is his successor, Frank Barnaby.

Contact with Other Organizations

In the case of SIPRI the contacts went further than by personal ties. The greater part of the work of the Pugwash Study Group on Biological Warfare (section 3.3.1) was taken over by SIPRI, which made it into one of its major projects. The current work at SIPRI had also been discussed at several Pugwash Conferences.

Pugwash has also been associated with the setting up of IPRA (International Peace Research Association). This organization arose initially from the need felt by some social scientists to have a movement similar to Pugwash but based mainly on social scientists. The first attempt to form a "Social Scientists' Pugwash" was made in 1963 at a meeting in Clarence, Switzerland, but the project never got off the ground. In 1964 IPRA was formed at a meeting in London. Initially it was agreed that the Secretaries-General of IPRA and Pugwash (Bert Roling and Joseph Rotblat) should attend each other's committee meetings as observers, but for a variety of reasons this arrangement has not been implemented.

There are growing contacts with some organizations of the United Nations family, quite apart from their sending observers to Conferences. Some activities which have arisen from these contacts are described in section 3.7. Recently, there have been informal meetings of Pugwashites with the Secretary-General of the United Nations and members of his staff concerned with disarmament.

3 PUGWASH ACTIVITIES

3.1 Conferences

The Conferences were initially the only Pugwash activity, and even today they remain the major activity. In the course of time the size, scope and nature of the Conferences have gradually changed.

In the early days, Conferences were held at irregular intervals, sometimes two Conferences following each other immediately; thus, during the first 10 years a total of 16 Conferences were held. With the introduction in 1967 of the new activity, Symposia, it was decided that Conferences should be held at yearly intervals. These Annual Conferences are usually held in September.

With the growing interest in Pugwash among the scientific community, there has been an ever increasing demand from scientists to attend the Conferences and their size has been steadily increasing, reaching the level of about 100 (see Table 5), with much larger numbers at the Quinquennial Conferences. The increase in the number of participants has brought about a change in procedure. Initially there were only plenary sessions with all participants attending. At the Seventh Conference in 1961 it was decided to introduce a system of Working Groups; this was necessitated not only by the larger numbers attending but also by the greater variety of topics discussed. The number of Working Groups varies from Conference to Conference but usually it is four or five; the average number of members in each Working Group is thus about 20, which is considered to be optimal for effective discussion.

More than half of the Conference time is taken up by sessions of Working Groups; the remaining time is in plenary sessions, each session lasting half a day (morning or afternoon). The Conference always starts with a plenary session. At one period this session became practically a formal ceremony, and included the reading of messages of greetings from Heads of State and various scientific organizations. More recently the formal part was reduced to about one hour and the remainder of the first plenary session is spent on a report and discussion on Pugwash activities during the past year. One or two of the plenary sessions near the end of the Conference are taken by reading reports from Working Groups, and the last session includes a discussion on future activities. In the earlier days the last session used to be taken up with the drafting of a public statement from the whole Conference. This became more and more difficult and time-consuming, and, after the Twelfth Conference, when it took seven hours to draft a statement, it was decided to abandon the practice of issuing public statements from the Conference and to leave it to the Continuing Committee to publish a statement in its own name.

In the recent years some plenary sessions in mid-Conference began to be used as a kind of teach-in on specialized topics, such as specific aspects of environmental pollution or of population problems. Several experts in the given field are invited to give reviews of the subject or present their own views on it; this is followed by comments from a number of invited discussants and finally by a discussion from the floor. These plenary sessions serve the useful purpose of introducing new topics to Pugwash, or of bringing the participants up-to-date in established Pugwash topics.

The topics for discussion at the Conferences also underwent a considerable change. Initially the main purpose of the Conferences was to seek a solution to the problems created by the introduction of weapons of mass destruction. **Disarmament and its various ramifications were, therefore,** discussed in great detail. Another natural topic for Pugwash was the social responsibility of scientists. In the course of time other subjects began to demand the attention of Pugwash scientists; these subjects included international co-operation in science and technology; the various problems of the developing nations, and, in particular, the role that science can play in accelerating their development; and, more recently, problems of the environment and of the population explosion. The question of the emphasis to be given to each of these subjects is frequently discussed by the Continuing Committee, as well as at the Quinquennial Conferences. The consensus is that problems of disarmament and world security still call for the most urgent attention and **should**, therefore, occupy the bulk of the Pugwash effort. But it is recognized that the other subjects must also be discussed, partly because of their growing interest in the community and partly because they are often associated with security problems. In a typical Pugwash Conference, three Working Groups might deal with some aspects of disarmament, one with the environment or with international collaboration, and one with problems of developing nations.

The outcome of the discussions in each Working Group is a report prepared by the conveners and approved by the whole Working Group. These reports are read out at a plenary session, so that other members of the Conference may learn about them and have an opportunity to comment and suggest amendments. Since the reports are considered as documents from each Working Group and not from the Conference as a whole, it is up to each Group to accept or not to accept the suggestions made at the plenary session. Sometimes the Continuing Committee agrees to release a report from a Working Group as a public document. The public statement issued by the Continuing Committee after each Conference is largely based on the reports from the Working Groups.

A detailed account of each of the Conferences, showing the gradual evolvement of procedure and increase in scope of interest, is given in Chapter 4.

3.2 Symposia

When Pugwash started, it was virtually the only international forum where scientists from East and West met to debate problems of the arms race and world security; few other scientists studied these problems, and consequently significant and substantive results could be expected from Pugwash debates. The situation changed considerably in the course of a few years. Largely stimulated by Pugwash, a number of individual scientists began to study these problems on a full-time basis and became experts in them; moreover, several institutes were set up specifically aimed at studying these issues with a full-time staff and secretariat. Under these circumstances the gathering of "amateurs," meeting for a few days and covering a very wide range of topics, could hardly be expected to compete successfully with the professionals. There are still valid reasons for meetings of "amateurs," such as at Pugwash Conferences; for example, to present to independent scientists the results of the work of the professional institutes for a critical evaluation, or to provide a forum for the critique of the working of different international organizations. Nevertheless, it was felt that Pugwash should return to its earlier role of making original contributions to the solution of problems facing mankind.

At the Ronneby Conference it was decided to realize this need by introducing a new type of activity, Symposia. These were envisaged to follow the pattern of small specialized scientific conferences. Each Symposium would consist of about 30 participants and be concerned with one specific topic which would be studied in depth. The finding of the Symposia would be discussed at the Annual Pugwash Conferences and, when it was deemed appropriate, the proceedings of a Symposium would be published in the form of a Pugwash Monograph.

To help the National Pugwash Groups in selecting topics for Symposia, a list of suitable topics was drawn up by the Continuing Committee. This list is shown in Table 10; as is seen, it covers all aspects of Pugwash activities. This list was intended only as a guide, and as seen from Table 11, a few of these topics were indeed taken up, but some Pugwash Groups decided to use topics other than those on the list.

The First Symposium, organized by the British Pugwash Group, was held in April 1968; by April 1972, 16 Symposia had been held, an average of four per year; this is within the original expectation of three to five per year. On the other hand, the standard of the discussions at the Symposia was not always up to expectation. In some cases the discussion tended to be rather general and platitudinous; this was particularly true at Symposia for which the topic was too broad and ill-defined. Nevertheless, the Symposia did, on the whole, fulfil their aim of providing a forum for some detailed and expert discussion, as well as to bring more scientists into Pugwash.

The proceedings of three Symposia, the First, Third and Tenth (Table 11), were considered to be of sufficient importance to be published as Pugwash Monographs. The first two Monographs were published by the Souvenir Press in London, and the third by The MIT Press in Cambridge, Massachusetts. The proceedings of the Fourth and Eighth Symposia were also considered to be worthy of publication, but this did not materialize due to delays with the publishers. The results of some other Symposia were transmitted to interested organizations. Thus, the findings of the Eighth Symposium were forwarded to the Second World Food Congress; those of the Ninth Symposium were presented at a UNESCO meeting of Ministers of the European Member States responsible for science policy; the recommendations of the Twelfth Symposium were sent to all members of the Conference of the Committee on Disarmament in Geneva in the hope that they would facilitate the reaching of an agreement on banning biological warfare; the background paper and recommendations of the Thirteenth Symposium were circulated to a number of Research Councils and Universities; and the recommendations of the Fourteenth Symposium were sent to U Thant (see section 3.7.5).

3.3 Study Groups

Before the introduction of Symposia, specific topics of interest to Pugwash which required several meetings were tackled by means of Study Groups. Some of these were directly under the auspices of the Continuing Committee, others were farmed out to outside bodies. In the first category were the Study Groups on Biological Warfare and on European Security.

3.3.1 Biological Warfare Study Group.

It was mainly due to the initiative of Martin Kaplan that the Biological Warfare Study Group was set up. Kaplan participated in all discussions on this subject since the Fifth Conference at Pugwash in 1959. There were informal talks on that topic during the Dubrovnik Conference, but the Study Group was set up formally at the Karlovy Vary Conference in 1964. Since then the Group has met six times: in January 1965 in Geneva, April 1965 in Trieste, October 1965 and September 1966 in Stockholm, and in May 1967 and again in May 1969 in Marianske Lazne. The attendance at the meetings ranged from 12 to 26, with the participants coming from 16 countries. The total number of participants was 64 (see Table 13), but the actual membership at each meeting varied considerably, and was selected according to the topic under discussion.

In discussing the means of preventing the development of biological weapons, and the difficulties in differentiating between defensive and offensive work in laboratories, the Group paid particular attention to procedures of inspection of the work of such laboratories. The Group put forward a pilot scheme of voluntary inspection of laboratories in different countries. This experiment was carried out in 1966 by a team headed by Carl Heden. Four laboratories were inspected, which represented different areas of specialization, as well as political structure; they were in Austria, Czechoslovakia, Denmark and Sweden. These inspections proved highly successful, and provided the basis for an inspection programme carried out on a much larger scale by SIPRI in the period 1967-1969.

Related to the above is the need of developing methods of rapid detection of microbiological agents, including viruses and toxins, which might be used in biological warfare. The meeting of the Study Group in Stockholm in September 1966 included a number of experts in this field, who have assessed the present-day techniques for rapid detection, and put forward recommendations for research work to be carried out by an international team. This was taken a step further in the Twelfth Symposium in Geneva 1971 (see section 3.2).

In 1967 most of the work of the Biological Warfare Study Group was taken over by SIPRI; with its much greater financial resources and permanent staff it was able to move much faster than Pugwash. The meetings of the Study Group in 1967 and 1969 were largely concerned with reviewing the progress made by SIPRI and putting forward suggestions for further work. At that stage the Biological Warfare Study Group became also concerned with the status of tear gas and other harassing agents (CN, CS and DH).

Members of the Study Group were involved in drafting a submission on biological and chemical warfare to U Thant (see section 3.7.5). Another achievement of the Study Group was to prepare the ground for a resolution to prohibit the use of biological weapons unanimously adopted at the 10th International Congress for Microbiology in Mexico City in April 1970.

3.3.2 European Security. The Study Group on European Security was started by the simultaneous and independent initiative of the Czechoslovak and Danish Pugwash Groups. The need for such a Study Group emerged at the Karlovy Vary Conference, when European problems were discussed at length. A regional meeting of European Pugwash scientists, held in Geneva in April 1964 (see section 2.6), further debated this topic, and the Study Group was set up formally at a meeting in Prague in December 1965. Antonín Šnejdárek and David Adler were appointed permanent Co-Chairmen of the Group; in 1968 Robert Leclerc took over from Adler. Three meetings were held in 1966: in March in Halsingborg, in May in Geneva, and in September in Jablonna; two meetings in 1967: in February in Zagreb, and in May in Marianske Lazne; and two more meetings in 1968: in February in Kiel, and in May in Marianske Lazne. The attendance at these meetings grew rapidly from 12 to 50, with participants coming from 16 European countries, about equally divided between NATO and Warsaw Pact countries, plus Austria and Sweden. A feature of this Study Group was that the majority of the participants came from the social sciences.

The work of the Study Group was concerned with three main problems: Germany, security in Europe, and integrational processes. The presence of scientists from both parts of Germany gave some poignancy to the discussion on the German issue, which included the problem of frontiers, a peace treaty and reunification. Under the heading "Security in Europe" the topics included denuclearized zones in Europe, procedures for the enforcement of collateral disarmament measures, and the role of IAEA. In relation to integrational processes, political, economic and scientific co-operation in Europe was discussed at length. Nearly 40 papers were prepared by the members of the Group during the first year of study, and the results were presented at the Sopot Conference. During the second year the Study Group prepared three reports: on non-proliferation, on European co-operation and integrational processes, and on European security; these reports were discussed at the Ronneby Conference.

By the end of the third year the range of topics that had arisen in the discussions of the Study Group had grown so wide that it was difficult to maintain cohesion, and the Continuing Committee decided that the objects of the Study Group might be better achieved by organizing several Symposia, each concerned with one aspect of European security.

3.3.3 East-West Study Group. The United States-Soviet Union Study Group on disarmament and arms control is not strictly a Pugwash activity, but the initiative for it, as well as the contacts, came from Pugwash. The American Academy of Arts and Sciences, together with the Soviet Academy of Sciences, were the joint sponsors of the Group, with Mikhail Millionshchikov and Paul Doty as Co-Chairmen. A grant was obtained from the Ford

Foundation to cover expenses when the Group met in the United States; for meetings in the Soviet Union, the Soviet Academy provided funds.

The first meeting of the Study Group took place in June 1964 at Harvard University. Five Soviet and 9 American scientists participated, with a few others from the United States attending for short periods. The topics discussed by the group included the "nuclear umbrella"; the first stages of disarmament; the various aspects of non-proliferation, including a ban on the transfer of technical information or of fissile materials; a moratorium on the sale of plutonium; and the ABM problem.

It was planned to hold further meetings alternatively in the Soviet Union and the United States, and the next meeting was scheduled for 1965, in Moscow. However, due to the Vietnam crisis, this meeting was put off. During the next few years contact between members of the Group was maintained chiefly on the occasions of Pugwash Conferences. However, a full meeting of the Group was held in August 1971 in Moscow.

3.3.4 Study Group on Development. In an entirely different category is the Study Group on Development. Its setting up was triggered by complaints from some of the Pugwashites who were particularly interested in the problem of developing nations. They felt that the Pugwash effort in this area was haphazard and limited merely to discussions in one of the Working Groups at Conferences; moreover, due to the changing composition of the Working Groups, these discussions tended to be repetitious and general. It was felt by these Pugwashites that the problems of developing countries demand a different approach than other problems tackled by Pugwash, and that a Standing Committee should be set up with the task of organizing Pugwash activities in the whole sphere of developing nations. The Continuing Committee accepted the proposal that developing nations pose a special problem, but decided that instead of a Standing Committee, a Study Group should be set up initially for a period of two years, with the task of working out a programme of Pugwash involvement in problems of development, and specifically to prepare plans for Symposia and other activities to be undertaken by Pugwash, all these plans to be put before the Continuing Committee for approval.

The Study Group was set up at the Fontana Conference in 1970 and formally approved by the Continuing Committee in April 1971. It consists of Victor Rabinowitch (United States) as convener, with John Katili (Indonesia), Bernard Laponche (France), Igor Mojeiko (Soviet Union), Thomas Odhiambo (Kenya), Geoffrey Oldham (United Kingdom), Ashok Parthasarathi (India), Frank Torto (Ghana), and Carlos Varsavsky (Argentina), with Ignacy Malecki (UNESCO) as observer. The Study Group met for the first time in Paris in April 1971, and prepared a preliminary programme of Symposia of different types and on various topics; these plans are still to be implemented.

3.4 Regional Conferences

3.4.1 European. It is often convenient for National Groups from a given geographical area to convene regional Conferences to discuss problems of common interest. The forerunner of this type of Conference were the meetings of European Pugwash Groups which were held in Geneva between 1959 and 1964 (section 2.6). They were made possible by the efforts of Martin Kaplan and James Wise.

The discussions at these meetings included the problem of Germany. An interesting feature of the meeting held in March 1963 was a joint paper by two German scientists, one from the German Federal Republic (Gerd Burkhardt) and the other from the German Democratic Republic (Max Steenbeck), in which a possible solution to the German problem was outlined. This may have been the first successful attempt at a common approach to this issue by scientists from both parts of Germany.

3.4.2 South-East Asian. As already pointed out (section 2.6), regional Conferences are of special interest to the scientists in other continents, and with the greater emphasis on the problems of the developing countries, regional Conferences are likely to become of increasing importance to the Pugwash Movement. The first regional Pugwash Conference of scientists in South-East Asian countries was held in Melbourne, January 23-27, 1967. It was attended by 26 scientists from nine countries: Australia, Ceylon, India, Indonesia, Japan, Malaysia, New Zealand, Pakistan, and Singapore.

The theme of the Conference was "Scientific, Technical and Industrial Development in South-East Asia," and the programme envisaged three main topics for discussion: (a) definition of crucial areas in which the application of science and technology will most rapidly improve living standards, and prerequisites for success in these areas; (b) problems of security and their effect on the development of science and technology; and (c) education and training; role of tertiary institutes; the question of developing a technician force. Seventeen papers relating to these topics were submitted by participants.

The Conference, which took place in the International House of the University of Melbourne, started with an introductory session to which the Press and guests were invited; this meeting was addressed by, among others, Sir Macfarlane Burnet, President of the Australian Academy of Science, which was associated with the Conference. The actual work of the Conference started on the following day, with plenary sessions in which each of the three items of the programme was taken up in turn. The discussion helped to crystallize topics of special interest, and these were then taken up in three Working Groups on the following subjects: (1) regional co-operation in development and education; (2) food sciences and technology in developing countries; and (3) problems of security and development. Apart from more detailed discussion of these problems, the Working Groups also drafted reports which formed the basis of a public statement from the Conference. These drafts were discussed on the last day of the meeting, and the statement was accepted unanimously (the text of the statement is given in Appendix 20).

Although the majority of the participants were newcomers to Pugwash, the usual spirit of Pugwash Conferences soon became evident in the tone of the discussions. The special needs of the South-East Asian region naturally came to the fore, and some specific proposals were made in this respect. The Vietnam issue was also an obvious topic, and the agreement reached on this is reflected in the statement.

The main weakness of the Conference was the absence of scientists from several countries in the region, particularly China and Vietnam. Despite this, the Melbourne meeting was an undoubted success and confirmed the great value of such regional Conferences. The participants were unanimous in asking for further meetings in the region, perhaps in a location which would make it possible for more countries to be represented. Attempts were made to convene the next Conference in Ceylon, but this plan has not materialized so far.

Another regional Conference is planned for 1972 or 1973 in Ibadan in Nigeria. It will be attended by scientists from the African continent, and one of its aims will be to set up an African Pugwash Group.

3.5 International Activities of National Pugwash Groups

Apart from being host to the Annual Conferences and organizing Symposia, some National Pugwash Groups carry out activities of an international character. An example is the International Summer School of Disarmament and Arms Control, organized by the Italian Pugwash Group, which is held every two years. Edoardo Amaldi is the director, and Carlo Schaerf the organizing secretary of the School, which is "intended for people who, either already having a professional interest in the field or who, being specialists in related fields, would like to play a more active and technically competent role in this direction." The School has an inter-disciplinary character, and the subjects range from the technical and scientific aspects to the sociological and political implications of disarmament and arms control.

The first School was held in June 1966 in Frascati, near Rome; the second in July 1968 in Pavia, near Milan; the third in August 1970 in Castello Duino, near Trieste; the fourth is to be held in August 1972 in Padova. The lecturers are mostly Pugwashites invited from several countries, and the students have come from some 20 countries. A measure of the success of the School is the growth from 22 students in 1966 to 60 in 1970. Apart from talks given by individual lecturers, characteristic features of the School are the seminars and round-table discussions in which both the lecturers and the students take an active part.

Another activity which has become a regular feature is the contact which the British Pugwash Group maintains with the International Youth Science Fortnight. This is an annual event in which some 500 budding scientists (school leavers or first year of University) from many countries come to London to visit various educational institutes, listen to lectures, and take part in discussions on science and society. Since 1969, one day of the Fortnight has been devoted to Pugwash. Pugwashites from the United Kingdom and several other countries come to give talks and to lead discussion groups on various topics of interest to Pugwash. These Pugwash days have proved very stimulating both to the experts and to the audience, and constitute a valuable contact between Pugwash and the younger generation.

3.6 Special Meetings

Apart from organizing the Annual Conferences and Symposia, the Continuing Committee has, from time to time, called small conferences on special topics. Due to their nature these meetings were kept strictly private, and nothing was written about them until the passage of time had made the issues less sensitive.

3.6.1 The Test Ban Problem.

One of the subjects of particular concern to Pugwash from the early days was the reaching of an agreement to ban tests of nuclear weapons. The discussions at several Pugwash Conferences having shown that the areas of agreement were considerable, it was thought that a meeting of a small group of experts might be useful in helping to bridge the gap. After the Tenth Conference in London, when the idea of the "black boxes" was put forward (section 4.9), arrangements were made for such a meeting to discuss the scheme in more detail. The sudden death of Topchiev, who was to lead the Soviet group, caused this plan to be postponed for a few months. In March 1963, the Secretary-General convened a special meeting to discuss the technical and political aspects of the nuclear test ban problem. It was held at the Ciba Foundation in London. There were 12 participants, 6 from the United States, 3 from the Soviet Union, 3 from the United Kingdom, with the Secretary-General in the Chair. Most of the participants from the three countries were experts in seismology and related subjects, and most of them were influential with their governments. The small size of the meeting, the standing of the participants, and the fact that the meeting was completely private, made it possible to conduct a detailed, erudite and fruitful discussion on the whole subject. The technical problems associated with underground explosions and the political issues of on-site inspections were thoroughly explored. A number of specific proposals emerged from these debates, and it was agreed that these should be submitted directly by the participants to the governments concerned. A document drawn up by the participants concludes: "The meeting considers that the clarity now attained in the scientific and technical aspects of the problem provides a sufficient basis for the governments to arrive at an agreement for the conclusion of a test ban treaty in the near future." It is believed that this meeting has substantially helped in reaching the agreement on the partial test-ban treaty three months later.

3.6.2 The Vietnam Crisis.

The Vietnam war has been discussed at several Pugwash Conferences, and each time the need to bring the war to an end was strongly urged; but beyond these general expressions of opinion, there were no concrete ideas about the solution of the crisis. It was thought, however, that more tangible results might be obtained in private discussion involving mainly scientists from the United States and the Soviet Union. The first such private meeting was held in August 1965 at the Ciba Foundation in London; present were 3 scientists each from the United States and the Soviet Union, and 2 from the United Kingdom. At this meeting the

relative attitudes of both sides were reviewed and realistic conditions
for terminating the war were discussed. No specific proposals emerged,
but the meeting helped to produce a clearer picture of the whole situation
and prepared the ground for further discussion.

The second meeting was held in Paris in June 1967. One of the reasons for
calling this meeting was to see whether Pugwash could help in the Middle
East crisis, but the opportunity was taken to discuss further the Vietnam
situation. The meeting was attended by 3 scientists from France, 3 from
the United States, 2 from the Soviet Union, and the Secretary-General.
This time the discussions centred round certain specific conditions to
enable both sides to come to the negotiating table. As a result of the
deliberations it was agreed that a mission consisting of French scientists
should go to Hanoi and convey a message from the United States Government
to the North Vietnam Government containing conditions for the termination
of war activities. This mission did take place and an exchange of messages
was thereby achieved. There are good reasons for the belief that the start
of official negotiations between the United States and Vietnam in the
spring of 1968 was the direct outcome of this mission.

3.7 Other Activities of the Continuing Committee
Apart from the functions already described, the Continuing Committee is
occasionally involved in other activities. Some of these are private interventions in time of crisis, others involve public declarations or semi-public submissions.

3.7.1 The Cuban Crisis.
A striking example of a private intervention was
the action taken by the Committee during the Cuban crisis in October 1962.
At the start of the crisis, the Secretary-General transmitted a cable from
the American Pugwash scientists to their colleagues in the Soviet Union,
asking them to urge the Soviet Government to re-route the ships to Cuba
so as to avoid a clash, and at the same time pledging themselves to urge
the United States Government not to take any precipitate action. Following this, the Secretary-General called an emergency meeting of influential
scientists from the United States and the Soviet Union to discuss means of
solving the crisis. For several days he was in almost continuous telephone communication with Washington and Moscow. Such a meeting could obviously not be held without the approval of the highest authorities in the
countries concerned, but this approval was very quickly obtained, and an
agreement was reached to hold the meeting in London within a few days;
however, the resolution of the crisis made the meeting unnecessary. While
it is impossible to say how useful this meeting would have been if it had
been held, the very fact that in a time of crisis it was possible to plan,
at very short notice, for a meeting of eminent scientists, with top level
approval for it, shows the importance of the channel of communication provided by Pugwash.

3.7.2 The India-Pakistan Conflict.
The tension between India and Pakistan
has always been of concern to Pugwash, and in 1963 a meeting was arranged
in Geneva among influential scientists from both countries to discuss the
possibility of closer scientific and technological collaboration between

Other Activities of the Continuing Committee

India and Pakistan and thus open the way to better general relations. The atmosphere at that meeting was very cordial and the outcome promising. Further discussions were held in 1964 during the Udaipur Conference; it was then agreed that Pugwash Officers should pay visits to the Heads of Government of both countries. A talk between Cecil Powell and Pandit Nehru did take place, but the visit to Ayub Khan did not materialize.

At the end of 1965 the Continuing Committee sent a cable to Tashkent, where the Indian and Pakistani Heads of State were meeting with Mr. Kosygin, urging them to bring the India-Pakistan conflict to an end.

3.7.3 The Middle-East Conflict. In May 1967, when the Arab-Israeli conflict became critical, the Continuing Committee decided to send letters to the Presidents of Egypt and Israel offering assistance in arranging a private meeting between scientists from each of the two countries with a few members of the Continuing Committee to discuss ways of easing the tension in that area of the world. A reply came very quickly from President Shazar of Israel accepting the suggestion, but no reply came from President Nasser, probably because of the outbreak of hostilities in the Six Day War.

3.7.4 The Situation in Argentina and Brazil. Another type of intervention was the open letter sent by the Continuing Committee to the President of the Argentinian Republic in 1966, referring to the persecution of scientists in Argentina and calling attention to the disastrous effects this may have on this country. A similar letter was sent in 1969 to the President of Brazil when persecution of scientists began in that country.

3.7.5 Submissions to the United Nations. In 1969 a request came from U Thant for a report on biological and chemical warfare to help the group of consultant-experts which was set up by the United Nations General Assembly in order to prepare a report on the effects of the possible use of chemical and bacteriological weapons. Several members of the Pugwash Biological Warfare Study Group prepared a document which was submitted to U Thant; the point made in the submission about tear gas and other harassing agents was taken up by U Thant in his recommendations to the members of the United Nations.

In the spring of 1971 U Thant again called on Pugwash to prepare a submission which would help another group of consultant-experts to prepare a report on the economic and social consequences of the arms race and military expenditure. This time the Continuing Committee itself prepared a statement during its meeting in Frascati in April 1971, based on a draft prepared by a British Group. The statement was submitted to U Thant together with an Appendix containing the recommendations of the Fourteenth Symposium in Leipzig.

3.7.6 Public Statements. Apart from the public statements issued after the Annual Conferences, the Continuing Committee issues from time to time statements on special topics. In 1959 a public statement was made on the urgent need to ban nuclear tests. In 1967 a statement was issued containing comments on the non-proliferation treaty, the text of which appears in Appendix 21.

3.8 Publications

The two official, but limited, publications of Pugwash are the Proceedings of the Conferences and the Pugwash Newsletter. Both are edited by the Secretary-General and issued from the Central Office. Initially the Proceedings of the Conference varied very much in size and style. The Proceedings of the First Conference were never issued; those of the Second Conference contained a verbatim transcript of all discussions and totalled about 1,000 pages; but since the Twelfth Conference they have been uniform in format and layout of material. Each volume contains the papers submitted by the participants, the public statement, the reports of the Working Groups and a summary of the discussions at the plenary sessions.

The Proceedings of the Second, Third, Fourth and Fifth Conferences were typed and produced in Mr. Cyrus Eaton's office. For the Sixth, Seventh and Eighth Conferences the host country (the Soviet Union and the United States) prepared the Proceedings. The Central Office took over the task starting from the Ninth Conference. The volumes are typewritten in the Central Office and reproduced, by a photographic process, by a commercial firm. The Proceedings vary in size from 230 to 550 pages.

The Proceedings are distributed gratis to all those who attended any of the past Conferences (participants and observers) as well as to Heads of State or Government. They also go to a number of individuals and organizations interested in Pugwash, but the recipients are advised that the contents are for personal use and not for publication. Eleven hundred copies of each volume are printed.

The other publication is the Pugwash Newsletter, which was started in July 1963. It appears quarterly, and by 1972 nine volumes have been published, each of 80-120 pages of print in double column. The Newsletter contains information about Pugwash events; reports on Symposia, with summaries of the discussions at them; reports from Working Groups at Conferences; and articles from individual Pugwashites. Thirteen hundred copies are printed of each issue; the distribution is the same as for the Proceedings, but extra copies are sent to some National Groups.

Apart from the History of Pugwash by J. Rotblat (the first edition under the title *Science and World Affairs* appeared in 1962; the second edition under the title *Pugwash--The First Ten Years* appeared in 1967) the only other Pugwash publications on the open market are the Pugwash Monographs which contain the proceedings of some Symposia; three of these have appeared so far (see section 3.2).

Another open publication was a volume containing the proceedings of the first International Summer School on Disarmament and Arms Control held in 1966 (see section 3.5).

This Chapter continues the history of the Pugwash Conferences following the First Conference described in Chapter 1. The account is presented in historical order and reflects the changing attitudes and interests in the course of time.

4.1 Second Conference: Lac Beauport, March 31-April 11, 1958, "The Dangers of the Present Situation, and Ways and Means of Diminishing Them"

Having agreed with Cyrus Eaton that the Second Conference would be held in Lac Beauport (see section 1.7), letters of invitation, signed by Bertrand Russell, were sent to 47 scientists. Of these, 22 accepted, the same number as at the First Conference, but the composition was largely different; only 9 of the participants of the First Conference were present. Of the 22 scientists, 8 came from the United States, 4 each from the Soviet Union and the United Kingdom, 2 from Canada, and one each from Australia, China, France and West Germany. The numerical predominance of participants from the United States, the Soviet Union and the United Kingdom was deliberate, as it was felt that these were the key countries on whose decisions must depend the establishment of a lasting peace. This pattern was followed in most of the subsequent conferences dealing with disarmament and world security. In selecting participants, the Committee was conscious of the need to include persons who had made a special study of disarmament problems.

The meeting took place in the Hotel Manoir Saint-Castin, which was taken over by Cyrus Eaton for the duration of the Conference. To allow more time for informal talks and for thought, the Conference was arranged to last 12 days, the longest of all Pugwash Conferences. Formal sessions were held either in the mornings or afternoons, and the chair at these sessions was taken by participants in rotation. There was no pre-arranged programme, and no papers were pre-circulated. The agenda was made up from day to day, as ideas developed and as new topics emerged from the discussion.

The scientific secretariat at the Conference was under the charge of Patricia Lindop, who had assisted Joseph Rotblat in the preparatory work in London, and who, in this and subsequent conferences, gave unsparingly of her time and energy. Together with Betty Royon, Eaton's personal assistant, they achieved a high standard of efficiency, so that not only the papers which were written by participants *ad hoc*, but the proceedings of each session were prepared, duplicated, and ready for distribution at the following session. The collection of all papers read at the Conference, together with the proceedings of the sessions, made up four volumes of nearly 1,000 pages; these volumes were subsequently circulated to the participants.

The subjects discussed came under three main headings: the dangers of the present situation; the means of eliminating the immediate dangers; and the means of relaxing tension. Each of these contained a number of topics, some of a general nature, such as short- and long-term policies aimed at establishing peace, and others more specific, e.g., problems of bases on foreign territory. A great deal of time was spent on discussing an agreement to ban nuclear weapons tests, and the technical problems of inspection which the enforcement of such an agreement would require. One session was devoted to a debate on the biological hazards of radiation and another to the exchange of students and scientists. Finally, taking a look a longer way ahead, the Conference discussed, during one session, the problem of the population explosion and its consequences.

In accordance with the initial decision, no statement was issued by the Conference, but a communiqué, listing the participants and the topics discussed (Appendix 3), was released at the end. The participants also decided to send the papers read at the Conference to the Heads of State or Government of 15 countries, to the Pope and to the Secretary-General of the United Nations. Some of them, e.g., Premier Khrushchev, President Tito, Prime Ministers Nehru and Diefenbaker, replied at length, expressing their appreciation of the work of the Conference. Acknowledgements were also received from the Department of State on behalf of President Eisenhower and from an aide to the Pope. This practice of sending the Proceedings to Heads of State was followed at the subsequent conferences.

The main value of the Lac Beauport Conference lay in the frank exchange of views among the participants. The topics covered a wide range of subjects, but in spite of this, the discussions were kept at a very high level. Many topics which were later to figure prominently at official disarmament talks, as well as at Pugwash Conferences, such as the minimum deterrent, non-proliferation of nuclear weapons, or problems of on-site inspections, were brought up for the first time here. Most of the issues were highly complex, both technically and politically, and, in view of the entirely different approaches taken by various participants to many of the problems, it was hardly to be expected that agreement would be reached on their solutions. In many instances the scientists from the West received, for the first time, reasoned objections to their views from scientists in the East, and vice-versa. This confrontation of ideas, of prejudices, and of causes of mistrust, was in itself very valuable, as it gave an opportunity for better understanding of motivation of others and, in some cases, removed misunderstandings and dispelled fears. At the end of the Conference all participants were much more informed and in a better position to study the problems. It was their unanimous opinion that this type of conference helped to clarify thinking, and that further meetings devoted to more detailed studies of the problems of disarmament should be held. Lac Beauport became the prototype for future conferences on various aspects of disarmament and arms control.

4.2 Third Conference: Kitzbühel and Vienna, September 14-20, 1958, "Dangers of the Atomic Age and What Scientists Can Do about Them"

When the Continuing Committee decided at its first meeting (section 1.7) to convene a more general conference in Europe, it was not at all clear how to finance such a large gathering. This matter was largely solved thanks to the intervention of Hans Thirring. An enthusiastic supporter of the Pugwash Movement, and participant of the First Conference, Thirring, who had considerable influence in Austria, approached the Theodor-Körner Foundation for support and received a very warm response. The Director of the Foundation, Dr. Bruno Kreisky (later Federal Chancellor of the Austrian Republic) attended, with Thirring, the meeting of the Continuing Committee held in London in June, 1958. The Committee accepted the generous offer of the Körner Foundation to provide hospitality for all participants during their stay in Austria at a conference to be held in Kitzbühel in the Tyrol, with a final session in Vienna.

There remained the problem of travelling expenses. These turned out to be not too heavy, since many participants from overseas were attending various other conferences in Europe. Grants towards these expenses were obtained from the Soviet Academy of Sciences, the New Hope Foundation, Cyrus Eaton, William Swartz, and a number of other individuals in the United States. In addition to the monetary donation, Eaton sent to Kitzbühel, at his own expense, three members of his staff to run the secretariat.

Since the purpose of the Conference was to deal with the general problem of the social implications of science, as well as to discuss future activities, a wider participation was secured. Furthermore, it was agreed to admit observers to the sessions, although the Press was still excluded. Altogether there were 101 persons present, of whom 70 were participating scientists, 14 were observers and guests, and 17 were members of the secretariat, interpreters, etc. The guests included Mr. and Mrs. Cyrus Eaton. Many participants brought their wives, and a few had their children with them. The 70 participants came from 20 countries, the largest groups being from the United States (20), the Soviet Union (10), and Great Britain (7). No Chinese scientists attended, but an apology for their absence came from the Chinese Academy of Sciences.

The main part of the Conference took place in Kitzbühel. The Grand Hotel was given over exclusively to the Conference, and all participants had rooms and meals there. Owing to the large number of Soviet scientists, some of whom did not know English, it was necessary to install in the conference room equipment for simultaneous interpretation between English and Russian. Although it was consequently necessary for participants to speak into microphones, the informality of the meetings was not seriously diminished. As at previous conferences, the informal talks among participants at meals and in the evenings proved to be of great value by helping to clear up misunderstandings and by stimulating new ideas.

Formal sessions took place twice daily, during five days, except for one afternoon when the participants went on an excursion to the mountains. This practice of a break for an excursion half-way through the Conference, became a feature of most of the subsequent Conferences.

The main topics discussed at the formal sessions were the following: the consequences of a nuclear war; technological aspects of disarmament; political aspects of disarmament; living in the scientific age; international co-operation; and the responsibilities of scientists. To allow more time for discussion, each session was introduced by a rapporteur who presented a brief background for discussion of the topic and a summary of the relevant papers submitted.

One session was devoted to future plans. It was generally agreed that the Pugwash Conferences had been very successful and worthwhile, and that they should continue; the debate centred round the most suitable character of these future activities. One paper read at the Conference recommended the formation of a definite organization with a well-defined membership, subscription, central office, and own journal. Most participants felt that the time was too early for formal organization, and that the activities should continue, as hitherto, on a rather loose and informal basis. An *ad hoc* committee was nominated to consider this problem. In reporting back to the Conference this committee expressed the view that the most important function of meetings of the Pugwash type is to provide a means whereby scientists from many nations can meet, attempt to understand each other and frankly exchange their views regarding the serious problems which now confront the world, and that, therefore, the meetings themselves were as important as the subject of the meetings. The committee recommended that further conferences should be held to discuss specific concrete problems, but that the gatherings be kept unofficial and informal. The choice of topics for discussion was to be left to the discretion of the Continuing Committee, but the *ad hoc* committee believed that the efforts should be concentrated on "topics which are directly related to the easing of international tensions, the establishment of systems of mutual security, the elimination of war as an instrument of national policy, nuclear control and disarmament, and the role of the scientist in creating a peaceful and abundant world." The committee also recommended discussions on other topics related to these broad subjects, e.g., the potential contributions of science and technology to the development of the underdeveloped nations, and international exchange of scientists. Finally, the Committee urged that attempts be made to diversify the composition of future meetings, and whenever possible to include competent representatives of the social sciences.

These recommendations were unanimously approved by the Conference. The participants gave full endorsement to the past work of the Continuing Committee and asked its members to continue in office; they also decided that the membership be enlarged by the addition of 5 more persons (section 2.1).

One of the major outcomes of the Kitzbühel Conference was the adoption of a public statement. When the Continuing Committee first decided to call the Kitzbühel Conference, it did so with the intention that a statement should be issued at the end, if a substantial majority of the participants were in favour of it. The first draft of such a statement was discussed by the members of the Continuing Committee during the London meeting in June 1958. The amended draft was distributed to all participants at the start of the Kitzbühel Conference, with a request for comments and amendments. These comments were considered by a special Drafting Committee, which met several times during the Conference and produced an amended draft for discussion at one of the plenary sessions. The final version was discussed at the last session held on the morning of September 19, and it was accepted *nem. con.*, with only Szilard abstaining.

Although the statement was adopted by the Conference at Kitzbühel, it was not released until the Press Conference which took place later that same day in Vienna; for this reason the statement was given the name the "Vienna Declaration," the full text of which is given in Appendix 4.

The importance of the Vienna Declaration is that it was accepted by a large number of scientists, who represented a very wide spectrum of political and ideological opinions, who occupied responsible positions in their own countries, and who carefully scrutinized every sentence and pondered over every paragraph. The principles of the Vienna Declaration have been endorsed by several thousand scientists from all over the world in a questionnaire which was subsequently sent out by the Continuing Committee (section 1.9), as well as by many other groups and societies.

After the conclusion of the Kitzbühel meeting the participants travelled to Vienna, where a formal meeting took place on the morning of Saturday, September 20, in the Austrian Academy of Sciences. This meeting, attended by many scientists and diplomats, was addressed by the President of the Federal Republic of Austria, Dr. Adolf Scharf, and by the Chairman of the Continuing Committee, Lord Russell, as well as by other participants. After a luncheon given to the participants by the Austrian President, the Conference resumed at the City Hall Auditorium (Wiener Stadthalle), where ten of the participants addressed an audience of about 10,000 people. This was probably the largest meeting arranged by Pugwash, and a fitting conclusion to a very successful Conference.

4.3 Fourth Conference: Baden, June 25-July 4, 1959, "Arms Control and World Security"

In pursuit of the recommendations of the Kitzbühel Conference, the first task of the enlarged Continuing Committee was to organize further conferences dealing with specific topics. It was decided that the first of these should be a meeting of the type held previously at Lac Beauport, i.e., a private conference, with no intention of issuing a public statement, and taken up entirely with the subject of world security. This decision was prompted by the deadlock reached in the official negotiations at Geneva on the suspension of nuclear tests and by the failure of the ten-nation conference on surprise attack.

The Continuing Committee felt that a meeting in a neutral country might be most suitable and, once again, Austria was chosen. Thanks to Thirring's help, accommodation for participants was found in the Hotel Kur Esplanade in Baden, near Vienna. This was the first Conference that was organized entirely without Eaton's financial help. The American members of the Committee were successful in the collection of the necessary funds. One donor, Mrs. Agnes Meyer, gave a sufficiently large sum to cover most of the travelling expenses and secretarial assistance. There was also a donation from the Körner Foundation.

The number of participants was 25, roughly the same as in the first two Conferences. Following the instruction from the Kitzbühel Conference, several disciplines were represented in addition to the natural sciences, e.g., military history, psychiatry, political science and international law.

As in Lac Beauport there was no pre-arranged programme and there were only 8 formal sessions, the rest of the time being spent on informal talks. The discussion at the meetings was based on 20 papers presented by participants. Most of the papers were related to the theme of the Conference, "Arms Control and World Security," and the topics discussed included the following: security problems and surprise attack; the prevention of the spread of nuclear weapons; the control of nuclear testing; military disengagement and other European measures; the control of missiles and satellites; and the psychological aspects of the arms race. Several of the papers, however, dealt with other topics, e.g., with the role and responsibilities of scientists. The discussion at some sessions became very heated, particularly on the deadlock in the Geneva negotiations on a test ban treaty, when there was some mutual accusation between the American and the Soviet participants. The discussion revealed that much of the mistrust resulted from a lack of understanding of the different ways of handling reports of official negotiations in the respective countries.

Although it had been decided that no statement would be issued from this Conference, a brief communiqué (Appendix 5) was released before the end of the Conference. This was made necessary by the demands from members of the Press, who were pestering the participants for interviews. The communiqué stressed that the Pugwash Conferences are private but not secret and that the discussions are fruitful largely because of the privacy in which they are held.

The Baden Conference suffered to a certain extent from lack of proper organization. Even so, some progress in the slow and arduous process of reducing areas of divergence of opinion was made. One of the notable results of the Baden Conference was the realization that the detailed and extensive study required in order to find a solution to the problem of world security would be best achieved by setting up international study groups working, if possible, full time. The following were thought to be suitable projects for such study groups: prevention of surprise attack; technical aspects of disarmament and world security; failure of the United Nations to operate properly in the disarmament area; problems of control of means of delivery; n-th country problem; and non-violent means of solving disputes.

4.4 Fifth Conference: Pugwash, August 24-29, 1959, "Biological and Chemical Warfare"

At the Kitzbühel Conference, several speakers drew attention to the rapid development of biological and chemical weapons and to the magnitude of the disaster which might follow from their use in war. As one of the potential threats to mankind arising from the development of science, biological and chemical warfare clearly comes within the purview of the Pugwash Movement, but there were not enough experts on the subject present at Kitzbühel to make any authoritative assessment. For this reason, the Continuing Committee decided to call a special conference on this topic, with the purpose of assessing the potentialities of biological and chemical weapons and of discussing possible methods of controlling them.

Since the topic was so different from those discussed at previous conferences, quite a new slate of participants had to be invited. Much help and advice in planning this Conference was obtained from Martin Kaplan, a very active Pugwashite, who later attended many Pugwash Conferences as an official World Health Organization observer. Invitations went out to 38 scientists, 26 of whom, from 8 countries, accepted. They represented the various disciplines involved, i.e., chemistry, biochemistry, plant biology, microbiology, virology, epidemiology, genetics, molecular biology, radiobiology, and--for the purpose of assessing the factors in the delivery of these weapons--meteorology. Only 8 of the participants had attended a previous Pugwash Conference; they were present mainly to make a comparison between biological and chemical weapons on the one hand, and nuclear weapons on the other. The participants included eminent authorities in their subjects, some of whom had made a special study of the problems of biological and chemical weapons.

This Conference was supported financially by Cyrus Eaton, who paid the travelling expenses of most of the participants and provided hospitality at Pugwash. Those who attended the First Pugwash Conference noted the greatly improved facilities. Instead of meeting in a primitive assembly room, the Fifth Conference was held in the gymnasium of a new up-to-date school building. The secretariat, under Betty Royon, had all modern equipment and a sufficiently large technical staff to cope with the work. Patricia Lindop, who participated in her own right as a radiobiologist, was again responsible for the scientific aspects of the secretariat.

The Fifth Conference differed from the earlier ones in yet another important aspect: there was very little divergence of opinion between Eastern and Western participants on the major topics of discussion. In this respect, the Conference resembled an ordinary scientific meeting dealing with technical matters. However, the inspiration for the meeting was the realization of the dreadful consequences which would follow any extensive use of chemical or biological weapons, and much time was taken up discussing methods of avoiding their use.

The topics discussed included the following: a general review of the use of communicable diseases; the potentialities of bacteria, viruses and rickettsiae; the possibility of novel agents of disease being produced through mutations; animal and plant diseases; epidemiological potentialities; the potentialities of chemical weapons, including physiological and psychological poisons; problems of the delivery of biological and chemical weapons; problems of international control of such weapons and the verification of claims that they had been used. In the course of discussion, a comparison was also made between the destructive power of these and nuclear weapons. A large part of the Conference was devoted to the consideration of the problem of secrecy in planning and preparing for biological and chemical, as well as nuclear, warfare.

One of the purposes of calling this Conference was to formulate, if possible, a document embodying the findings of the meeting and its recommendations. A draft of such a document was prepared by the Steering Committee of the Conference and was carefully discussed at two plenary sessions. It was then adopted unanimously. The statement (Appendix 6) is a fairly long document which describes the nature of chemical and biological weapons, and the reason why they pose an important problem bearing on international relations. It goes on to make recommendations about methods of controlling these weapons, and ends up with the same conclusions as previous Pugwash Conferences that "no ban of a single type of weapon, no agreement that leaves the general threat of war in existence, can protect mankind sufficiently. We, therefore, must look forward to a day when the preservation of peace will transcend the ambitions of individual nations."

The Fifth Conference was probably the first serious discussion between scientists from the East and West on the dangers of chemical and biological warfare, and the Proceedings are a unique document containing an erudite assessment of the problem. The study of biological warfare, started at this Conference, was taken up several years later in one of the Pugwash Study Groups (section 3.3.1).

4.5 Sixth Conference: Moscow, November 27-December 5, 1960, "Disarmament and World Security"

Since the exchange of views on disarmament and arms control was primarily intended to influence the thinking of the governments of the nuclear powers, the Continuing Committee felt that at least some of the Conferences should be held in these countries. Accordingly, it was decided to explore the possibility of organizing the next two conferences on disarmament in the Soviet Union and in the United States. After an exchange of letters between Russell and Topchiev, a formal invitation came from the latter, on behalf of the Soviet Academy of Sciences, to hold the next Pugwash Conference in Moscow.

At the meeting of the Continuing Committee in London in December 1959, it was agreed that this Conference should again be of the Lac Beauport type, i.e., a private meeting, and that a statement would be issued only if a substantial degree of unanimity were obtained. It was initially planned to hold the Conference in April, 1960, but this did not allow sufficient time for preparation, and so it was decided to hold it in September.

Invitations went out, over Lord Russell's signature, to a number of scientists, and acceptances were received from 53 of them from 11 countries. The Soviet group in Moscow worked hard during the summer to prepare for the Conference. However, at the beginning of August a request came from the United States members of the Continuing Committee to postpone the Conference until the late autumn. The reason for this request was the presidential election which was due to take place on November 3. Some of the United States scientists were involved in the election campaign and would not have been able to come to Moscow in September. It was also thought that in the heat of the election campaign the purpose of the Moscow Conference might have been misconstrued. A special meeting of the Continuing Committee was called in London in September and it was agreed to postpone the Conference until the end of November.

New invitations went out, and although some of the people who had previously accepted were unable to attend on the new date, many others accepted. In the end there were 75 persons from 15 countries, the largest number at any Pugwash Conference held until then. Once again the largest group (23) came from the United States, but the number of Soviet scientists (21) was nearly equal. The British group numbered 8 and the Chinese 4. The list of Soviet participants was very impressive, containing some of their most famous scientists. There were also many new, but very well-known names on the lists from other countries. Moreover, there was a larger proportion than usual of persons who might be termed scholars rather than scientists in the strict sense--political scientists, strategists, sociologists, lawyers.

The travelling expenses of the participants were met from funds collected mainly in the United States. During the stay in Moscow, the participants, as well as their wives, were the guests of the Soviet Academy of Sciences. All participants were accommodated in the Metropole Hotel, and ate together in a private dining room. There was an impressive evening social programme, including ballet performances in the Bolshoi Theatre. The hospitality extended after the Conference, when the participants were offered a choice of excursions to Leningrad, Kiev, the Crimea, etc., as the guests of the Academy; a number of the participants availed themselves of this offer.

The Conference itself took place in the "House of Friendship," which is used as a centre for the promotion of international relations. Vladimir Pavlichenko was in charge of the secretariat, which had all the necessary technical equipment for the efficient management of the Conference Office. Of the 52 papers read at the Conference, many were handed in at the last minute, but all were translated, duplicated and distributed within a few days. The texts of all papers, as well as all the proceedings of the meeting, were collected and subsequently issued to participants, in a bound volume of 800 pages.

The meetings were held in a room with a large U-shaped table, around which all the participants were seated. Simultaneous interpretation between English and Russian was provided, and there were enough microphones for people to be able to speak from their seats. This helped in maintaining the informality of the proceedings.

The Conference started with a formal session, during which messages of greeting were read out from Premier Khrushchev, Lord Russell, the President of the Soviet Academy, Alexander Nesmeyanov, and the President of the United States National Academy of Sciences, Detlev Bronk. During the Conference it was announced that all participants were invited to a reception by Premier Khrushchev at the Kremlin; this had to be cancelled owing to his indisposition, but some participants met Khrushchev after the end of the Conference.

The first day was somewhat formal, but soon the ice was broken and the discussions became more free. Two sessions were held every day, with selected participants taking the chair in rotation. The topics for discussion at the sessions were: history of the arms race and disarmament negotiations; the dangers of the continued arms race; the current status of negotiations on the banning of nuclear tests; problems of world security systems; plans for comprehensive disarmament; political, economic and technical problems of arms limitation and disarmament; surprise attack; control of delivery; the foundation of a stable world; the creation of a suitable climate of opinion; and the scientist's role and responsibilities.

Although the divergence of opinion on the methods of achieving a secure world was still marked, there was a considerable narrowing of the differences. At one stage Peter Kapitza called for a blackboard and drew on it a graph showing the relation between the state of armament and military penetrability. Later Jerome Wiesner used the blackboard to draw graphs showing the correlation between the degree of disarmament and the necessary measures of control. This quantitative approach, so familiar to the participants, transformed the whole meeting and made for much more rapid progress.

Apart from the formal sessions, the informal talks again proved to be of the utmost value. In fact, the programme of the Conference was changed in order to free one afternoon for informal talks, in groups of 5 to 20 people. This proved so successful that a second afternoon was set aside for further informal talks.

In addition, there was plenty of opportunity for private conversations, especially since the Soviet scientists invited their foreign colleagues to their homes for meals.

At the last session, the Conference adopted, with 3 abstentions, a statement which was prepared by the Continuing Committee and discussed at plenary sessions (Appendix 7). This statement reasserted the belief of the participants in the basic principles set out in the Vienna Declaration and briefly summarized the work and achievements of the Moscow Conference.

It is very difficult to assess such achievements accurately, but there are usually various indications which enable one to judge whether a conference has been successful or not. It seems to be the general opinion that the Moscow Conference was of very great significance. It also marked the turning point of the attitude of the Western powers, which was initially aloof and suspicious of Pugwash, to one of approval and respect. From the interest taken in it by the governments of the Great Powers and their favourable reaction to the scheduling of more conferences, it is safe to conclude that the Moscow Conference had the greatest impact on public opinion and official circles achieved by any Pugwash Conference until then. In the opinion of one participant expressed during a television programme, the Moscow Conference was the most important event in the field of disarmament during 1960. It is also of significance that two of the United States participants in the Moscow Conference (Jerome Wiesner and Walt Rostow) were soon afterwards appointed by President Kennedy to important posts in his government.

4.6 Seventh Conference: Stowe, September 5-9, 1961, "International Cooperation in Pure and Applied Science"

Arising out of the discussion at the Kitzbühel Conference, the Continuing Committee considered early in 1959 the desirability of convening a conference concerned with the problem of international scientific collaboration. This was thought to fall within the purview of the Pugwash Conferences, not only because of the direct advantages to science and general welfare which would result from such collaboration, but also because of the development of the climate of mutual trust which it was hoped would follow. It was felt, however, that this type of conference could more easily be convened by one of the Academies of Sciences, and the Committee decided to pass on the idea to the National Academy of Sciences of the United States.

Although the response from the Academy was favourable and some exchange of correspondence took place between the Presidents of the United States and Soviet Academies, it became apparent by 1961 that no action was to be expected from these quarters in the near future. When, therefore, the United States Planning Committee met early in 1961 to discuss plans for a conference on disarmament (section 4.7), Rabinowitch put forward a suggestion that the proposed conference on international scientific collaboration should be held in the United States just prior to the one on disarmament. This proposal was subsequently accepted by the Pugwash Continuing Committee when it met in London in March 1961.

Originally it had been planned to hold the Seventh Conference in Woods Hole, Massachusetts, and the Eighth Conference in Aspen, Colorado, but it turned out that the accommodation at Woods Hole was inadequate and that the altitude of Aspen might prevent some people from attending for reasons of health. It was, therefore, decided that both Conferences be held at the same place, at the Lodge at Smuggler's Notch, a few miles from Stowe, in Vermont. Situated in beautiful countryside, at the foot of Mount Mansfield, the Lodge offered all the amenities of a first class hotel, and the seclusion of the place greatly helped in creating a feeling of community among the participants.

It had been planned that the participation should be roughly 15 each from the Soviet Union and the United States, with 20 from other countries. For various reasons, however, the attendance from the Soviet Union and other countries was somewhat smaller. The Chinese scientists did not accept the invitation extended to them, although there was an understanding from the United States Government that visas would have been issued to them; one scientist from Eastern Germany who had accepted the invitation was not granted a visa. On the other hand, the number of scientists from the United States who wished to attend was far greater than scheduled. To avoid making the United States representation too large, it was agreed that some of them would attend in the role of observers.

Among the observers were the Presidents of the United States National Academy of Sciences and the American Academy of Arts and Sciences; both these institutions acted as hosts to the Conferences and the Presidents gave speeches of welcome at the opening session. Messages were also received from President Kennedy and Premier Khrushchev. In addition, the Governor of Vermont came to Stowe to the first meeting to welcome the participants.

This Conference differed from the earlier ones not only in the topic of discussion but also in the method of work. The subject of international scientific collaboration lends itself to natural division into various scientific disciplines, and the Committee felt that better progress could be made if, instead of plenary sessions, much of the discussion took place in Working Groups. Consequently, after the first day of plenary sessions, at which there was a general discussion on the history and methodology of international scientific collaboration, the Conference divided into six Working Groups, in two main classes: (A) Earth Sciences, Space Research, Life Sciences, and Physical Sciences; (B) Assistance to Developing Nations, and Exchange of Scientists and Scientific Information. Each participant could choose two Working Groups, one each from class A and B, since the meetings of these two classes were held at different times. After a full day of discussion in the Working Groups there was a plenary session at which preliminary reports from the Groups were given. The Working Groups then went back to prepare their final reports, which were discussed again at the last plenary session and finally incorporated in a statement from the whole Conference. This method turned out to be very fruitful, as it allowed a large amount of work to be done in a short time, and it was followed--with some minor variations--at most of the future conferences.

The statement from the Conference (Appendix 8), which was accepted unanimously, is one of the longest to be produced by any of the Pugwash Conferences. It lists some 50 projects which the Conference considered worthy of international collaboration. Many of these are not original ideas; some of the projects have been under consideration by other international institutions, particularly the International Council of Scientific Unions. In the case of other projects the statement indicates the most appropriate of existing international institutions to undertake them. The main emphasis was on projects which could help to create more trust among nations. In this respect one suggestion in the statement deserves special attention, i.e., the setting up of an inter-continental Science Centre, which would contain a number of institutes and research projects designed for the best utilization of the very expensive machines to be built there, such as particle accelerators and computers. It was estimated that the cost of such a Centre would be of the order of five thousand million dollars. The wording of the statement relating to the siting of this Centre, "the astute location of such a striking epitome of science...could have extraordinarily great significance in improving the tone of the present political situation," clearly suggests Berlin. There was a full and frank discussion during two of the plenary sessions on the political advantages to be gained from such a move, and although it was decided not to mention the city specifically in the statement, the opinion expressed by representatives from both East and West was almost unanimous in support of this suggestion.

Despite the increased political tension (see section 4.7), the atmosphere throughout the Conference was calm and friendly. Except for several problems relating to aid to less developed countries, exchange of scientists, genetics and population growth, the discussion of which revealed a considerable divergence of opinion between East and West, there were hardly any serious differences, and the Conference ended with the gratifying feeling by all participants of having made a number of constructive proposals which, if implemented, could greatly contribute towards establishing a stable world. The implementation of some of these proposals was indeed taken up subsequently at government level.

4.7 Eighth Conference: Stowe, September 11-16, 1961, "Disarmament and World Security"

When the decision was made by the Continuing Committee to convene a conference in Moscow, it was also agreed that it should be followed by a conference of the same type, to be held in the United States. Immediately after the Moscow Conference, a Planning Committee was set up in the United States, under the chairmanship of Harrison Brown, with Paul Doty, Bentley Glass, Richard Leghorn and Eugene Rabinowitch as members. It was largely due to this Committee, and especially to Harrison Brown's tactful guidance during the meetings, that the Conference turned out to be a success despite the heavy handicaps.

Apart from obtaining the agreement of the United States National Academy of Sciences and of the American Academy of Arts and Sciences to act as hosts, the Planning Committee managed to secure funds for the necessary expenses of the Seventh and Eighth Conferences, totalling about $100,000; a major contribution to this was made by the Ford Foundation. The Planning Committee also prepared the programme which, like that of the Seventh Conference, envisaged the division of the participants into working groups.

The total number and distribution by countries of the participants were very similar to those for the Seventh Conference. In fact, nearly half of the participants, including all of the Soviet members, were the same as at the Seventh Conference. In the American group, on the other hand, there were many newcomers, including eminent and influential scientists; one of them was Henry Kissinger, who later became President Nixon's assistant for national security affairs. The British group contained among the participants and observers a high proportion of scientists who were serving as advisers to the British Government. The participation of these scientists was evidence of the recognition by the Western Governments of the important role played by the Pugwash Conferences in the disarmament field.

It had been intended that the Eighth Conference would resume the discussion on disarmament problems where it was left off in Moscow, and there had been great hopes of making good progress. But the worsening of the political scene in the summer of 1961, due to many causes, and in particular to the event which occurred just prior to the Conference, i.e., the resumption of tests of nuclear weapons by the Soviet Government, had cast a deep shadow over the gathering. Some of the Western participants came with the feeling that there was no point in further talks, but the majority believed that the deterioration of the political situation made it even more imperative for scientists to continue their efforts in this field. The friendly atmosphere established during the previous week at the Seventh Conference had also greatly helped to overcome the crisis. Even so, there was some mutual recrimination during the two plenary sessions on the first day of the Conference. On the following day, however, the participants divided into five Working Groups and got down to earnest work, which, on the whole, was carried out in a spirit of co-operation, and which was marked by considerable success. In particular, the first Group, which discussed reduction of production and elimination of fissile materials and stockpiles, was quickly able to reach agreement on all items, and produced a document concisely summarizing the problem and putting forward concrete suggestions for solving it.

The second Working Group, on weapons delivery systems, found the going a bit hard at the beginning; but after receiving reinforcement from the members of the first Group, it too produced a document specifying a sequence of events that might lead to the dismantling of delivery systems.

The third Group dealt with the first steps of a disarmament plan and the ways of achieving a specific degree of disarmament while maintaining a strategic balance between the two blocs. Although this was a much more difficult task than the more technical problems attacked by the first two Groups, there was remarkable agreement, and the specific proposals made by this Group marked a real step forward from the position reached at the Moscow Conference.

The fourth and fifth Groups dealt with much broader problems--those of general and complete disarmament and of the preconditions to possible success at negotiations. Because of the general nature of these topics the discussion tended to be more diffuse and no specific conclusions were reached. Nevertheless, the reports produced by these Groups contain several important projects for further study.

Altogether, the five Working Groups performed their tasks successfully, and their final reports contain a number of valuable suggestions.

Apart from receiving reports from the Working Groups, the last plenary session of the Conference was spent on a discussion on the text of a statement from the Conference. A great deal of controversy had been going on behind the scenes in regard to the advisability or inadvisability of issuing a statement. Some participants felt that, under the circumstances, no statement should be issued except for a communiqué listing the people present and topics discussed. Other participants felt that in view of the real progress which had been made, some statement embodying the findings ought to be issued. Eventually a compromise was reached on a very brief statement (see Appendix 9), but even this was not acceptable to all attending, and five of the United States participants abstained. This was the largest percentage of abstentions recorded in any Pugwash meeting, and was a reflection of the tense political situation which existed in September 1961. However, in spite of the controversy over the statement, the fact that influential scientists from East and West could meet at a time of such a crisis and reach agreement on a number of important issues gave proof of the strength of the Pugwash Conferences and of the special role which the scientist can play in suggesting solutions to political problems.

4.8 Ninth Conference: Cambridge, August 25-30, 1962, "Problems of Disarmament and World Security"

By 1962 the Pugwash Conferences had been going for five years, and the Continuing Committee felt that the time had come to review past activities and make plans for the future. It was thought that this, as well as the election of a new Continuing Committee, should be made by a widely representative group of scientists, and that for this reason a large conference should be convened in London to which all participants in the past Pugwash Conferences would be invited. It was realized, however, that such a big meeting would not be conducive to a detailed discussion on the various aspects of disarmament. In order not to leave this topic off the agenda for too long a period, the Continuing Committee decided that the London meeting be preceded by a smaller Conference, to be held a few days earlier in Cambridge, and wholly concerned with disarmament problems.

It had been assumed that all those invited to Cambridge, would then go to London to participate in the Tenth Conference, and in this way minimize travelling expenses. Actually, a few of the Cambridge participants were unable to stay for another week, and a few did not wish to take part in the London Conference, so that 17 out of the 67 participants in Cambridge, did not go to London. In Cambridge, there were also 18 observers, who included some who had come for the Tenth Conference but arrived earlier, and others who occupied official advisory posts with their governments; in accordance with established practice it was felt that they should be given the status of observer rather than of full participant. As at the previous Conferences, the largest groups came from the United States and the Soviet Union.

Nevill Mott, who was Chairman of the British Organizing Committee, was at the time Master of Gonville and Caius College, and thanks to him participants were housed in the newly built Harvey Court of the College; the meetings themselves were held in the old teaching and common rooms of Caius College. Compared with some previous Conferences the standard of food and accommodation was somewhat austere, but this was more than compensated by the specific charm of Cambridge. The academic calm and air of detachment of life in an ancient College provided an ideal setting for the Conference; many old problems were thrashed out and new ideas debated in informal talks while walking along the cloisters or the Backs.

It had been decided to follow the example of the Seventh and Eighth Conferences, and to concentrate the discussions in Working Groups. On the first day two plenary sessions were held at which 5 keynote papers were given. The purpose of these papers was to review the current status of the disarmament negotiations and to assess the possibilities for the future. After these plenary sessions, the Conference divided into five Working Groups, which met for the next 4 1/2 days, with the exception of one afternoon, when a plenary session was held to receive preliminary reports from the Groups. The topics of the five Working Groups were (1) problems of reduction and elimination under international control of weapons of mass destruction and of their means of delivery; (2) problems of balanced reduction and elimination of conventional armaments; (3) political and technical measures contributing to the lessening of international tensions (including the nuclear test ban and consideration of activities in space); (4) problems of security in a disarmed world; (5) economic aspects of disarmament. This last Group, under the chairmanship of Robert Neild, finished its task very quickly (perhaps because it had only six members!) and produced a report which was subsequently unanimously accepted by the whole Conference. There was much more controversy in the other Working Groups, and this was reflected in the discussions at the final plenary session which was held on the afternoon of the last day, when the reports from all Working Groups were presented for reception by the Conference as a whole. The reports of Working Groups 3 and 4 produced some argument, and it was agreed that appendices should be attached to the reports of these Groups, with the comments of those who did not fully subscribe to them, or wished to express their own opinions.

In view of the proximity of the London Conference it was decided not to issue a public statement from the Cambridge Conference. Instead, one of the members of the Continuing Committee (Bentley Glass), was asked to prepare a resume of the work of the Conference, for presentation at the London Conference. The text of this report is given in Appendix 10.

4.9 Tenth Conference: London, September 3-7, 1962, "Scientists and World Affairs"

The main purpose of the Tenth Pugwash Conference was to debate Pugwash itself; to review past activities, adopt a programme for future activities, and elect a new Continuing Committee. It was felt that, in the first instance, all those who participated in any of the past Conferences should be given an opportunity to attend and discuss these issues. Invitations were, therefore, sent out to the 179 living Pugwashites who had been full participants in any of the eight previous Pugwash Conferences. Forty percent of these (72) were able to come, which is a very good response considering the many calls which are always made on such scientists, and the fact that many of them had themselves to pay the expenses of travelling and accommodation. Additional invitations were then sent out by the Continuing Committee, with particular emphasis on bringing in scientists from a large number of countries. Eventually, the total number of participants was 175 from 36 countries. This included 9 scientists who had attended previous Pugwash Conferences as observers, and 17 who came for the first time to the Cambridge Conference. Thus, more than half of all participants had some previous experience of a Pugwash Conference. In addition, there were 40 observers and 5 guests.

Of the countries from which scientists came to previous Pugwash Conferences only two were missing: China and the German Democratic Republic. The Academia Sinica sent a polite letter of refusal. The scientists from the German Democratic Republic could not come because of the severe travel restrictions imposed on them by the NATO countries.

The organization of such a large Conference demanded a considerable effort. The British Organizing Committee, which was also responsible for organizing the Ninth Conference, appointed Mick Esdale (Patricia Lindop's husband) as administrator for both Conferences. The main task for the Organizing Committee was to secure funds to cover the expenses. The Royal Society agreed to be the sponsor of both Conferences, as well as to open an account in its name into which donations could be paid. A public appeal was launched, and this was followed by a number of letters to individual firms and foundations in Great Britain. The response was satisfactory and brought in over ₤ 11,000. However, this was not sufficient to cover the organizational costs as well as hospitality for both Conferences, and the Organizing Committee decided to offer hospitality to all participants in Cambridge, but only to those in the London Conference for whom it was essential.

One of the main problems in planning the London Conference was how to maintain the usual spirit of informality and personal intimacy at such a large gathering. From this point of view it was considered important that the participants should be given the maximum opportunity of being together outside the formal sessions, by being accommodated in the same hotel, and having meals together. The Hotel Russell was chosen as coming nearest to fulfilling these requirements. All this, however, did not suffice to dispel completely the somewhat formal atmosphere, particularly since throughout the Conference the participants met at plenary sessions, sitting in a huge hall with rows and rows of chairs facing the platform. The air of respectability, as illustrated, for example, by the opening of the Conference by a Cabinet Minister, or by the official reception given to the participants by Her Majesty's Government, was also somewhat foreign to Pugwash Conferences. Still, these drawbacks had to be balanced against the need of having the largest possible gathering of scientists when making decisions about the future of the Movement.

The large attendance raised the question of publicity. Some members of the Continuing Committee felt that it would be impossible to exclude the Press, and that therefore all the sessions should be open. Others feared that the presence of the Press would stifle free discussion and make the Conference even more formal. A compromise was reached to admit the Press for the formal opening, and to invite the science editors of a number of journals and newspapers as observers. It was also agreed to hold press conferences during and at the end of the Conference; these were conducted by John Maddox and Gerald Leach, who were appointed press officers for the Cambridge and London Conferences.

The Conference started with a formal opening ceremony, to which a number of representatives of universities and learned societies were invited, as well as members of the Press, radio and television. The chair was taken by Nevill Mott, and the platform included the members of the Continuing Committee, as well as the signatories of the Russell-Einstein Manifesto: Bertrand Russell, Leopold Infeld, Linus Pauling, Cecil Powell, Joseph Rotblat and Hideki Yukawa. The remaining two of the then surviving signatories, Max Born and Herman Muller, sent messages which were read out by Russell.

The Conference was officially opened by Lord Hailsham, who was then Minister for Science in the British Government. Following this, messages of greetings were read from Prime Minister Harold Macmillan of Great Britain, Premier Nikita Khrushchev of the Soviet Union, President John Kennedy of the United States, Prime Minister Jawaharlal Nehru of India, President Mohammed Ayub Khan of Pakistan, President Josip Tito of Yugoslavia, President Antonin Novotny of Czechoslovakia, President Kwame Nkrumah of Ghana, and the Secretary-General of the United Nations, U Thant.

Next, the President of the Royal Society, Howard (later Lord) Florey, welcomed the Conference on behalf of the Royal Society. This was followed by messages of greetings from Frederick Seitz, President of the National Academy of Science of the United States, and from the Presidium of the Academy of Sciences of the Soviet Union.

Bertrand Russell then welcomed the participants as Chairman of the Continuing Committee. He recalled the circumstances which gave rise to the Pugwash Movement, and summarized the task ahead: "Our common purpose is the survival of Man, which is in jeopardy. It is impossible to imagine a more important purpose." Russell received a standing ovation. This was the last time he appeared at a Pugwash Conference.

The opening ceremony ended with a report of the work of the Continuing Committee given by the Secretary-General; the text of this report is enclosed as Appendix 11.

After the guests and the Press left, the Conference got down to business. Its first task was to set up three standing committees: on future activities, with 13 members; on future organization, with 6 members; and on drafting a statement, with 5 members. The members of the Continuing Committee were not included in the standing committees, but were available for consultation.

On the afternoon of the first day the Conference received and discussed reports of the activities of all Pugwash National Groups.

During the next three days the Conference settled down to its main purpose, to discuss the various areas of Pugwash activities. Each session of 3 1/2 hours duration was taken up by one of the main topics of the Conference, i.e., the position of the scientist in the community; science and world security; international scientific collaboration; science in aid of developing nations; and science and education. The Continuing Committee had invited three of four papers on each topic, and each session started with summaries of these papers. This was followed by a discussion from the floor, often based on relevant papers submitted by the participants; altogether there were 80 papers.

Despite the large number of participants the discussions were orderly, lively and informative, and on some occasions remarkably fruitful. Thus, during the session on world security, Igor Tamm put forward the idea, conceived during the Conference in informal talks with other Soviet and

American participants, of ending the deadlock on the test ban negotiations by the installation of unmanned automatic seismic stations in areas of seismic activity. This so-called "black box" idea received a great deal of publicity, as it was mentioned in the public statement issued by the Conference. It was soon afterwards taken up at government level, and figured in an exchange of letters between Kennedy and Khrushchev a few months later.

While the discussions were going on in the plenary sessions, the three standing committees held frequent meetings to prepare their reports. These reports were submitted and discussed on the last day of the Conference.

The main task before the standing committee on future activities was how to reconcile the great variety of activities which had been suggested for Pugwash with effectiveness and with the limited resources. The committee came out in favour of making the achievement of disarmament and permanent peace the main Pugwash activity, although it recommended the inclusion of subjects less directly related to this topic. The report of this committee, which was unanimously accepted by the whole Conference, is given in Appendix 12.

The standing committee on future organization was mainly concerned with the composition of the new Continuing Committee. It recommended that the Continuing Committee should consist of 14 members: the Chairman and Secretary-General *ex officio*; 3 members each from the United States and the Soviet Union; 2 each from the United Kingdom and Western Europe; and one each from East Europe and Asia. Places should also be left for addition in the future of scientists from China and other regions, such as Latin America and Africa. To provide continuity, the present members of the Continuing Committee should be re-elected. The report recommended that all members of the Continuing Committee should be scientists, and that the Secretary-General should be a scientist, preferably active in research. The Secretary-General should carry out the work between meetings of the Continuing Committee, and should have the authority to act in matters of urgency. Finally, the report recommended that the official name of the Movement be "Pugwash Conferences on Science and World Affairs," but that national groups should be free to abbreviate this name, or use any part of it.

This report was also unanimously adopted by the Conference. The Conference then re-elected Bertrand Russell as Chairman, and Joseph Rotblat as Secretary-General. The newly elected members of the Continuing Committee were: Edoardo Amaldi (Italy) and Herbert Marcovich (France), to represent Western European countries; Leopold Infeld (Poland), to represent Eastern European countries; and Vikram Sarabhai (India), to represent Asian countries.

In the last session the Conference discussed the draft of the public statement prepared by the standing committee. In accordance with previous practice, it was agreed that the statement would become a document of the

Conference, and released to the Press as such, only if it had the approval of a considerable majority (85 to 90 percent) of the participants. The draft was then considered by the Conference paragraph by paragraph. Some items evoked considerable discussion, and a few amendments were accepted by the Conference. The whole statement (Appendix 13) was then adopted by the Conference without dissent, but five participants asked to be recorded as abstainers from the statement.

This first Quinquennial Conference had fulfilled its objects: it outlined the field of future activities of the Pugwash Movement, and gave it a sound organizational structure. Above all, it reaffirmed the need of scientists to be concerned with problems of disarmament and world security, and expressed its belief that scientists can make a special contribution to these problems. "We reassert our conviction that the goal of full disarmament and permanent peace is realistic and urgent. This work is truly to be seen as a part of a long struggle for the progress of mankind, and it is one in which scientists have a responsible part to play. We call upon scientists everywhere in the world to join us in this task."

4.10 Eleventh Conference: Dubrovnik, September 20-25, 1963, "Current Problems of Disarmament and World Security"

During the London Conference invitations were received from scientists in India, Yugoslavia and Czechoslovakia to hold Pugwash Conferences in these countries. Considerations of climate made it advisable to hold the conference in India in the early months of the year, but to avoid too long an interval between conferences, it was decided that the Eleventh Conference be held in Yugoslavia.

An active Pugwash Group had been in existence for some time in Yugoslavia, under the chairmanship of Ivan Supek. The Group set up an Organizing Committee which managed to secure sufficient funds to offer hospitality to all participants and to cover organizational expenses. The Council of the Yugoslav Academies of Science agreed to sponsor the Conference.

The choice of the site of the Conference was largely dictated by considerations of transport and accommodation facilities, as well as by the desire to return to a small place where all participants could be together all the time. Dubrovnik, with its grace and loveliness, met all these needs. The meetings were held in the spacious and beautifully designed Umjetnicka Galerija (Art Gallery), and the participants were accommodated in the Neptune Hotel, some distance from the centre of Dubrovnik. This necessitated the use of minibuses to transport the participants twice daily to and from the meeting place, but this caused little inconvenience. The weather was excellent throughout, and some of the Working Groups held their meetings on the beach.

The Conference took place a few months after the signing of the Partial Test Ban Treaty in Moscow, and this first tangible evidence of progress in disarmament, towards which Pugwash has contributed so much, had created a feeling of exhilaration and hopeful expectation of further successes. This mood was reflected in the official messages received from

Kennedy, Khrushchev, Macmillan, Novotny and Walter Ulbricht (Chairman of the Council of State of the German Democratic Republic), as well as in the speech made at the opening ceremony by the Vice-President of Yugoslavia on behalf of President Tito. It was also clearly evident in the tone of the debates and in the choice of topics for discussion.

Among the topics for the five Working Groups, three were specifically concerned with further steps towards disarmament. In particular, the discussion centred around the problems of abolition of delivery systems; inspection and control in the first stage of disarmament; surprise attack; the importance of non-proliferation of nuclear weapons, with a detailed analysis of the consequences of such proliferation; the need to control the transfer of fissile materials through the International Atomic Energy Agency; the need for the extension of the Test Ban Treaty, with a suggestion for joint seismological studies; nuclear guarantees; and the ban on the use of outer space for military purposes. Many of these items were later taken up at official level and some were incorporated into treaties.

The remaining two Working Groups dealt with problems which came up at Pugwash for the first time in a detailed discussion. One was concerned with denuclearized zones, especially in Europe. This was prompted by the realization that the lack of political settlement in Europe, particularly in Germany, may be the main stumbling block to progress in disarmament agreements. This topic was tackled a few months earlier at a meeting in Geneva of representatives of European Pugwash Groups, at which scientists from both parts of Germany were present (see section 3.4.1). It was then agreed that a paper on the German question should be prepared jointly by two scientists, one from the German Federal Republic and one from the German Democratic Republic. This paper, outlining the areas of agreement as well as of disagreement, was presented at the Dubrovnik Conference, and was a good starting point in a useful discussion, which was a forerunner for many debates on this problem at future conferences.

The subject of the fifth Working Group, the role of non-aligned nations in disarmament and world security, was taken up partly because of the interest in this problem of the Yugoslav Group, and partly because of the increasing importance of the non-aligned nations in disarmament negotiations at that time.

The timetable of the Conference was modelled on that of the Cambridge Conference, i.e., plenary sessions at the beginning, with several keynote papers, followed by meetings of the Working Groups. The first of these papers was given by Vladimir Kirillin who, after the death of Topchiev, became the leader of the Soviet Pugwash Group and took his place on the Continuing Committee at the meeting which was held in Dubrovnik just prior to the Conference.

At this meeting too Bernard Feld took part for the first time, after the resignation of Harrison Brown from the Committee. Feld, who had participated in most of the previous Pugwash Conferences, became the chairman of the American Pugwash Committee in early 1963, and ever since has taken a leading part in Pugwash work, both in the United States and in the international arena.

At its meeting in Dubrovnik the Committee discussed the question of a statement from the Conference. Initially, it had been intended not to issue any statement, but some members pointed out that many of the findings of the Working Groups would be worthy of publication. As a compromise it was agreed that a statement would be issued from the Continuing Committee, but that the approval of the Conference be sought for the publication of parts of the reports from the Working Groups. This procedure was discussed at length at the last session of the Conference, but eventually it was approved. The two steps in the procedure were, first, the acceptance of the reports from the Working Groups as documents from the Conference as a whole, and second, the approval by the Conference of those parts of the reports which were to be included in the public statement.

All reports from the Working Groups were accepted *nem. con.*, except one dealing with denuclearized zones in Europe, which was accepted with some reservations from a few scientists from the Eastern bloc. The items to be included in the public statements were then approved by the Conference. The final text of this statement (Appendix 14) was subsequently prepared by the Continuing Committee. While listing the substantial progress made and the novel ideas which emerged at the Conference, it concludes: "In spite of widespread agreement on many important issues amongst members of the Conference, a number of questions remained unresolved and several novel suggestions require further consideration."

4.11 Twelfth Conference: Udaipur, January 27-February 1, 1964, "Current Problems of Disarmament and World Security"

Seven years after the date when the First Conference was planned to be held in New Delhi, Pugwash finally came to India. In the meantime, an active Pugwash group had come into existence in India, with Vikram Sarabhai as its prime mover. An Organizing Committee, under the chairmanship of Homi Bhabha, was set up to prepare the Twelfth Conference. The Committee managed to secure the necessary funds for the organization of the Conference and to offer full hospitality to all participants. In addition, a grant of ₤6,000 was made to the Continuing Committee for assistance in travelling expenses; in view of the great distances involved for the majority of participants, this grant made all the difference in ensuring a good attendance.

The Lake Palace Hotel in Udaipur was chosen for the site of the Conference. Formerly the palace of the Maharana of Mewar, the Hotel stands on an artificial island in the middle of a lake. The exotic splendour of this island-paradise gave the Conference a dreamlike quality, but it did not take long for the participants to settle down to face the real issues before them, some of which were highlighted by the contrast between the setting of the Conference and the general standard of living in India.

Although the theme of the Conference was the same as that in Dubrovnik, the emphasis was much more on developing nations and on the interrelation between development and security. The number of participants from developing nations was higher than at previous Conferences, although not as high as the Committee wished; out of a total of 56 participants, 11 came from countries which are usually classified as "developing."

Mr. Nehru had expressed the wish to come to Udaipur and meet the participants, but illness prevented him from undertaking the journey. In his place, Mrs. Indira Gandhi, who later succeeded her father, came to Udaipur where she spent some time in talks with members of the Conference. Mr. and Mrs. Cyrus Eaton, who happened to be in India at the time, also paid a visit to the Conference.

The Conference started with the, by then traditional, opening ceremony, which was chaired by Homi Bhabha. Messages of greetings were received from the President of India, S. Radhakrishnan, and Prime Minister Jawaharlal Nehru, President Lyndon Johnson of the United States, Premier Nikita Khrushchev of the Soviet Union, President Ayub Khan of Pakistan, Prime Minister Jozef Cyrankiewicz of Poland, and Chancellor Ludwig Erhard of the Federal German Republic.

In the plenary session, following the formal opening, a keynote paper on "Disarmament, Security and Economic Development" was given by Mikhail Millionshchikov, who was participating in a Pugwash Conference for the first time. Shortly afterwards he became a member of the Continuing Committee, and chairman of the Soviet Pugwash Group, after the retirement of Kirillin; from then on Millionshchikov took an ever-increasing and leading part in Pugwash activities.

Most of the Conference time was taken up in Working Groups, four of which were set up on the following topics: (1) organization for collective security; (2) implications for disarmament and world security of a wider dispersal of military power; (3) the relation between the economic problems of the developing nations and world security; (4) priorities for science and technology in developing nations. Much of the agenda of the first two Working Groups was taken up with the dangers arising from the wider dissemination of nuclear weapons, and with the measures necessary to bring about a non-proliferation treaty. In Working Group 3 the interrelation between disarmament and economic development was discussed in some detail, and proposals were made for more international collaboration which would help both in economic development and world security. Among other ideas it was suggested that Pugwash scientists should volunteer their services, in the field of their speciality, to international teams working on problems of developing countries. Working Group 4 made a detailed analysis of the optimal methods of organizing science and technology in the developing nations, the type of education and research which is most suitable for these nations, and the best ways to achieve international co-operation for this purpose. A very long report from this Group concluded with an appendix listing sixteen suggestions and recommendations.

The reports from all Working Groups were read and discussed at the plenary sessions on the last day of the Conference. Several suggestions for amendments, made in these discussions, were approved by the Working Groups, and the amended reports were subsequently accepted by the Conference as a whole. Reservations from a United States participant in relation to the report of Working Group 2, and from Soviet participants in relation to the report of Working Group 3, were recorded.

The absence of China in disarmament negotiations was very much on the mind of the participants, and the urgent need to re-establish contact with Chinese scientists at Pugwash Conferences was stressed both in the working groups and in the plenary sessions. At the last session the Conference unanimously adopted the following resolution: "The Twelfth Pugwash Conference at Udaipur greatly regrets the absence from its deliberation of any participants from the People's Republic of China and urges the Academia Sinica to send several Chinese scientists to participate in the Thirteenth and all subsequent Pugwash Conferences."

The final session was taken up with a discussion on the public statement to be issued from the Conference. The letter of invitation to participants had stated that, should the findings merit publication, the Conference would be asked to discuss the desirability of issuing a public statement. With this in mind, the Continuing Committee appointed a small subcommittee to prepare a draft of a statement. This draft came up at the last plenary session, and was discussed at very great length before it was finally given unanimous approval. This session, which lasted for seven hours, the longest ever at a Pugwash Conference, made it abundantly clear that it is not practicable to draft a public statement at such a large gathering.

The statement (Appendix 15) summarizes the findings of the Working Groups, although it does not fully reflect the many ideas which emerged during the discussions and the great care taken in debating some of the issues. Apart from the progress made on specific disarmament topics the main achievement of the Udaipur Conference was in stressing the close relationship between world security and development, and in confirming that the subject of developing nations comes within the purview of Pugwash.

4.12 Thirteenth Conference: Karlovy Vary, September 13-19, 1964, "Disarmament and Peaceful Collaboration among Nations"

At a meeting of the Continuing Committee held in Udaipur immediately after the Twelfth Conference, there was a considerable discussion about the timetable and procedure at Pugwash Conferences. It was felt that the amount of time allocated to the Working Groups to carry out their tasks, i.e., to prepare the agenda, hold substantive discussions, and draft reports to the plenary sessions, was altogether too short, and that because of this the selection of topics for discussion was not as thoughtful, and the debates themselves not as detailed, as might have been if more time were available. An extension of the available time was not feasible, since many participants could not afford to be away from their other duties for more than a week. A compromise solution was reached that a small number of people should meet before the Conference to prepare the detailed agenda for the Working Groups.

Thirteenth Conference

Remembering the tedious debate on the public statement at the Udaipur Conference, the Committee decided that at the next Conference, there would be no public statement from the Conference as a whole, but that the Continuing Committee would issue a statement to the Press which would summarize the main findings and conclusions of the Working Groups. It was also agreed that this decision would be stated in the letters of invitation to participants.

Having made these general arrangements, the Committee then decided that the next Conference be held in Czechoslovakia, in September 1964. The Czechoslovak Pugwash Group had been in existence for some time, with its own office in Prague, and with several very active members, including Frantisek Sorm, the President of the Academy of Sciences, Ivan Malek, a Vice-President of the Academy, and Theodor Nemec, the Secretary of the Group. Nemec, an ardent supporter of Pugwash, has spent much time and effort on Pugwash work, both within Czechoslovakia and outside.

The Czechoslovak Academy of Sciences sponsored the Conference and offered hospitality to all participants during their stay at the preparatory meeting in Prague and the main Conference in Karlovy Vary.

The preparatory meeting took place in the International Hotel in Prague, where the exclusive suite on the top of the Hotel was taken over for this purpose. Thirty-seven scientists from 13 countries took part in this meeting, which lasted 9-12 September. After a joint session to explain the procedure, the participants divided into five groups, each working on a detailed breakdown of the agenda previously prepared by the Continuing Committee in the light of the papers submitted to the Conference. This preparatory meeting was very useful for the main Conference, as it enabled the participants to get down to business from the start, but the three days allotted for the preparatory work turned out to be too much; some of the groups, having finished the preparation of the agenda, started substantive discussions while still in Prague.

On the afternoon of 12 September, the members of the preparatory meeting, together with the participants of the main Conference who had in the meantime arrived in Prague, were transported by coaches to Karlovy Vary. Counting participants, many with their wives and families, observers, co-ordinators of Working Groups, translators and interpreters, secretaries and technical assistants, altogether 239 persons came to Karlovy Vary.

All of them were accommodated in the stately Moskva Pupp Hotel, where the meetings were also held. The tremendous effort put in by the Czechoslovak Organizing Committee, and the attention to detail, were evident at every step, from hiring of a film unit to produce a first-rate documentary film on Pugwash, to asking the chef of the Pupp Hotel to cook a special Pugwash dish at the banquet held during the Conference, when every one of the participants was also presented with one of the famous Moser wine glasses. Receptions were given by the Municipality of Karlovy Vary, and the climax of the social programme was a barbecue party on a nearby hill, with huge bonfires, roast pigs and native music and dancing.

This and other types of social programmes at Pugwash Conferences, not only provide the participants with a pleasant entertainment, but greatly help to relax the atmosphere and to create conditions for friendly informal talks which are an essential part of Pugwash discussions.

In order to provide the maximum time for discussion in the Working Groups it was decided to dispense with the keynote papers at the plenary sessions. The Conference started with a ceremonial opening session, in the full splendour of the famous Grand Hall in the Hotel. Frantisek Sorm formally opened the Conference, and messages of greetings were read from Antonin Novotny, President of Czechoslovakia, Premier Nikita Khrushchev of the Soviet Union, Prime Ministers Alec Douglas-Home of the United Kingdom, Jozef Cyrankiewicz of Poland, and Tage Erlander of Sweden, and from U Thant.

Most of the plenary sessions on the first day were taken up with presenting the agenda for the Working Groups prepared in Prague. The rest of the time of the Conference was spent in Working Groups, and only at the end were there two plenary sessions to receive the reports.

The theme of the Conference being "Disarmament and Peaceful Collaboration among Nations," the discussion centred around specific problems of disarmament and world security on the one hand, and on methods of peaceful collaboration on the other. The first aspect was discussed in four Working Groups with the following topics: (1) measures for reducing tensions and the dangers of war, especially in Central Europe; (2) measures to prevent the further spread of nuclear weapons; (3) progress towards comprehensive disarmament; (4) problems of collective security. Most of these topics had come up at previous Conferences, but the more detailed leisurely study at Karlovy Vary enabled a greater measure of agreement to be reached, particularly on Europe and on the problem of proliferation of nuclear weapons. The topic of Working Group 5 was arms control and peaceful collaboration among nations; under this heading the Group discussed the role and responsibility of scientists in advancing the cause of peace, and the long term consequences of disarmament in the development of science and technology.

During the Conference the Swedish participants announced the decision of the Swedish Government to set up an international institute for research on problems relating to peace (section 2.11). This was warmly greeted by the whole Conference, and Working Group 5 spent some time on discussing suitable projects to be undertaken by the Institute.

In addition to the five Working Groups, a special Working Group on biological warfare was set up during the Conference, to take advantage of the presence in Karlovy Vary of a number of scientists with authoritative knowledge of this subject. The continuing research and development of biological weapons made it necessary to discuss this problem again, particularly since it was thought that the outlook for controlling biological warfare activities may be more promising than appeared in 1959 at the Fifth Pugwash Conference. This meeting was the first of a series to be held subsequently by the Study Group on Biological Warfare (section 3.3.1).

At the last plenary session, when the reports from the Working Groups were read, there was some lively discussion, particularly on the suggestion that states should declare not to be the first to use nuclear weapons, and on the travel restrictions on scientists from the German Democratic Republic imposed by the Allied Travel Office in Berlin. A few suggestions for amendments of the reports were accepted by the Working Groups, and the Conference gave its endorsement to the final reports as documents from the Working Groups.

After the conclusion of the Conference, the Continuing Committee drafted a public statement, based on the reports of the Working Groups. The statement (Appendix 16) summarizes the work of the Conference by collating first the conclusions from the different Working Groups dealing with immediate steps towards disarmament, and then those relating to more distant targets. Although fairly brief, the statement reflects the very large measure of agreement reached and the progress on many stormy issues, and which made the Karlovy Vary Conference one of the most successful of the Pugwash Conferences.

4.13 Fourteenth Conference: Venice, April 11-16, 1965, "International Co-operation for Science and Disarmament"

The United Nations designated 1965 to be "International Co-operation Year,' and the Continuing Committee decided that the Pugwash Conference to be held in that year in Venice should be mostly concerned with problems of international co-operation in science, although not neglecting the disarmament topic.

The Italian Organizing Committee, with Gilberto Bernardini as Chairman, succeeded in getting the Accademia Nazionale dei Lincei and the Italian Physical Society to sponsor the Conference; funds were also secured for organizational expenses and for a proportion of the cost of the accommodation of participants. The Fondazione Giorgio Cini had offered their premises on the Isola San Giorgio Maggiore for the meeting.

In accordance with the pattern adopted in Czechoslovakia, it was decided that the main Conference be preceded by a preparatory meeting. The Continuing Committee received an invitation from Abdus Salam, the Director of the International Centre for Theoretical Physics in Trieste, to hold the preparatory meeting there, with full hospitality offered.

The preparatory meeting, which was organized by Paolo Budini, took place 8-10 April. The 35 participants were accommodated in the Jolly Hotel in Trieste, and the meetings were held in the premises of the Associazione Fra I Laureati dell'Universita di Trieste. Apart from the work on the agenda there was also a meeting of the Study Group on Biological Warfare.

For the main Conference in Venice it was not possible to accommodate all participants in one hotel; the dispersal among three hotels, one being separated from the other two by a stretch of water, somewhat reduced the opportunities for private meetings in the evenings. On the other hand, the site of the meetings themselves, on the San Giorgio Island, provided an excellent setting, combining seclusion with spaciousness, and creating the right atmosphere.

However, neither these favourable surroundings, nor the efficient secretariat and the social entertainment provided by the organizers, Bruno Bertotti and Giovanni Giacometti, managed to disperse the heavy shadow cast by the dangerous situation developing in Vietnam, and which occupied much of the time of the Conference, although originally not on the agenda.

The Conference started in the traditional way, with a formal session which was addressed by two members of the Italian Government, the Under-Secretary of State for Foreign Affairs, Mario Zagari, and the Minister of Scientific Research and Technology, Carlo Arnaudi. Messages of greetings were received from the President of Italy, Giuseppe Saragat, Prime Minister Harold Wilson of the United Kingdom, President Kwame Nkrumah of Ghana, and U Thant.

Immediately after the opening, the Conference got down to its task in the Working Groups, and the only plenary sessions of the Conference were held at the end of the meeting to receive the reports.

In accordance with the decision about the programme, the subject matter of the Conference was divided into two parts. One, dealing with international co-operation, was split into 3 Working Groups on the following topics: (1) national, regional and international institutes and their implications; (2) problems of international co-operation in science; (3) international co-operation in science education. The other part was concerned with disarmament, and had 2 Working Groups: (4) current problems of arms control and disarmament, and (5) problems of general and complete disarmament. It was in these two Working Groups that the Vietnam situation was discussed, mostly in joint meetings which, because of the interest in the subject by members of other Working Groups, had sometimes more than 50 participants. A great deal of time was spent in these meetings on an attempt to draft a statement on Vietnam which could be issued from the Conference as a whole; this was also discussed at the plenary sessions at the end. Eventually, a text of a statement to be included in the public statement from the Continuing Committee was approved by the Conference, but this was non-committal and hardly did justice to the earnest and thoughtful exchange of views at the meetings of the Working Groups, and to the specific schemes that had been suggested for the solution of the Vietnam problem.

The considerable time taken up on the Vietnam issue was bound to be detrimental to progress on other items on the agenda of Working Groups 4 and 5; nevertheless, they managed to get a useful discussion on interim measures towards arms limitation or reduction; measures to reduce tension; extension of the test ban treaty; various impediments to disarmament; and the United Nations peace-keeping machinery.

By contrast, the Working Groups on international co-operation in science found very little of controversial substance. They discussed the role of research institutes in the advancement of science; the principles governing the establishment of international research centres; problems concerning the relations between universities and large scientific institutes; the International Biological Programme; storage and retrieval of information; and the various steps to be taken to improve science education.

All these problems are often debated by numerous other bodies; however, due to their unique nature and approach, the Pugwash Conferences are in a position to discuss them in a manner unhampered by official commitments and, because of this, it is often possible to reach agreement quicker and to make recommendations for implementation by other official organizations. At the Venice Conference, the idea was put forward of an International Science Foundation to be set up by the United Nations.

A joint meeting of Working Groups 1 and 2 discussed further the plans to set up SIPRI (see section 2.11) and made proposals for projects to be undertaken by the Institute. Another joint meeting of several Working Groups also discussed the idea of an International Year for the Preparation of Disarmament, to be proclaimed by the United Nations and organized along the lines of the International Geophysical Year.

Finally, the Conference received a detailed report from the Study Group on Biological Warfare, which had met twice since the Karlovy Vary Conference. The plans for further work of this Study Group, outlined in the report, were accepted by the whole Conference.

These concrete proposals which emerged from the Conference, and are included in the statement (Appendix 17), have stressed the many areas of fruitful collaboration and have done much to offset the gloom caused by the Vietnam war.

4.14 Fifteenth Conference: Addis Ababa, December 29, 1965–January 3, 1966, "Science in Aid of Developing Countries"

Although disarmament and the East-West conflict are the major areas of interest to Pugwash, the potential danger arising from the enormous, and increasing, disparity between the developed and developing countries must be of great concern to scientists, and consequently a legitimate subject for discussion at Pugwash Conferences. This topic came up to a certain degree at some earlier Conferences, but the Continuing Committee felt that a whole Conference should be devoted to it, and that it should be held in one of the developing countries. An intimation had been received that Kwame Nkrumah would be glad to have a Pugwash Conference in Ghana, but it was felt that the choice should be for a country more likely to be acceptable to all scientists in Africa. Ethiopia fulfilled these conditions, and a tentative approach was, therefore, made through Gordon Wolstenholme, the Director of the Ciba Foundation in London. Dr. Wolstenholme has taken an active part in the organization of science in Ethiopia, in particular in the setting up of the Haile Sellassie Prize Trust. His letter brought a quick response, followed by an invitation to the Continuing Committee to hold the Fifteenth Conference in Addis Ababa under the joint sponsorship of the Haile Sellassie I University and the Haile Sellassie I Foundation.

An Organizing Committee was set up in Addis Ababa with Kassa Wolde Mariam, the President of the Haile Sellassie I University, as Chairman. Full hospitality was offered to participants during their stay in Ethiopia.

The Continuing Committee felt that the success of the Conference depended on the participation of a large number of scientists from developing countries. This created financial problems, since travelling expenses were substantial, and since hardly any means existed in the developing countries to offer grants for such a purpose. However, UNESCO and the Carnegie Endowment responded to an appeal and, together with other sources, provided funds to enable a number of scientists to attend. A few of those who accepted were unable to come at the last minute, and the Conference ended up with 63 participants, from 31 countries, and 23 observers. More than half came from Africa, Latin America and Asia, and nearly 60 percent of all members attended a Pugwash Conference for the first time.

The participants were accommodated in the Ghion Imperial Hotel, a modern and first-class establishment. All the meetings took place in the Africa Hall, with its spacious and splendidly equipped meeting rooms. From the point of view of conference amenities, such as simultaneous translations, reproduction of documents and secretarial facilities, the Addis Ababa Conference exceeded in up-to-dateness all the past Conferences held in the affluent countries. At the same time the organizers provided ample opportunity for participants to learn something of the native culture and customs. The New Year was seen in at the University with an Ethiopian-style dinner and music; there was a whole day trip to the Blue Nile; and there was a reception at the Palace, at which every participant was personally greeted by the Emperor, Haile Sellassie. The tone of the whole Conference was set by the Emperor in the speech he made at the formal opening, and in which he exhorted scientists to turn their attention to the problems of poverty, fear, ignorance, and disease. "In a world made strong and prosperous through the force of man's intellect, it is a further challenge to that intellect that science can be charged to solve the unique problems of development; for all mankind must share in the better life which progress has made possible."

Although the usual procedure of dividing into Working Groups was followed at this Conference, it was decided to start with plenary sessions at which papers introducing the topics of the Working Groups would be given by scientists from the developing countries. This was in line with the aim that the scientists from the developing countries should present the problems as they are in reality, and then jointly with their colleagues from the advanced countries try to find practical solutions.

The first day of the Conference was taken up on these introductory discussions. Actually, because of the Emperor's other engagements, the first plenary session started before the formal opening ceremony, which took place in the afternoon.

The rest of the time was spent in meetings of the Working Groups, with a plenary session towards the end, to discuss the preliminary reports from the Working Groups, and a final plenary session to receive the final reports.

Four of the Working Groups were concerned with aspects of the application of education, science and technology to development. The topics for these Groups were: (1) education in developing countries; (2) organization of scientific institutions and research in developing countries; (3) scientific approach in aid to developing countries; (4) special problems of developing countries, including international aspects of development, development planning, industrialization, food and people, protein and nutrition, water development, and conservation.

The topic of the fifth Working Group was security problems of developing countries. Under this heading the Group discussed the attitudes of developing countries towards security problems, the economic burden of armaments on developing countries, current conflicts (including Vietnam and Rhodesia), the role of the United Nations in the security of developing countries, regional organizations and security problems, the role and responsibilities of nations for promoting security, and non-proliferation of nuclear weapons.

In all the Groups the discussion was amicable, with very little controversy. All groups produced substantive reports, which were subsequently summarized by the Continuing Committee in the public statement (Appendix 18).

The Addis Ababa Conference was a big step forward for Pugwash. New subjects were discussed and new approaches made. With a majority of participants attending for the first time, it was amazing how very quickly the new members attuned themselves to the Pugwash spirit and Pugwash-type discussions. Requests were made during the Conference for more meetings of this type, and for a larger representation on the Continuing Committee of scientists from the developing countries. The response to a questionnaire subsequently sent out by Eugene Rabinowitch provided further evidence of the desire of scientists from these countries to have more Pugwash Conferences of the Addis Ababa type.

4.15 Sixteenth Conference: Sopot, September 11-16, 1966, "Disarmament and World Security, Especially in Europe"

The efforts of Leopold Infeld, a signatory of the Russell-Einstein Manifesto and a member of the Continuing Committee since 1962, resulted in the setting up in 1964 of a Pugwash Group in Poland, with Ignacy Malecki as chairman, and Karol Lapter as secretary. This committee, which soon became very active in Pugwash work, issued an invitation to the Continuing Committee to hold the Sixteenth Pugwash Conference in Poland, under the sponsorship of the Polish Academy of Sciences. Sopot, a resort on the Baltic coast, was suggested as the site of the Conference, with Jablonna, near Warsaw, for the preparatory meeting.

At this Conference, Pugwash returned to its usual topic, disarmament, and in particular to the relation between disarmament and Europe. For this reason, the participants were drawn mainly from the nuclear powers and European countries. By contrast with the Fifteenth Conference, about three-quarters of the participants had been to one or more previous Pugwash Conferences, and were familiar with their procedure.

Of the four Working Groups, two were concerned with Europe, and the other two with aspects of general and complete disarmament. In the first two Groups the Conference benefited from the work of the Study Group on European Security, which had met several times during the past year, and which had a meeting in Jablonna just prior to the Conference (section 3.3.2).

The estate in Jablonna, often used by the Polish Academy for scientific conferences, was given over to Pugwash for meetings of the Continuing Committee, the Study Group on European Security, and the preparatory meeting. The latter, with some 25 participants, met to discuss the draft agenda prepared by the Continuing Committee. Only minor amendments were made, and the whole meeting was over in a short time.

On 10 September all members of the Conference were taken by coaches from Warsaw to Sopot, visiting on the way a number of historical and industrial centres. In Sopot the participants were accommodated in the spacious Grand Hotel, one of the largest in Poland, which was completely taken over for the Conference. Full hospitality was offered to participants, and the organizers had not spared effort or expense to make the stay both pleasant and memorable. The social programme enabled participants to learn something about the country, so rich in historical monuments; the outings included an excursion to Westerplatte, the starting place of World War II, and to the site of a Nazi concentration camp.

As usual, the Conference started with a formal opening ceremony presided over by Ignacy Malecki. The Deputy Prime Minister of Poland, Eugeniusz Szyr, addressed the assembly, and there were messages of greetings from U Thant, Tage Erlander, the Prime Minister of Sweden, and Walter Ulbricht, Chairman of the State Council of the German Democratic Republic. No messages came this time from the heads of any of the great powers.

After the opening ceremony, there was a short plenary session in which Mikhail Millionshchikov and Bernard Feld gave brief reviews of the current situation in disarmament negotiations. This was followed by reports of the work of two Pugwash Study Groups, on European Security and Biological Warfare. The Conference then started its proper work in the Groups.

As in Venice, the Vietnam issue loomed large at the Conference. It was inevitable that the war in Vietnam should be discussed; indeed, it would have been inconceivable for a Pugwash Conference to ignore the terrible tragedy of the Vietnamese people, and the threat of the escalation of the conflict. In order to avoid this subject monopolizing the Conference to the detriment of the other subjects on the agenda, the Continuing Committee decided that the Vietnam issue should be taken up specifically only in Working Group 3, which had "current conflicts" on its agenda. However, in order to give all members of the Conference an opportunity to express themselves on this problem, a special plenary session was arranged for one evening, instead of a visit to the opera.

Rudolf Peierls, who in the absence of Powell presided over the meeting of the Continuing Committee held in Jablonna, took the chair at this session. It was not an easy meeting. One after the other participants spoke, not mincing words in expressing horror and indignation at the happenings in Vietnam. Most of the speakers bitterly attacked the bombing of the North Vietnamese by the Americans and their use of chemical weapons, while a few speakers drew attention to the atrocities committed by the other side. Some participants stressed the responsibility of scientists to use their influence in urging their governments to do everything possible to bring the combatants to the negotiating table. Naturally, such a large gathering could not be expected to get down to a detailed analysis of the situation and to discuss methods of solving the problem. This had to be left to Working Group 3, which devoted several of its sessions to this issue. The discussion in the Group yielded a surprising measure of agreement, but it was decided that the ideas which emerged from it should be conveyed by participants directly to governments, rather than be put into the public statement.

The topics for the Working Groups were: (1) disarmament in Europe; (2) reduction of tensions and political settlements in Europe; (3) main problems of progress towards general and complete disarmament; (4) measures for arms limitation. The items discussed in the first two Working Groups included collective measures in Europe, such as the freeze of nuclear weapons; non-proliferation; denuclearization; military forces and conventional weapons in Europe; and observation posts. All these topics had been discussed at previous Conferences, and the areas of disagreement between East and West had become well-defined, but each time some new idea emerges, which makes it possible to remove at least some of the divergence. It is for these small measures of progress, which usually result from joint discussions, that it is considered well worthwhile to return to these issues time and time again.

In the Working Group dealing with progress towards general and complete disarmament, the position of China was discussed at length, and the Group was again unanimous in stressing the need to bring China into disarmament discussions. Among measures for arms limitation discussed in Working Group 4, a number of specific subjects were considered in some detail, such as the extension of the test ban agreement, coupled with an idea of a seismic detection club, non-proliferation, nuclear-free zones, nuclear freeze proposals and the need for an adequate control system to ensure the peaceful utilization of fissile materials from reactors.

The reports of the Working Groups were discussed at a plenary session at the end of the Conference. There was a lively debate on some of these reports, and a few amendments were accepted by the Working Groups. These reports formed the basis for the public statement drafted by the Continuing Committee after the end of the Conference, and which was issued at a Press conference the following day (Appendix 19).

4.16 Seventeenth Conference: Ronneby, September 3-8, 1967, "Scientists and World Affairs"

At the Tenth Conference in London in 1962, it was suggested that every 4 or 5 years there should be a large Conference with the same aims as the London Conference, i.e., to make decisions about future activities and to elect a new governing body. The Continuing Committee decided in 1964 that a Conference of this nature be held in 1967, and Sweden was suggested as the host country. The organization of a large Conference can be undertaken only by a very active National Pugwash Group which, in addition, must be able to acquire the necessary funds. The Swedish Pugwash Group fulfilled these criteria. Largely thanks to its energetic secretary, Rolf Björnerstedt, the Swedish Group was one of the most active at that time. Its particular interest was the Biological Warfare Study Group, in which it played a major role and organized the pilot scheme of inspection of microbiological laboratories (see section 3.3.1). The setting up of the Stockholm International Peace Research Institute (SIPRI) in 1966, of which Björnerstedt was an Assistant Director, until Robert Neild was appointed Director in 1967, was also very helpful in this respect; the governing board of SIPRI agreed to provide the major proportion of the financial needs of the Conference.

A Swedish Organizing Committee was set up with Arne Engström as Chairman and Björnerstedt as Secretary; its members included Hannes Alfvén, Martin Fehrm, Carl Hedén and Jan Prawitz. After surveying several possible sites, it was decided that the Conference be held in Ronneby, in the south of Sweden. The Ronneby Brunn Hotel had all the necessary facilities for meetings, as well as enough rooms to accommodate all expected participants and associates.

As in the case of the London Conference, letters of invitation were sent to all who participated in any of the previous 16 Conferences. At that time there was a total of 408 living participants, and nearly half of them accepted the invitation. However, a number of those who had initially accepted cancelled at the last moment, due to lack of funds for travelling expenses, so that only 117 of them came to Ronneby. On the other hand, many scientists were invited to Ronneby for the first time, so that the total number of participants was 180, slightly larger than at the London Conference. They came from 44 countries, which was the largest number of countries in any Pugwash Conference until then. There were also 14 observers.

The Continuing Committee felt that it ought to give guidance to the Conference about plans for future activities and organization; for this reason these problems, as well as the programme of the Conference, were discussed at several meetings of the Continuing Committee. The idea of instituting specialized symposia, subsequently adopted by the Ronneby Conference, was conceived at these meetings. A special sub-committee was set up to prepare a detailed programme; it met with the Swedish Organizing Committee in Stockholm in December 1966. The Continuing Committee itself met for 2 days in the Malmen Hotel in Stockholm a few days before the start of the Conference. This was followed by a 2-day meeting, in the same place, of a number of participants invited by the Continuing Committee to help in preparing the plans for future activities.

The question of publicity, and the possibility of admitting the Press to the plenary sessions, were discussed by the Continuing Committee. It was decided to invite the Press for the formal opening sessions, including the report to be given by the Secretary-General, but not to the remaining sessions. Instead, Press conferences were arranged for every day, which were attended by the chairmen of the plenary sessions or conveners of Working Groups. Nigel Calder was appointed Press Officer for the Conference, and at the Press conferences he gave admirable summaries of the discussions.

The Conference started on the morning of Sunday, September 3 with an opening ceremony presided over by Arne Engström. The Conference was formally opened by the Prime Minister of Sweden, Tage Erlander, who came specially to Ronneby and spent 2 days with the participants. In his speech the Prime Minister referred to the many current conflicts and tensions in the world, and to the particular responsibility of scientists to build the road to peace in co-operation with politicians.

There was a rather large number of messages of greetings from statesmen and scientific institutions. In the first category, messages of greetings were received from U Thant; the Presidents of Austria (Franz Jonas), Czechoslovakia (Antonin Novotny), Italy (Guiseppe Saragat), and Pakistan (Mohammed Ayub Khan); the Governor General of Australia (Lord Casey); the Prime Minister of India (Indira Gandhi); the Chairman of the Council of State of the German Democratic Republic (Walter Ulbricht); and the Foreign Ministers of the German Federal Republic (Willy Brandt) and of Poland (Adam Rapacki). These were followed by messages of greetings from the Royal Swedish Academy of Sciences, the Royal Swedish Academy of Engineering Sciences, the Royal Society, the Academies of Sciences of the Soviet Union, the United States, Czechoslovakia, the German Democratic Republic, Australia, Poland, Hungary, Israel; the Italian Accademia dei Lincei; the Science Council of Japan, and the American Academy of Arts and Sciences.

The Secretary-General then gave a report on the work of the Continuing Committee during the past 5 years; this included a survey of the work of the National Pugwash Groups and obituaries of 14 Pugwashites who had died since 1962; the text of this report is given in Appendix 22.

After reconvening in private session, the Conference discussed the report; this was continued in the afternoon when reports were also given of the work of the Pugwash Study Groups, of SIPRI and IPRA (see section 2.11).

During the first session the Conference also set up two Standing Committees. One, concerned with future activities, had 12 members; many of these had already started work at Stockholm, two days before the Conference; this Committee elected Sir Gordon Sutherland as its Chairman. The other, on future organization, had 5 members and was chaired by Sir John Cockcroft. Both of these committees held meetings throughout the

Conference, either separately or conjointly. The members of the Continuing Committee were deliberately not included in the Standing Committees, but many of them were frequently called in for consultations.

While the two Standing Committees were busy in the background, the Conference went on with its programme which consisted of plenary sessions and Working Groups. Apart from the plenary session on "Responsibilities of Scientists," held on the first day and in which there was a general and lively discussion from the floor, the plenary sessions on the mornings of the three following days had all been structured by the Continuing Committee in the form of symposia, each opened by three keynote speakers. The first symposium was on "Arms Control, Peacekeeping and Security," and the papers were given by Mikhail Millionshchikov, Vikram Sarabhai and Jerome Wiesner. (Actually Wiesner had to cancel at the last moment and his paper was read by Frank Long.) The second symposium on "New Approaches in Disarmament" started off with papers by Lev Artsimovitch, John Cockcroft and Alva Myrdal. The third symposium was on "International Co-operation and Development" and the papers were given by Harrison Brown, Rolando Garcia and Ivan Malek.

Vigorous discussions followed the papers in all three symposia, with some interesting and original ideas. The topics tackled at these plenary sessions were further debated in Working Groups. Due to the large number of participants, seven Working Groups were set up and their task was to discuss most of the problems of interest to Pugwash under the following headings: (1) arms control and disarmament; (2) peacekeeping and security; (3) new approaches in disarmament; (4) international programmes in science; (5) education, technology and development; (6) the special responsibilities of scientists; and (7) current conflicts and their resolution. This last Group was an afterthought and was set up with the intention of concentrating the consideration of sensitive problems, such as the situation in Vietnam, in the Middle East, and in Nigeria in one Group; even so Vietnam was brought up in two other Groups. The debates in the seventh Group were the most heated at the Conference; on the Middle East the discussion was long and passionate, and no solution was agreed to. On the other hand, there was general agreement on specific measures to bring to an end the conflict in Vietnam; in this respect there was remarkable progress since the Sopot Conference.

Group 5, concerned with the problems of developing nations, had before it a proposal from Carl Djerassi on the need to establish Centres of Excellence for basic research in developing countries; as a typical example of the location of such a centre he mentioned Nairobi. This suggestion was soon afterwards taken up by the Kenyan entomologist, Thomas Odhiambo, and the East African Academy of Sciences. Subsequently, a meeting of representatives from several Academies of Sciences decided to set up an international Centre for Insect Physiology and Ecology in Nairobi, with Odhiambo as Director. ICIPE is now a flourishing research centre.

All Working Groups prepared reports which were read out at a plenary session on the last day of the Conference. At its last plenary session the

Eighteenth Conference 73

Conference got down to decide about the future of Pugwash. The Standing Committee on Future Activities presented its report which contained an analysis of the raison d'être of Pugwash and of the scope of its activities, as well as specific proposals for the future; the text of this report is given in Appendix 23. The Standing Committee on Future Organization then presented its report, in which it recommended the establishment of the post of President of Pugwash and an enlargement of the Continuing Committee; it also proposed a budget for the Central Office of $50,000 per annum. After brief discussions both reports were accepted by acclamation.

The Conference then elected Sir John Cockcroft as First President of Pugwash. All the serving members of the Continuing Committee were re-elected with Cecil Powell as Chairman of the Committee. Joseph Rotblat and Patricia Lindop were re-elected as Secretary-General and Assistant Secretary-General, respectively.

It had been the intention of the Continuing Committee that this large Conference should issue a public statement and a drafting committee was set up at the beginning of the Conference. The draft of a statement prepared by this committee was circulated to members of the Conference and debated at the closing session. The discussion was very long and heated, and it became clear from its tone that there was a great deal of opposition to the proposed statement. In accordance with Pugwash practice not to issue any statement unless it commands the support of a very substantial majority, it was decided to abandon the idea of a statement from the Conference as a whole. It was agreed, however, that the Continuing Committee might issue a statement under its own name; this was prepared after the end of the Conference (Appendix 24).

The lack of agreement on a public statement from the whole Conference, although disappointing, did not mar the achievements of the Conference. Apart from the very informative discussions in the plenary sessions and Working Groups on practically all aspects of interest to Pugwash, the main achievement of the Ronneby Conference was to agree on a new type of activity, i.e., Symposia, which provided forums for detailed discussions on important issues, gave more scope for National Pugwash Groups, and opened up the possibility of bringing in more scientists to Pugwash. The new organizational structure and the specific proposals about the budget and staffing of the Central Office, also served to consolidate the programme for Pugwash for the next 5 years.

4.17 Eighteenth Conference: Nice, September 11-16, 1968, "Current Problems of Peace, Security and Development"

In the earlier plans for the Seventeenth and Eighteenth Conferences it was envisaged that both would be held in Scandinavia, the first in Sweden and the second in Denmark. However, the Danish Pugwash Group did not manage to acquire the necessary funds for a Conference and decided to organize a symposium instead. The French Group then gallantly stepped in and, despite the short notice, offered to organize the 1968 Conference. A Pugwash Group in France had been in existence almost from the beginning; one of the Continuing Committee meetings in 1959 was held in Royaumont, near Paris, and French scientists played a vital role in the private negotiations on bringing the Vietnam war to an end (see section 3.6.2). The prime movers in the French Group were Herbert Marcovich, a member of the Continuing Committee since 1962, and Etienne Bauer, who took on the main task of organizing the Conference.

Although Paris was contemplated as the venue, it was decided to keep away from big cities, and Nice was chosen as a place offering a more relaxed atmosphere. The Plaza Hotel had all the necessary amenities, meeting rooms and accommodation for the size of the Conference, which was back to what it used to be before Ronneby. There were 81 participants from 28 countries, as well as 12 observers. A novel feature was the invitation of science writers. Since the public statements issued by the Continuing Committee evoked little response from the Press, it was decided to try to improve communication, at least with the scientific community, by inviting a small number of representatives of science journals, so that they could write reports from firsthand experience. Eight science writers from France and the United Kingdom were invited. In this first experiment the Continuing Committee proceeded somewhat cautiously, and allowed the science writers to participate only in the plenary sessions; their exclusion from the Working Groups naturally caused resentment; nevertheless, the science writers performed their task conscientiously, and the reporting of the Nice Conference was indeed much better than for many previous Conferences.

During the year since the Ronneby Conference, Pugwash had lost its first President, John Cockcroft, as well as the person invited to succeed him, Lord Florey. Following the decision to make the office of President a rotating one, with one-year tenure, the French Group invited Francis Perrin to be the President of the Nice Conference. He presided over the first and the last plenary sessions.

In accordance with the decision at Ronneby to reduce to a minimum the formal ceremony at the opening sessions, there was only one message of greetings, from U Thant, following the opening speech by the President. Tribute was paid to the memory of Cockcroft, and the Conference immediately got down to the business on its agenda, i.e., to receive reports of Pugwash Symposia. During the first year of operation of this new activity, three Symposia were held, in London, in Marianske Lazne and in Krogerup (see Table 11). In fact, just prior to the Nice Conference, there was a continuation of the Second Symposium, since it was felt that the subject matter had not been adequately covered when the Symposium met in Marianske Lazne in May. Eighteen persons, most of whom participated in Marianske Lazne, took part in the second part of the Symposium which was held in the Plaza Hotel from 8-10 September, in parallel with a meeting of the Continuing Committee.

Although the proceedings and recommendations of Symposia are written up in the Pugwash Newsletters, it was thought useful to give full reports on these first Symposia to the Nice Conference, in order to hear comments on this new venture from the plenum. Accordingly, the first three plenary sessions were given over to reports and discussions on the three Symposia. In the third plenary session there was also a report on the work of SIPRI; this dealt mainly with its study groups on monitoring underground explosions and on chemical weapons.

On the afternoon of the second day the Conference split into four Working Groups which met during most of the remaining time of the Conference. The topics of the Working Groups were (1) arms control and disarmament; (2) regional arms control; (3) current problems; and (4) scientific and technological manpower problems in developing countries. As to be expected, the most heated debates took place in the Working Groups on current problems, which included on its agenda Nigeria, the Middle East, Vietnam and Czechoslovakia.

The military intervention in Czechoslovakia occurred just three weeks before the start of the Conference, and this event was bound to influence the atmosphere of the meeting. A few Pugwashites had, in fact, suggested that the Conference be postponed, but the Executive Committee decided to go ahead as planned, arguing that it is in times of political crisis that Pugwash Conferences are most needed. This view was endorsed by all participants at Nice, and the tone and scope of the discussion there gave it full justification. Czechoslovakia figured prominently at the Conference, in papers submitted, in discussions at plenary sessions and, in particular, in the Working Group on current conflicts, which included a Czechoslovak scientist. Members of other Working Groups joined the Group when it discussed Czechoslovakia. After a really frank exchange of views the text of a resolution was worked out; it was unanimously adopted by the Working Group, although in the plenary session some opposition to it was expressed. The general view was that not only was this delicate situation handled skilfully, but that the Movement emerged from it strengthened by its resolve not to evade sensitive areas but to tackle them in the Pugwash spirit.

The other Working Groups tackled a variety of problems concerned with the more usual aspects of world security. While confirming the vital necessity of general and complete disarmament, it was thought that some partial measures of arms control might be practicable and realizable in the near future. Among these were limitations on nuclear weapons and on arms trade, a freeze on military manpower and on military expenditure. In this connection, it was suggested that a United Nations Conference be called to assess the military expenditure of nations, a suggestion taken up two years later by the United Nations General Assembly.

The reports of the Working Groups were read at plenary sessions at the end of the Conference, and were used by the Continuing Committee in the statement issued after the Conference (Appendix 25).

An event at the Nice Conference worthy of mention was an informal evening session with a group of French students to discuss their problems. After the massive student unrest in Paris in May 1968, this was still a topical issue, and the opportunity was taken to enquire at first hand the nature of the students' grievances. Although the discussion was inconclusive, it gave Pugwash an inkling of the nature of the generation gap and an incentive to establish further contacts with students.

4.18 Nineteenth Conference: Sochi, October 22-27, 1969, "World Security, Disarmament and Development"

After nearly 10 years the Continuing Committee felt that it was time for Pugwash to return to the two countries with the largest Groups, the Soviet Union and the United States. It was decided to have the Conferences in the same order as in 1960 and 1961, i.e., in the Soviet Union in 1969, and in the United States in 1970. At the nomination of the Soviet Pugwash Group, the Continuing Committee elected Mikhail Millionshchikov as President of Pugwash for the 1968-1969 session; he took up office at the end of the Nice Conference. As in 1960, the Conference was sponsored by the Soviet Academy of Sciences and all participants were the guests of the Academy during their stay in the Soviet Union.

Although Annual Conferences are usually held in early September, the Soviet Pugwash Group asked for the Conference to be held in late October. This was partly dictated by the location of the Conference in Sochi, a resort on the Black Sea, where the climate was more amenable at the end of October.

The meetings were held in the Intourist Hotel which had enough rooms for all the Working Groups, secretariat, etc., but not to accommodate all members of the Conference. Because of this, most of the participants stayed in the Magnolia Hotel, about a mile away, but the main meals were taken in the Intourist Hotel by all members of the Conference, so that opportunities for informal talks were not significantly impaired by this separation.

There was not enough time after the Nice Conference for the Continuing Committee to prepare the programme for the Conference. This was left to the Executive Committee which met in Moscow in February 1969 to work out a detailed programme and a list of topics for the Working Groups. Apart from attention to world security problems, necessitated by the acceleration of the arms race, it was thought that European security and chemical and biological weapons should be given close scrutiny in view of these issues being taken up in various official bodies. The tackling of so many problems necessitated the invitation of a somewhat larger number of participants than in former Annual Conferences. Altogether, there were 101 scientists from 29 countries, as well as 10 official observers. As usual, the host country was allowed a larger quota and there were 21 Soviet scientists participating.

There were again 8 science writers, from France, the United Kingdom, the United States, and the Soviet Union, but this time the science writers were allowed to attend the meetings of the Working Groups as well as the plenary sessions. The science writers did not abuse this privilege in their reporting of the Conference, which again was quite extensive.

Nineteenth Conference

The Conference started with a formal session in which the President, Mikhail Millionshchikov, gave an opening address in which he summarized the achievements of Pugwash and the aims of the Conference. He then read a message of greetings from the Prime Minister of the Soviet Union, Alexei Kosygin, as well as greetings from the Presidium of the Soviet Academy of Sciences. A message of greetings from U Thant was read by Ralph Bunche, and the participants were welcomed to Sochi by the Chairman of the Krasnodar District.

Pugwash had suffered a grievous loss about two months earlier by the sudden death of Cecil Powell, the chairman of the Continuing Committee, while on a trip which was to bring him to Sochi. In the opening session, Pugwash honoured his memory and several tributes were paid to Powell's scientific achievements, to his work in the social implications of science, and to his leadership in Pugwash.

As usual, the work of the Conference was divided between plenary sessions and Working Groups. In two of the plenary sessions reports were given on the Fourth, Fifth and Sixth Symposia, which were held in 1969, as well as on the meeting of the Biological Warfare Study Group which was held in Marianske Lazne in May 1969. However, another plenary session was of a novel character: a prepared panel discussion on one topic, the deployment of anti-ballistic missile systems. This topic was at that time being hotly debated, particularly in the United States, and it was felt that Pugwash participants should be given a full review of the subject, as well as an opportunity to comment on it. Bernard Feld, who organized the panel discussion, was in the chair; the main speaker was George Rathjens, who was followed immediately by Georgi Arbatov. In the ensuing debate, in which 14 discussants took part, all the ramifications and implications of the deployment of ABM's on the arms race, and their influence on the forthcoming SALT negotiations were brought to the fore from various angles. It was the general opinion that this type of panel discussion fulfilled an important function at a Pugwash Conference, both educationally, by giving members of the Conference full information on the current status of a vital issue, and substantively, by providing a forum for exchange of views and original suggestions.

The five Working Groups dealt with the following topics: (1) measures for terminating current military conflicts and keeping the peace; (2) European security; (3) reduction and elimination of nuclear weapons and delivery systems; (4) disarmament in the non-nuclear field and further steps towards general and complete disarmament; and (5) modern science and developing countries. Under these headings a great variety of topics was discussed, sometimes overlapping, and requiring two Groups to meet in joint session, and sometimes dividing into sub-groups; these often met during meal times and evenings. One of the Working Groups went back to its deliberations late at night after the banquet and worked until the morning. The Group dealing with nuclear weapons and delivery systems was strongly aware of the possibility of another escalation in the arms race between the United States and the Soviet Union and the great danger which may result from this; they felt that the scientists have a great responsibility in explaining the seriousness of the situation to the general public and shaking them out of their complacency. The Working Group on European Security was also cognizant of the danger resulting from the existence of two military blocs in Europe and of the opportunities which were beginning to emerge for the initiation of formal talks between governments on security in Europe. There were requests in this Group to discuss further the Czechoslovak issue but this was opposed by the Czechoslovak Pugwash Group, which in a letter to the Continuing Committee praised the stand taken at the Nice Conference but asked not to discuss Czechoslovakia as a separate item. Working Group 4 spent most of its time on ways and means of eliminating chemical and biological weapons. This required some rather technical considerations. Working Group 5 recommended the establishment of an International Foundation for Scientific and Technical Development to support research in developing nations, and it spelled out in detail its terms of reference and framework. The Working Group on current conflicts discussed Vietnam, the Middle East and Nigeria (with 3 Nigerian scientists, one from the Federal state and two from Biafra) but not much further progress was made beyond Nice.

The tenseness resulting from concentration on such sensitive areas was made more bearable by the varied social programme provided by the organizers, which included receptions, the planting of Friendship Trees, film shows, a circus show, and an excursion to Pitsunda. There was also a banquet with gypsy music and dances. Mr. Cyrus Eaton, who with Mrs. Eaton were the guests of the Soviet Academy, addressed the Conference at the banquet; the opportunity was also taken to congratulate Philip Noel-Baker on his forthcoming eightieth birthday.

In the last two days of the Conference, the Working Groups presented their reports to the plenary sessions. In addition to the five Working Groups there was also a report from an *ad hoc* group on the effects of nuclear weapons tests; this was set up to look into the claim of Professor Sternglass about infant mortality resulting from tests of nuclear weapons. As usual, the Continuing Committee used these reports as the basis for the statement which was issued after the end of the Conference (Appendix 26). Apart from the need to reaffirm the original goals of Pugwash and to extend them to include new problems, such as of developing nations, the statement stressed the need for all scientists to concern themselves with these life-or-death issues, and in particular to involve the younger generation.

4.19 Twentieth Conference: Fontana, September 9-15, 1970, "Peace and International Co-operation: A Programme for the Seventies"

1970 was a busy year for the American Pugwash Group. Numerically the strongest of the National Groups, and playing an important role in all Pugwash Conferences, the United States Group had since 1961 concentrated mainly on meetings of American Pugwashites within the United States. But in 1970 the Group made its impact on the international arena by organizing two Symposia and the Annual Conference. Bernard Feld, the Chairman of the United States Pugwash Group, was the prime mover in preparing the Tenth Symposium, on the Impact of New Technologies on the Arms Race, which was held in June in Racine, Wisconsin. The discussion of this Symposium, which was pitched at a high level of technical know-how, was subsequently published as a monograph by The M.I.T. Press. The Eleventh Symposium, which was held in Stanford, California, in September, came about mainly through the efforts of Eugene Rabinowitch, and was concerned with problems of developing nations and what scientists can do about them. But the main effort went into the organization of the Annual Conference. In addition to the National Academy of Sciences, and the American Academy of Arts and Sciences, this Conference was also sponsored by the Adlai Stevenson Institute of International Affairs, in Chicago. Its Director, William Polk, gave the organizers of the Conference his wholehearted support, both financially and by lending his staff and publicity resources.

Because of the location of the Adlai Stevenson Institute, it was initially intended to have the Conference in Chicago, but the advantages of having it away from a large city persuaded the organizers to choose a site in the nearby state of Wisconsin. Fontana, a small town on Lake Geneva, has a splendid hotel, the Abbey, which offered all the facilities for the Conference. Indeed, the luxurious accommodation and first-class cuisine set a standard which will be difficult to surpass, as far as material needs are concerned.

Despite the heavy travelling expenses for most of the participants, there was a very good response to invitations, and the Conference had 98 participants from 31 countries; this included 23 from the United States. There were also 9 official observers. The invitation of science writers from the United States presented a difficult problem. There were so many candidates under this category, all eager to come, that to select a few would have been very embarrassing for the organizers. In the end, it was decided not to have any science writers from the United States, and there were only 2 from other countries, one each from the United Kingdom and the Soviet Union. However, a very large number of journalists, representing many American newspapers, descended on the Abbey Hotel; they were not allowed to attend the meetings but they interviewed many participants and were kept informed about the progress by daily Press conferences. The relations with the Press were admirably handled by Howard Lewis of the United States National Academy of Sciences, who served as Press Officer of the Conference.

Another, and new, category of attendees was students. In some of the past Conferences, young people, usually undergraduates or post-graduates from the local university, were brought in to help in the organization, e.g., to run errands, provide liaison between Working Groups, and generally help in the secretariat. It was the initiative of the United States Group to extend the involvement of these people by allowing them to sit in the plenary sessions and the Working Groups and, subject to agreement of the chairmen, to participate in the discussion. At Fontana there were 24 young people in the category of student-participants. Almost all of them were postgraduates, taking higher degree courses or engaged on research projects. Their selection was somewhat haphazard. American participants in the Pugwash Conferences were asked to submit names of suitable candidates from among members of their university departments or from other institutes. To avoid travel expenses, all but one of the 24 came from America; but 8 of these were foreign students who happened to be in the United States for a period of study. The only student who travelled from another country was a Swede, Jan Fjellander, who was invited because of his earlier contacts with Pugwash in connection with a conference on "Threats and Promises of Science" which he had organized with a group of young people from several European countries.

The students applied themselves eagerly to their assignments; they worked very hard in the secretariat, as well as taking an active part in the debates in the Conference. A special evening session was organized during the Conference, with one of the students in the chair, and a number of them presenting their views about the Conference and Pugwash in general.

Eugene Rabinowitch was the President of Pugwash for the 1969-1970 session, and he opened the Conference with an impassioned speech in which he outlined the tasks of Pugwash; he called, in particular, for a vigorous involvement of Pugwash in an effort to apply the economic and intellectual forces of all nations to the advancement of underdeveloped countries.

Messages of greetings were read from U Thant and Bruno Kreisky, the Federal Chancellor of the Austrian Republic. These messages were followed by speeches of welcome from the three co-sponsors of the Conference, the Adlai Stevenson Institute, the National Academy of Sciences, and the American Academy of Arts and Sciences. There was also a greeting from the Presidium of the Soviet Academy of Sciences.

Once again an important loss to Pugwash had to be recorded in the opening session: the death in February 1971 of the founder of the Pugwash Movement, Bertrand Russell, and a tribute was paid to his memory.

The rest of the first plenary session was taken up with a report on the activities of the past year and a discussion on the two last Symposia held in the United States.

Following the successful example of Sochi, there were two plenary sessions structured as panel discussions on specific topics, both new to Pugwash. One was on "International Aspects of Environmental Pollution and the Depletion of Natural Resources." It was opened by three invited speakers, one of them being a chief organizer of the 1972 United Nations Conference on the Human Environment. Several more invited discussants then made their contribution, followed by a lively discussion from the floor which had to be terminated due to the late hour, after a session lasting more than 4 hours.

The subject of the second panel discussion was "Problems of Population and Economic Growth." This was started by three invited speakers, followed by discussion from the floor. Although population problems were occasionally mentioned in previous Pugwash Conferences, this was the first time that a whole plenary session had been devoted to it; it was clear from the interest shown by participants that this topic will recur on the Pugwash agenda.

As usual, the main work of the Conference was centered in the Working Groups. There were five of them on the following topics: (1) international security problems; (2) European security arrangements; (3) disarmament and arms limitation; (4) international co-operation in science and technology; and (5) science, technology and development. Current conflicts were this time discussed in the first Working Group, which also dealt with arms trade. The possible role of Europe, as a factor influencing relations between the superpowers, was discussed in the second Working Group. The third Working Group dealt with SALT, the extension of the Test Ban Treaty, nuclear proliferation, weapons on the seabed, and chemical and biological weapons. The fourth Group spent most of its time on environmental pollution and the role of Pugwash in promoting international co-operation.

The Group dealing with developing countries was very anxious to see the further effort in this direction put on a properly organized basis, and representatives of the Group presented these views to the Continuing Committee at a special meeting; the outcome of this was the setting up of a special Study Group on Development (see section 3.3.4).

All the Working Groups produced reports of their work which were read out and discussed at a plenary session near the end of the Conference. These reports, with minor omissions, were used by the Continuing Committee in the public statement issued after the conclusion of the Conference (Appendix 27).

At the last session there was a report on current work in SIPRI, as well as a discussion on Pugwash activities for the next year. The Conference was then informed of the decision of the Continuing Committee to revert to the resolution at Ronneby to have a permanent post of President. This was followed by the announcement that Hannes Alfvén was invited and has accepted to become President. He confirmed this in a speech in which he promised to do his best to help to achieve the objective of Pugwash, a promise which he soon made good, after receiving the 1970 Nobel Prize in Physics, by making Pugwash the theme of his discourse at the Nobel Laureates reunion in Lindau in 1971.

4.20 Twenty-First Conference: Sinaia, August 26-31, 1971, "Problems of World Security, Environment and Development"

Although Romanian scientists had attended practically every Conference since 1962, there was no National Group in Romania, nor other organized Pugwash activities. The situation changed in 1969, when Corneliu Penescu attended for the first time the Pugwash Conference in Sochi. With his zeal and outstanding organizational skill he threw himself whole-heartedly into the task of bringing Pugwash to Romania. He was the prime mover of the Association of Scientists in Romania, which provided the resources and the members of the Organizing Committee of the Twenty-First Pugwash Conference.

The site chosen for the Conference, Sinaia, a tourist resort in the Carpathians, provided a perfect setting, with its relaxed atmosphere, beautiful scenery and excellent weather. The whole of the Palas Hotel was taken over for the accommodation of the participants. All meetings were held in the nearby House of Culture, which was also taken over for the duration of the Conference. Originally built as a casino, it contained a magnificent set of rooms for plenary sessions, working groups, and secretariat, and for informal chats.

As usual, the Continuing Committee decided on the geographical distribution of the participants in the light of the programme of the Conference. But, whether it was due to the increasing popularity of Pugwash in the scientific community, or to the attractions of the Conference site, there were numerous requests from National Groups to increase their quotas. These requests could not be granted because the total number of members of the Conference was limited by the accommodation available in the Palas Hotel. As it was, and despite some last minute cancellations, there were 97 participants from 31 countries, plus 9 observers. There also were 19 students, mostly from Romania. An unusually large number of participants brought their wives and members of families.

The Romanian organizers offered an extensive social programme of excursions, receptions and film shows. A special event was the reception given by the President of Romania, Nicolae Ceausescu. This was held in Bucharest, and the participants with their wives made a special trip to the capital one afternoon, returning late in the evening. Instead of formal speeches, President Ceaucescu talked informally to individuals or groups of participants; the members of his cabinet did the same, thus ensuring a very friendly and informal atmosphere.

The actual proceedings of the Conference took their usual course. Professor Penescu, as the President of the Conference, opened the first session and read a message from President Ceausescu; a message of greetings was also read from U Thant, and there were speeches of welcome from the Romanian Academy of Sciences, and the Mayor of Sinaia. The President of Pugwash, Hannes Alfvén, then gave a presidential address in which he referred to the most pressing areas for Pugwash activities, particularly to the need to tackle the population problem. This was followed by a report on the past year's activities given by the Secretary-General, and a discussion on the Fifteenth Symposium on tactical arms limitation in Europe, which had just taken place in Finland.

The Conference then divided into 5 Working Groups which began their meetings on the first day. As had become customary, there also were three plenary sessions in the form of panel discussions on specific topics. In order not to take away too much time from the Working Groups, two of these sessions were held in the evening. One plenary session was on "Water Pollution," and consisted of a number of speeches by experts in this field. Another session, equally erudite, had as its theme the "General Consequences of the Green Revolution." Both of these are somewhat unusual topics for Pugwash, but they were organized because of the growing interest of Pugwash in problems of the environment and developing countries.

The third plenary session was on a politically topical subject, "The Human Problems of East Pakistan and the Refugees." This session was arranged because of the strong feelings of many participants that Pugwash must discuss the tragic plight of the regugees. Efforts were made to invite to this discussion Pakistani scientists from both West and East, so that the views of both sides of the conflict could be presented. These efforts were unsuccessful, but there were among the participants a number of people with intimate knowledge and experience of the situation in Bangladesh and India, as well as experts in the problems of refugees, so that the discussion was highly informative. As a result of this session, the Continuing Committee included in its statement an appeal to all parties concerned to take steps to alleviate the suffering of the refugees, as well as to reduce tensions in the region which threaten international peace.

The topics of the five Working Groups were as follows: (1) European security problems; (2) improved international mechanisms for resolution of local conflicts and for peace-keeping; (3) international security and further steps towards disarmament; (4) international aspects of environmental problems; and (5) economic and technological co-operation amongst nations, in particular for development. The Groups on European security and on international security came out with specific proposals for the settlement of problems facing the Continent; these reflected the growing possibility of a European Security Conference being convened in the near future. Working Group 3 also made a number of cogent suggestions concerning SALT and other aspects of disarmament. Much of the discussion in Working Group 5 centred on the population problem and on its control by contraceptive methods.

It is obvious that Pugwash is devoting an increasing proportion of its time to "new" problems, such as the environment, population, and developing countries, but this does not mean a decrease of interest or effort on the main issue of the dangers from the existence of weapons of mass destruction and the arms race. The greater range of subjects debated has been made possible by the larger number of participants, which leaves enough scientists for full discussion in the Working Groups dealing with the subjects which are the prime interest to Pugwash, i.e., world security and steps towards disarmament. Indeed, the chief emphasis in Pugwash is still on the avoidance of a nuclear war and the achievement of general and complete disarmament. This is reflected in the relative space devoted to the different topics in the statement from the Continuing Committee on the Sinaia Conference (Appendix 28).

5 SUMMING UP

In the course of 15 years, the Pugwash Conferences on Science and World Affairs have become established as an important and effective channel of communication between scientists for the study and discussion of many of the complex issues which confront mankind at the present time. The participation in these conferences of eminent scientists from East and West, and the constructive proposals which have emerged from the discussions, particularly in relation to disarmament, have secured for the Pugwash Conferences the respect of the scientific community, of governments, and of many sectors of society. The name "Pugwash" has become a symbol of successful international debate on controversial issues, and the conferences are cited as a model for similar efforts in other fields of human relations.

The success of the Pugwash Conferences is the result of resolute efforts of a group of scientists, determined to retain an independent and unbiased outlook, and anxious to build and consolidate international understanding and co-operation. The Pugwash Conferences have shown that it is possible to apply the scientific approach, which has proved so successful in science and technology, to problems which are only indirectly related to science. They have shown that even when dealing with highly controversial matters, it is possible to tell the truth, without being abusive, to be candid, without trying to embarrass, provided that there is a common approach based on scientific objectivity and mutual respect.

Another aspect of the Pugwash Movement is that it represents an excursion into a new type of activity by scientists, the fulfilment of their social responsibilities. The important role played by science in modern society, and the special opportunities and competence of scientists, put on them the duty to help mankind to avert the dangers which are arising from the progress of science and technology, and to assist in the development of a new world, in which the beneficial applications of science can be fully developed.

Since 1955, when the Russell-Einstein Manifesto was issued, the world situation, as far as it affects the aims of Pugwash, has changed considerably. All nations now accept the view that a nuclear war would be an unmitigated catastrophe, and that no side would emerge as a real victor from such a war. Much has also been achieved in bringing nations together to talk about various aspects of world security. Whereas at the beginning, Pugwash was the only channel of communication between East and West for debate on these issues, nowadays many channels are open, and with the inclusion of China in the United Nations, there are great hopes of extending the lines of communication.

Above all, there has been a dramatic change in the attitude and the involvement of scientists in issues facing mankind. Stimulated by Pugwash in some measure, many scientists have made the study of the problems of disarmament and arms control their main occupation. The increasing awareness in society of the importance of research on peace and conflict, has resulted in the setting up of a number of national, and a few international, institutes, where scholars from both the social and the natural sciences carry out full-time research on these problems. The usefulness of closer international collaboration in science and technology is often linked with the need to establish a better climate for East-West understanding and good will, and this has brought forth projects for new institutions, from an international university to regional institutes, and many scientists are involved in their planning. Other scientists, responding to the realization by society of the importance of a proper organization of science, have made science policy their chief interest and became professionally involved in science planning and administration. The special problems of developing countries have been taken up as a subject of study by social scientists in universities and academies of science. In the affluent countries, society is becoming increasingly concerned with some negative aspects of the peaceful applications of science, e.g., pollution of the environment, or the possible interference with the natural evolution of mankind by "genetic engineering"; many scientists are worried about the possible misuses for war purposes of their academic research and often find that their pursuits pose before them many new moral and ethical problems. This has given rise to the setting up of societies specifically concerned with the social responsibilities and moral obligations of scientists.

All these developments mean that one of the aims of Pugwash, to get scientists to think and work on the various aspects of the impact of science on society, has been largely achieved, and it may be argued that Pugwash should now retire and hand over the remaining tasks to these professional or specialized bodies. On the other hand, it may be argued that the uniqueness of Pugwash as an "amateur" body, in bringing together individuals without commitments and allegiances, and the very fact that over the years it managed to maintain its independence and yet retain the confidence of governments in both East and West, are sufficiently compelling reasons to continue its existence. In any case, the main aims of Pugwash are still to be fulfilled. Although the foreboding of imminent catastrophe expressed in the Russell-Einstein Manifesto has not come true, and we have managed to avoid a world-wide conflagration so far--in a small part perhaps thanks to the existence of Pugwash--the dangers facing mankind have not disappeared. The arms race continues unabated, and is indeed accelerating; the sophistication of weapons of mass destruction and of their means of delivery is increasing, making an accidental outbreak of war ever more probable. The discrepancy in the standard of living between nations is increasing rather than decreasing. The world is in a turmoil, with the ideological differences as pronounced as ever, and with many local conflicts threatening to engulf the whole globe. Clearly, the initial aims of Pugwash, as expressed in the Russell-Einstein Manifesto and in the Vienna Declaration, are still to be achieved, and this alone calls for further and more intense efforts by scientists from all countries and various disciplines to fulfill these objectives. Pugwash remains one of the most effective vehicles for such efforts.

By increasing the scope of its activities, and by bringing in more scientists, young and dynamic as well as senior and respectable, Pugwash, with its unique structure, world-wide links, and established reputation for objectivity and independence, could serve as the rallying point for the diverse activities of scientists. It could be the central forum for critique of efforts by other groups of scientists, assessment of their results, and generation of new ideas. Thus, Pugwash could become the source of inspiration and hope for the strivings of scientists to create a stable and happy future for mankind.

Table 1. Changes in the Membership of the Continuing Committee

United Kingdom

Cecil Powell[+]	1957–1969	Edward Bullard	1958–1959		
↓		↓			
Patricia Lindop	1970–	Nevill Mott	1959–1963		
		↓			
		Rudolf Peierls	1963–		

United States

Eugene Rabinowitch	1957–	Victor Weisskopf	1958–1959	Bentley Glass	1958–1967
		↓		↓	
		Harrison Brown	1959–1963	Frank Long	1967–1971
		↓		↓	
		Bernard Feld	1963–	Carl Djerassi	1971–

Soviet Union

Dmitri Skobeltzyn	1957–1963	Alexander Topchiev[+]	1958–1962	Evgeniy Fedorov	1958–1963
↓		↓		↓	
Lev Artsimovitch	1963–	Vladimir Kirillin	1963–1964	Vladimir Khvostov[+]	1963–1972
		↓			
		Mikhail Millionshchikov	1964–		

Western Europe

Eduardo Amaldi (Italy)	1962–	Herbert Marcovich (France)	1962–	Rolf Björnerstedt (Sweden)	1968–1969
				↓	
				Ole Maaløe	1969–

Eastern Europe

Leopold Infeld[+] (Poland)	1962–1968	Ivan Málek (Czechoslovakia)	1965–	Ivan Supek (Yugoslavia)	1968–
↓					
Ignacy Malecki (Poland)	1968–1969				
↓					
Anguel Balevski (Bulgaria)	1970–				

[+] Deceased

Table 1. Changes in the Membership of the Continuing Committee (Continued)

Asia
Vikram Sarabhai[+] (India)	1962–1971

Africa
Wilbert Chagula (Tanzania) ↓	1967–1971
Frank Torto (Ghana)	1971–

Latin America
Carlos Varsavsky (Argentina)	1969–

Table 2. National Pugwash Groups

Australia	India
Austria	Israel
Belgium	Italy
Bulgaria	Japan
Canada	Netherlands
Czechoslovakia	Nigeria
Denmark	Norway
Egypt	Poland
Ethiopia	Romania
Finland	Soviet Union
France	Sweden
German Democratic Republic	Switzerland
German Federal Republic	United Kingdom
Ghana	United States
Hungary	Yugoslavia

Table 3. List of Participants in the 21 Pugwash Conferences Held Between 1957 and 1971

(The numbers after the name denote the serial number of the Conferences attended)

Country	Participant	Conferences
Afghanistan	Ghazanfar, Dr. S.A.S.	15
Argentina	Garcia, Dr. R.V.	15, 17
	Varsavsky, Dr. C.M.	18, 19, 20
Australia	Burton, Dr. J.	6, 10, 11
	Crawford, Sir John	7
	Encel, Prof. S.	18
	Fowler, Dr. K.	13
	Hughes, Dr. Helen	15
	Inall, Dr. E.K.	19
	+Martyn, Dr. D.F.	14
	Miller, Prof. J.D.B.	10
	Nicholls, F.G.	15
	Oliphant, Sir Mark	1, 2, 3, 8, 9, 10, 12
	Rathgeber, Dr. H.D.	17
Austria	Breitenecker, Dr. M.	10
	Jungk, Dr. R.	16, 17
	Kohler, Prof. F.	21
	Mainx, Prof. F.	10
	Steinmaurer, Prof. R.	10
	Thirring, Prof. H.	1, 3, 4, 6, 7, 10, 11, 14
	Weinzierl, Prof. P.	19
Belgium	Baudoux, Prof. P.	18, 21
	Coppieters, Prof. E.	19
	+Leclercq, Prof. R.	16, 17, 20
Brazil	Ianni, Dr. O.	12
	Kerr, Prof. W.E.	11, 15
	Lattes, Prof. C.M.C.	10
	Leite Lopes, Prof. J.	17
	Pavan, Prof. C.	7
	Sala, Dr. O.	9
Bulgaria	Balevski, Acad. A.T.	20, 21
	Bratanov, Acad. K.	17, 19, 20, 21
	Nadjakov, Acad. G.	3, 6, 7, 8, 9, 10, 11, 17, 18, 19, 20, 21

+ Deceased

Table 3. List of Participants in the 21 Pugwash Conferences Held Between 1957 and 1971 (Continued)

Country	Participant	Conferences
Canada	Alcock, Dr. N.Z.	10, 11, 16, 17
	Boyd, W.	13, 17
	Burns, E.L.M.	20
	+Chisholm, Dr. Brock G.	1, 3, 5, 10
	Dobell, P.C.	19
	Dolman, Prof. C.E.	5
	+Foster, Prof. J.S.	1
	Holmes, J.W.	20
	Kerr, Prof. D.	5
	Legault, Dr. A.	21
	Ouellet, Dr. C.	2
	Polanyi, Prof. J.C.	6, 8, 10, 12
	Watson-Watt, Sir Robert	2, 3, 4, 5, 6
Ceylon	Baptist, Dr. N.G.	15, 17, 18, 19
Chile	Barzelatto, Dr. J.	21
Peoples' Republic of China	Chang-Wei, Prof.	6
	Chou Pei-Yuan, Prof.	1, 2, 4, 6
	Feng Ping-Fu	6
	Yu Kwang-Yuan, Prof.	6
Colombia	Groot, Dr. H.	15
Czechoslovakia	+Brdička, Prof. R.	6
	Filkorn, Prof. V.	17
	Hacik, Prof. V.	19
	Hajdu, Dr. V.	17
	+Husa, Prof. V.	6, 10
	Knapp, Prof. V.	3, 11
	Kopal, Dr. V.	6
	Kožešník, Prof. J.	3, 13, 17
	Liska, Dr. L.	17
	Macek, Acad. J.	10
	Málek, Acad. I.	10, 11, 12, 13, 14, 15, 16, 17, 19
	Moravec, Dr. J.	19, 21
	Němec, T.	9, 10, 13, 14, 16, 17, 18, 19
	+Procházka, Acad. V.	9, 10
	Šiška, Acad. K.	13, 20
	Šnejdárek, Dr. A.	13, 16, 17
	Šorm, Acad. F.	10, 13, 16
	Urban, Dr. L.	9
	Zoubek, Acad. V.	20
Dahomey	Quirino, Dr. L.	15

Summing Up   93

Table 3. List of Participants in the 21 Pugwash Conferences Held Between 1957 and 1971 (Continued)

Country	Participant	Conferences
Denmark	Adler, D.J.	13, 14, 16, 17
	Boserup, A.	17, 19, 20, 21
	Kofoed-Hansen, Prof. O.M.	9, 10, 11, 13
	Maaløe, Prof. O.	10, 13, 14, 17, 19, 20, 21
	Magnus, Dr. P. von	5
	Ølgaard, Dr. P.L.	16
	Pihl, Prof. M.	3
	Wilhjelm, Dr. J.	16, 17
Egypt	Abdel-Meguid, Dr. A.R.	14, 15
	Eissa, Dr. N.A.H.	19, 20
	El-Bedewi, Prof. F.A.	17, 18, 19, 20, 21
	El Hamamsy, Dr. Leila S.	14
	Lakany, Dr. M.A.	15, 16, 17
	Mahfouz, Prof. M.M.	20, 21
	Morcos, Dr. S.R.	10
Ethiopia	Aklilu Lemma, Prof.	15, 17
	Aseffa Tekle, Dr.	15, 17
	Duri, Prof. M.	15
	Gouin, Prof. P.	15
	Kassa Wolde Mariam	15
	Mengesha, Dr. Melak H.	15
	Whipple, Prof. R.O.	15, 17
Finland	Broms, Prof. B.	21
	Jansson, Prof. J.M.	18
	Miettinen, Prof. J.K.	20, 21
	Saukkonen, Prof. J.J.	17
France	Auger, Prof. P.V.	18
	Bauer, E.	15, 16, 17, 18, 19, 20
	Biquard, P.	13
	Bussac, Dr. J.	18
	Dubarle, Father Pierre-Leon	3, 10, 11
	Genevey, P.	21
	Gregory, Prof. B.P.	2, 3, 6, 10
	Gros, Dr. A.	10
	Gueron, G.	10, 17
	Gueron, Prof. J.	3, 10
	Joxe, A.	12, 13, 16
	Klein, Dr. J.	18
	†Lacassagne, Prof. A.M.B.	1, 3
	Laponche, Dr. B.	17, 18, 20
	Lestel, J.	14
	Lwoff, Prof. A.	5, 10
	Magat, Prof. M.	10, 12, 14, 17, 18, 19

Table 3. List of Participants in the 21 Pugwash Conferences Held Between 1957 and 1971 (Continued)

France (Continued)	Marcovich, Dr. H.	6, 10, 11, 12, 14, 15, 16, 18, 19, 20, 21
	Meyrowitz, Dr. H.	17
	Moch, Jr.	11, 13, 14, 17, 18, 19, 21
	Perrin, Prof. F.	8, 9, 11, 17, 18, 19, 20
	Piganiol, Prof. P.	10
	Rodriques, Prof. A.M.	18
	Rosenstiehl, Prof. P.	8, 9, 10, 14, 18
	Roth, Prof. E.	17, 18
	Rudali, Dr. G.	21
	Thibault, Prof. P.	5
	Thorner, D.	21
German Democratic Republic	+Barwich, Prof. H.	6, 11
	Ersil, Prof. W.	19
	Hess, Dr. P.	13, 17
	Kolesnyk, Dr. A.	16, 17, 19
	Kröger, Prof. H.	16, 17, 19, 20, 21
	Kuczynski, Prof. J.	13, 15
	Lösche, Prof. A.	17
	Pose, Prof. H.	6
	Rienäcker, Prof. G.	3, 11, 12, 13, 16
	Steinbrück, Prof. P.W.	21
	Wünsche, Prof. H.	17, 20
	Zorn, B.	21
German Federal Republic	Afheldt, H.	10, 11, 13, 14, 16, 17, 18, 19, 21
	Albrecht, Dr. U.	20, 21
	+Born, Prof. M.	3
	+Burkhardt, Prof. G.	3, 6, 7, 8, 9, 10, 13, 14
	Bussche, A. von dem	15
	Delbrück, Dr. J.	17
	Franz, Dr. H.	10
	Friedrich-Freska, Prof. H.	10, 17
	Glubrecht, Prof. H.	19, 20, 21
	Heimendahl, Dr. E.	6
	Hönl, Prof. H.	3
	Jensen, Prof. J.H.D.	14
	+Kliefoth, Prof. W.	3, 17
	Lenz, Prof. H.	3, 10
	Menzel, Prof. E.	9, 10, 12, 16, 17, 19
	Raiser, Prof. L.	16, 17
	Rumpf, Prof. H.	11
	Weizsäcker, Prof. C.E. von	2, 4
	Wolf, Prof. K.A.	10

Table 3. List of Participants in the 21 Pugwash Conferences Held Between 1957 and 1971 (Continued)

Country	Participant	Conferences
Ghana	Abbiw-Jackson, D.K.	11
	Quartey, Prof. J.A.K.	10
	Torto, Prof. F.G.	15, 17, 18, 20, 21
	Yanney-Wilson, Dr. J.	10
Greece	Dimissianos, Dr. B.	11
	Vatistas, Dr. S.	10
Hungary	Bognar, Prof. J.	12
	Bognar, Prof. R.	10, 11, 17
	Csáki, Prof. F.	20
	Haraszti, Prof. G.	21
	Janossy, Prof. L.	3
	Kende, Dr. I.	17
	Lang, Dr. I.	21
	Pal, Prof. L.	10, 13, 17
	Reczei, Prof. L.	16, 17, 18
	Rusznyak, Acad. I.	6
	Straub, Prof. F.B.	7, 8, 9, 10, 13
	Szabolcsi, Acad. M.	19, 20
	Vas, Acad. K.	19, 21
Iceland	Gunnarsson, Dr. O.	10, 17
India	Ahuja, Dr. M.L.	5
	+Bhabha, Dr. H.J.	3, 12
	Bhagavantam, Prof. S.	20
	Desai, Prof. M.J.	16
	Gupta, Prof. S.	21
	Kothari, Prof. D.S.	12
	+Krishnan, Sir K.S.	3
	+Mahalanobis, Prof. P.C.	3, 10, 18
	Menon, Prof. M.G.K.	11, 12, 14, 15, 17, 18
	Parthasarathi, A.	19, 20
	Rahman, A.	15
	+Sarabhai, Prof. V.A.	9, 12, 13, 15, 16, 18, 20, 21
	Thacker, Prof. M.S.	12
	Zaheer, Dr. S.H.	12, 17, 18, 19, 21
Indonesia	Prawirohardjo, Dr. S.	14
	Soedjatmoko, Dr. S.	20
Ireland	+Conway, Dr. E.J.	10
	O'Ceallaigh, Dr. C.	17

Table 3. List of Participants in the 21 Pugwash Conferences Held Between 1957 and 1971 (Continued)

Country	Name	Conferences
Israel	+Boyko, Dr. H.	10
	+de Shalit, Prof. A.	12, 15
	Feldman, Prof. M.	17
	Freier, S.	16, 18, 20
	Friedlander, Prof. S.	20, 21
	Keynan, Prof. A.	14, 20
	Lifson, Prof. S.Z.	19, 21
	Peter, Dr. Y.	15
	Sela, Prof. M.	10
	Stein, Prof. G.	14, 17, 19
Italy	Aloisi, Prof. M.	14
	Amaldi, Prof. E.	3, 14, 17, 18, 19, 21
	Arangio-Ruiz, Prof. G.	14
	+Bassini, Prof. G.L.	17
	Bernardini, Prof. G.	7, 14
	Bertotti, Prof. B.	12
	+Boeri, Prof. E.	3
	Buzzati-Traverso, Prof. A.A.	10, 11, 13, 14
	Calogero, Prof. F.	14, 17, 19, 20
	Favilli, Prof. G.	10
	Forlati, Dr. Laura	13, 14
	Giacometti, Prof. G.	16, 18, 20
	Jona-Lasinio, Dr. G.	13
	Mezzetti, Prof. L.	10
	Pascolini, Dr. A.	20, 21
	Schaerf, Prof. C.	18, 19, 21
Japan	Fukushima, Prof. Y.	21
	Kamefuchi, Prof. S.	10
	Konuma, Dr. M.	14
	Matumoto, Prof. K.	18
	Miyake, Prof. Y.	3, 12, 17
	Ogawa, Prof. I.	1, 3, 10, 17
	Sakamoto, Prof. Y.	20
	+Sakata, Prof. S.	3
	Sawada, Prof. S.	20
	Tanaka, Prof. S.	18
	Tomonaga, Prof. S.	1, 3
	Toyoda, Prof. T.	7, 8, 17, 20
	Yamada, Prof. E.	12, 17
	Yukawa, Prof. H.	1, 3, 9, 10
Kenya	Odhiambo, Prof. T.R.	20
	Wasawo, Prof. D.P.S.	15, 17
Lebanon	Raven, Prof. T.	10

Table 3. List of Participants in the 21 Pugwash Conferences Held Between 1957 and 1971 (Continued)

Madagascar	Ramiadrasoa, Dr. A.	18
Malaysia	Oppenheim, Sir Alexander	10
	Sandosham, Prof. A.A.	12, 17
Mongolia	Sodnom, Prof. N.	19
Netherlands	Boskma, Dr. P.	13, 19, 20
	Gorter, Prof. C.J.	10
	Kwee, Dr. S.L.	10, 17
	Landheer, Prof. B.	12, 17
	Nijboer, Prof. B.R.A.	3, 10, 21
	Röling, Prof. B.V.A.	6, 7, 8, 9, 13, 14
	Slotemaker de Bruine, G.H.	10
	Smith, Prof. P.B.	15, 17, 18, 19, 21
	Tolhoek, Prof. H.A.	10, 11, 12, 16
	Valkenburgh, Dr. P.	11
	Van der Woude, Dr. A.	19, 20
New Zealand	Read, Dr. J.	10
	Walker, Prof. D.	10
Nigeria	Awe, Prof. O.	19
	Bassir, Prof. O.	15, 17, 18, 21
	Ezeilo, Prof. J.O.C.	19
	Fagbemi, Dr. O.J.	20
	Obi, Dr. C.	10
	Onwumechili, Prof. C.A.	19
Norway	Cyvin, Dr. S.	16, 17
	Eide, Prof. A.	18, 20
	Evang, Dr. K.	17
	Förland, Dr. T.	10, 13, 20
	Galtung, Prof. J.	12, 13, 15, 16, 17, 18, 19
	Höivik, Dr. T.	21
	Randers, Dr. G.	3
	Thee, Prof. M.	21
	Wergeland, Dr. H.	10
Pakistan	Salam, Prof. A.	9, 10, 12, 17
Peru	Pozo-Olano, Prof. J.D.	15, 17

Table 3. List of Participants in the 21 Pugwash Conferences Held Between 1957 and 1971 (Continued)

Poland	Adamczewski, Prof. I.	16, 17, 18, 21
	Bukowski, Prof. J.	17, 18
	Danysz, Prof. M.	1, 10, 13
	Dobrosielski, Prof. M.	17, 18
	+Infeld, Prof. L.	3, 9, 10, 11, 12, 13, 14, 16
	Klafkowski, Prof. A.	16
	Kumaniecki, Prof. K.	6
	Lapter, Prof. K.D.	10, 11, 13, 14, 15, 16
	Lewandowski, B.	20
	Malecki, Prof. I.	14, 15, 16, 17, 19
	Nowacki, Prof. P.J.	21
	Popiolek, Prof. K.	19
	Šach, Dr. J.	20, 21
	Śmialowski, Prof. M.	20
	Stefański, Prof. W.	6
	Szulkin, Prof. P.	6
	Wieczorek, Dr. W.	19
	Wojtaszek, Dr. E.	19
Romania	+Agarbiceanu, Prof. I.	13, 14, 16
	Ceoceonica, Dr. V.	21
	Curievici, Prof. I.	21
	Dragulescu, Acad. C.	12, 13, 21
	Dumitrescu, Acad. D.	11
	Foias, Prof. C.I.	19
	Gherman, Prof. O.	21
	Hanga, Prof. V.	13, 16, 17, 18
	Hulubei, Acad. H.	9, 10
	Ionescu, Dr. V.	21
	Ionescu, Prof. T.	21
	Negucioiu, Prof. A.	21
	Nicolescu, Acad. M.	13
	Penescu, Prof. C.	19, 20, 21
	Tanase, Prof. A.	21
	Teodorescu, Acad. N.	21
	Tripsa, Prof. I.	21
	Trutia, Prof. A.	21
Senegal	Faye, Dr. B.	20, 21
Sierra Leone	Lardner, G.E.A.	15

Table 3. List of Participants in the 21 Pugwash Conferences Held Between 1957 and 1971 (Continued)

Soviet Union	Aboltin, Prof. V.Y.	15, 16, 17, 18, 19
	Alexandrov, Acad. A.P.	6
	Andreyev, Prof. P.V.	13, 14, 15, 16
	Arbatov, Prof. G.A.	19, 20, 21
	Artsimovitch, Acad. L.A.	9, 10, 11, 13, 14, 16, 17, 18, 19, 20
	+Arzumanyan, Acad. A.A.	6, 11
	Bazanov, Dr. N.I.	10
	Besedin, Dr. G.P.	10
	Blagonravov, Acad. A.A.	6, 7, 8, 9, 10, 11, 13
	Bogolubov, Acad. N.N.	3, 4, 6, 7, 8, 9, 10, 11, 13
	Dobrotin, Prof. N.A.	3
	Dubinin, Acad. M.M.	5, 6, 7, 8, 9, 10, 12, 13, 14, 16, 17, 18, 19
	Emelyanov, Prof. V.S.	6, 9, 10, 12, 14, 16, 17, 18, 19, 20
	Engelhardt, Acad. V.A.	17, 18, 19, 20, 21
	Ermakov, Prof. A.N.	20
	Essenov, Acad. S.E.	17
	Fedorov, Acad. E.K.	3, 4, 6
	Gafurov, Prof. B.G.	15
	Griniewsky, Prof. O.A.	15
	Gryzlov, Prof. A.A.	17
	Gverdziteli, Prof. I.G.	18
	Gvishiani, Dr. Ludmila	19, 20, 21
	Imshenetsky, Prof. A.A.	5, 6, 17, 19
	Inozemtsev, Prof. N.N.	9, 10
	+Isakov, Prof. I.S.	6
	Kapitza, Acad. P.L.	6, 17, 18
	+Kargin, Acad. V.A.	9, 10, 15, 16, 17
	Kashkai, Acad. M.A.	17
	Khohlov, Prof. R.V.	19
	+Khvostov, Acad. V.M.	6, 7, 8, 9, 10, 11, 12, 13, 14, 16, 18, 19
	Kirillin, Acad. V.A.	11
	Korneev, Dr. S.G.T.	10
	+Korovin, Prof. E.A.	3, 6
	Kovalev, Prof. M.I.	12
	Kozhevnikov, Prof. I.J.	9, 10
	Kuleshov, Dr. V.F.	19, 20
	Kuzin, Prof. A.M.	1, 2, 3, 9, 10, 13
	Leipunski, Prof. O.	9, 10
	Lozinski, Prof. V.V.	12
	Matulis, Acad. Y.	17
	+Medvedev, Prof. S.S.	13, 17
	Millionshchikov, Acad. M.D.	12, 13, 14, 15, 16, 17, 18, 19, 20

Table 3. List of Participants in the 21 Pugwash Conferences Held Between 1957 and 1971 (Continued)

Soviet Union (Continued)	Novikov, Prof. D.P.	19
	Pavlichenko, V.P.	3, 4, 5, 10, 11, 12, 13, 14, 15
	Platanov, Dr. Y.P.	17
	Plaude, Acad. K.K.	17
	Pochitalin, I.G.	17, 18, 19, 20, 21
	Primakov, Dr. E.M.	20
	Prokhorov, Acad. A.M.	18
	Reutov, Acad. O.	19, 20, 21
	Riznichenko, Prof. J.	9, 10
	+Rubinstein, Prof. M.I.	6, 9, 10, 12, 13, 14, 15, 17
	Sadovsky, Prof. M.A.	6
	Semenov, Acad. N.N.	6
	Shelepin, Prof. M.	17
	Shustov, Dr. V.V.	19
	+Sisakyan, Acad. N.M.	4, 7, 8
	Skobeltzyn, Acad. D.V.	1, 2, 3, 6
	Smorodintsev, Prof. A.A.	5
	Sokolov, Dr. I.A.	17, 18, 19, 20, 21
	Solodovnikov, Prof. V.G.	19
	+Talensky, Prof. N.A.	4, 6, 7, 8, 9, 10, 11, 12, 13, 14, 16
	+Tamm, Acad. I.E.	6, 7, 8, 9, 10
	Timofeev, Prof. T.	21
	+Topchiev, Acad. A.V.	1, 2, 3, 6, 7, 8, 9, 10
	Tupolev, Acad. A.N.	6, 9, 10, 11, 14
	Vavilov, Dr. V.S.	3
	Vernov, Prof. A.N.	9, 10
	Vinogradov, Acad. A.P.	2, 3, 4, 6, 11, 13, 14, 16, 17, 18, 19, 21
	Voslensky, Prof. M.S.	17, 19, 21
	Vul, Prof. B.M.	11, 12, 14, 16, 19
South Africa	Schumann, Dr. T.E.W.	10
Spain	Catala de Alemany Prof. J.	10, 17
	Leal, J.L.	19
	Sampedro, Prof. J.	21
Sudan	Hassan Ishag, Prof. M.	15
	Nagger, Dr. K.E.	17

Table 3. List of Participants in the 21 Pugwash Conferences Held Between 1957 and 1971 (Continued)

Sweden	Ahnlund, Dr. Katarina	17
	Alfvén, Prof. H.	13, 14, 17, 20, 21
	Birnbaum, Dr. K.	16
	Björnerstedt, Dr. R.	14, 16, 17
	Dedijer, Dr. S.	15
	Engström, Prof. A.	11, 17
	Eriksson, B.E.	20
	Fehrm, M.	17
	Funke, Dr. G.W.	10, 12
	Hedén, Prof. C.-G.	17
	Herlofson, Prof. N.	18, 19, 21
	Lindberg, Prof. O.	10
	Nilsson, Dr. S.	17, 18
	Prawitz, J.	14, 16, 17, 19
	Revesz, Dr. L.	10, 17
	Sparring, Dr. A.	17, 21
	Sven Gard, Prof.	5
	Tammelin, Dr. L.-E.	17
	+Tiselius, Prof. A.	17
Switzerland	Dominicé, Prof. C.	20
	Freymond, Prof. J.	21
	Goldschmidt-Clermont, Dr. Y.	17
	Heitler, Prof. W.	10
	+Houtermans, Prof. F.G.	10
	Meyer, Prof. K.P.	11, 17
Tanzania	Chagula, Dr. W.K.	15, 17
Thailand	Chiowanich, Dr. Panee	15, 17
	Puranananda, Dr. C.	12
Togo	Agblemagnon, Dr. N.	17
Uganda	Crawford, Prof. M.	12
United Kingdom	Barnaby, Dr. C.F.	17, 18, 19
	+Bawden, Sir Frederick	5, 10
	Beckman, Dr. J.	21
	+Bernal, Prof. J.D.	10
	Blackett, Lord	4, 8, 9, 10, 11
	Bondi, Prof. H.	14, 16
	+Boyd-Orr, Lord	3
	Brown, Dr. L.M.	16
	Buchan, A.	6, 9
	Bullard, Sir Edward	7, 8, 9
	Burcham, Prof. W.E.	10
	Burhop, Prof. E.H.S.	10

Table 3. List of Participants in the 21 Pugwash Conferences Held Between 1957 and 1971 (Continued)

United Kingdom (Continued)	Calder, N.	17
	Carlton, Dr. D.	21
	Chain, Prof. E.B.	17
	Childs, Dr. E.C.	15
	+Cockcroft, Sir John	8, 9, 10, 11, 17
	Cohen, Prof. J.	10, 17
	+Darwin, Sir Charles	2, 10
	Davies, Prof. M.	17
	Ditchburn, Prof. R.W.	17
	Elton, Prof. L.R.B.	13, 17
	+Florey, Lord	10
	Flowers, Sir Brian	11, 13, 14, 16
	Frank, Prof. F.C.	18
	Frisch, Prof. O.R.	6, 10, 13
	Gutteridge, W.F.	15, 16, 17, 18, 19, 21
	Haddow, Sir Alexander	6, 7, 10
	Hodgkin, Prof. Dorothy	10, 17
	Hodgson, Dr. P.E.	17
	Howard, Prof. M.E.	8, 9, 19
	Huxley, Sir Julian	10
	Jackson, Lady	20
	Jones, Dr. G.O.	17
	Lindop, Prof. Patricia J.	5, 10, 13, 14, 15, 18, 19, 20, 21
	Lipman, Prof. N.	18
	Lockspeiser, Sir Ben	6, 7, 10
	+Lonsdale, Dame Kathleen	3, 10
	Manley, Prof. G.	5, 10
	Martin, Prof. A.	17, 20
	Martin, Sir David	10, 14
	Mendl, Dr. W.	19
	Mott, Sir Nevill	9, 10, 11
	Neild, Prof. R.R.	12, 17
	Noel-Baker, P.	6, 8, 9, 10, 11, 13, 14, 19, 20
	Oldham, Dr. C.H.G.	17, 21
	Peierls, Sir Rudolf	6, 9, 12, 13, 14, 16, 17, 18, 19, 20, 21
	Penney, Lord	8, 9
	Peters, Sir Rudolph	10
	Pirani, Prof. F.	12
	Pirie, N.W.	10, 19, 21
	Pollock, Prof. M.R.	21
	+Powell, Prof. C.F.	1, 2, 3, 4, 6, 9, 10, 11, 12, 13, 15, 17, 18
	Pryce, Prof. M.H.L.	3
	de Reuck, A.	20
	Ritchie-Calder, Lord	10

Table 3. List of Participants in the 21 Pugwash Conferences Held Between 1957 and 1971 (Continued)

United Kingdom (Continued)	Rotblat, Prof. J.	1, 2, 3, 4, 5, 6, 7, 8, 9, 10, 11, 12, 13, 14, 15, 16, 17, 18, 19, 20, 21
	+Russell, The Earl	3, 10
	Stoker, Prof. M.G.P.	5, 10
	Sutherland, Sir Gordon	12, 14, 15, 17
	Thomson, Sir George	3, 10
	Waddington, Prof. C.H.	2, 10
	Watson, Dr. C.J.H.	19
	Wolstenholme, Dr. G.E.W.	15
	Young, Wayland (Lord Kennet)	9, 10
United States	Adams, Mrs. Ruth	13, 17
	Bergmann, Prof. P.G.	10, 17
	Bernard, Prof. Viola W.	10
	Bethe, Prof. H.A.	8
	Boulding, Prof. K.E.	10, 12, 16
	Bowie, Prof. R.R.	8
	Brennan, Dr. D.G.	6, 8, 9, 10, 18
	Brode, Prof. R.B.	10
	Brown, Prof. H.	3, 4, 6, 7, 8, 9, 10, 11, 12, 13, 14, 15, 17, 18, 20
	Bunn, Prof. G.	20, 21
	Burhoe, Dr. R.W.	10
	Cavers, Dr. D.F.	1, 3
	Coleman, Prof. J.	15
	Commoner, Prof. B.	10
	Consolazio, Dr. W.V.	7, 10
	+Coryell, Prof. C.	3
	Davidon, Prof. W.C.	3, 10, 17
	Dillon, Dr. W.S.	17
	Djerassi, Prof. C.	17, 18, 19, 20, 21
	Doty, Prof. P.	1, 6, 7, 8, 9, 11, 13, 16, 18, 19, 20
	Dyson, Prof. F.J.	9, 10, 16
	Edsall, Prof. J.T.	2, 6, 10
	Feld, Prof. B.T.	3, 4, 6, 8, 9, 10, 11, 12, 13, 14, 15, 16, 17, 18, 19, 20, 21
	Fischer, Prof. G.	6
	Fisher, Prof. R.	11
	Frank, Prof. J.D.	4, 10, 17
	Frisch, Prof. D.	6
	+Gardner, Dr. T.	8
	Garwin, Prof. R.L.	17, 19, 21

Table 3. List of Participants in the 21 Pugwash Conferences Held Between 1957 and 1971 (Continued)

United States (Continued)	Gell-Mann, Prof. M.	12
	Glaser, Prof. D.A.	11, 13, 19
	Glass, Prof. B.	3, 5, 6, 7, 8, 9, 10, 11, 13, 14, 16, 17, 18, 20
	Gomer, Prof. R.	9
	+Grodzins, Prof. M.	2, 3, 4, 6
	Hansen, K.R.	19, 20
	Herriott, Prof. R.M.	10, 17
	Higgins, Dr. C.C.	5
	Higinbotham, Dr. W.A.	2, 6
	Hill, Dr. D.L.	3
	Hoagland, Prof. H.	10
	Hoffmann, Prof. S.	21
	Holton, Prof. G.	17
	Inglis, Prof. D.R.	6, 10, 17
	+Iselin, Dr. C.O'D.	7
	Kalkstein, Dr. M.	10, 17
	Kaplan, Dr. M.M.	3, 5, 7, 10
	Katz, A.H.	6, 10
	Kaysen, Prof. C.	12
	Kissinger, Prof. H.A.	8, 9, 10, 13, 16
	Kistiakowsky, Prof. G.	8, 20
	Kleiman, R.	18
	Klineberg, Dr. O.	10
	Kybal, Dr. D.	6
	Lall, Mrs. Betty G.	13, 16, 18
	+Lauritsen, Prof. C.C.	8, 17
	Leake, Prof. C.D.	5, 7, 17
	Leghorn, R.S.	2, 4, 6, 9, 10
	Leontief, Prof. W.	9, 10, 14, 19
	Lipson, Prof. L.	8, 10
	Long, Prof. F.A.	11, 14, 16, 17, 18, 20
	Marshak, Prof. R.	17
	Mayer, Prof. J.	17
	Mead, Dr. Margaret	10
	Meselson, Prof. M.	10, 11, 13, 14, 20
	Morgenthau, Prof. H.J.	13, 17, 19, 21
	Muench, Prof. H.	5
	+Muller, Prof. H.J.	1, 3
	Muller, Prof. S.	16, 17, 18, 20
	Munger, Prof. E.S.	15, 17
	Munk, Prof. W.	9
	Orear, Prof. J.	3, 6, 7, 9, 10, 13
	Palevsky, Dr. H.	3, 10, 17
	Panofsky, Prof. W.K.H.	8
	Parsons, Prof. T.	17, 18
	Pauling, Prof. L.	2, 3, 7, 10
	Phelps, Prof. J.B.	6, 10, 17

Table 3. List of Participants in the 21 Pugwash Conferences Held Between 1957 and 1971 (Continued)

United States (Continued)	Pickering, Dr. W.H.	7
	Piel, Dr. G.	7
	Polk, Prof. W.R.	20
	Purcell, Prof. E.M.	8
	Rabi, Prof. I.I.	7, 8, 9, 11, 17
	Rabinowitch, Prof. E.	1, 2, 3, 4, 5, 6, 7, 8, 9, 10, 11, 13, 14, 15, 16, 17, 18, 19, 20, 21
	Rabinowitch, Dr. V.	17, 20, 21
	Rathjens, Prof. G.W.	17, 19, 20
	Revelle, Prof. R.	4, 7, 10, 12, 14, 15, 17, 19, 20
	Rich, Prof. A.	5, 6, 7, 10, 11, 12, 13, 15, 16, 17, 19
	Rollefson, Prof. R.	14, 17
	Rosebury, Prof. T.	5, 10
	Rosecrance, Prof. R.	21
	Rosenblith, Prof. W.	7
	Rostow, Prof. W.W.	6
	Ruina, Prof. J.	12, 17, 19
	Sabin, Dr. A.B.	10
	Schelling, Prof. T.C.	6
	Schultz, Prof. T.W.	20, 21
	Seitz, Prof. F.	3, 9, 12
	Selove, Prof. W.	1, 3
	Shils, Prof. E.	10
	Shulman, Prof. M.D.	11, 16, 19, 20
	Skolnikoff, Dr. E.	17
	Sohn, Prof. L.B.	6, 8, 9, 14, 17
	Spingarn, Dr. J.	4
	Staley, Prof. E.	7, 12
	Swartz, W.	20, 21
	+Szilard, Prof. L.	1, 2, 3, 4, 6, 8, 9, 11
	Todd, W.M.	20
	Toll, Dr. J.S.	10
	Townes, Dr. C.H.	8, 9
	Voss, J.	17, 20
	Weinberg, Dr. A.M.	3, 7, 17
	Weinberg, Prof. S.	20
	Weisskopf, Prof. V.F.	1, 3, 4, 10
	Wiesner, Prof. J.B.	2, 4, 6, 13
	Wigner, Prof. E.P.	3, 4, 7
	Wilson, Dr. R.R.	20
	Wolfe, Dr. H.C.	10
	York, Prof. E.	19, 21
	Zacharias, Prof. J.R.	7
	Zucker, Dr. A.	21

Table 3. List of Participants in the 21 Pugwash Conferences Held Between 1957 and 1971 (Continued)

West Indies	Martin, S.L.	15
Yugoslavia	Bartos, Acad. M.	11
	Benko, Prof. V.	19
	Berberovic, Prof. L.	21
	Butozan, Prof. V.	16
	Calic, Dr. D.	10
	Kanazir, Acad. D.	11
	Knapp, Dr. V.	13
	Kuhelj, Acad. A.	10, 11
	Markovic, Dr. M.	14, 17
	Mates, L.	11, 17, 20
	Osredkar, Prof. M.	18
	Sahovic, Dr. M.	20, 21
	Savic, Prof. P.	3
	Supek, Acad. I.	9, 10, 11, 12, 14, 15, 18, 20
	Tanovic, Prof. A.	19
	Vavpetic, Acad. L.	13, 17
Zambia	Goma, Prof. L.K.H.	18

Table 4. Geographical Distribution of Participants

Country	No. Participants	No. Attendances	Country	No. Participants	No. Attendances
Afghanistan	1	1	Japan	14	27
Argentina	2	5	Kenya	2	3
Australia	11	19	Lebanon	1	1
Austria	7	15	Madagascar	1	1
Belgium	3	6	Malaysia	2	3
Brazil	6	7	Mongolia	1	1
Bulgaria	3	18	Netherlands	11	30
Canada	13	27	New Zealand	2	2
Ceylon	1	4	Nigeria	6	9
Chile	1	1	Norway	9	19
China	4	7	Pakistan	1	4
Colombia	1	1	Peru	1	2
Czechoslovakia	19	45	Poland	18	42
Dahomey	1	1	Romania	18	28
Denmark	8	24	Senegal	1	2
Egypt	7	16	Sierra Leone	1	1
Ethiopia	7	10	South Africa	1	1
Finland	4	5	Soviet Union	71	246
France	28	78	Spain	3	4
German Democratic Republic	12	26	Sudan	2	2
			Sweden	19	35
German Federal Republic	19	47	Switzerland	6	7
			Tanzania	1	2
			Thailand	2	3
Ghana	4	8	Togo	1	1
Greece	2	2	Uganda	1	1
Hungary	13	25	United Kingdom	65	177
Iceland	1	2	United States	119	342
India	14	34			
Indonesia	2	2	West Indies	1	1
Ireland	2	2	Yugoslavia	16	29
Israel	10	18	Zambia	1	1
Italy	16	34			

Table 5. Attendance at Pugwash Conferences

Serial Number	Date	Location	No. Participants	No. Countries	% Participants Attending for the First Time
1	July, 1957	Pugwash, Canada	22	10	100
2	March-April, 1958	Lac Beauport, Canada	22	8	59
3	September, 1958	Kitzbühel, Austria	70	20	66
4	June-July, 1959	Baden, Austria	25	7	24
5	August, 1959	Pugwash, Canada	26	8	59
6	Nov.-Dec., 1960	Moscow, U.S.S.R.	75	15	56
7	September, 1961	Stowe, U.S.A.	41	12	34
8	September, 1961	Stowe, U.S.A.	43	11	33
9	August, 1962	Cambridge, U.K.	67	19	33
10	September, 1962	London, U.K.	175	36	43
11	September, 1963	Dubrovnik, Yugoslavia	64	24	30
12	Jan.-Feb., 1964	Udaipur, India	56	25	39
13	September, 1964	Karlovy Vary, Czechoslovakia	74	19	25
14	April, 1965	Venice, Italy	68	20	25
15	Dec. 1965-Jan. 1966	Addis Ababa, Ethiopia	63	31	57
16	September, 1966	Sopot, Poland	69	22	25
17	September, 1967	Ronneby, Sweden	180	44	35
18	September, 1968	Nice, France	81	29	27
19	October, 1969	Sochi, U.S.S.R.	101	29	38
20	September, 1970	Fontana, U.S.A.	98	31	35
21	August, 1971	Sinaia, Romania	97	31	37

Table 6. Classification of Participants by Profession or Field of Study

	Number		% Total
A. Philosophy, Mathematics and Education			
1. Philosophy	14		
2. Mathematics	17		
3. Education and organization of science	21	52	8
B. Physical Sciences			
4. Physics (including Biophysics and Geophysics)	198		
5. Chemistry (Physical, Inorganic, Organic and Crystallography)	49		
6. Technology (Electronics and Engineering)	31		
7. Other (Geography, Oceanography, etc.)	13	291	47
C. Biological and Medical Sciences			
8. Biology (including Microbiology, Bacteriology and Biology)	30		
9. Biochemistry and Physiology	17		
10. Medicine and Pathology	20		
11. Radiobiology	11		
12. Genetics	11		
13. Psychology and Psychiatry	8		
14. Other (Anthropology, Botany, Nutrition, etc.)	13	110	18
D. Social Sciences			
15. Economics (including Political Economy)	33		
16. History	20		
17. Law (including International Law)	35		
18. International Relations	45		
19. Politics and Sociology	34	167	27
Total		620	100

Table 7. List of Observers and Scientific Staff in the 21 Pugwash Conferences Held Between 1957 and 1971

(The numbers after the names denote the serial number of the conferences attended.)

Australia	Burton, Dr. J.	9
	Fitzgerald, Prof. P.	10
	Makinson, Dr. R.E.B.	10
Austria	Jungk, Dr. R.	3, 10
	Schwarcz, E.	3
	Thirring, Prof. H.	8
Canada	Alcock, Dr. N.Z.	9
	Joubin, Dr. F.R.	10
Czechoslovakia	Hajdu, Dr. V.	16
	Němec, T.	11
Denmark	Maaløe, Prof. O.	11
	Michelsen, B.	10
	Ulrich, Dr. J.W.	10
Ethiopia	Abebe Kebede	15
	Abu Sharr, Dr. I.	15
	Asseffa Seifu	15
	Baxter, Prof. R.M.	15
	Burling, Dr. R.L.	15
	Dierauf, Prof. E.	15
	Endalkachew Mekonnen	15
	Jacobsen, Prof. G.S.	15
	Paz, Prof. I.	15
	Rowse, E.A.A.	15
	Taye, Talahun	15
	Urban, Dr. E.K.	15
	Winid, Prof. B.	15
France	Genevey, P.	9, 11, 12
	Scalabre, G.	18
German Democratic Republic	Hess, Dr. P.	11
German Federal Republic	+Burkhardt, Prof. G.	11
	Häfele, Prof. W.	17
	Heimendahl, Dr. E.	11
	Nerlich, Dr. U.	9

+ Deceased

Table 7. List of Observers and Scientific Staff in the 21 Pugwash Conferences Held Between 1957 and 1971 (Continued)

India	Pant, Dr. P.	12
	Trivedi, V.C.	12, 13
Italy	Bertotti, Prof. B.	14
	Budini, Prof. P.	14
	Giacometti, Prof. G.	14
Netherlands	Fieyra, J.	10
	ten Cate, L.O.	10
	Terwisscha van Scheltinga, F.J.A.	9, 13
Poland	Blusztajn, Dr. M.	15
	Bukowski, Prof. J.	15
	Kopecki, Prof. K.	15
	Kruczkowski, Dr. A.	15
	Lider, J.	15
Soviet Union	Bazanov, Dr. N.I.	7, 8, 9
	Besedin, Dr. G.P.	9
	Griniewsky, Prof. O.A.	14
	Korneev, Dr. S.G.T.	7, 8, 9
	Nesmeyanov, Acad. A.N.	6
	Pavlichenko, V.P.	1, 2, 6, 7, 8, 9
	Shustov, Dr. V.V.	16
	Voslensky, Prof. M.S.	14
South Africa	King, J.A.	10
Sweden	Björnerstedt, Dr. R.	13
	Fehrm, M.	12
	Myrdal, Mrs. Alva	17
	Paulsson, Dr. Inger	17
United Kingdom	Allan, Dr. H.R.	10
	Allibone, Dr. T.E.	10
	Bull, Hedley	10, 14, 16
	Burhop, Prof. E.H.S.	1, 3
	+Buzzard, Sir Anthony	10
	Calder, N.	10
	Campbell-Smith, Mrs. S.	10
	Catlin, Sir George	10
	Clow, Dr. A.	10
	Davy, J.	14
	Flowers, Sir Brian	9
	Fraser, Dr. R.G.J.	10
	Frisch, Prof. O.R.	9
	Goldsmith, M.	10

Table 7. List of Observers and Scientific Staff in the 21 Pugwash Conferences Held Between 1957 and 1971 (Continued)

United Kingdom (Continued)	+Haslett, A.W.	10
	Hutchinson, Prof. G.W.	10
	+Isaacs, Dr. A.	10
	Kendrew, Dr. J.C.	9
	+King-Hall, Lord	10
	Leach, G.	9, 10, 11
	Levitt, Dr. W.	10
	Lindop, Prof. Patricia J.	2, 3, 6, 7, 8, 9, 11, 12
	Lockspeiser, Sir Ben	8
	Maddox, J.	9, 10, 13
	Margerison, Dr. T.	10
	Neild, Prof. R.R.	9
	Nicholson, E. Max	10
	Noel-Baker, P.	3
	Pirani, Prof. F.	10
	Pirie, Dr. Antoinette	10
	Price, B.T.	9, 11
	Scott, Sir Oliver	10
	Simpson, Miss Esther	10
	Willmore, Dr. A.P.	10
	Wright, J.K.	13, 16
	Young, Wayland (Lord Kennet)	6, 7, 8
	Zuckerman, Lord	8, 9
United States	Adams, Mrs. Ruth	1, 4, 6, 7, 8, 9, 10, 11
	Bronk, Dr. D.	7
	Clemens, Prof. W.C., Jr.	10
	Commoner, Prof. B.	3
	Cowen, R.C.	10
	Dillon, Dr. W.S.	15
	Erikson, Prof. E.	12
	Finkelstein, L.S.	12
	Hibbs, Dr. A.R.	9
	Hoagland, Prof. H.	7
	Katz, A. H.	8, 9
	Kissinger, Prof. H.A.	11
	Lang, D.	11
	Mezerik, A.G.	3
	Orear, Prof. J.	8
	Piel, Dr. G.	12
	Platig, Dr. E.R.	10, 15
	Rabinowitch, Dr. V.	9, 10, 11, 13, 14
	Rathjens, Prof. G.W.	10
	Reif, Prof. F.	10
	Sailor, Dr. V.L.	3
	Sands, Prof. M.	8
	Scoville, Dr. H.	17

Table 7. List of Observers and Scientific Staff in the 21 Pugwash Conferences Held Between 1957 and 1971 (Continued)

United States (Continued)	Stone, S.	16
	Stulman, J.	15
	Swartz, W.	17, 18
	Szilard, Dr. Gertrud W.	17
	Townes, Dr. C.H.	7
Yugoslavia	Knapp, Dr. V.	11
	Lazanski, M.	11
	Moljk, Prof. A.	11
ECA	Gardiner, R.K.A.	15
	Sundralingam, Dr. A.	15
FAO	Akin Deko, Chief, G.	15
	Aubrac, R.	18, 19, 20, 21
	Richie, T.E.	17
IAEA	Grigorieff, Dr. W.W.	3
	Lopez-Menchero, E.	21
	McKnight, A.D.	18
	Sanders, B.	21
	Seligman, Dr. H.	17
	Zheludev, I.S.	19
ICSU	Blaskovic, Acad. D.	13
SIPRI	Berner, O.	17
	Blackaby, F.	18
	Neild, R.R.	18, 19, 20, 21
	Němec, T.	20, 21
	Perry-Robinson, J.	18, 19
	Sinyak, Dr. K.	19
U.N.	Blickenstaff, D.	12
	Björnerstedt, Dr. R.	18, 20
	+Bunche, Dr. R.J.	13, 19
	Desai, Dr. R.C.	20
	Epstein, W.	14
	Gollong, P.B.W.	21
	Gresford, G.	17, 18
	Kutakov, Dr. L.N.	18, 20
	Kutovoj, Dr. E.Y.	19
	Mussard, J.A.	20
	Nesterenko, A.N.	16, 17
	Pastinen, I.	21
	Petrovsky, V.	16
	Pierson, J.H.G.	14, 15
	Suslov, V.P.	13
	Vejvoda, M.L.	15

Table 7. List of Observers and Scientific Staff in the 21 Pugwash Conferences Held Between 1957 and 1971 (Continued)

UNESCO	Ajumogobia, F.I.	15
	Alpert. Dr. H.	19
	Awokoya, S.O.	19
	+Bertrand, Dr. A.	14
	+Burkhardt, Prof. G.	17
	+Hochfeld, Dr. J.	13
	Kovda, Dr. V.A.	10
	Krause, Dr. R.	13
	Makagiansar, Dr. M.	18
	Malecki, Prof. I.	20, 21
	Matveyev, Prof. A.	14, 15
	Maybury, Dr. R.	12
	Mills, W.A.	11
	Roderick, Dr. H.	10
	Tha Hla, Prof.	11
	Uchida, T.	21
UQP	Elim, Dr. R.S.	17
WHO	Kaplan, Dr. M.M.	11, 12, 13, 14, 16, 17, 18, 19, 20

Table 8. List of Science Writers in the 18th, 19th and 20th Conferences

(The numbers after the names denote the serial number of the conferences attended.)

France	Berg. S.	18
	Fisson, P.	18
	Thuillier, Prof. P.	18
	Ullmann, M.	18
	Vichney, N.	18, 19
Soviet Union	Anichkin, O.N.	19
	Kolesnichenko, T.A.	20
	Liustiberg, V.F.	19
	Vasiliev, O.S.	19
United Kingdom	Clarke, R.	18, 19
	Stubbs, Dr. P.	18
	Tooze, Dr. J.	18
	Wade, N.M.L.	20
United States	Bengelsdorf, Dr. I.S.	19
	Kleiman, R.	19
	Sullivan, W.S.	19

Table 9. List of Student Participants in the 20th and 21st Conferences

(The numbers after the names denote the serial number of the conferences attended.)

Brazil	de Melo, J.L.P.	20
Canada	Greenwood, T.	20
Egypt	Allam, A-W.I.	20
India	Parekh, B.	20
Iran	Ansari, M.	20
Netherlands	Plougonven, C.	20
Portugal	Branco, G. da F.C.	20
Philippines	Macaranas, F.M.	20
Romania	Bologa, Liana	21
	Cornea, Mihaela	21
	Cosma, M.	21
	Durobantu, A.	21
	Ene, Balasa	21
	Mihailescu, M.	21
	Mindra, M.	21
	Nicuta, D.	21
	Popa, D.	21
	Popov, M.	21
	Roman, G.C.	21
	Sanda, Denisa M.	21
	Stane, Mioara	21
	Vulcan, Cristina	21
	Zamfirescu, Elena	21
Sweden	Fjellander, J.R.	20
United States	Bloch, P.C.	20
	Cahn, Anne	20
	Conway, P.	20
	Davis, J.C.	20
	Djerassi, D.	20, 21
	Feld, Elizabeth	20, 21
	Hagengruber, R.L.	20
	Hammond, A.	20
	Hardy, B.H.	20
	Harriman, R.L.	21
	Rosenthal, M.	20
	Schaich, T.	20

Table 9. List of Student Participants in the 20th and 21st Conferences (Continued)

United States (Continued)	Stephenson, G.R.	20
	Swartz, R.	20, 21
	Timbie, J.	20
	Walton, B.	20

Table 10. List of Suggested Topics for Pugwash Symposia (Prepared in 1968)

1. Definition of "nuclear umbrella" and "minimum deterrent."
2. Comprehensive test ban.
3. Seismic detection.
4. Reduction in intermediate range missile systems.
5. Effects of new technological developments on the nuclear arms race, and on prospects for arms control.
6. Nuclear submarines and sonar detection systems, and other aspects of arms control in the oceans.
7. Traffic in conventional arms.
8. Economic aspects of armaments.
9. Nuclear-free zones.
10. Regional arms control and disarmament measures in Europe.
11. Chemical warfare.
12. Meaning and prospects of long-term disarmament (or conditions for a stable world).
13. Peaceful settlement of disputes and other international problems.
14. Disarmament measures after the non-proliferation treaty.
15. Crisis management--with particular reference to Berlin, Cuba, Suez, Vietnam.
16. Methods of reducing friction in special areas (Europe, Middle East, S.E. Asia, etc.).
17. Treaty to ban military research.
18. Economic aspects of energy production (with particular reference to nuclear power).
19. World Science Centre and International Science Foundation.
20. Role of science and scientists in national and world affairs.
21. Social changes caused by the scientific and technological revolution.
22. Ethical guidelines for scientists.

Table 10. List of Suggested Topics for Pugwash Symposia (Prepared in 1968) (Continued)

23. Ethical problems for biologists and biological medical scientists arising from the possibility of biological warfare.

24. The role of scientific methods in the study of international relations.

25. A European Institute of Science and Technology with emphasis on East-West collaboration.

26. Co-existence and democracy.

27. An International Council for study of conflicts.

28. Best use of scientific resources by developing nations.

29. Problems of technology transfer to developing countries.

30. Multilateral and bilateral technical assistance programmes.

31. Population problem as it affects developing countries especially in Asia.

32. Resources of the oceans.

33. Use of communications satellites.

34. Problems of rural development in developing countries.

35. Power supplies for thinly populated areas.

Table 11. Pugwash Symposia

Serial Number	Date	Location	Topic	No. Participants	No. Countries	% Participants from Host Country	% Participants Attending for the First Time
I	April 1968	London, United Kingdom	Control of Peaceful Uses of Atomic Energy (with particular reference to non-proliferation)	40	16	28	50
II	May and September, 1968	Marianske Lasne, Czechoslovakia and Nice, France	Scientific and Technical Co-operation in Europe as a contribution to European Security	36	17	19	36
III	July 1968	Krogerup, Denmark	Implications of the Deployment of Anti-Ballistic Missile Systems	27	12	19	41
IV	April 1969	London, United Kingdom	Economic Aspects of Energy Production (with particular reference to nuclear power)	32	14	25	66

Table 11. Pugwash Symposia (Continued)

V	May 1969	Marianske Lazne, Czechoslovakia	Role of Science and Scientists in National and World Affairs	27	11	15	26
VI	September, 1969	Elsinor, Denmark	An International Agency for the Collection and Dissemination of Information on Potential Crises	22	9	23	50
VII	December, 1969	Radziejowice, Poland	Arms Control and Disarmament Measures in Europe	19	9	42	42
VIII	May 1970	Oberursel, German Federal Republic	Overcoming Protein Malnutrition in Developing Countries	29	11	31	86
IX	June 1970	Noordwijk, Netherlands	The Setting Up of Institutions for European Scientific and Technical Co-operation	35	13	31	34
X	June 1970	Racine, United States	Impact of New Technologies on the Arms Race	39	11	57	62

Table 11. Pugwash Symposia (Continued)

Serial Number	Date	Location	Topic	No. Participants	No. Countries	% Participants from Host Country	% Participants Attending for the First Time
XI	September, 1970	Stanford, United States	What Can Scientists Do for Development?	48	16	52	63
XII	February, 1971	Geneva, Switzerland	Rapid Detection and Identification of Microbiological Agents	28	9	25	64
XIII	April 1971	Frascati, Italy	Social Aspects of Technological Change	40	12	22	37
XIV	April 1971	Leipzig, German Democratic Republic	Economic and Social Aspects of Disarmament	33	14	33	52
XV	August 1971	Lahti, Finland	Tactical Arms Limitation in Europe	27	12	26	56
XVI	April 1972	Dubrovnik, Yugoslavia	Necessity, Opportunities and Obstacles for European Collaboration	33	15	18	36

Table 12. List of Participants in the 16 Pugwash Symposia Held Between 1968 and 1972

Country	Participant	Symposia
Argentina	Varsavsky, Dr. C.M.	XI
Austria	Breitenecker, Dr. M.	IX
	Rothschild, Prof. K.W.	XIV
Belgium	Baudoux, Prof. P.	II
	Coppieters, Prof. E.	XIV
	Stroot, Prof. J.P.	II, VII, IX, XVI
Brazil	Kirschner, Prof. P.	XI
Bulgaria	Denchev, Dr. A.	IV
	Kamenov, Acad. E.J.	XIV
	Zachariev, Prof. I.	XIV
Canada	Greenwood, T.	X
	Hopper, Dr. W.D.	XI
	Lewis, Dr. W.B.	IV
	von Riekhoff, Dr. H.	XV
Ceylon	Baptist, Prof. N.G.	VIII
Chile	Barzelatto, Dr. J.	XI
Colombia	Cobos, Dr. F.	VIII
	Leon-Betancourt, Dr. A.	XI
Cuba	Preston, Dr. T.	VIII
Czechoslovakia	Bucek, Dr. J.	I
	Hajdu, Dr. V.	III
	Hajek, Prof. J.	VI
	Málek, Acad. I.	II, V
	Markvart, Dr. J.	IV
	Maydl, Dr. P.	XVI
	Němec, T.	II, V
	Sedlak, Dr. J.	XVI
	Siska, Acad. K.	XVI
	Sojak, Dr. V.	XIV
	Šorm, Acad. F.	II, V
	Tondl, Prof. L.	II, V
	Zeleny, Prof. I.	XIII

+ Deceased

Table 12. List of Participants in the 16 Pugwash Symposia Held Between 1968 and 1972 (Continued)

Country	Participant	Symposia
Denmark	Björl, Prof. E.	VI
	Boserup, A.	III, VI
	von Bülow, H.	IV
	Gottlieb, H.	V, VI
	Maaløe, Prof. O.	II, III, VI, IX, XII, XIII, XVI
	von Magnus, Prof. Preben	XII
	Mortensen, K.	III
	Ølgaard, Dr. P.L.	I, X, XV
	Petersen, N.	III
	Rehberg, Prof. P.K.B.	III
	Seidenfaden, Dr. G.	VI
Finland	Broms, Prof. B.	XV
	Forssell, Dr. O.G.	XIV
	Gyllenberg, Prof. H.G.	XII
	Jansson, Prof. J.M.	VII, XV
	Jauho, Prof. P.	XV
	Kuhlberg, S.	XV, XVI
	Miettinen, Prof. J.K.	XV
	Saukonnen, Prof. J.J.	II
	Valtanen, J.	XV
	Väryrynen, R.	XV
	Weckstrom, Dr. P.M.J.	XII
France	Bauer, E.	II, V
	Bussac, Dr. J.	I, IV
	Gueron, Prof. J.	IV, IX, X
	Hassner, Prof. P.	XVI
	Joxe, Dr. A.	XIV
	Klein, Dr. J.	III, VII
	Magat, Prof. M.	II
	Marcovich, Dr. H.	II, V, XI, XIII, XVI
	Moch, J.	VI
	Perrin, Prof. F.	I, IV
German Democratic Republic	Bollinger, Prof. K.	XIV
	Ernst, K-D.	XIV
	Ersil, Prof. W.	V
	Faulstich, Prof. H.	I
	Geyer, Dr. H.M.	XIV
	Hahn, Prof. G.	XIV
	Hess, Prof. P.	XIV, XV
	Kolesnyk, Dr. A.	I, II, V, XIV
	Kröger, Prof. H.	XIV, XVI
	Kuczynski, Acad. J.	XIII, XIV
	Leibnitz, Prof. E.	XIV
	Schlesinger, H.	XIV
	Zorn, B.	XIV

Table 12. List of Participants in the 16 Pugwash Symposia Held Between 1968 and 1972 (Continued)

Country	Participant	Symposia
German Federal Republic	Afheldt, H.H.	I, III, VII, X
	Albrecht, Dr. U.	XIV
	Bredow, Dr. W.F.	XVI
	Cremer, Prof. H.D.	VIII
	Delbrück, Dr. J.	I
	Esche, H.	VIII
	Glubrecht, Prof. H.	VIII, XI
	Häfele, Prof. W.	X
	Heinrichs, Dr. J.	VIII, XIII
	Ipsen, Dr. K.	XV
	Joos, Dr. H.	II, IX
	Kaiser, Prof. K.	XV
	Kind, B.	VIII
	Korte, Dr. R.	VIII
	Kraut, Prof. H.	VIII
	Kreye, O.	VIII
	Reich, U.P.	VII
	von Weizsäcker, Dr. E.U.	V
	Wilbrandt, Prof. H.	VIII
Ghana	Torto, Prof. F.G.	XI, XVI
Hungary	Bati, Dr. L.	II
	Fono, Dr. A.	IV
	Kende, Dr. I.	VII, XIV
	Lengyel, Prof. S.	V
	Levai, Prof. A.	IV
	Szendy, Dr. K.	IV
India	Chadha, Dr. M.S.	XI
	Devadas, Dr. R.P.	VIII
	Gopalan, Dr. C.	VIII
	Krishnaswamy, Dr. P.R.	VIII
	Menon, Prof. M.G.K.	I
	Nag Chaudhuri, Dr. B.D.	XI
	Pal, Prof. Y.	XI
	Parpia, Dr. H.A.B.	VIII
	Parthasarathi, A.	XI
	Ramanna, Dr. R.	X
	+Sarabhai, Prof. V.A.	I
Indonesia	Katili, Prof. J.	XI
Israel	Freier, S.	I, III, X
	Vital, Dr. D.	I
	Yiftah, Prof. S.	IV
Italy	Amaldi, Prof. E.	XIII
	Amati, Dr. P.	II

Table 12. List of Participants in the 16 Pugwash Symposia Held Between 1968 and 1972 (Continued)

Country	Participant	Symposia
Italy (Continued)	Bertotti, Prof. B.	XIII
	Brunelli, Prof. B.	X, XIII
	Budini, Prof. P.	IX
	Calogero, Prof. F.	I, III, XIII
	Calogero, Mrs. Louisa	I
	Cini, M.	XIII
	Gallino, Prof. L.	XIII
	Mazza, Dr. M.	IV
	Pascolini, Dr. A.	XIII
	Schaerf, Prof. C.	XIII
	Scossiroli, Prof. R.E.	XIII
Japan	Okita, Dr. S.	XI
Kenya	Odhiambo, Prof. T.R.	XI
Netherlands	Alting von Geusau, Prof. F.A.M.	I, IX
	Bannier, J.H.	IX
	Bartlema, Dr. H.C.	XII
	Boskma, Dr. P.	VI, IX
	de Charro, F. Th.	IX
	De Wilde, Prof. J.	XI
	Hoogland, Dr. W.	IX
	Jaquet, Dr. L.G.M.	XVI
	Landheer, Prof. B.	IX
	Quik, H.G.	II, IX
	Rörsh, Prof. A.	IX
	Smith, Prof. P.B.	II, IX
	de Vries, Dr. C.	IX
	Wierda, W.	III
	Wouthuysen, Prof. S.	IX
Norway	Eide, Mrs. W.B.	VIII
	Gleditsch, N.P.	XIV
	Holst, J.J.	XV
	Omland, Dr. T.	XII
	Rosenquist, Prof. I.T.	I, IV
	Sannes, Prof. J.	II
	Thee, Dr. M.	VI
Peru	Bacigalupo, Dr. A.	XI
Poland	Adamczewski, Prof. I.	II
	Bukowski, Prof. J.	VII
	Karkoszka, A.	VII
	Kuratowski, Prof. L.	VII
	Ludwiczak, Z.	VII

Table 12. List of Participants in the 16 Pugwash Symposia Held Between 1968 and 1972 (Continued)

Poland (Continued)	Malecki, Prof. I.	II, V
	Nowacki, Prof. P.J.	I, IV
	Olszewski, Prof. E.	VII
	Popkiewicz, Prof. J.	XIV
	Rybicki, Prof. Z.	IX
	Sach, Dr. J.	VII
	Skowronski, A.	XV
	Towpik, Dr. A.	VII
	Wieczorek, Dr. W.	VII, XIV
Romania	Dragulescu, Acad. C.	II
	Gherman, Prof. O.	XVI
	Hanga, Prof. V.	II
	Nita, Prof. M.	III
	Pavelescu, Dr. D.	II
	Penescu, Prof. C.	XVI
Soviet Union	Aboltin, Prof. V.Y.	II, VI, XIV
	Alferov, Dr. V.V.	V
	Belikov, Prof. V.M.	VIII
	Emelyanov, Prof. V.S.	I, II, IV, V, VI, X, XVI
	Engelhardt, Acad. V.A.	IX
	Gvishiani, Dr. Ludmila	XIII
	Kaftanov, Prof. V.	IX
	Karlov, Dr. M.V.	XV
	Khabarin, Dr. N.V.	I, IV
	+Khvostov, Acad. V.	XIII
	Kozinets, Dr. O.I.	X
	Kuleshov, Dr. V.	IV, VII, IX, XIII
	Mikhaltsev, Dr. I.	X
	Millionshchikov, Acad. M.D.	XIII, XVI
	Milovidov, Dr. I.V.	III
	Pochitalin, I.G.	III, XIII, XVI
	Sagdeyev, Dr. R.	X
	Silin, Prof. V.	XV
	Sinyak, Prof. K.	V, XII
	Skryabin, Prof. G.	VIII
	Sychev, Dr. V.	X
	Timofeev, Prof. T.	XIII
	Vinogradov, Acad. A.P.	III
	Voslensky, Prof. M.S.	VII, XIV
	Zelenin, Prof. A.V.	XII
Sweden	Alfvén, Prof. H.	XIII, XVI
	Backstränd, G.	IX
	Birnbaum, Dr. K.E.	VII, XVI
	Collen, Dr. B.	I
	Diczfalusy, Prof. E.R.	XI

Table 12. List of Participants in the 16 Pugwash Symposia Held Between 1968 and 1972 (Continued)

Sweden (Continued)	Hedén, Prof. C-G.	V, XII
	Herlofson, Prof. N.	I, II, III
	Ljunggren, Dr. A.M.O.	XII
	Magnusson, G.L.	III
	Prawitz, J.	I, III, IV, X, XV
	Tammelin, Dr. L.E.	XII
	Thore, Dr. A.	XII
Switzerland	Bloch, Prof. H.	XII
	Bonifas, Prof. V.	XII
	Fey, Prof. H.	XII
	Kellenberger, Dr. E.	XII
	Mach, Dr. B.	XII
	Mende, T.	VI
	Schwarz, Prof. U.	XVI
	Ungar, Dr. J.	XII
	Wiesmann, Prof. E.	XII
United Kingdom	Astor, Hon. David	VI
	Balogh, Lord	XIV
	Barnaby, Dr. C. F.	I, II, III, IV, V, VII
	Beamish, Crooke, J.	IV
	Beckman, Dr. J.	I
	Bondi, Prof. H.	IX
	Carlton, Dr. D.	I, III, XIII, XIV, XV
	Elliott, Dr. G.	I
	Fielding, R.J.	VII, XVI
	Gott, H.	IV
	Groom, A.J.R.	III
	Gutteridge, W.F.	XIV, XVI
	Haigh, Dr. C.P.	IV
	Higgins, R.	VI
	Hodgkin, Prof. Dorothy	V
	Holmes, R.	IV
	Kennet, Lord	XIII, XV
	Lindop, Prof. Patricia	XII
	Lipman, Dr. N.	I
	Lloyd, B.D.	IV
	+Lonsdale, Dame Kathleen	V
	Maddox, J.	I
	Martin, Prof. A.	I
	Mendl, Dr. W.	I
	Oldham, Dr. C.H.G.	XI
	Pease, Dr. R.S.	IX
	Peierls, Sir Rudolf	I, II, V
	Pirie, N.W.	VIII
	+Powell, Prof. C.F.	I, II
	Price, B.T.	X

Table 12. List of Participants in the 16 Pugwash Symposia Held Between 1968 and 1972 (Continued)

United Kingdom (Continued)	Rotblat, Prof. J.	I, II, III, IV, V, VI, VIII, IX, XI, XII, XIII, XIV, XVI
	Searby, P.J.	IV
	Smart, I.	X, XV
	Taylor, Dr. C.E.D.	XII
United States	Adams, Mrs. Ruth	XI
	Alexander, B.	X
	Anderson, Dr. V.C.	X
	Bloch, Prof. F.	XI
	Boulding, Prof. K.E.	VI
	Bunn, Prof. G.	X
	Campbell, Dr. J.C.	XVI
	Chayes, Prof. A.	X
	Coleman, Prof. J.M.	XI
	Copeland, B.K.W.	XI
	Davidon, Prof. W.	V
	Davidson, Dr. W.D.	XIII
	Djerassi, Prof. C.	XI
	Doty, Prof. P.	X
	Eden, Prof. M.	VI, IX
	Eicher, Dr. C.K.	VIII
	Engel, J.	XI
	Feld, Prof. B.T.	III, V, X, XIV
	Frank, Prof. C.R.	XI
	Frisch, Dr. Rose	VIII
	Fubini, E.	X
	Gilinsky, Dr. V.	XV
	Goldberg, Dr. L.J.	XII
	Goodman, Mrs. Rita	X
	Goss, G.	X
	Hall, W.	XI
	Hammond, Dr. R.P.	IV
	Hansen, K.R.	XI
	Heggie, R.G.	XI
	Hirschman, Prof. A.O.	XI
	Hoag, Dr. D.G.	X
	Indik, Prof. B.	VI
	Inglis, Dr. D.	I
	Kirk, Prof. D.	XI
	Kistiakowsky, Prof. G.B.	X
	Kleinjans, Dr. E.	XI
	Landsberg, H.	XIII
	Lennette, Dr. E.	XII
	Long, Prof. F.A.	V, X, XIII
	McCorkle, T.	X
	McKenzie, Dr. J.	X

Table 12. List of Participants in the 16 Pugwash Symposia Held Between 1968 and 1972 (Continued)

United States (Continued)	Mark, Dr. J.C.	X
	Melman, Prof. S.	XIV
	Mitz, Dr. M.	XII
	Morgenthau, Prof. H.J.	XV
	Nash, Prof. M.	XI
	Paffrath, L.	X
	Pomerance, Mrs. Jo	I
	Ponnamperuma, Dr. C.	XI
	Rabi, Prof. I.I.	IX
	Rabinowitch, Prof. E.	V, XI, XIII, XVI
	Rabinowitch, Dr. V.	XI
	Rachwartono, R.	XI
	Rathjens, Dr. G.W.	III, X
	Read, Dr. J.	X
	Resnick, Dr. J.	X
	Revelle, Prof. R.	XI
	Rice, Prof. H.L.	XI
	Rich, Prof. A.	V
	Rochlin, Dr. R.S.	I
	Rosecrance, Prof. R.	XV
	Ruina, Prof. J.P.	X, XV
	Singer, Prof. J.D.	VI
	Skolnikoff, Dr. E.	XIII
	Sohns, Dr. E.R.	XI
	Sproull, Dr. R.	X
	Stone, Dr. J.J.	III
	Szilard, Mrs. Gertrud	XI
	Udis, Dr. B.	XIV
	Vietmeyer, Dr. N.D.	XI
	Voss, J.	XI
	Weinberg, Prof. S.	X
	Weiss, Dr. C., Jr.	XI
	Weisskopf, Prof. V.F.	IX
	Wiesner, Dr. J.B.	I
	York, Dr. H.	XV
West Indies	Jelliffe, Prof. D.	VIII
	Jelliffe, Mrs. E.F.P.	VIII
Yugoslavia	Acimovic, Prof. L.	XVI
	Alaga, Prof. G.	IX
	Andrassy, Acad. J.	XVI
	Bakotic, Prof. B.	XVI
	Buzina, Prof. R.	VIII
	Gamulin, Prof. T.	XVI
	Katicic, Prof. N.	XV
	Knapp, Prof. V.	IV
	Popovic, Dr. D.	IV

Table 12. List of Participants in the 16 Pugwash Symposia Held Between 1968 and 1972 (Continued)

Yugoslavia (Continued)	Rajh, Dr. Z.	II
	Sahovic, Dr. M.	XVI
	Sajovic, Dr. D.	IV
	Supek, Acad. I.	I, XVI
	Supek, Prof. R.	XIII
Zaire	Lofo, Prof. J.M.	XIII
CERN	Amati, Prof. D.	II, IX
	Charpak, Dr. G.	II, IX
	Goldschmidt-Clermont, Dr. Y.	II, IX
	Kowarski, Dr. L.	IX
FAO	Aubrac, R.	XIII
	Biro, A.	XIII
	Kapsiotis, Dr. G.D.	VIII
	Quaix, H.	XIII
	Wrigley, Dr. J.	XIII
FAO/IAEA	Luse, Dr. R.	VIII
IAEA	Krymm, R.	IV
	Sanders, B.	I
	Shmelev, V.	I
	Spinrad, Dr. B.	IV
ICSU	Baker, F.G.W.	XIII
OECD	Cade, Dr. J.	XIII
	King, Dr. A.	II
SIPRI	Blackaby, F.	VI
	Leitenberg, Prof. M.	III, XV
	Neild, R.	III, VI
J.N.	Björnerstedt, Dr. R.R.	XVI
	Kutovoj, Dr. E.	XIV
	Nagelstein, Dr. E.W.	VIII
	Petrovsky, V.	X
UNDP	Kretzmann, Dr. E.M.J.	XI
UNESCO	Buzzati-Traverso, Prof. A.	XI
	Chapdelaine, M.	XIII
	Clarke, R.	XIII
	de Hemptinne, Y.	V
	Macioti, Dr. M.	XVI
	Malecki, Prof. I.	IX

Table 12. List of Participants in the 16 Pugwash Symposia Held Between 1968 and 1972 (Continued)

World Bank	Abdel Meguid, Dr. A.R.	XI
WHO	Faulk, Dr. W.P.	XII
	Ferreira, Dr. W.	XII
	Handler, J.	VI
	Kaplan, Dr. M.M.	II, IX, XII, XIII

Table 13. Participants in Meetings of the Study Group on Biological Warfare

Australia	Prof. R. C. Nairn
Austria	Prof. F. Mainx
Czechoslovakia	Acad. D. Blaskovic
	Dr. J. Franek
	Mr. B. Kozak
	Acad. I. Malek
	Dr. J. Moravec
	Prof. K. Raska
	Dr. J. Riha
	Dr. M. J. Sterzl
Denmark	Dr. J. Leerhøy
	Prof. O. Maaløe
France	Prof. A. Kirn
	Prof. A. Lwoff
	Dr. H. Marcovich
	Dr. H. Meyrowitz
German Federal Republic	+Prof. G. Burkhardt
	Dr. E. von Weizsäcker
Hungary	Prof. F. B. Straub
Israel	Dr. R. Goldwasser
	Prof. A. Keynan
Italy	Prof. B. de Bernard
	Prof. A. A. Buzzati-Traverso
	Prof. G. A. Maccacaro
Netherlands	Dr. I. F. Ph. Hers
Poland	Dr. J. Jeljaszewicz
	Prof. K. D. Lapter
Soviet Union	Dr. V. V. Alferov
	Acad. M. M. Dubinin
	Acad. A. A. Imshenetsky
	Prof. A. M. Kuzin
	Dr. L. Melnikov
	+Prof. N. A. Talensky
	Acad. A. P. Vinogradov
	Prof. V. Zhdanov

Table 13. Participants in Meetings of the Study Group on Biological Warfare (Continued)

Sweden	Dr. R. Björnerstedt
	Prof. T. Caspersson
	Mr. M. Fehrm
	Prof. Sven Gard
	Prof. C-G. Hedén
	Dr. M. Ritzen
	Dr. L. E. Tammelin
	+Prof. A. Tiselius
	Dr. B. Zacharias
Switzerland	Dr. J. Ungar
United Kingdom	Dr. J. H. Humphrey
	Prof. Patricia J. Lindop
	Prof. J. Rotblat
	Dr. C. E. D. Taylor
United States	Dr. I. Bennett
	Prof. P. Doty
	Dr. G. Edsall
	Prof. B. T. Feld
	Prof. D. Glaser
	Prof. B. Glass
	Dr. M. M. Kaplan
	Prof. M. Meselson
	Prof. A. Rich
SIPRI	Mr. O. Berner
	Dr. A. Ljungren
	Mr. T. Němec
	Mr. J. Perry Robinson
	Dr. K. M. Sinyak
Western European Union	Mr. E. Mostacci

APPENDICES

THE RUSSELL-EINSTEIN MANIFESTO

In the tragic situation which confronts humanity, we feel that scientists should assemble in conference to appraise the perils that have arisen as a result of the development of weapons of mass destruction, and to discuss a resolution in the spirit of the appended draft.

We are speaking on this occasion, not as members of this or that nation, continent, or creed, but as human beings, members of the species Man, whose continued existence is in doubt. The world is full of conflicts; and, overshadowing all minor conflicts, the titanic struggle between Communism and anti-Communism.

Almost everybody who is politically conscious has strong feelings about one or more of these issues; but we want you, if you can, to set aside such feelings and consider yourselves only as members of a biological species which has had a remarkable history, and whose disappearance none of us can desire.

We shall try to say no single word which should appeal to one group rather than to another. All, equally, are in peril, and, if the peril is understood, there is hope that they may collectively avert it.

We have to learn to think in a new way. We have to learn to ask ourselves, not what steps can be taken to give military victory to whatever group we prefer, for there no longer are such steps; the question we have to ask ourselves is: what steps can be taken to prevent a military contest of which the issue must be disastrous to all parties?

The general public, and even many men in position of authority, have not realized what would be involved in a war with nuclear bombs. The general public still thinks in terms of the obliteration of cities. It is understood that the new bombs are more powerful than the old, and that, while one A-bomb could obliterate Hiroshima, one H-bomb could obliterate the largest cities, such as London, New York, and Moscow.

No doubt in an H-bomb war great cities would be obliterated. But this is one of the minor disasters that would have to be faced. If everybody in London, New York, and Moscow were exterminated, the world might, in the course of a few centuries, recover from the blow. But we now know, especially since the Bikini test, that nuclear bombs can gradually spread destruction over a very much wider area than had been supposed.

It is stated on very good authority that a bomb can now be manufactured which will be 2,500 times as powerful as that which destroyed Hiroshima. Such a bomb, if exploded near the ground or under water, sends radioactive particles into the upper air. They sink gradually and reach the surface of the earth in the form of a deadly dust or rain. It was this dust which infected the Japanese fishermen and their catch of fish.

No one knows how widely such lethal radio-active particles might be diffused, but the best authorities are unanimous in saying that a war with

Appendix 1   138

H-bombs might quite possibly put an end to the human race. It is feared that if many H-bombs are used there will be universal death—sudden only for a minority, but for the majority a slow torture of disease and disintegration.

Many warnings have been uttered by eminent men of science and by authorities in military strategy. None of them will say that the worst results are certain. What they do say is that these results are possible, and no one can be sure that they will not be realized. We have not yet found that the views of experts on this question depend in any degree upon their politics or prejudices. They depend only, so far as our researches have revealed, upon the extent of the particular expert's knowledge. We have found that the men who know most are the most gloomy.

Here, then, is the problem which we present to you, stark and dreadful and inescapable: Shall we put an end to the human race; or shall mankind renounce war?* People will not face this alternative because it is so difficult to abolish war.

The abolition of war will demand distasteful limitations of national sovereignty.** But what perhaps impedes understanding of the situation more than anything else is that the term "mankind" feels vague and abstract. People scarcely realize in imagination that the danger is to themselves and their children and their grandchildren, and not only to a dimly apprehended humanity. They can scarcely bring themselves to grasp that they, individually, and those whom they love are in imminent danger of perishing agonizingly. And so they hope that perhaps war may be allowed to continue provided modern weapons are prohibited.

This hope is illusory. Whatever agreements not to use H-bombs had been reached in time of peace, they would no longer be considered binding in time of war, and both sides would set to work to manufacture H-bombs as soon as war broke out, for, if one side manufactured the bombs and the other did not, the side that manufactured them would inevitably be victorious.

Although an agreement to renounce nuclear weapons as part of a general reduction of armaments*** would not afford an ultimate solution, it would serve certain important purposes. First: any agreement between East and West is to the good insofar as it tends to diminish tension. Second: the abolition of thermo-nuclear weapons, if each side believed that the other had carried it out sincerely, would lessen the fear of a sudden attack in the style of Pearl Harbour, which at present keeps both sides in a state of nervous apprehension. We should, therefore, welcome such an agreement, though only as a first step.

---
*Professor Joliot-Curie wishes to add the words: "as a means of settling differences between States."
**Professor Joliot-Curie wishes to add that these limitations are to be agreed by all and in the interests of all.
***Professor Muller makes the reservation that this be taken to mean "a concomitant balanced reduction of all armaments."

The Russell-Einstein Manifesto

Most of us are not neutral in feeling, but as human beings, we have to remember that, if the issues between East and West are to be decided in any manner that can give any possible satisfaction to anybody, whether Communist or anti-Communist, whether Asian or European or American, whether White or Black, then these issues must not be decided by war. We should wish this to be understood, both in the East and in the West.

There lies before us, if we choose, continual progress in happiness, knowledge, and wisdom. Shall we, instead, choose death, because we cannot forget our quarrels? We appeal, as human beings, to human beings: remember your humanity, and forget the rest. If you can do so, the way lies open to a new Paradise; if you cannot, there lies before you the risk of universal death.

Resolution
We invite this Congress, and through it the scientists of the world and the general public, to subscribe to the following resolution:

"In view of the fact that in any future world war nuclear weapons will certainly be employed, and that such weapons threaten the continued existence of mankind, we urge the Governments of the world to realize, and to acknowledge publicly, that their purpose cannot be furthered by a world war, and we urge them, consequently, to find peaceful means for the settlement of all matters of dispute between them."

Professor Max Born (Professor of Theoretical Physics at Berlin, Frankfurt, and Gottingen, and of Natural Philosophy, Edinburgh; Nobel Prize in physics).

Professor P. W. Bridgman (Professor of Physics, Harvard University; Nobel Prize in physics).

Professor Albert Einstein.

Professor L. Infeld (Professor of Theoretical Physics, University of Warsaw).

Professor J. F. Joliot-Curie (Professor of Physics at the Collège de France; Nobel Prize in chemistry).

Professor H. J. Muller (Professor of Zoology at University of Indiana; Nobel Prize in physiology and medicine).

Professor Linus Pauling (Professor of Chemistry, California Institute of Technology; Nobel Prize in chemistry).

Professor C. F. Powell (Professor of Physics, Bristol University; Nobel Prize in physics).

Professor J. Rotblat (Professor of Physics, University of London; Medical College of St. Bartholomew's Hospital).

Appendix 1   140

Bertrand Russell.

Professor Hideki Yukawa (Professor of Theoretical Physics, Kyoto University; Nobel Prize in physics).

STATEMENT FROM THE FIRST PUGWASH CONFERENCE, HELD IN PUGWASH, JULY 7-10, 1957

At the invitation of Lord Russell, and through the generous hospitality of Mr. Cyrus Eaton, a group of scientists, drawn from ten nations and widely representative of different political, economic and other opinions, met in Conference at Pugwash, Nova Scotia, between July 7 and 10, 1957. Mr. Y. Shimonaka and others also provided valuable assistance.

The meeting originated in the suggestion contained in the Russell-Einstein appeal, that scientists should meet to assess the perils to humanity which have arisen as a result of the development of weapons of mass destruction. Two years have passed since that statement was issued but the dangers remain. In fact, the stockpiles of nuclear weapons have increased, new nations have joined the ranks of those producing weapons, or trying to produce them, whilst serious misgivings have been expressed as to whether the continued testing of such weapons may not result in damage to the population. The general belief that a full-scale nuclear war would bring universal disaster upon mankind, and the recognition that it is technically possible for both the two great contending forces to visit any desired degree of destruction upon an enemy, as well as certain political developments, have created an atmosphere in which it was possible for us to meet, and to discuss dispassionately, many important and highly controversial issues.

The international problems which have arisen as a result of the development of atomic energy are of two kinds, technical and political. A gathering of men of science can discuss with special competence only the scientific and technical implications of atomic energy. Such discussion, however, can be fruitful only if it takes into account the political problems which are the background to international negotiations. The signatories of the Russell-Einstein appeal affirmed their intention to say nothing which might seem to favour one rather than the other of the two great groups of powers into which the world is divided. In attempting to formulate the conclusions which followed from our discussions, we too have tried to avoid any exacerbation of the differences between nations which might follow, for example, from emphasis on technical considerations unwelcome to one or other of the two great powers.

Men of science are now well aware that the fruits of their labours are of paramount importance for the future of mankind, and they are thus compelled to consider the political implications of their work. Their opinions on politics are as diverse as those of other men. These facts make it difficult for a conference such as the present to issue an agreed statement on matters which are controversial. The discussion of such issues, however, allowed the points of difference and the areas of agreement to be defined, and led to a measure of mutual understanding of the opinions of one another.

The main work of the meeting was centered around three principal topics: (1) the hazards arising from the use of atomic energy in peace and war;

(2) problems of the control of nuclear weapons; and (3) the social responsibility of scientists. Three committees were established to give detailed consideration to these topics. Their reports to the conference are given in the statements appended to this document, but the principal conclusions bearing on the hazards of atomic energy may be briefly summarized as follows:

Committee I on nuclear hazards, made an independent assessment of the effects of the nuclear tests carried out hitherto. From the details given in the appendix, it may be seen that the hazard, compared with others to which mankind is subject from natural causes, is small. Nevertheless, because of the world-wide distribution of fission products, and the fact that some areas may be subject to effects much above the average, close attention to the dangers should be maintained, especially if tests of bombs which give large radioactive fallout continue to be made.

The committee also considered the hazards arising from the peace-time use of industrial atomic power, or the application of radiations in medicine and industry. Although these hazards must be viewed in the light of the great benefits which will flow from such applications, means of greatly reducing the attendant hazards are available and should be widely adopted.

The above-mentioned estimates of the hazards which have arisen from test explosions, permitted a closer examination to be made of the probable consequences of an unrestricted nuclear war. This examination led to the unquestioned conclusion that a general war with nuclear weapons would indeed represent a disaster of unprecedented magnitude. The radiological hazards would be thousands of times greater than those due to the **fallout effects** of test explosions. In the combatant countries, hundreds of millions of people would be killed outright by the blast and heat, and by the ionizing radiation produced at the instant of explosion whether bombs of the so-called "clean" or "dirty" kind were employed. If "dirty" bombs were used, large areas would be made uninhabitable for extended periods of time, and additional hundreds of millions of people would die from delayed effects of radiation from local fallout, some in the exposed population from direct radiation injury, and some in succeeding generations as a result of genetic effects. But even countries not directly hit by bombs would suffer through global fallout, which, under certain conditions, might be of such intensity as to cause large-scale genetic and other injury.

It is against the background of the fearful consequences for humanity of a general war with nuclear weapons that the conclusions of Committee II, which considered problems of control, must be viewed. The principal objective of all nations must be the abolition of war and the threat of war hanging over mankind. War must be finally eliminated, not merely regulated by limiting the weapons which may be used. For this purpose, it is necessary to reduce tension among the nations; to promote mutual understanding among the people; to strive for the ending of the arms race; and to provide an adequate control system so as to give substantial protection, and permit the development of mutual confidence.

One of the greatest difficulties in international affairs in recent years has sprung from the fact that in a period of delicate strategic balance, even secondary questions acquire strategic significance; in such a situation, they are rarely subject to agreed solutions because any particular solution appears to be to the strategic advantage of one rather than another of the powers. We believe that it is unrealistic to depend upon any sudden increase in mutual confidence and that it is more likely to grow from small beginnings. In this situation, even small agreements covering limited fields could be of great importance.

In the present circumstances, we believe that the greatest peril comes from the possibility that a war might break out between two smaller nations, that Russia and America might intervene militarily on opposite sides, and that such a war might be fought by using atomic bombs in combat. We believe it would be very difficult to limit a local war of this kind-- particularly if it is fought with atomic weapons in the tactical area-- and that what may start out as a local war may end as a general atomic catastrophe. In order to avert this danger, political settlements aimed specifically at eliminating the risk of the outbreak of a local war between smaller nations are needed.

The conclusions of Committee III on the responsibilities of scientists state our common conviction that we should do all in our power to prevent war and to assist in establishing a permanent and universal peace. This we can do by contributing to the task of public enlightenment concerning the great dilemma of our times; and by serving to the full extent of our opportunities in the formation of national policies. The Committee gives a statement of beliefs and aspirations suitable for scientists in the modern world.

Finally, we should like to give expression to the high degree of unanimity we have found among all the members of the Conference on *fundamental aims*. We are all convinced that mankind must abolish war or suffer catastrophe; that the dilemma of opposing power groups and the arms race must be broken; and that the establishment of lasting peace will mark the opening of a new and triumphant epoch for the whole of mankind. We earnestly hope that our conference may make a modest contribution to these great aims.

Report of Committee One: Radiation Hazards

The effects of radiation, from nuclear tests, from peaceful applications, and from the possible wartime use of nuclear weapons, have been the subject of much concern and study. We have felt it desirable at this meeting to consider the available facts bearing on these problems.

With regard to the effects of nuclear testing we have found that separate calculations carried out independently in Great Britain, Japan, the U.S.A. and the U.S.S.R. have yielded results in good agreement with one another on the amount of fallout and on its effects.

A principal effect is due to strontium-90. If, as some evidence indicates, the production of leukaemia and bone cancer by radiation is proportional to the dose, even down to very small doses, then we estimate that the tests conducted over the past six years will be responsible for an increase of about 1 per cent over the natural incidence of leukaemia and bone cancer during the next few decades. Over the next 30 years, this increase would amount to about a hundred thousand additional cases of leukaemia and bone cancer. The correct numbers may be several times larger or smaller. These additional cases could, however, not be identified among the 10 million or so normal cases of the same diseases.

A second principal effect of global fallout consists of genetic mutations. We estimate that these will cause serious injury to about as many individuals as those in whom leukaemia or bone cancer will be produced by the strontium-90. However, the genetic effects from a given amount of fallout, unlike the effects of strontium-90 will be scattered over many generations.

Peacetime uses of radiation, such as x-rays in medicine, or nuclear power production, will also be responsible for the delivery of radiation to large numbers of people. Genetic and long-term somatic effects will result from this radiation, in amounts depending on how much radiation is received by the reproductive cells and by other parts of the body.

It is important, in evaluating the effects from various sources of radiation, to try to put them in proper perspective. For example, the radiation received by the average individual from medical x-rays, is, in countries of more highly-developed techniques, considerably greater than the fallout radiation from tests at the recent rate. This does not mean, however, either that we should stop using x-rays, or that we should not be concerned about fallout from tests. Great benefits to man are obtained from the use of x-rays, as well as from the industrial use of nuclear energy. The new awareness concerning the deleterious effects of radiation is leading to greatly improved techniques in the use of x-rays, and to more rigorous precaution in the application of nuclear energy. By these means it will be possible to reduce the doses received from medical and industrial radiation to levels that are justifiable in the light of the benefits obtained. It is useful to remember that modern industrialized society involves many developments with harmful side effects, as in the case, for example, of the fumes from automobiles and from industrial establishments. Accurate evaluation of the damage caused in this way has not been made but, even if it should turn out to be considerable, no one would expect to stop using all automobile engines or noxious industrial processes.

With regard to fallout effects from tests, it should be recognized that the effects are global, and exerted upon citizens of all countries, regardless of whether they or their governments have approved the holding of tests. In these circumstances, the usual criteria as to whether a given hazard is justifiable cannot be applied. According to the figures given above, many individuals will be affected, although the numbers represent only a small percentage increase over normally occurring effects, and it will not be possible to say, for example, which specific case of leukaemia

The First Pugwash Conference

is due to fallout and which is a natural case. It should also be realized that appreciable areas of the world will experience higher than average effects from fallout.

We now come to the consideration of the effects of a nuclear war. It cannot be disputed that a full-scale nuclear war would be an utter catastrophe. Its effects would be thousands of times greater than the fallout effects from nuclear tests. In the combatant countries, hundreds of millions of people would be killed outright, by the flash and heat, and by the ionizing radiation produced at the instant of explosion. If so-called "dirty" bombs were used, large areas would be made uninhabitable for extended periods of time, and additional hundreds of millions of people would probably die from delayed effects of local fallout radiation; some in the exposed population from direct radiation injury and some in succeeding generations as a result of genetic effects. Even countries not directly hit by bombs would suffer through global fallout, which under certain conditions might be of such intensity as to cause large-scale genetic and other injury.

Report of Committee Two

In this age of atomic weapons, the objective of all nations must be the abolition of war and even the threat of war from the life of mankind. War must be eliminated, not merely regulated by limiting the weapons to be used. The advancement of this objective calls for:

1. The lessening of tensions among nations and the promotion of mutual understanding among their peoples.

2. The ending of the arms race.

3. The provision of reasonable safeguards in the arms control system to give substantial protection and build up mutual confidence. The development of atomic armaments has now gone so far that a completely effective and reliable control system appears to be no longer possible.

4. The initiation of a step-by-step process to develop as satisfactory a set of controls and safeguards as practicable. The prompt suspension of nuclear bomb tests could be a good first step for this purpose.

Report of Committee Three

It is our conviction that the paramount responsibility of scientists outside their professional work is to do all in their power to prevent war and to help establish a permanent and universal peace. This they can do by contributing to the full measure of their capabilities to public enlightenment on the destructive and constructive potentialities of science and by contributing to the full extent of their opportunities in the formation of national policies.

To this aim, scientists of all countries without regard to political and economic systems can dedicate themselves because they share certain common beliefs. Following are some of them:

Appendix 2

1. With the penetration of science into the world of atomic nuclei, humanity has entered a new epoch.

2. The development of science and technology has paramount importance for the future of all mankind. This imposes upon scientists the obligation to be more actively concerned with matters of public policy, and upon political leaders the duty to take fully into account the scientific and technological facts.

3. As a consequence of man's mastery of nuclear forces, a war can now cause immeasurable damage to mankind.

4. If the achievements of science are rationally employed, they could enormously increase the well-being of all men.

5. Scientific and technical progress is irreversible. With humanity basing much of its technological progress on the manipulation of nuclear forces, it is of paramount importance that war be made permanently and universally impossible.

6. In the past, nations have often resorted to force in the quest for natural resources and fruits of labour. These methods must now be replaced by a common effort to create wealth for all.

7. The security of mankind demands that no section of it shall have the capacity to destroy the other. The developments of science and technology tend to break down barriers between nations and, in effect, to unify mankind.

8. The need of all parts of mankind to co-operate in the growth of the total sum of human knowledge and wealth, despite ideological and other differences which may divide them, is permanent and not a matter of temporary "co-existence" of different political or economic systems.

9. Tradition tends to place the emphasis in the education of youth on separate ideals of single nations, including the glorification of wars. The atomic age urgently requires a modification of these traditions. Without abandoning loyalty to national heritage or fundamental principles of the different societies, education must emphasize the fundamental and permanent community of the interests of mankind, in peace and co-operation, irrespective of national boundaries and differences in economic or political systems.

10. Science has a well proven tradition of international co-operation. We hope that this co-operation can be strengthened and extended into other fields of human endeavour.

11. Science develops most effectively when it is free from interference by any dogma imposed from the outside, and permitted to question all postulates, including her own. Without this freedom of scientific thought and the freedom to exchange information and ideas, full utilization of the constructive possibilities of science will not be possible.

The First Pugwash Conference

Participants

Australia
Prof. M. L. E. Oliphant

Austria
Prof. H. Thirring

Canada
Dr. G. Brock Chisholm, Prof. J. S. Foster

China
Prof. Chou Pei Yuan

France
Prof. A. M. B. Lacassagne

Japan
Prof. I. Ogawa, Prof. S. Tomonaga, Prof. H. Yukawa

Poland
Prof. M. Danysz

U.K.
Prof. C. F. Powell, Prof. J. Rotblat

U.S.A.
Prof. D. F. Cavers, Prof. P. Doty, Prof. H. J. Muller, Prof. E. Rabinowitch, Prof. W. Selove, Prof. L. Szilard, Prof. V. Weisskopf

U.S.S.R.
Prof. A. M. Kuzin, Acad. D. V. Skobeltzyn, Acad. A. V. Topchiev

Professors Foster and Szilard abstained from the statement.

Observers and Scientific Staff

U.K.
Dr. E. H. S. Burhop

U.S.A.
Mrs. Ruth Adams

U.S.S.R.
Mr. V. P. Pavlichenko

3 STATEMENT FROM THE SECOND PUGWASH CONFERENCE, HELD IN LAC BEAUPORT, MARCH 31-APRIL 11, 1958

During the past two weeks an international conference of scientists has taken place at Lac Beauport, Quebec, to discuss the dangers resulting from the present atomic arms race, and means of diminishing them. A list of those attending is given below.

The Conference was made possible by the generous hospitality and assistance of Mr. and Mrs. Cyrus Eaton, and it originated in the following way.

In 1955, a public statement was issued by Lord Russell, Albert Einstein, and nine other scientists, directing attention to the dangers which had arisen as a result of the development of weapons of mass destruction, and calling for a meeting of scientists which would make a true and independent assessment of the hazards. A meeting for this purpose was held in Pugwash, Nova Scotia, in July, 1957, which was attended by 22 scientists. That meeting published a statement concerning the dangers arising from test-explosions of nuclear weapons and the consequences which would arise from their use in warfare; the problems of control of nuclear weapons; and the responsibilities of scientists.

The meeting at Pugwash set up a Continuing Committee of which Lord Russell was the Chairman, and Professor Powell, Professor Rotblat, Professor Rabinowitch, and Academician Skobeltzyn were members. The Committee was instructed to call further meetings should they appear desirable.

Since the meeting in Pugwash, there has been a further intensification of the arms race. At a meeting of the Continuing Committee in London December last, it was decided to call the present Conference. All the scientists invited warmly supported the objectives of the meeting, although some were unable to attend.

In calling the present Conference, the aim was to provide an opportunity for private discussion in which there could be a frank and friendly exchange of views on the many difficult issues which stand in the way of a general settlement among the powers and the establishment of a lasting peace.

Most of the discussions of the Conference were grouped under three main headings: the dangers of the present situation; means of diminishing the immediate dangers; and means of relaxing tension.

The topics discussed included: dangers of wars arising from technological accidents or as a result of conflicts between small nations; the biological hazards consequent on fallout; the problems arising from the possibility of the acquisition of nuclear weapons by additional nations; problems posed by the development of long-range rockets; problems of bases on foreign territory; problems of large conventional forces; the political and technological aspects of a ban on tests; the problems of general political and military stabilization; short and long-term policies aimed at establishing peace; the co-operation between nations in joint projects of a constructive nature; exchange of students and scientists; and measures for promoting international trust.

The Conference showed that in spite of different approaches to particular problems, there was a common agreement on the nature and magnitude of the grave dangers of our present situation, and a common desire to contribute to their removal by bringing about lasting peace through political settlements, and ultimately through far-reaching disarmament. The friendly atmosphere of the meeting, and a sense of common purpose, contributed greatly to the usefulness of the discussion.

Even in a short conference, it was found possible to make a serious appraisal of some of the decisive problems of our times. In a period of technological and scientific advance of unprecedented speed, we believe that scientists have a special responsibility and a special competence to promote informed opinion. With this aim in mind, the materials of this Conference will be made available to interested governments. It is not our intention, however, at this time to publish the details of our discussions and conclusions. Rather, each of us will seek to present the results of the Conference to scientists and others who may be interested.

The Conference recognizes the need to hold further meetings, some of which may differ from the present one in the number of participants and in general type. It favours the plan presented by the Continuing Committee to hold another Conference in September, probably in Austria, which will be more broadly representative and with a larger number of participants. In addition to discussing the findings of the present Conference, the next meeting will deal with the long-term problem, "Peace in the Atomic Age."

Participants

Australia
Prof. M. L. E. Oliphant

Canada
Prof. Cyrias Ouellet, Sir Robert Watson-Watt

China
Prof. Chou Pei Yuan

Federal German Republic
Prof. C. F. von Weizsäcker

France
Prof. Bernard Gregory

U.K.
Sir Charles G. Darwin, Prof. C. F. Powell, Prof. J. Rotblat, Prof. C. H. Waddington

Appendix 3 150

U.S.A.
Prof. John Edsall, Prof. Morton Grodzins, Dr. William A. Higinbotham, Col. Richard S. Leghorn, Prof. Linus Pauling, Prof. Eugene Rabinowitch, Prof. Leo Szilard, Prof. Jerome B. Wiesner

U.S.S.R.
Prof. A. M. Kuzin, Acad. D. V. Skobeltzyn, Acad. A. V. Topchiev, Acad. A. P. Vinogradov

Observers and Scientific Staff

U.K.
Dr. Patricia J. Lindop

U.S.S.R.
Mr. V. P. Pavlichenko

4 STATEMENT FROM THE THIRD PUGWASH CONFERENCE, HELD IN KITZBÜHEL AND VIENNA, SEPTEMBER 14-20, 1958

VIENNA DECLARATION

1. Necessity to End Wars

We meet in Kitzbühel and in Vienna at a time when it has become evident that the development of nuclear weapons makes it possible for man to destroy civilization and, indeed, himself; the means of destruction are being made ever more efficient. The scientists attending our meetings have long been concerned with this development, and they are unanimous in the opinion that a full-scale nuclear war would be a world-wide catastrophe of unprecedented magnitude.

In our opinion defence against nuclear attack is very difficult. Unfounded faith in defensive measures may even contribute to an outbreak of war.

Although the nations may agree to eliminate nuclear weapons and other weapons of mass destruction from the arsenals of the world, the knowledge of how to produce such weapons can never be destroyed. They remain for all time a potential threat for mankind. In any future major war, each belligerent state will feel not only free but compelled to undertake immediate production of nuclear weapons; for no state, when at war, can be sure that such steps are not being taken by the enemy. We believe that, in such a situation, a major industrial power would require less than one year to begin accumulating weapons. From then on, the only restraint against their employment in war would be agreements not to use them, which were concluded in times of peace. The decisive power of nuclear weapons, however, would make the temptation to use them almost irresistible, particularly to leaders who are facing defeat. It appears, therefore, that atomic weapons are likely to be employed in any future major war with all their terrible consequences.

It is sometimes suggested that localized wars, with limited objective, might still be fought without catastrophic consequences. History shows, however, that the risk of local conflicts growing into major wars is too great to be acceptable in the age of weapons of mass destruction. Mankind must, therefore, set itself the task of eliminating all wars, including local wars.

2. Requirements for Ending the Arms Race

The armaments race is the result of distrust between states; it also contributes to this distrust. Any step that mitigates the arms race, and leads to even small reductions in armaments and armed forces, on an equitable basis and subject to necessary control, is therefore desirable. We welcome all steps in this direction and, in particular, the recent agreement in Geneva between representatives of East and West about the feasibility of detecting test-explosions. As scientists, we take particular pleasure in the fact that this unanimous agreement, the first after a long series of unsuccessful international disarmament negotiations, was made possible by mutual understanding and a common objective approach by scientists from different countries. We note with satisfaction that the governments of the U.S.A., U.S.S.R., and U.K. have approved the statements and the conclusion contained in the report of the technical experts. This is a significant success; we most earnestly hope that this approval will soon be followed by an international agreement leading to the cessation of all nuclear weapon tests and an effective system of control. This would be a first step toward the relaxation of international tension and the end of the arms race.

It is generally agreed that any agreement on disarmament, and in particular nuclear disarmament, requires measures of control to protect every party from possible evasion. Through their technical competence, scientists are well aware that effective control will in some cases be relatively easy, while it is very difficult in others. For example, the conference of experts in Geneva has agreed that the cessation of bomb tests could be monitored by a suitable network of detecting stations. On the other hand, it will be a technical problem of great difficulty to account fully for existing stocks of nuclear weapons and other means of mass destruction. An agreement to cease production of nuclear weapons presents a problem of intermediate technical difficulty between these two extreme examples.

We recognize that the accumulation of large stocks of nuclear weapons has made a completely reliable system of controls for far-reaching nuclear disarmament extremely difficult, perhaps impossible. For this disarmament to become possible, nations may have to depend, in addition to a practical degree of technical verification, on a combination of political agreements, of successful international security arrangements, and of experience of successful co-operation in various areas. Together, these can create the climate of mutual trust, which does not now exist, and an assurance that nations recognize the mutual political advantages of avoiding suspicion.

Recognizing the difficulties of the technological situation, scientists feel an obligation to impress on their peoples and on their governments the need for policies which will encourage international trust and reduce mutual apprehension. Mutual apprehensions cannot be reduced by assertions of good will; their reduction will require political adjustment and the establishment of active co-operation.

3. What War Would Mean

Our conclusions about the possible consequences of war have been supported by reports and papers submitted to our Conference. These documents indicate that if, in a future war, a substantial proportion of the nuclear weapons already manufactured were delivered against urban targets, most centres of civilization in the belligerent countries would be totally destroyed, and most of their populations killed. This would be true whether the **bombs used derived most of their power from fusion reactions** (so-called "clean" bombs) or principally from fission reactions (so-called "dirty" bombs). In addition to destroying major centres of population and industry, such bombs would also wreck the economy of the country attacked, through the destruction of vital means of distribution and communication.

Major states have already accumulated large stocks of "dirty" nuclear weapons; it appears that they are continuing to do so. From a strictly military point of view, dirty bombs have advantages in some situations; this makes likely their use in a major way.

The local fallout resulting from extensive use of 'dirty" bombs would cause the death of a large part of the population in the country attacked. Following their explosion in large numbers (each explosion equivalent to that of millions of tons of ordinary chemical explosive), radioactive fallout would be distributed, not only over the territory to which they were delivered but, in varying intensity, over the rest of the earth's surface. Many millions of deaths would thus be produced, not only in belligerent but also in non-belligerent countries, by the acute effects of radiation.

There would be, further, substantial long-term radiation damage, to human and other organisms everywhere, from somatic effects such as leukaemia, bone cancer, and shortening of the life span; and from genetic damage affecting the hereditary traits transmitted to the progeny.

Knowledge of human genetics is not yet sufficient to allow precise predictions of consequences likely to arise from the considerable increase in the rate of mutation which would ensue from unrestricted nuclear war. However, geneticists believe that they may well be serious for the future of a surviving world population.

It is sometimes suggested that in a future war, the use of nuclear weapons might be restricted to objectives such as military bases, troop concentrations, airfields, and other communication centres; and that attacks on large centres of population could thus be avoided.

Even tactical weapons now have a large radius of action; cities and towns are commonly closely associated with centres of supply and transportation. We, therefore, believe that even a "restricted" war would lead, despite attempted limitation of targets, to widespread devastation of the territory in which it took place, and to the destruction of much of its population. Further, an agreement not to use cities for military purposes, entered into in order to justify their immunity from attack, is unlikely to be maintained to the end of a war, particularly by the losing side. The latter would also be strongly tempted to use nuclear bombs against the population centres of the enemy, in the hope of breaking his will to continue the war.

4. Hazards of Bomb Tests

At our first conference it had been agreed that while the biological hazards of bomb tests may be small compared with similar hazards to which mankind is exposed from other sources, hazards from tests exist and should receive close and continual study. Since then, an extensive investigation by the United Nations Scientific Committee on the Effects of Atomic Radiation has been carried out and its authoritative conclusions published. In this case, too, scientists from many different countries have been able to arrive at a unanimous agreement. Their conclusions confirm that the bomb tests produce a definite hazard and that they will claim a significant number of victims in present and following generations. Though the magnitude of the genetic damage appears to be relatively small compared with that produced by natural causes, the incidence of leukaemia and bone cancer due to the radioactivity from test explosions may, in the estimate of the U.N. committee, add significantly to the natural incidence of these diseases. This conclusions depends on the assumption (not shared by all authorities in the field) that these effects can be produced even by the smallest amount of radiation. This uncertainty calls for extensive study and, in the meantime, for a prudent acceptance of the most pessimistic assumption. It lends emphasis to the generally agreed conclusion that all unnecessary exposure of mankind to radiation is undesirable and should be avoided.

It goes without saying that the biological damage from a war, in which many nuclear bombs would be used, would be incomparably larger than that from tests; the main immediate problem before mankind is thus the establishment of conditions that would eliminate war.

5. Science and International Co-operation

We believe that, as scientists, we have an important contribution to make toward establishing trust and co-operation among nations. Science is, by long tradition, an international undertaking. Scientists with different national allegiances easily find a common basis of understanding; they use the same concepts and the same methods; they work toward common intellectual goals, despite differences in philosophical, economic, or political views. The rapidly growing importance of science on the affairs of mankind increases the importance of the community of understanding.

The ability of scientists all over the world to understand one another, and to work together, is an excellent instrument for bridging the gap between nations and for uniting them around common aims. We believe that working together in every field where international co-operation proves possible makes an important contribution toward establishing an appreciation of the community of nations. It can contribute to the development of the climate of mutual trust, which is necessary for the resolution of political conflicts between nations, and which is an essential background to effective disarmament. We hope scientists everywhere will recognize their responsibility, to mankind and to their own nations, to contribute thought, time, and energy to the furthering of international co-operation.

Several international scientific undertakings have already had considerable success. We mention only the century-old, world wide co-operation in weather science, the two International Polar Years which preceded (by seventy-five and twenty-five years, respectively), the present International Geophysical Year, and the Atoms-for-Peace Conferences. We earnestly hope that efforts will be made to initiate similar collaboration in other fields of study. Certainly they will have the enthusiastic support of scientists all over the world.

We call for an increase in the unrestricted flow of scientific information among nations, and for a wide exchange of scientists. We believe that nations which build their national security on secrecy of scientific developments sacrifice the interests of peace, and of the progress of science, for temporary advantages. It is our belief that science can best serve mankind if it is free from interference by any dogma imposed from outside, and if it exercises its right to question all postulates, including its own.

6. Technology in the Service of Peace

In our time, pure and applied science have become increasingly interdependent. The achievements of fundamental, experimental and theoretical science are more and more rapidly transformed into new technological developments. This accelerated trend is manifest, alike in the creation of weapons of increased destructiveness, and in the development of means for the increased wealth and well-being of mankind. We believe that the tradition of mutual understanding and of international co-operation, which have long existed in fundamental science, can and should be extended to many fields of technology. The International Atomic Energy Agency, for example, aims not merely at co-operation for establishing facts about atomic energy, but also at helping the nations of the world to develop a new source of energy as a basis for the improvement of their material welfare. We believe that international co-operation in this and other fields, such as economic development and the promotion of health, should be greatly strengthened.

The extremely low level of living in the industrially underdeveloped countries of the world is and will remain a source of international tension. We see an urgent need to forward studies and programmes for the effective industrialization of these countries. This would not only improve the level of living of the majority of the population of the world; it would also help to reduce the sources of conflict between the highly industrialized powers. Such studies would offer fruitful scope for co-operative efforts between scientists of all nations.

The great increase in the ease and speed of communications, and our increasing understanding of how the forces of nature influence the living conditions of nations in different parts of the world, show us, in a way not previously possible, the extent to which the prosperity of individual nations is connected with, and dependent upon, that of mankind as a whole; and how rapidly it could be increased by common international effort. We believe that through such common effort, the co-existence between nations of different social and economic structure can become not merely peaceful and competitive, but to an increasing degree co-operative, and therefore more stable.

As scientists, we are deeply aware of the great change in the condition of mankind which has been brought about by the modern development and application of science. Given peace, mankind stands at the beginning of a great scientific age. Science can provide mankind with an ever increasing understanding of the forces of nature and the means of harnessing them. This will bring about a great increase in the well-being, health, and prosperity of all men.

7. The Responsibility of Scientists

We believe it to be a responsibility of scientists in all countries to contribute to the education of the peoples by spreading among them a wide understanding of the dangers and potentialities offered by the unprecedented growth of science. We appeal to our colleagues everywhere to contribute to this effort, both through enlightenment of adult populations, and through education of the coming generations. In particular, education should stress improvement of all forms of human relations and should eliminate any glorification of war and violence.

Scientists are, because of their special knowledge, well equipped for early awareness of the danger and the promise arising from scientific discoveries. Hence, they have a special competence and a special responsibility in relation to the most pressing problems of our times.

In the present conditions of distrust between nations, and of the race for military supremacy which arises from it, all branches of science--physics, chemistry, biology, psychology--have become increasingly involved in military developments. In the eyes of the people of many countries, science has become associated with the development of weapons. Scientists are either admired for their contribution to national security, or damned for having brought mankind into jeopardy by their invention of weapons of mass destruction. The increasing material support which science now enjoys in many countries is mainly due to its importance, direct or indirect, to the military strength of the nation and to its degree of success in the arms race. This diverts science from its true purpose, which is to increase human knowledge, and to promote man's mastery over the forces of nature for the benefit of all.

We deplore the conditions which lead to this situation, and appeal to all peoples and their governments to establish conditions of lasting and stable peace.

Participants

Australia
Prof. M. L. E. Oliphant

Austria
Prof. Hans Thirring

Bulgaria
Acad. G. Nadjakov

Canada
Dr. Brock Chisholm, Sir Robert Watson-Watt

Czechoslovakia
Dr. Viktor Knapp, Dr. J. Kožešník

Denmark
Prof. Mogens Pihl

The Third Pugwash Conference

Federal German Republic
Prof. Max Born, Prof. G. Burkhardt, Prof. Helmut Hönl, Prof. Werner Kliefoth, Dr. Hanfried Lenz

France
Father Pierre-Leon Dubarle, Dr. Bernard Gregory, Dr. J. Gueron, Prof. Antoine Lacassagne

German Democratic Republic
Prof. Gunther Rienäcker

Hungary
Prof. Lajos Janossy

India
Dr. H. J. Bhabha, Sir K. S. Krishnan, Prof. P. C. Mahalanobis

Italy
Prof. E. Amaldi, Prof. E. Boeri

Japan
Prof. Yasuo Miyake, Prof. Iwao Ogawa, Prof. Schoichi Sakata, Prof. S. Tomonaga, Prof. Hideki Yukawa

Netherlands
Prof. B. R. A. Nijboer

Norway
Dr. Gunnar Randers

Poland
Prof. Leopold Infeld

U.K.
Lord Boyd-Orr, Dame Kathleen Lonsdale, Prof. C. F. Powell, Prof. M. H. L. Pryce, Prof. J. Rotblat, The Earl Russell, Sir George Thomson

U.S.A.
Prof. Harrison Brown, Dr. David Cavers, Prof. Charles Coryell, Prof. William Davidon, Prof. Bernard Feld, Prof. Bentley Glass, Prof. Morton Grodzins, Mr. David Hill, Dr. Martin Kaplan, Prof. H. J. Muller, Prof. Jay Orear, Dr. Harry Palevsky, Prof. Linus Pauling, Prof. Eugene Rabinowitch, Prof. Frederick Seitz, Prof. Walter Selove, Prof. Leo Szilard, Dr. Alvin Weinberg, Prof. Victor Weisskopf, Prof. Eugene Wigner

U.S.S.R.
Acad. N. N. Bogolubov, Prof. N. A. Dobrotin, Acad. E. K. Fedorov, Prof. E. A. Korovin, Prof. A. M. Kuzin, Mr. V. P. Pavlichenko, Acad. D. V. Skobeltzyn, Acad. A. V. Topchiev, Dr. V. S. Vavilov, Acad. A. P. Vinogradov

Appendix 4

Yugoslavia
Prof. Paul Savic

Observers and Scientific Staff

Austria
Dr. R. Jungk, Mr. E. Schwarcz

U.K.
Dr. E. H. S. Burhop, Dr. Patricia Lindop, Mr. P. Noel Baker

U.S.A.
Prof. B. Commoner, Mr. A. G. Mezerik, Dr. V. L. Sailor

IAEA
Dr. W. W. Grigorieff

5 STATEMENT FROM THE FOURTH PUGWASH CONFERENCE, HELD IN BADEN, JUNE 25-JULY 4, 1959

Twenty-five internationally-known scientists are meeting in Baden bei Wien, Austria, June 25 to July 4, to discuss problems of "Arms Control and World Security" which have arisen from the military applications of scientific discoveries.

This is the fourth of a continuing series of meetings, the first of which was held in Pugwash, Nova Scotia, in July 1957. Many of the scientists present have also attended former "Pugwash" meetings.

The value of the discussions lies in the fact that they are private, but not secret; organized, but not formal. The participants were invited in their personal capacities and not as representatives of national or other organizations. The meeting is intended to increase the depth of understanding and the width of view of each participant in the fields under discussion; it did not have the aim of formulating any formal recommendations.

Many subjects were discussed, dealing with the different aspects of the problem of armaments control and world security. Frank and extensive discussions were carried out in the spirit of complete frankness and desire for mutual understanding.

Participants

Austria
Prof. Hans Thirring

Canada
Sir Robert Watson-Watt

People's Republic of China
Prof. Chou Pei Yuan

Federal German Republic
Prof. C. F. von Weizsäcker

U.K.
Prof. P. M. S. Blackett, Prof. C. F. Powell, Prof. Joseph Rotblat

U.S.A.
Prof. Harrison Brown, Prof. Bernard T. Feld, Dr. Jerome Frank, Dr. Morton Grodzins, Col. Richard Leghorn, Prof. Eugene Rabinowitch, Dr. Roger Revelle, Dr. J. Spingarn, Prof. Leo Szilard, Prof. Victor Weisskopf, Dr. Jerome B. Wiesner, Prof. Eugene P. Wigner

Appendix 5

U.S.S.R.
Acad. N. N. Bogolubov, Acad. E. K. Fedorov, Mr. V. P. Pavlichenko,
Acad. N. M. Sisakian, Prof. N. A. Talensky, Acad. A. P. Vinogradov

Scientific Staff

U.S.A.
Mrs. Ruth Adams

STATEMENT FROM THE FIFTH PUGWASH CONFERENCE, HELD IN PUGWASH, AUGUST 24-29, 1959

The fifth in the series of Pugwash Conferences of scientists, aimed at assessing the dangers to humanity arising from developments of modern science and technology, has met in Pugwash, Nova Scotia, on August 24-29, as guests of Mr. Cyrus Eaton. Twenty-six scientists from eight nations attended the Conference.

The purpose of the Conference was to assess the potentialities of chemical and biological agents as weapons, and to explore possible means for preventing their production or use in war.

The subject of chemical and biological warfare has been shrouded in official secrecy. For years large projects have existed in several countries with the stated purpose of developing defence means against such weapons. We have no direct information about the results of these projects, but inevitably they increase the efficiency and destructiveness of various types of biological and chemical weapons, and result in the development of new techniques. Judging from the number of technical workers involved in such projects and the money expended, much knowledge related to the production and delivery of micro-organisms for war purposes has probably been gained. Moreover, unsupported statements appear which suggest that such weapons have enormous lethal or incapacitating effects against man, can destroy plants and animals, and have advantages under certain conditions of war. Recently, a concerted effort appears to have been made to suggest that these weapons are more "humane" than other means of warfare.

We have discussed the general nature of such weapons as well as the properties of the individual agents and their methods of delivery, and have compared them with other weapons. Our discussions suggest that the difficulties of establishing a stable and lasting peace are aggravated by the fact that all nations, whether or not they possess nuclear weapons, might produce biological and chemical weapons; international tension would consequently be increased.

Potentialities of Biological and Chemical Weapons

Biological weapons--microbes, viruses and their toxic products--can be delivered and dispersed in such a way that fatal or incapacitating diseases might be produced over large areas. They can be produced cheaply on a significant scale, even in a country whose technological development is not highly advanced. Such weapons could be used either alone or together with others. The attack could be local or massive or could consist of individual acts of sabotage. The agent could be selected to cause a great many primary casualties, or to initiate epidemics.

Infective agents or toxins used as biological weapons would presumably have the following characteristics: (a) lethal or incapacitating when applied in small amounts; (b) remain potent when stored or dispersed; (c) the diseases they produce should not be preventable by simple sanitary precautions, or by customary practices of immunization; (d) neither the

Appendix 6   162

agents themselves nor the diseases they produce should be easily identifiable; (e) the diseases they produce should not be curable by customary drugs or antibiotics. Many well-known biological agents possess several or all of the foregoing attributes. The simultaneous use of two or more pathogenic organisms might assist the spread of infection and confuse diagnosis.

Highly virulent strains of some pathogenic agents can easily be selected, as can strains of virulent bacteria resistant to all usual antibiotics, drugs and to some disinfectants. Recent advances in microbial genetics make it possible to produce variants, some of which may be even more suitable for biological warfare than naturally occurring strains.

Quantitative information on the infectivity and toxicity for man of biological agents that might be used as weapons is too meagre for their effects to be compared at all accurately with those of nuclear weapons. However, a surprise attack on a city might in time cause numbers of casualties approaching those caused by a small atomic bomb. An attack with an infective agent, originally meant to be localized, might lead to an epidemic because of abnormal routes of delivery, the large number of primary casualties, or the disorganization of public health.

The meteorological and other conditions required for biological or chemical attacks on man are so exacting that the military effects will be far from certain. The necessary conditions for a successful attack might prevail only on some days and at limited times of the day, and would be subject to the errors of meteorological forecasting. The discharged material, instead of moving into and staying in the intended area, might recoil on the aggressor. Biological weapons would presumably be stabilized to withstand exposure to the atmosphere and so might remain active for long periods and ultimately fall anywhere.

Attacks on economically useful animals are subject to many of the same limitations as attacks on man. The most likely use of biological warfare on animals would be to disrupt the economy, which could be done by introducing various infections that spread very rapidly, and some of which are transmissible to man.

There are also agents that could be used to destroy crops, but their effects are unlikely to be important compared with attacks on human beings and animals. Chemicals such as plant hormones would produce the quickest and perhaps the most serious results, but to be effective would have to be applied over great areas. Some infectious diseases of plants could also be damaging, and their introduction could adversely affect the economy of a region for a long time; but most spread too slowly to influence the outcome of a war.

Chemical weapons ("poison gas" or other poisonous substances) were used in the first World War and on several subsequent occasions. In recent years new poisonous substances have been produced which are many times as active as the earlier agents. Means for their bulk production have also been improved, as have procedures for their dissemination over areas very much larger than those covered during chemical attacks in World War I. The production of chemical warfare agents could easily be disguised as peacetime chemical industry, or such industry could be quickly converted to produce them.

The so-called nerve gases, which are chemically similar to certain insecticides, are extremely potent and cheap, and cannot easily be countered with effective defensive measures. Masks and appropriate clothing can partially protect against them, but it is difficult to apply such protection to large populations; and it is unlikely that nerve gas casualties could be treated with antidotes soon enough after an attack to prevent serious consequences. New types of hallucinating agents or of poisons that give rise to transient mental disorganization, without recognizable permanent injury, have been advocated as a means of "humanizing" war. Although they do not kill directly, their use could have serious consequences, because individuals or groups of people exposed to them behave unpredictably and often irresponsibly. The extremely high level of toxicity of new types of poisonous materials, as well as the means available for their delivery, permit their effects to be compared with those of certain types of atomic weapons.

Summarizing the previous paragraphs, biological and chemical agents clearly represent considerable additions to modern arsenals. Yet, we realize that nuclear weapons, particularly modern hydrogen bombs, have a destructive power several orders of magnitude greater than chemical or biological weapons. As means of immediate and certain destruction, these weapons cannot compare with hydrogen bombs. The dependence of biological weapons on uncontrollable factors, such as meteorological conditions, and the difficulty of confining the effects to the attacked territory, make them especially unpredictable in scope and effect.

World-wide apprehension about biological and chemical weapons can be allayed only by measures tending to assure that they will not be produced or used. But, however difficult the international control of atomic weapons may be, the international control of biological and chemical weapons by any system of inspection seems incomparably more difficult.

The first reason is that the specific weapons, or combinations of weapons, likely to be used in a particular instance cannot be foreseen.

The second is that chemical or biological weapons can be selected and prepared in ordinary chemical or microbiological laboratories. The fact that no elaborate or large-scale facilities are needed makes it difficult to identify possible places of preparation for biological or chemical warfare. Even elaborate installations would resemble those normally used in vaccine or antibiotic production. It follows that small and large nations, whether industrially undeveloped or highly industrialized, might secretly prepare to use such weapons; and with each added nation possessing such capabilities, the danger of war would mount.

A third reason is that means of dispersal of chemical and biological agents of warfare are diverse, including planes, submarines and missiles, as well as saboteurs. Their delivery therefore cannot be prevented because it would require a ban on all forms of transport, civil as well as military.

If control by inspection is so extremely difficult, what alternative ways are there to decrease the danger that chemical and biological weapons will be used? It seems clear that international renunciation of the use of such weapons, as in the 1925 Geneva Protocol, cannot allay apprehension unless *all* nations, small as well as large, ratify such an agreement without reservation. This is the first necessary step.

Secrecy is clearly essential to preparations for biological and chemical warfare. On the one hand, it enables any nation planning aggression to depend upon the element of surprise, and upon the opponent's lack of effective counter measures taken in advance. On the other hand, the unknown is, of itself, a potent cause of human anxiety, and is even more so when associated with weapons of any kind. Any actual danger there may be will certainly be exaggerated wherever information about any aspect of the situation is denied. Secrecy on the part of possible enemies is even more productive of anxiety, suspicion and hostility, and may precipitate hostile reactions. Free and frank revelation of all scientific and technical developments is essential to a degree of mutual trust necessary to resolve the acute tensions that now plague the world.

The most hopeful approach to international regulation therefore seems to comprise (a) a general agreement to prohibit the use of such weapons, and (b) the renunciation of official secrecy and security controls over microbiological, toxicological, pharmaceutical and chemical-biological research.

In considering how to implement the second of the foregoing proposals, we note the already excellent effects of the report of the U.N. Scientific Committee on the Effects of Atomic Radiation. A comparable scientific committee, or a permanent U.N. Scientific Commission on biological and chemical modes of warfare, could help to dispel apprehension. A subsidiary function of either group might be to investigate impartially the claims by plaintiff nations that others had openly or surreptitiously used methods of biological or chemical warfare against them.

The very existence of such a Commission might in time arouse the conscience of the individual scientists of all nations, the only ultimately effective safeguard against violations.

In agreement with the Third Pugwash Conference in Vienna, we repeat that, in the end, only the absolute prevention of war will preserve human life and civilization in the face of chemical and biological as well as nuclear weapons. No ban of a single type of weapon, no agreement that leaves the general threat of war in existence, can protect mankind sufficiently. We, therefore, must look forward to a day when the preservation of peace will transcend the ambitions of individual nations.

Trust between nations cannot be established by proclamation, but only by experience, particularly by experience in co-operative work towards common aims. There is already an extensive interchange of scientific information and people in the sciences basic to the problems discussed in this statement. We must build on this. The Commission proposed to collect and evaluate information bearing on chemical and microbiological warfare should serve not only to allay the fears of mankind that new and ever more horrible weapons of such types will be invented, but further to dispel the miasma of secrecy that fosters international suspicion and tension, and in its place to extend the benevolent application of microbiological and chemical knowledge for the benefit of all men.

Participants

Canada
Dr. Brock Chisholm, Prof. Claude E. Dolman, Prof. Donald Kerr, Sir Robert Watson-Watt

Denmark
Dr. Preben von Magnus

France
Dr. Andre Lwoff, Dr. Pierre Thibault

India
Dr. M. L. Ahuja

Sweden
Prof. Sven Gard

U.K.
Mr. F. C. Bawden, Dr. Patricia J. Lindop, Prof. Gordon Manley, Prof. Joseph Rotblat, Prof. M. G. P. Stoker

U.S.A.
Prof. H. Bentley Glass, Dr. Charles C. Higgins, Dr. Martin M. Kaplan, Prof. Chauncey D. Leake, Prof. Hugo Muench, Prof. Eugene Rabinowitch, Prof. Alexander Rich, Prof. Theodor Rosebury

U.S.S.R.
Acad. Mikhail M. Dubinin, Prof. Alexander A. Imshenetsky, Mr. Vladimir P. Pavlichenko, Prof. A. A. Smorodintsev

7 STATEMENT FROM THE SIXTH PUGWASH CONFERENCE, HELD IN MOSCOW, NOVEMBER 27–DECEMBER 5, 1960

The sixth International Conference of Scientists, organized by the Pugwash Continuing Committee, has been held in Moscow from November 27 to December 5, 1960, and has been attended by 75 scientists from 15 countries. Its discussions have been devoted to the problems of disarmament and world security.

The beliefs and aspirations of the scientists who participated in the previous conferences were expressed in the Vienna Declaration of September 1958, which **was** adopted by the members of the Third Conference who met in Kitzbühel, Austria. This declaration expressed the belief that the development of nuclear and other weapons of mass destruction makes it imperative to exclude them, and indeed, war itself, from the life of mankind. It stated that this aim should be achieved through disarmament under effective control, and by promoting widespread constructive co-operation between all nations. It expressed confidence that soon an agreement on cessation of nuclear weapons tests would be reached.

In the past two years new tensions have appeared in international relations; and in the face of these developments we reassert our firm belief in the validity of those basic principles of the Vienna Declaration set out above.

We consider of great importance the resolution unanimously adopted by the General Assembly of the United Nations in 1959 on the need to establish a peaceful world in which all means of warfare shall have been abolished under effective control. In agreement with this aim of complete and general disarmament, under effective control, we have had discussions of the means whereby this aim could be put into effect. We have also given detailed consideration to the nature and the time sequence of the stages in plans for disarmament, and the measures of international control for their effective verification, and have reached a common understanding on some of these matters of substance. We have agreed that, to be generally acceptable, such plans must ensure that at no time, as disarmament proceeds, is any substantial military advantage gained from it by any of the powers.

We have also agreed that successful completion of a disarmament plan will require that the present suspicions and artificial barriers between nations be gradually reduced and replaced by a growing sense of common interest, mutual understanding, and confidence. Progress in disarmament itself will be a most important factor in this change in the climate of public opinion. The fundamental interests of all states and peoples and the acute danger of accidental war require early and substantial progress in disarmament, in order that the successful and mutually satisfactory implementation of concrete measures may both reduce common dangers, and lead to an increase in public confidence in the possibility of attaining the main goals.

The following were among other important topics which were considered: the history and dangers of the arms race, the ban on tests of nuclear weapons, surprise attack, measures for maintaining peace during and after disarmament, the particular role of scientists in the creation of friendly relations between states and peoples, and measures of positive collaboration between them, including improvement of the welfare of peoples in the economically less developed areas of the world. The working papers submitted to the Conference, coming from scientists of many countries, showed that much work had been done, and the resulting discussions were correspondingly well informed.

The discussions have proceeded in a cordial and constructive atmosphere with a growing readiness by the participants to make serious efforts to understand different points of view. This has permitted a number of misunderstandings to be removed, and differences of view to be more clearly understood.

The frankness of the discussions and the participation in our Moscow meeting of many outstanding scientists, some for the first time, lead us to believe that the Pugwash Conferences are making a growing contribution towards overcoming the grave danger of the present world situation, and encourage us to continue them. The next conference on the subject of disarmament and world security will be held in the course of 1961, and it is proposed to organize it in the U.S.A. We also intend to proceed with plans for other conferences, dealing with the problems of constructive co-operation between nations in pure and applied science.

The present situation is one of great danger and great opportunity brought about by the scientific and technological triumphs of our time. The overriding task is to prevent the outbreak of a devastating war and to establish a stable peace in which war is impossible. In the light of the experience of our conference, we reaffirm both the responsibility and the competence of scientists to help in solving the problems arising from applications of their work.

In the tasks of the immediate future, of helping to secure early and substantial measures towards complete disarmament, of promoting widespread scientific co-operation and friendly relations between scientists on an international scale, and the widespread application of science for the benefit of man, we need all the goodwill and all the creative intellectual power we can muster. We ask scientists all over the world to contribute to the study and solution of these problems, which are crucial for the future of mankind.

Participants

Australia
Dr. J. Burton

Austria
Professor H. Thirring

Bulgaria
Professor G. Nadjakov

Appendix 7   168

Canada
Professor J. Polanyi, Sir Robert Watson-Watt

People's Republic of China
Professor Chou Pei-Yuan, Professor Yu Kwang-Yuan, Professor Chang Wei,
Mr. Feng Ping-Fu

Czechoslovakia
Professor R. Brdička, Professor V. Husa, Professor V. Kopal

Federal German Republic
Professor G. Burkhardt, Dr. E. Heimendahl

France
Dr. B. P. Gregory, Dr. H. Marcovich

German Democratic Republic
Professor H. Barwich, Professor H. Pose

Hungary
Professor I. Rusznyak

Netherlands
Professor B. V. A. Röling

Poland
Professor K. Kumaniecki, Professor W. Stefanski, Professor P. Szulkin

U.K.
The Hon. A. Buchan, Professor O. R. Frisch, Professor A. Haddow, Sir Ben
Lockspeiser, The Rt. Hon. P. Noel-Baker, Professor R. E. Peierls, Professor C. F. Powell, Professor J. Rotblat

U.S.A.
Professor D. Brennan, Professor Harrison Brown, Professor P. Doty,
Professor J. Edsall, Professor B. Feld, Professor G. Fischer, Professor D.
Frisch, Professor Bentley Glass, Professor M. Grodzins, Dr. W. Higinbotham,
Professor D. Inglis, Mr. A. Katz, Dr. D. Kybal, Mr. R. Leghorn, Professor
J. Orear, Dr. J. Phelps, Professor E. Rabinowitch, Professor A. Rich,
Professor W. W. Rostow, Professor T. Schelling, Professor L. Sohn,
Professor L. Szilard, Professor J. Wiesner

U.S.S.R.
Academician A. P. Alexandrov, Corr. Member A. A. Arzumanyan, Academician
A. A. Blagonravov, Academician N. N. Bogolubov, Academician M. M. Dubinin,
Corr. Member V. S. Emelyanov, Academician E. K. Fedorov, Corr. Member
A. A. Imshenetsky, Corr. Member I. S. Isakov, Academician P. L. Kapitza,
Corr. Member V. M. Khvostov, Corr. Member E. A. Korovin, Professor M. I.
Rubinstein, Corr. Member M. A. Sadovsky, Academician N. N. Semenov, Academician D. V. Skobeltzyn, Professor N. A. Talensky, Academician I. E.
Tamm, Academician A. V. Topchiev, Academician A. N. Tupolev, Academician
A. P. Vinogradov

The above statement was adopted by the Conference *nem. con.*, with the following abstaining: Professors Brennan, Schelling and Szilard.

Observers and Scientific Staff

U.K.
Dr. Patricia J. Lindop, Mr. Wayland Young

U.S.A.
Mrs. Ruth Adams

U.S.S.R.
Acad. A. N. Nesmeyanov, Mr. V. P. Pavlichenko

8 STATEMENT FROM THE SEVENTH PUGWASH CONFERENCE, HELD IN STOWE, SEPTEMBER 5-9, 1961

The Seventh Conference on Science and World Affairs was held at Stowe, Vermont, September 5-9, 1961. Forty-one scientists from 12 countries attended the Conference.

This Conference had as its theme "International Co-operation in Pure and Applied Science." Our previous conferences have been chiefly concerned with ways of preventing the misuse of science in the wholesale destruction of mankind. In this Conference at Stowe, we have turned to the discussion of constructive international co-operation in science, because it is a way to create trust between nations, a trust which develops from common interests and from experience in working together.

Science misused by nations to foster competitive interests as world powers makes possible the destruction of mankind. Science used co-operatively by all nations for the increase of human knowledge and the improvement of man's productive capacity can give all men on earth a satisfactory and worthwhile life. Scientists bear a responsibility both to foster the constructive use of science and to help in preventing its destructive use.

The deliberations of the Conference were carried out in plenary sessions and in meetings of working groups. These groups were six in number as follows: I. Co-operation in the Earth Sciences; II. Co-operation in Space Research; III. Co-operation in the Life Sciences; IV. Co-operation in the Physical Sciences; V. Co-operation in Assistance to Developing Nations; VI. Exchange of Scientists and Scientific Information.

Similar suggestions for co-operative research activities arose **independently from different working groups. This is reflected in several places** in this statement. This is a welcome indication of the essential unity in science. The discussions were carried on in a spirit of friendly co-operation and full agreement was reached by the entire Conference on the suggestions enumerated below.

I. CO-OPERATION IN THE EARTH SCIENCES

The planet earth is the common abode of all humans. They have a common interest, both intellectual and practical, in increasing the knowledge of the structure and dynamics of the earth.

As the work of the IGY has demonstrated, the earth sciences present an especially appropriate and fruitful field in international collaboration. The work in these fields must be carried forward on an international scale, as no one country is likely to provide sufficient funds to conduct on its own the world-wide investigations which are required.

In recognition of the developing sociological and engineering problems posed by the present trends in earth sciences, we recommend the **enlisting** of the social and engineering sciences in this work.

The following concrete proposals are made.

A. A Survey of the Entire Ocean in Three Dimensions

1. **The Ocean Floor.** We propose an international programme to develop a detailed map of the floor of the world ocean, including sub-bottom reflecting layers. This programme would require, in the first instance, international agreements on exchange of data and methods, including intercalibration of instruments.

2. **Waters of the Ocean.** An international programme to survey and map the three dimensional distributions of temperatures, salinity, density, dissolved oxygen, and nutrient salts, under average conditions, of the ocean, and synoptic surveys to develop the broad picture of seasonal and shorter-period changes in more limited areas, as well as the study of the interactions among the major bodies of water in the ocean.

3. **Ocean Life.** An international survey and mapping showing the major biological provinces of the ocean and determination of the fertility of the waters at all levels in the food chain and the standing crop of food material available for human use.

Prosecution of the foregoing programme would necessarily involve the establishment of world-wide navigation and communication systems and allocation of radio-frequencies for earth-science measurements which would serve many other significant objectives. These matters, as well as the new ocean-wide surveys recommended above, fall within the province of the International Oceanographic Commission (IOC).

B. Earth's Crust and Mantle

1. **Deep Drilling Programme.** The objective of drilling through the earth's crust to the mantle at selected points around the globe presents many unsolved technical problems which call for international collaboration. We agree, therefore, that the calling of an international conference on these problems is an urgent first step. The conference would provide for the exchange and pooling of drilling techniques developed by present national programmes and would consider methods for the solution of such unsolved problems as the re-entry and management of high temperatures to be encountered in depth even at oceanic sites. The survey and selection of drilling sites would be a primary responsibility of this conference. The conference could also undertake the establishment of scientific objectives for the drilling programme. We further agree that the execution of the programme would benefit from the continuous exchange of technique and personnel, and that the full exchange of information and of samples is imperative for the success of the programme. It is recommended that when the prime contractor for the United States Mohole Project is selected, arrangements should be made for such meetings and the exchange of accumulated experiences.

C. Total Environmental Forecasting

The water-air interface appears to be the primary site of heat, water vapour and momentum exchange between the oceans and the atmosphere, and so the key to short-term and long-term forecasting of weather, climate, and changes in the ocean. Together, the oceans and atmosphere constitute a huge and complex heat engine. To some degree the ocean-half of this system acts as the fly wheel over both short and long time periods. Studies of these phenomena must necessarily be conducted on a long-term and worldwide basis.

An international conference should be called to consider and to organize the establishment of a world-wide network of radio-telemetering observational buoys. This system of buoys would render continuous reports on atmospheric conditions and so contribute to the completion of the world weather map. It would also continuously monitor the energy and water vapour energy exchange between the ocean and the atmosphere, and would observe the changes in the flow of ocean currents in three dimensions. Over a sufficiently long period, such a network of buoys would help to assign reliable values to the rate of overturn of the ocean as a whole, a key problem in both climatological forecasts and in the safe disposal of radioactive wastes at sea. The hydrographic offices of the major maritime nations, as well as the World Meteorological Organization (WMO) should be encouraged to stimulate such a programme.

D. Resources

1. Fresh Water. The rising world population and the increasing concentration of that population in metropolitan centres is already pressing upon the water resources easily available for direct human consumption, for industrial purposes, and for agriculture. We agree that an international conference should be called to consider the organization of an International Hydrologic Decade for the study of the many unknowns that surround this ominous development.

The proposed conference would institute a world-wide survey of water resources and of the future course of water use. Such a programme would have the significant incidental benefit of attracting the interests of scientists to a field in which basic studies have been neglected. Subjects for immediate consideration are the qualities of water considered from the point of view of various uses, the economical desalting treatment of water, the recycling and the re-use of water. The conference necessary to set such studies in motion should be called by UNESCO.

2. Living Resources of the Ocean. Acre per acre, the oceans today sustain at least as large a plant crop on the average as does the land, yet man now gets only about one per cent of his food requirements from the sea. The oceans, therefore, offer a means for the rapid solution of the protein deficiency afflicting two-thirds of the world population. It is apparent that these resources can best be exploited to this end through international co-operation. The ultimate aim should be to elevate the fishing industry from a hunting industry to an agricultural technology. It has been estimated that existing fishery techniques could easily produce five times the present annual crop of fish, which is at present about 30 million metric tons. This yield could be even more greatly increased by development of means for helping the winds to overturn the oceans more rapidly. This is not an insurmountable undertaking, but experiments to this end must be conducted under international auspices (Food and Agricultural Organization--FAO, and Scientific Commission for Oceanographic Research--SCOR).

3. <u>Mineral Resources of the Ocean Floor</u>. Recent studies of the ocean floor show a vast reserve of minerals, especially nickel, cobalt, copper, and manganese. By means of bottom-photography organized on a world-wide basis, the potentiality of this reserve may be more fully assessed. The necessary observational programme could be organized by SCOR.

4. <u>Natural Catastrophes</u>. The forecasting, minimizing or eventual control of violent natural catastrophes is one objective of the earth sciences which will also require continuing international co-operation. Earthquakes, tsunamis, volcanic eruptions, hurricanes, and tornadoes constitute the principal hazards of this kind.

With respect to the first three, a better international seismological network, including better instrumentation and distribution of stations is required. More detailed studies of hurricanes and tornadoes would reveal whether or not man can exert some control over these phenomena.

To implement these programmes, we further recommend:

(a) That insofar as possible existing international organizations such as IOC, UNESCO, FAO, WMO, SCOR, SCAR*, etc., be the means of furthering these programmes.

(b) Since what is suggested here represents a long-term enlargement of their present activities, increased funds may have to be requested to finance continuing international conferences and studies in these various fields. At the outset, at any rate, the funds necessary to finance the travel of specialists to conferences so as to plan productive international programmes are relatively small, and within the means of the agencies suggested. If forward-looking programmes are agreed to, as was the case during IGY, it is likely that each nation will find means of financing its share of the total long-range programme.

(c) There is at present no effective means of promoting atmospheric research on a world-wide basis. WMO remains a data handling organization. At present, to suggest an international atmospheric research centre on a scale considerably larger than **the international meteorological research** institute at Stockholm, would tend to rob national centres. Thus it is recommended that this matter, however desirable, be deferred to one of our subsequent conferences. For the present a considerable acceleration of international atmospheric research seems impractical.

---

*Special Committee on Antarctic Research.

Appendix 8   174

(d) Of the many desirable studies suggested, the highest priority should be given to three:

  (i) The world-wide survey of the oceans, including their contents in three dimensions.

  (ii) The deep drilling programme, including systematic sampling of the unconsolidated sediments.

  (iii) The establishment of a total environmental, that is to say, atmosphere and ocean, forecasting service.

II. CO-OPERATION IN SPACE RESEARCH

Though believing that there should be close co-operation in space research, we realize that complete co-operation in this field, as in some others, will become possible only when the arms race is ended, international tensions are reduced, complete and general disarmament becomes a reality, and the need for secrecy disappears.

We believe, however, that certain advances in the presently established co-operation in space are possible now, and that certain others could be studied now with the hope of realization in the not too distant future.

A. First, we recommend an increase in the exchange of scientific information in areas such as the physics of space and the effects of the space environment on life. We further recommend periodic international symposia devoted to such subjects.

B. We also recommend the exchange of methods, and of information on instruments, for scientific **space** studies which have no military importance.

C. We recommend the orderly assignment and use of radio-frequencies in space. We support the initiative in this direction taken by the International Telecommunications Union, and hope that a final solution can be reached within two years.

D. We recommend the expansion of existing systems of satellite tracking stations. Bilateral agreements between different nations, including (within the limits of military security) an agreement between the United States and the U.S.S.R., on the common use of tracking stations; such a bilateral agreement could serve as the first step in this direction.

E. International agreement should be reached on a co-ordinated programme for the use of rockets and satellites during the Quiet Sun Year (planned for the second half of 1962).

F. Similar agreement should be reached on co-operation in the use of rockets and satellites in the projected world magnetic survey. This agreement should include arrangements for simultaneous observation from **satel**lites launched into different orbits by different nations. This co-operation could be organized in the framework of the Committee on Space Research (COSPAR).

G. We endorse in principle the desirability of international world-wide systems of communications satellites and of meteorological satellites since these would clearly be in the interests of all mankind. We realize that certain difficulties now stand in the way, but we hope that the governments of the United States and the U.S.S.R., as well as of other nations embarking on rocket and satellite programmes, will undertake a common study of the ways to overcome them.

H. We recommend that co-operation should be established in the instrumental study of the moon, and also that the basic principles of the International Antarctic Treaty be applied to the moon and other cosmic bodies.

I. We recommend the calling of an international conference or symposium to consider how to avoid the biological and radioactive contamination of extra-terrestrial bodies.

III. CO-OPERATION IN THE LIFE SCIENCES

Among the many fields of biology in which international co-operation is possible, some are particularly well suited by their nature and importance for combined efforts. These, which relate especially to the promotion of human welfare, have been given primary concern by us. It is very evident that world-wide betterment of human welfare could be produced if the already existing biological knowledge were to be properly disseminated and fully utilized. Among the most important considerations are the means of bringing this about, so that local facilities and resources can be optimally exploited. The following recommendations incorporate proposals designed to achieve this end, as well as to promote research for the discovery of new knowledge in the field of biology.

A. Biological Aspects of Food Resources

One of the most important problems facing humanity is that of assuring an adequate supply of food. While some areas have an abundant food supply, in others there is a low yield of food production and a correspondingly low level of nutrition. Adequate biological information now exists to enhance food production in these areas considerably, provided the knowledge is adequately diffused and applied. This can be done most effectively by the development of regional agricultural experiment stations, which can deal with the problem of developing agricultural methods suitable to the local terrain, as well as the long-term problem of breeding plants and animals which are able to thrive in the specific locality. These local agricultural experiment stations should be co-ordinated with an international centre. In this way it will be possible to teach agricultural practices which avoid errors experienced in the development of other areas, such as erosion of the soil, deforestation, overgrazing, etc. The implementation of this recommendation might be carried out through the establishment under the United Nations of an international centre and a large-scale international training programme, supplemented by inter-institutional

exchanges of personnel between countries. Although some work has been
carried out under the United Nations in this area, their programme should
be strengthened and extended considerably, especially in the newly developing countries.

Even though the majority of all life on this planet is synthesized in the
oceans, man has utilized this source of food only to a limited degree. It
is quite likely that the oceans can supply ten times more food for man
than the total being produced at the present time. This can be done by
developing methods for the cultivation of food in the oceans, rather than
the use of the inefficient and self-limiting hunting procedures employed
today. To do this we must greatly expand our knowledge of marine biology.
Fortunately, the international oceanographic research expeditions, such as
now planned for the exploration of the Indian Ocean, can afford a significant opportunity for increasing our knowledge of marine life. Another important means for expanding knowledge in this area is through the work of
marine biological laboratories, situated in many countries. Many of these
laboratories are now critically short of funds and need a wider basis of
support. We recommend that these laboratories be united into an international system, perhaps under the International Union of Biological Sciences, to ensure permanent support and increase in number.

B. Preservation and Promotion of Health

The health sciences offer one of the most rewarding meeting grounds for
international co-operation in science. Increased international co-operation and financial support is essential for the realization of important
advances in such fields as cancer, cardiovascular disease, immunology, infectious diseases, mental health, environmental sanitation, problems of
ageing, nutrition, human genetics, and others.

International institutes of health devoted to these problems should be established in one carefully chosen place to serve as a world centre of
medical research. Sufficient financial support of a long-term nature
should be provided to permit their efficient operation. Smaller subsidiary institutes oriented towards more specialized problems or regional
needs (space medicine, medical entomology, tropical medicine) should be
established in different countries.

Other urgent needs in the health sciences characteristically requiring
greater international co-operation and support include: (1) more effective and rapid dissemination of information on research and advances in
medical knowledge; (2) increased education and training of physicians and
allied scientific and auxiliary personnel at both undergraduate and postgraduate levels; (3) an extension of epidemiological studies and control
of important communicable diseases, such as malaria, tuberculosis, and in-
fluenza, as well as of chronic degenerative diseases; (4) genetic and im-
munologic studies of human population groups; and (5) problems of reproduction.

The central co-ordination and administration of these institutes and programmes should be entrusted to the World Health Organization of the United

Nations, which is the major operating international agency in the medical field. It is realized, however, that these additional tasks in the health sciences cannot be undertaken adequately unless the funds now being spent for these purposes are at least trebled.

C. The Environment and its Modification by Man

The exponential growth of human populations and the accompanying industrial, agricultural, and scientific activities have given rise to a number of serious problems including pollution of air and water resources which are of considerable biological importance. We now recognize that continual chemical pollution of the air (known as smog) is a characteristic feature associated with most metropolitan areas, and as such constitutes a problem of world-wide importance. The great increase of industrial growth has brought about extensive water pollution, which is lethal to aquatic organisms and renders the water unfit for human use. Especially grave are the problems involving contamination of air, soil, and water with radioactive substances. Included here, as well as the more obvious problem of fallout from nuclear explosions, there is the matter of the safe disposal of radioactive wastes. Even though several agencies of the United Nations have carried out extensive studies in the field of radioactive contamination, more international attention should be directed towards the problems of chemical pollution of air and water. We recommend that international conferences be scheduled on these topics.

Another of the more serious consequences of man's rapid growth is the extent to which it may bring about the extinction of many plant and animal species. There are large forest and game reserves in the newly-formed African countries which are seriously threatened today because of a shortage of funds and trained personnel who can maintain these preserves. This problem has been considered by a committee on ecology in the International Council of Scientific Unions. We believe that action on this problem should be taken by the United Nations in order to bring about prompt and effective results. If this is not done rapidly we will unfortunately suffer irreplaceable losses. Another aspect of this problem should be the establishment of a system of world-wide institutes for preserving indigenous strains of plants, animals, and micro-organisms. These may have enormous practical as well as theoretical benefits in future years.

D. "Endless Frontiers"

It has been said that the developments in biology during the next century will be as explosive as the growth of the physical sciences in the preceding century. This will undoubtedly offer new opportunities for international co-operation. At least two directions of this advance are already evident.

There has been a phenomenal development recently in our understanding of the structure and function of biological macromolecules and the central role of the nucleic acids and the mechanism which relates the nucleic acids to the protein molecules. This work has led to a significant insight into the molecular events which underlie cell division, as well as viral infection. These developments have a significant bearing on the

Appendix 8   178

problem of cancer as well as the broader fields of molecular evolution and the origin of life. Intense interest in this field has developed among scientists in all countries, and it may be possible to capitalize on this enthusiasm by developing an intercontinental institute of molecular biology. This institute could serve as a research and training centre for expediting the development of the subject and as an important continuing channel of communication in the biological field between "East" and "West" countries.

This proposal originated in both the biological and physical science working groups.

Both the United States and the Soviet Union have announced that they are planning to carry out manned exploration of space. It is not unreasonable to suggest that some of the biological developmental work be carried out in common. To implement this exploration it will be necessary for these proposed trips to develop a wide variety of equipment needed to maintain the human occupant for a prolonged period in a confined space. A considerable saving of time and money would ensue from joint research projects in this area. In addition, some of the instruments which man uses in space for his scientific investigations could be included in this co-operative programme. Joint precautions must be exerted to prevent the contamination of extra-terrestrial bodies by terrestrial organisms. Joint investigations of possible extra-terrestrial forms of life and macromolecules should be planned. We propose that these suggestions be forwarded to COSPAR for its consideration. It should be noted that the adoption of even a limited type of co-operation in space research would be of great symbolic value and have substantial popular appeal.

At the present time an International Biological Programme is under discussion by ICSU. Many of the projects described above may be included in this Programme, which, if carried out broadly and effectively, would have considerable scientific value as well as a favourable impact on public opinion.

IV. CO-OPERATION IN THE PHYSICAL SCIENCES

Modern physical science has in many of its aspects become very big and expensive. It therefore lends itself particularly well to intercontinental co-operation in which the costs are shared, and the results are made available to all mankind.

Four specific areas of physical science were identified as being ripe for vigorous action on an intercontinental basis. These areas were the following:

A. High Energy Physics
The field of high energy physics is an excellent one for co-operation between all countries of the world. This co-operation could centre around the establishment of a laboratory whose main research tool would be an accelerator of not less than 300×10^9 electron volts and of a design which would achieve success in the shortest possible time.

The Seventh Pugwash Conference

B. Controlled Thermonuclear and Plasma Research
In the field of controlled thermonuclear research there has been much effective exchange of information and scientists. This development is particularly significant since thermonuclear research, prior to 1955, was secret. We urge that such collaboration be broadened, in particular, that the world's thermonuclear laboratories remain open to scientists of all nations who can contribute to this interesting and potentially important field of research.

Although a new very large thermonuclear device is probably not needed immediately, still there is a large field of general research in plasma physics which could well be advanced by the establishment of an intercontinental laboratory.

C. Ultra-Heavy Element Chemistry
The production and study of the very heavy elements (atomic number 95 and above) and the resulting extension and elucidation of Mendeleev's periodic chart is a scientific investigation of great interest to mankind. Handling large quantities of the heavy elements is difficult and very expensive, and gives strong reason to pool the world's efforts in this field.

Two different devices are needed for such studies: high-flux reactors, and heavy-ion, high-current cyclotrons.

We recommend that an intercontinental centre devoted to investigation of the properties of the ultra-heavy elements be established. The centre probably should be equipped with the most powerful available heavy-ion cyclotron and with equipment for handling the materials. The ultra high-flux reactor (10^{16} neutrons/cm^2/sec), because of its hazard, probably should be located at a different, more isolated site.

D. Large-Scale Computers
The development of the large modern electronic computer with its enormous memory and high speed represents one of the most significant scientific events of the last two decades. The future development of these computing machines, with larger memories and higher speeds by orders of magnitude, would be of immense value to science. Such computing machines will cost sums of the order of magnitude of a large accelerator--perhaps as much as $\$100 \times 10^6$.

The development of such computers would be a suitable project for international co-operation. The utilization of such a machine will advance not only mathematics but all the physical sciences, and the biological sciences, particularly the unravelling of the structure of macromolecules. It would also find great utility in economics and other social sciences.

We recommend further study for such an intercontinental centre.

E. A Globular Cluster of Big Science Centres
It is our belief that the separate big science laboratories in high-energy physics, heavy-element chemistry, macromolecular biology, health research, and possibly thermonuclear research, will prosper better if they are

reasonably close together than if they are completely isolated from each other. We particularly believe that the intercontinental computing centre will be more viable and will be a better centre if it is the nucleus of such a cluster.

We therefore urge that the Intercontinental Scientific Laboratories be located in relative geographic proximity and that they be served by the Incontinental Computing Centre. Such an Intercontinental Science Centre, comprising much of what is called "Big Science," would represent a capital investment of the order of $\$5 \times 10^9$. It is our belief that the astute location of such a striking epitome of Science--the most characteristic theme of our modern civilization--could have extraordinarily great significance in improving the tone of the present political situation.

V. CO-OPERATION IN ASSISTANCE TO DEVELOPING NATIONS

We express the strong belief that assistance to developing countries is a duty and necessity for all countries.

This aid should be rendered so that it would not impair the independence of any country.

We express our support for greater international co-operation in assistance to developing nations. Such co-operation could help to reduce world tensions, to strengthen peace, and to further disarmament. Disarmament would in turn improve the climate for international co-operation in this and other fields and make available additional funds which could and, we hope, would be used to increase the assistance to developing nations. Clearly, the greatest co-operation and the release of maximum funds for the assistance programme could be achieved by complete disarmament.

Assistance, we believe, should be provided both on a bilateral and a multilateral basis, including a substantial expansion of assistance through the United Nations.

The problems of assistance to developing nations are different in different parts of the world, and should be studied as such. Scientists could assist in this study through a co-operative programme which should involve not only scientists of different countries but also specialists in different fields--biologists and physicists as well as anthropologists, economists and engineers.

Several programmes have to be undertaken simultaneously if technical assistance is to be successful. This includes both measures of immediate help as well as programmes which require long-range approach. Co-ordinated study of such programmes by scientists from different countries, including both scientists from the developed countries and those from the recipient countries, is required. Useful in this connection may be further spread of sister relations such as already exist between some universities in the developed and in the developing nations. Similar relations could be established between research institutes, agricultural stations, and other

centres of applied research. Particular attention should be given to
problems of adaptation of advanced technology to the needs and resources
of an underdeveloped area. Establishment of regional applied science research institutes appears desirable.

We believe that scientists have a definite role to play in the development
of assistance programmes and therefore suggest that we place special emphasis on this subject in one of our subsequent conferences. We believe
that this conference should include a large participation of representatives from the developing nations.

We welcome the recommendation from the Economic and Social Council (ECOSOC)
that a conference on science and technology in application to the problems
of new nations should be held next summer in Geneva under United Nations
sponsorship.

Among subjects related to the assistance to developing nations in which
scientists have a particular interest, are problems of education in all
its aspects--science education and general education, elementary education
and higher education. Another subject of interest to scientists is that
of natural resources of different areas and of their population trends.
Unprejudiced quantitative study of the latter topic should be carried out
on an international, co-operative basis. Another topic for similar co-operative research is world nutrition, including the study of reasons for
widespread occurrence of avoidable malnutrition in many parts of the world.
The problems of energy supply, particularly in areas in which the demand
for energy is diffused rather than concentrated in large industrial centres, calls for a similar study. We suggest that preliminary study groups
on these problems be organized prior to the above-mentioned conference.

We suggest that an international study be made of the advisability and
practicability of establishing an international fund to which individual
scientists from countries in which local funds are insufficient for this
purpose could apply for assistance in their scientific research.

VI. EXCHANGE OF SCIENTISTS AND SCIENTIFIC INFORMATION

By its very nature and tradition science is a universal enterprise. Not
only does the accumulating knowledge and understanding belong to all mankind, but the work of science moves forward most surely when it engages
the collaborative effort of scientists of all nations. The intimate character of this collaboration on questions of profound import to the life
of mankind serves to enhance the mutual trust and understanding of the
scientific community and of the nations from which its members are drawn.

The rapid exchange of information, mutual visits of scientists and their
working as guests in the laboratories of other scientists, constitute the
main pathways of scientific collaboration among scientists all over the
world. We note that there has been substantial progress in recent years
in the area of scientific exchange. Scholars of many nations have the
opportunity to meet and discuss scientific questions at international

conferences, symposia, and other meetings organized by international scientific organizations as well as by the national organizations of scientists and institutions of higher learning. In this epoch of accelerating progress in science the fostering of such international contacts and exchanges has become an increasingly urgent necessity. During the past decade, the accomplishments of the International Geophysical Year have provided triumphant demonstration of the fruitfulness of international co-operation in science. Moreover, the development of co-operative research among scientists of many countries and the consequent internationalization of Antarctica has given a concrete demonstration of how such co-operation can set precedents for constructive agreements among nations.

We express regret that there exist a number of difficulties which interfere in major ways with the further broadening of scientific collaboration and exchange.

A. Exchange of Scientists
We recommend that the planned exchange of scientific personnel initiated by the Bronk-Nesmeyanov and similar agreements should be considerably increased. The visits should be extended over periods sufficient for the completion of research projects. In addition to planned exchange, the framework of these agreements should allow for, and encourage, invitations to scientists in the country in which they are to visit, and for the invited scientists to be able to accept such invitations. We find that application of the *quid pro quo* principle to visits under the agreement (that is, the exchange of one solid state physicist for another solid state physicist, etc.) has tended to hamper fruitful exchange, and we urge that such regulations be set aside in future agreements.

The role of government bureaucracies in the administration of these agreements should be minimized. To implement this recommendation, we urge governments to expedite visas and passports for scientists, since past and present failures in this respect have seriously hampered scientific exchange.

We recommend that in addition to exchange via formal arrangements the other traditional forms of scientific exchange—personal visits and correspondence among scientists, attendance at international scientific meetings and at meetings of scientific societies of other nations, the framing of common plans for joint and parallel enterprises and so on—be encouraged and facilitated.

We recommend that the scientific organizations of various nations should consider ways to facilitate the travel of pre- and postdoctoral fellows across national boundaries to study for adequate periods of time (one year or more) at research centres and under teachers where their training and scientific maturation can be best enhanced.

B. Exchange of Information
Noting the obstacle to the exchange of scientific information presented by the mounting volume of current publication, which is increasing

exponentially and doubling about every decade, we feel that the situation calls for radical measures of rationalization to be designed and carried out through international agreement and co-operation. Among potentially useful measures are the following: to review and co-ordinate the character and content of journals published in all countries with a view to reducing the number and variety of journals which a scientist must follow to keep abreast of work in his discipline; to institute standard formats for the presentation of scientific papers; to formulate a standard system for the annotation of the contents of published papers suitable for coding and manipulation by machines for the storage and retrieval of information; to institute regional depots under international co-ordination to store complete experimental records and other documentation in support of the brief published papers; to make such material rapidly available to interested scientists; to consolidate the abstracting services now carried on independently in many countries, a measure that could reduce present duplication of effort by a conservatively estimated factor of three.

We recommend that measures be taken to bring significant work going forward in all countries to the attention of interested scientists. This objective could be served by the publication of international review journals of two types: interdisciplinary review journals written in relatively non-technical language for the benefit of scientists in different disciplines, and more specialized review journals which would keep scientists working in a given area abreast of the work going on in the same or related areas all over the world.

We urge that all governments open their postal systems to the untrammelled flow of scientific publications whatever their country of origin or destination.

Participants

Australia
Sir John Crawford

Austria
Prof. Hans Thirring

Brazil
Prof. C. Pavan

Bulgaria
Prof. G. Nadjakov

Federal German Republic
Prof. G. Burkhardt

Hungary
Prof. F. B. Straub

Appendix 8   184

Italy
Dr. G. Bernardini

Japan
Prof. T. Toyoda

Netherlands
Prof. B. V. A. Röling

U.K.
Sir Edward Bullard, Prof. A. Haddow, Sir Ben Lockspeiser, Prof. J. Rotblat

U.S.A.
Prof. Harrison Brown, Dr. William Consolazio, Prof. Paul Doty, Prof. Bentley Glass, Prof. C. O'D. Iselin, Dr. Martin Kaplan, Prof. Chauncey Leake, Prof. Jay Orear, Prof. Linus Pauling, Prof. W. Pickering, Mr. Gerard Piel, Prof. I. Rabi, Prof. Eugene Rabinowitch, Dr. Roger Revelle, Prof. Alexander Rich, Prof. Walter Rosenblith, Dr. Eugene Staley, Dr. Alvin Weinberg, Prof. Eugene Wigner, Prof. J. R. Zacharias

U.S.S.R.
Acad. A. A. Blagonravov, Acad. N. N. Bogolubov, Acad. M. M. Dubinin, Prof. V. M. Khvostov, Acad. N. M. Sisakian, Prof. N. A. Talensky, Acad. I. E. Tamm, Acad. A. V. Topchiev

Observers and Scientific Staff

U.K.
Dr. Patricia J. Lindop, Mr. Wayland Young

U.S.A.
Mrs. Ruth Adams, Dr. Detlev Bronk, Prof. H. Hoagland, Prof. Charles Townes

U.S.S.R.
Dr. N. I. Bazanov, Dr. S. G. T. Korneev, Mr. V. P. Pavlichenko

9 STATEMENT FROM THE EIGHTH PUGWASH CONFERENCE, HELD IN STOWE, SEPTEMBER 11-16, 1961

The Eighth Conference on Science and World Affairs was held at Stowe, Vermont, on September 11-16, 1961; its general subject was Disarmament and World Security.

It is gratifying that in such troubled times it proved possible for 43 scientists from 11 countries to meet in a friendly atmosphere and to examine together carefully the dangers which face the people of the world.

During the previous week the Seventh Conference, devoted to International Co-operation in Science, had outlined many important areas where co-operative action would be scientifically productive as well as effective in improving international understanding. In this Eighth Conference, a wide range of topics was discussed in plenary session, in separate working groups, and in private conversation.

The subjects of study which related in one way or another to the problems of attaining stable peace, world security, and general and complete disarmament included:

Cessation of production of fissile materials for military use and destruction of military nuclear stockpiles.
Elimination and control of means for weapons delivery.
Demilitarization of outer space.
Interdependence of international political settlements and disarmament.
Nuclear weapon tests.
Military disengagement, and creation of demilitarized and atom-free zones.
International security forces.
Methods of settlement of international disputes.
Rules of peaceful co-existence.
Organization of control and inspection over disarmament.
Conditions for creating trust and confidence among nations.

A variety of individual views was expressed. These were often quite divergent, but were explored in a frank manner. The participants found the discussions helpful in clarifying points of view, and common understanding was reached on a number of important issues. We hope this will open important avenues for constructive action.

The participants of the Conference are united in the realization of the danger of unleashing a nuclear war, which would cause untold destruction and bring death to innumerable people. We hope that the desire for peace and the revulsion against war, which are shared by all peoples, will make possible a peaceful resolution of the conflicts which have led to the present deterioration of the international situation, and make possible the attainment of complete and universal disarmament, and the establishment of stable peace on earth.

In the present crisis we reaffirm our belief in the general principles enunciated in the Vienna Declaration of September, 1958.

Appendix 9   186

This meeting kept open a much needed informal channel of communication among scientists concerned with the future of civilization.

For this reason it is hoped that similar conferences will be convened by the Continuing Committee at suitable intervals in the future. In addition, plans have been made to form continuing unofficial East-West study groups in order to devote more detailed attention to problems of the nature of those considered at the present Conference.

Participants

Australia
Sir Mark Oliphant

Bulgaria
Prof. G. Nadjakov

Canada
Prof. J. Polanyi

France
Dr. Francis Perrin, Mr. Pierre Rosenstiehl

German Federal Republic
Prof. G. Burkhardt

Hungary
Prof. F. B. Straub

Japan
Prof. Toshiyuki Toyoda

Netherlands
Prof. B. V. A. Röling

U.K.
Prof. P. M. S. Blackett, Sir Edward Bullard, Sir John Cockcroft, Mr. Michael Howard, Rt. Hon. Philip Noel-Baker, Sir William Penney, Prof. J. Rotblat

U.S.A.
Prof. Hans Bethe, Prof. R. R. Bowie, Dr. Donald Brennan, Prof. Harrison Brown, Prof. Paul Doty, Prof. B. T. Feld, Mr. Trevor Gardner, Prof. Bentley Glass, Prof. Henry Kissinger, Prof. George Kistiakowsky, Prof. Charles Lauritsen, Prof. Leon Lipson, Prof. W. Panofsky, Prof. E. M. Purcell, Prof. I. Rabi, Prof. Eugene Rabinowitch, Prof. Louis B. Sohn, Prof. Leo Szilard, Prof. Charles Townes

U.S.S.R.
Acad. A. A. Blagonravov, Acad. N. N. Bogolubov, Acad. M. M. Dubinin, Prof. V. M. Khvostov, Acad. N. M. Sisakian, Prof. N. A. Talensky, Acad. I. E. Tamm, Acad. A. V. Topchiev

Observers and Scientific Staff

Austria
Prof. H. Thirring

U.K.
Dr. Patricia Lindop, Sir Ben Lockspeiser, Mr. Wayland Young, Sir Solly Zuckerman

U.S.A.
Mrs. Ruth Adams, Mr. Amrom Katz, Prof. J. Orear, Prof. Matthew Sands

U.S.S.R.
Dr. N. I. Bazanov, Dr. S. G. T. Korneev, Mr. V. P. Pavlichenko

The National Academy of Sciences and the American Academy of Arts and Sciences were hosts to this as well as the preceding Conference. Both Conferences were organized by the United States Organizational Committee under the aegis of the International Continuing Committee of these Conferences.

The following did not join in the resolution:
Professor R. R. Bowie, Dr. Donald Brennan, Mr. Amrom Katz, Professor Henry Kissinger, Professor Leon Lipson

The following were absent during the discussion of the statement:
Mr. Trevor Gardner, Professor Charles Lauritsen, Professor I. Rabi

REPORT ON THE NINTH PUGWASH CONFERENCE, HELD IN CAMBRIDGE, AUGUST 25-30, 1962

Bentley Glass

The Ninth Pugwash Conference on Science and World Affairs met in Cambridge on 25th-30th August 1962. The general subject discussed by the 67 participants and 18 observers, representing 19 countries, was "Problems of Disarmament and World Security."

Formal papers were presented only during the two plenary sessions of the first day of the Conference. Harrison Brown considered the present possibility of achieving a nuclear test ban agreement. In the hope that the present failure of the governments concerned to reach an agreement rests not on a difference of principle, but rather on disagreements relating to timing and procedure, he suggested that a study of the probability that inspection following a seismic event would actually lead to a revelation of any military secrets of importance might reassure the U.S.S.R. Furthermore, secrecy on the part of the U.S.S.R. has probably resulted in the build-up of a much greater military installation in the United States than would otherwise have been likely. Another theme on which he touched was the increasing pressure to perform, in the absence of a nuclear test ban, experiments that significantly, and perhaps permanently, alter the human environment in ways deleterious to science and to life itself.

"The Present Stage of Disarmament Negotiations" was summarized by V. M. Khvostov, who pointed out that since the Stowe Conferences, two very significant developments have taken place, namely, first, the agreement between the Soviet Union and the United States on the principles of general and complete disarmament, and second, the inclusion of the neutral states in the negotiations. He also provided a summary and analysis of the Soviet draft proposals, which are expressed for the first time in the form and language of an international treaty. He followed this with a critique of the U.S. draft proposals, and concluded with a comment on the April proposal put forward by the eight neutral states.

The paper by Academician Topchiev dealt with the general deterioration of the situation in which disarmament negotiations must be conducted amidst explosions of nuclear weapons and in the atmosphere of an ever-accelerating arms race. He said, in summation: "The gap between acknowledging the necessity for disarmament and the actual moulding of people's will into reality does not diminish of its own accord, and sometimes it even increases." He pointed to many international measures proposed by the U.S.S.R. to relax tension and make disarmament possible--measures which need not await complete and total disarmament. He clarified the Soviet position on strict international control of the disarmament process. He pointed out that the U.S. proposal for a proportional disarmament, by a given percentage of weapons in each stage of disarmament, must react to the disadvantage of the power initially weaker, which would lose the advantage of military secrecy. He criticized the lack of "great and rapid steps in the disarmament process" proposed by the United States, and insisted that "the amount of control is to correspond to the character and amount of disarmament." In this respect he rejected the method of selective zonal control, proposed by Professors Sohn and Frisch at the Moscow Pugwash Conference and more recently embodied in the U.S. disarmament proposals. This method, like others proposed by the West, is "nothing less than an additional channel for espionage especially at the first stage." In concluding, Acad. Topchiev proposed that the Conference should elect a body to lead in the preparation of future measures of disarmament, in the form of an "International Year for the Preparation of Disarmament."

The paper by Louis B. Sohn was in the first instance a plea for a better atmosphere for the conduct of disarmament negotiations, one of less mutual recrimination among the powers, one of more willingness to accept impartial international jurisdiction in the settlement of disputes and accusations. A general reduction in the intensity of current disagreements in all corners of the world is a prerequisite, he believes, to a more reasonable approach to the arms problem. The methods of disarmament negotiations also need improvement, for they all too often show an unwillingness to deal with substantive issues. Sohn dealt with some of the specific issues: the command of the International Peace Force; the settlement of international disputes in their early stages; the development of international law; the formulation of rules of conduct relating to disarmament; and the establishment of really effective peacekeeping machinery. He proposed, at one juncture, a special and independent tribunal of "elder statesmen and other persons having a worldwide reputation for impartiality, knowledge of international affairs and familiarity with United Nations processes." This tribunal could act in a purely advisory capacity to the United Nations, but might grow to be something much stronger in the maintenance of peace. Sohn also pointed out that the faster the Soviet Union would like to disarm, the faster must be the build-up of the inspection system. Limited first-stage steps would require lesser amounts of inspection. Taking recognition of the Soviet objections to inspection prior to real disarmament, the new U.S. disarmament proposals substitute a progressive zonal inspection plan which Sohn believes can be modified to meet Soviet objections to any remaining danger of espionage.

The paper by P. M. S. Blackett, entitled "The Way Ahead," will in my estimation bear serious and repeated study by all groups interested in disarmament proposals, since it presents many far-sighted suggestions in its critical analysis of the current disarmament stalemate. Blackett emphasizes as all-important Clause 5 of the McCloy-Zorin agreement on the principles of general and complete disarmament.

"All measures of general and complete disarmament should be balanced so that at no stage of the implementation of the treaty could any state or group of states gain military advantage and that security is ensured equally for all." According to Blackett, both the Soviet and American draft treaties conflict with this essential requirement of balance in important ways. The Soviet requirement that in the first stage all foreign troops and bases should be eliminated would weaken Western defence in Europe more than that of the Soviet bloc. Alternatives are suggested. On the other hand, the recently accepted view that there is a great

Appendix 10

disparity of nuclear strengths between the powers, in favour of the United States, makes a proportional reduction of nuclear strength over a long period of years, as proposed by the U.S., work greatly to the disadvantage of the U.S.S.R. Blackett proposes for the first stage of disarmament a rapid reduction of the strategic nuclear forces to the same low and equal level--a minimum deterrent level; together with a reduction of conventional forces also to an equal and low level. In this way "Russia would have to pay a disarmament surtax on her greater manpower and America on her greater nuclear power." Each would sacrifice most where strongest. Blackett also considered the economic and political difficulties in the way of acceptance of a disarmament treaty, particularly in the United States. He is probably correct in seeing the need for a great educational campaign to reduce the opposition to disarmament in "free enterprise" countries, and likewise in supposing that the much longer duration of the disarmament stages in the American plan is related to "realistic estimates as to the time it might take to make drastic disarmament palatable politically to the American electorate."

Time will not permit much further description of this critical analysis, but I must mention the stress Blackett places on (1) the value of independent actions by individual nations and groups of nations, and the things he thinks Great Britain might do along these lines to ensure a bipolar rather than a multipolar danger of nuclear war; (2) the harm done to Soviet interests by excessive secrecy through the promotion of excessive American rearmament; and (3) the futility, as well as danger, of the counter-military target policy recently enunciated by Secretary McNamara.

Many interesting and valuable background papers were presented to the Conference for the use of one or another of the five Working Groups whose labours occupied most of the time during the Conference.

Working Group 1 (24 members) was concerned with problems of reduction and elimination under international control of weapons of mass destruction and of their means of delivery. This Working Group commenced discussions on the basis of agreement that a very substantial, or even complete, reduction of the means of delivery of nuclear weapons would constitute a satisfactory basis for the first stage of disarmament. Stage 2 would then involve the reduction or elimination of the nuclear weapons themselves. Definition of "means of delivery" and the precise degree of destruction to be attained during stage 1 proved more difficult. Some members declared for the complete destruction in stage 1 of all systems capable of delivering nuclear missiles, verification of the destruction, and dismantling of the factories producing delivery systems. Others proposed substantial reduction, to a minimum deterrent level maintaining the balance of force between the two sides, to be followed by a reduction to zero after all nations were convinced that disarmament had proceeded as planned and the measures to prevent rearmament were adequate. The entire Group agreed on the need for presenting to the International Disarmament Organization such data on the production of means of delivery of nuclear weapons as might be necessary to provide adequate control. Still a third proposal suggested the value of distinguishing between the means of delivery of large weapons and of small ones, which might more easily be controlled through the elimination of fissile material. Some overlap between stages 1 and 2 would occur on this plan.

Verification procedures should take account of the uncertainties of the disarmament process. An average uncertainty of the correct order of magnitude was thought to be about 10%. It was agreed that if reasonable suspicions were to arise that other factories than those declared as engaged in military productions were engaged in clandestine activities, such suspicion could be checked by extension of the verification procedures.

There was discussion by this Working Group of the relation of inspection to secrecy as an element of military security; of zonal sampling procedures; and of the relation of the elimination of foreign bases and of troops stationed abroad to the process of destruction of the means of delivery. No consensus was reached except that these problems all deserve further study. It was agreed, however, that the procedures envisaged for the elimination of nuclear weapons and the means of delivery would also be adequate for the elimination of biological and chemical weapons of mass destruction.

Working Group 2 (13 members) dealt with problems of balanced reduction and elimination of conventional armaments. Its first conclusions related to the desirability of the inclusion of the People's Republic of China in any such negotiations and agreements. The ceiling to be established would otherwise have to be modified in the light of the absence of the Chinese. Nevertheless, the nuclear powers, it was agreed, can discuss first steps in this area even in the absence of the Chinese.

With the unfairness of reductions on a percentage basis in mind, the Group agreed that fixed ceilings in manpower and in each category of weapons should be the aim. The first stage of conventional disarmament should take place during stage 1 of nuclear disarmament. At some stage all troops should withdraw to their own national boundaries, but there was disagreement as to precisely at what stage this was to be desired. Those favouring early withdrawal agreed, however, that regional defensive bases might be retained to the end of disarmament, if free of foreign troops, nuclear weapons or means of delivery, and if under national command. The Group further agreed that at each stage of disarmament a regional and global balance between conventional forces should be maintained.

Verification of disarmament should proceed as follows: (1) all states should specify their forces, including reserves, both in manpower and military material; (2) the International Control Organ should be given access to the relevant statistical data (including budgets and production records of plants producing conventional arms); (3) the International Control Organ should have the right to observe demobilization of units, destruction of the agreed quantities of weapons, and the conversion, dismantling, and reduction of capacity of arms-producing plants. It was further agreed that inspection for conventional disarmament need not be so detailed as for nuclear weapons, since a much greater violation would be required to achieve a decisive advantage. Inspection of sampling, inspection of limited zones on either side of a frontier, and inspection at major communication centres, including airports, over a larger area, were considered as alternative methods.

Working Group 3 (24 members) considered a variety of political and technical measures that could contribute to a lessening of international tensions. Subgroups worked on each of four areas. The first subgroup reaffirmed the need for a nuclear tests ban as a first step in general and complete disarmament. The proposal of the eight neutral nations in the 18-Nation Conference was held to be highly valuable as a basis of acceptable compromise. It might be used as a basis for a treaty; or it might be modified to allow, as a matter of principle, a small number of inspections over and above those carried out by invitation. Alternatively, it might be accepted in either of the foregoing forms for a limited term, say of two years, in order to establish the confidence needed for further procedure. Members of the Group expressed different opinions about these several possibilities; but all agreed that an early cessation of nuclear weapons testing, say by 1st January 1963, was "both possible and imperative." Not only all nuclear powers but also those nearing such capability should become signatories of the treaty.

Activities in space were the study of a second subgroup, which supported the recommendations in this area of the Seventh Pugwash Conference and welcomed the increasing exchange of information in this area under COSPAR and the United Nations Committee on the Peaceful Uses of Outer Space. The proposed agreement between the United States and the U.S.S.R. for collaboration in certain fields is most encouraging. The subgroup recommended this subject to the particular attention of the Tenth Conference. The use of outer space for military purposes was held to be a serious threat to mankind. Negotiations to prevent the equipment of space vehicles with military nuclear equipment should begin now. Experiments which endanger human life, or which change the space environment so as to jeopardize scientific studies, should be excluded. An international mechanism for controlling these matters and passing on the desirability of scientific experiments that might alter the space environment should be established. An international treaty, similar to the Antarctic Treaty, should be drafted to protect the interests of all nations in cosmic bodies. An agreement is needed for the safe return of all cosmonauts and space vehicles landing accidentally on foreign territory as a result of space experiments. Scientific research in space should be given a high priority, and an agreement made that it will not be interfered with by other uses of space. The aims of every space launching should be published in advance; and following any agreement on the destruction of nuclear delivery systems, effective controls should be established over the types of loads to be carried by rockets in peaceful explorations of space.

A third subgroup turned its attention to the problem of communication, and declared the existence of an urgent need for an international conference on this subject. The cultural lag between scientific advances and popular understanding makes attention to this question by the Tenth Pugwash

Conference very desirable. It should consider "whether it will be possible to convene a special conference of social scientists and other scholars who could contribute to solving this problem." The plans for a quarterly journal on disarmament were noted with approval, especially the emphasis on simultaneous publication in Russian and English, and perhaps in other languages. The subgroup also recommended all measures for increasing the flow of information and opinion between countries, especially through the reprinting of articles published in other countries.

A fourth subgroup dealt with political measures likely to reduce tension. It recommended the stabilization of existing frontiers and the neutralization of certain geographical areas; and it called on all states to avoid stimulating and fanning internal conflicts in other countries. Much wider and more systematic co-operation in scientific and technological enterprises should be developed, and increased technical assistance to developing nations should proceed on a co-operative rather than competitive basis. It was recommended that the Pugwash Continuing Committee should establish a continuing study group on International Co-operation to develop further such ideas as the formation of a World Centre of Scientific Research, perhaps in Berlin.

The "denuclearization" (which I take to mean the elimination of nuclear weapons' capability) of central Europe, including both parts of Germany, Poland, and Czechoslovakia would greatly allay apprehensions and reduce international tensions. Other areas might be treated similarly, e.g., the Balkans, Africa and the Far East. "Denuclearization" could be carried out within the framework of a general disarmament treaty so as not to upset the existing balance of power systems in Europe. For the fuller establishment of collective security, "the constitution, the organization, and the role of existing international bodies require early formal review, as provided for in the United Nations Charter." A consideration of conflicts involving non-aligned or neutral nations is recommended to the Continuing Committee. Finally, an early agreement to prevent the spread to any additional nation of nuclear weapons, or the information required to produce them, was endorsed.

All the reports of the four subgroups were accepted by the entire Working Group 3.

Working Group 4 (17 members) dealt with the problems of security in a disarmed world. In a world in which complete and general disarmament has been achieved and confidence assured in all countries that the terms of the disarmament treaty have been implemented everywhere, what machinery will be needed to maintain peace and prevent rearmament in the event of disputes? The Group agreed that each country must still retain a police force to keep internal order. These should be equipped only with light arms (including machine guns). The existence of such police forces indicates that the danger of war will not have been completely eliminated. Many causes of disputes and conflicts among states will remain, and probably cannot always be settled by direct negotiation, especially if there is no force or compulsion to reach an agreement. The International Court

Appendix 10   194

will play an important role, but its jurisdiction is not accepted by every state, and in any event it can only interpret international law, not make new laws or rule on situations not covered by existing law or treaties. Disputes might arise in particular from charges that a state was violating the terms of the disarmament treaty. (It is assumed that that treaty will have established an international control authority with right of unlimited inspection and functioning without a veto.) Disputes referred to the Security Council might meet with failure to act, in case a permanent member of the Security Council used the veto power. Most members of the Group did not feel that the veto right in the Security Council ought to be abolished, though perhaps the list of member states with the veto power should be altered, in accordance with provisions of the United Nations Charter.

For all the foregoing reasons, unresolved conflicts of interest will remain, "and the question of how this can be remedied requires further study."

The Group did not consider that it could be possible or desirable to lay down rules for every contingency. "The world must be allowed to develop."

The temptation to resort to force, by using the state's police force or by illegally rearming, requires an international police force. The Group could not agree whether this would be better constituted from national contingents drawn from the police forces of member states, or whether it should be "a separate body of individuals organized by the United Nations." It should, in any case, be "equipped with light arms and such other equipment as the Security Council may from time to time find necessary for effective enforcement action in accordance with the United Nations Charter." It should not possess nuclear weapons or other weapons of mass destruction.

The Working Group was unable to agree on the question of command of the international police force. Obviously it must be prevented from becoming a new instrument of tyranny. It is, therefore, not reasonable to expect agreement on a single commander. Whether a command by three, or by five, representatives of various groups of member nations, either permanent or varying from situation to situation, would be effective is a problem that requires further study.

Most important was the agreement of the Group that "the international police force must not interfere in the internal affairs of states, except where internal actions violate the disarmament treaty or endanger international security." To define "internal affairs" will not be simple, but it was agreed that "in case of an attempt to change a government by force (revolution or counter-revolution), the military intervention by police forces of another state in favour of either side in the civil strife would be regarded as armed interference and would be prohibited." This agreement represents a significant step in our thinking.

It was agreed that in the disarmed world "it is important to prohibit war propaganda and incitement to rearmament." There was much discussion of how to do this.

Finally, and in a disarmed world even as now, stability will be favoured by increased international co-operation in scientific, technological, educational, and other fields.

Working Group 5 (6 members) boldly attacked the problems of the economics of disarmament and completed its report in the space of a single day. In this achievement it was significantly aided by the conclusions of the United Nations Study Group on the Economic and Social Consequences of Disarmament, with which it fully concurred.

The transfer of men and machines from the satisfaction of military demands to peaceful purposes can be done smoothly if
"(a) the general level of demand and production is maintained;
 (b) measures are taken to ensure that alternative jobs are provided in regions where defence industry is now concentrated or aid is given to workers to move elsewhere;
 (c) retraining facilities are provided for those whose skills become redundant or are inadequate for civil life."

The Group asserted its belief that these conditions can be satisfied by appropriate national policies. Demobilization after World War II and in the mid-fifties in many countries demonstrates that the task, analysed in some detail by the Group, is not impossible.

Scientists and technicians fill a special place in this picture. Used in large numbers in military research and development, they must be successfully redeployed to contribute to peaceful technology. "All governments already accept responsibility for promoting and financing research.... To meet the needs of disarmament nations must find ways of financing and organizing peaceful research directly instead of through military budgets." They should begin to do this now, while remembering that space research, civil aircraft, and peaceful uses of atomic energy are not the only lines to be pursued. There are many opportunities in industry, transport, energy, automation, research into techniques useful in underdeveloped countries, and there is a great need for a larger supply of teachers and technicians for those countries.

The Group agrees that international trade should on the whole be benefited by disarmament. Aid to developing countries can be greatly increased under disarmament.

The fear of disarmament is in part owing to economic fears. If these are ungrounded--all the nations participating in the United Nations study having expressed confidence in their ability to handle the problems of transition--these economic fears must be dispelled. Within two years, or more easily in three or four years, but preferably not longer, the economic readjustment to disarmament could be carried through if sufficient planning and preparation are made in advance. A large amount of public education is needed ere all of this can be done.

In conclusion may I say that if the advances in agreement seem small and the areas of difficulty seem large in these considerations of disarmament problems, it is, in the first place, because we are getting deeper into them and grappling with more technical matters than at first; and secondly, it is because we are advancing even further beyond the matters considered by our official negotiators at Geneva. We have no reason for discouragement. Even the least advance in these considerations may make possible the breakthrough to a disarmed and peaceful world.

Participants

Australia
Sir Mark Oliphant

Brazil
Dr. Oscar Sala

Bulgaria
Prof. G. Nadjakov

Czechoslovakia
Mr. Theodor Němec, Acad. Vladimir Procházka, Dr. Ludek Urban

Denmark
Prof. O. M. Kofoed-Hansen

Federal German Republic
Prof. G. Burkhardt, Prof. E. Menzel

France
Prof. F. Perrin, Prof. Pierre Rosenstiehl

Hungary
Prof. F. B. Straub

India
Prof. V. Sarabhai

Japan
Prof. H. Yukawa

Netherlands
Prof. B. V. A. Röling

Pakistan
Prof. Abdus Salam

Poland
Prof. Leopold Infeld

Rumania
Acad. H. Hulubei

U.K.
Prof. P. M. S. Blackett, Mr. Alastair Buchan, Sir Edward Bullard, Sir John Cockcroft, Mr. Michael Howard, Sir Nevill Mott, Mr. Philip Noel-Baker, Prof. R. E. Peierls, Sir William Penney, Prof. C. F. Powell, Prof. J. Rotblat, Mr. Wayland Young

U.S.A.
Dr. D. G. Brennan, Prof. Harrison Brown, Prof. Paul Doty, Prof. Freeman J. Dyson, Prof. Bernard T. Feld, Prof. Bentley Glass, Prof. Robert Gomer, Dr. Henry Kissinger, Mr. R. S. Leghorn, Prof. Wassily Leontief, Prof. W. Munk, Prof. Jay Orear, Prof. Isidor I. Rabi, Prof. Eugene Rabinowitch, Prof. Frederick Seitz, Prof. Louis B. Sohn, Prof. Leo Szilard, Prof. Charles H. Townes

U.S.S.R.
Acad. L. A. Artsimovitch, Acad. A. A. Blagonravov, Acad. N. N. Bogolubov, Acad. M. M. Dubinin, Prof. V. S. Emelyanov, Dr. N. N. Inozemtsev, Acad. V. A. Kargin, Prof. V. M. Khvostov, Prof. I. J. Kozhevnikov, Prof. A. M. Kuzin, Prof. O. Leipunsky, Prof. J. Riznichenko, Prof. M. I. Rubinstein, Prof. N. A. Talensky, Acad. I. E. Tamm, Acad. A. V. Topchiev, Acad. A. N. Tupolev, Prof. A. N. Vernov

Yugoslavia
Prof. Ivan Supek

Observers and Scientific Staff

Australia
Dr. John Burton

Canada
Dr. N. Z. Alcock

Federal German Republic
Dr. U. Nerlich

France
Mr. Pierre Genevey

Netherlands
Mr. F. J. A. Terwisscha van Scheltinga

U.K.
Prof. B. H. Flowers, Prof. O. R. Frisch, Dr. J. C. Kendrew, Mr. Gerald Leach, Dr. Patricia Lindop, Mr. John Maddox, Mr. Robert Neild, Mr. B. T. Price, Prof. Sir Solly Zuckerman

Appendix 10

U.S.A.
Mrs. Ruth Adams, Dr. Albert R. Hibbs, Mr. Amrom H. Katz, Mr. Victor Rabinowitch

U.S.S.R.
Dr. N. Bazanov, Dr. G. P. Besedin, Dr. S. G. T. Korneev, Mr. V. Pavlichenko

11 THE WORK OF THE PUGWASH CONTINUING COMMITTEE (REPORT TO THE TENTH PUGWASH CONFERENCE IN LONDON)

J. Rotblat

Five years ago, at the end of the First Conference in Pugwash, an informal Committee was set up, under the chairmanship of Lord Russell, to convene further conferences. This Committee consisted of four people: Professors Powell and Rabinowitch, Academician Skobeltzyn and myself. About a year later, at the Kitzbühel Conference in September 1958, the Committee was enlarged to nine members, so as to make three each from the United States, the Soviet Union and Great Britain. The additional members were Professors Weisskopf and Glass, Academicians Topchiev and Fedorov, and Sir Edward Bullard. Professor Weisskopf and Sir Edward Bullard were later replaced by Professor Brown and Sir Nevill Mott. It was this Committee which conducted the affairs of the so-called Pugwash Conferences on Science and World Affairs, and which convened the present Conference.

Five years in office is long enough for any governing body and the time has come for the Committee to lay down its mandate. As has been indicated in the letter of invitation, the purpose of this Conference is to receive and discuss reports of past activities, and on this basis to reach decisions about future activities and organization. This is, therefore, a suitable time for the outgoing Committee to give a report of its work during the past five years.

I do not intend to present a detailed account of all our Conferences. Lord Russell has just reminded you of the origins of Pugwash. Most of you will have received a copy of the "History of the Pugwash Conferences," which I hope you will have found time to read. I shall, therefore, speak mainly about the general principles underlying the work of the Continuing Committee.

International Conferences

Our main task was to organize international conferences, and the first things we had to decide were: the type of conferences to convene, their scope, and who should be invited. Before the Committee met for the first time in December 1957, a questionnaire was sent out to a number of scientists in Great Britain and the United States about the nature of the meetings to be called. From the replies it appeared that two types of conference were about equally favoured: the first, to discuss urgent political problems such as disarmament, with the aim of influencing governments; and the second, to study the social implications of scientific progress, aiming mainly at educating and clarifying the thinking of scientists themselves. There was also a call, from a minority of scientists, for large meetings which would be aimed at influencing the general public. It is interesting to note that a strikingly similar result was obtained a few years later, when an opinion poll was taken among a much larger group of scientists from many countries, both East and West.

Using those expressions of opinions as a guide, the Committee organized two Conferences in 1958: the Lac Beauport meeting devoted to disarmament and the Kitzbühel-Vienna Conference designed to deal with the more general problem of the role of the scientist in the atomic age.

In subsequent meetings, however, we did not observe this equal division; in fact, almost all of the following Conferences, the Fourth, Fifth, Sixth and Eighth, as well as the Ninth which has just finished in Cambridge, were all concerned with various aspects of the arms race and disarmament. Only the Seventh Conference, at Stowe last year, dealt with the more general topic of international scientific co-operation.

The reason for this specialization in disarmament problems should be obvious. The threat of a nuclear war represents at the moment the greatest danger to mankind. Disarmament must, therefore, be given the highest priority. But there may have been additional reasons. We had to prove ourselves. We had to show that scientists can preserve their integrity and make objective judgments even when discussing political problems. We had further to show that contrary to what has often been said about scientists we were not naive and woolly about these complex issues, that we could not only discuss them sensibly and objectively, but also make significant contributions towards their solution. What better test case could there be than disarmament, which had been discussed at various international forums for a long time without much progress!

I think that it will be generally accepted that we have passed the test. We have shown that although our participants represent an extremely wide spectrum of political opinion, we can maintain an unbiased outlook and can give sympathetic understanding to other people's difficulties and their points of view. We have proved that by applying some of the virtues of the scientific method to non-scientific problems we can reach a far greater measure of agreement than has ever been reached by non-scientists. Above all, we have managed to establish a very useful channel of communication between East and West. The best proof of our success is the changed attitude of the Western Governments; initially indifferent and even suspicious, they are now interested and sympathetic. This is demonstrated in many ways, not the least by the participation in our conferences of scientists who hold important advisory positions to their governments on disarmament problems.

Although disarmament must still remain our topic of first priority, we now have to pay more attention to other problems. Even a disarmed world would not be a safe world if the many causes of mistrust and tensions were allowed to remain. One of these is the disparity in the standard of living in different parts of the world. Science, properly organized, can do a great deal to help developing nations in their struggle for economic and cultural advancement. We are very conscious of this need, and for several years the Continuing Committee has been planning a conference on this topic. Much thought went into its preparation but for various reasons we have been unable to bring it about. However, a proposal for such a conference will be put before you this week. Another means of creating more trust in the world is by international collaboration in science. We devoted the Seventh Conference to this topic and we hope to pursue the matter further both this week and at future meetings. We are also being called upon to tackle the more fundamental issues which make for an unstable world, such as psycho-social behaviour and, above all, the whole approach to education. We shall have an opportunity at this Conference to discuss whether these issues should come within the scope of Pugwash activities.

We are, of course, aware that these problems are being discussed by other bodies and organizations. We are conscious of the anxieties just expressed by the President of the Royal Society. I should like to take this opportunity to state clearly that it is not our intention to duplicate the efforts of others. In particular, we are anxious not to encroach on the excellent work which is being carried out by several international organizations, such as ICSU, UNESCO or other United Nations Agencies. But experience over the past five years has shown that we have a special role which does not overlap those of the other organizations. Our function is not to run new projects but to stimulate their initiation. Our main purpose is to provide original and critical thinking, to study the various issues which have arisen from the progress of science, and to make constructive suggestions which, we hope, will be taken up by other bodies. I have already indicated some reasons why, it seems to me, our efforts have proved successful. Another important reason is our independence, the fact that we come to Pugwash Conferences representing nobody but ourselves.

Selection of Participants

This brings me to the method of selection of participants in the Conferences. From the beginning we established the principle that scientists should be invited individually and not as representatives of this or that group. We never refer to participants from a given country as a delegation from that country. In fact, we frequently observe at Conferences a greater measure of agreement among scientists from different countries than among those from a single country. This independence of outlook is, I hope, a fundamental characteristic of scientists. Science does not accept any dogma; it has no respect for authority or established tradition other than that arrived at on scientific grounds. Academic freedom of the scientist is the condition *sine qua non* for the existence and progress of science, and the same must apply to our conferences. But just as there exist differences of opinion amongst scientists on scientific matters, there are differences among scientists on political issues, and it has been our **aim** to balance the participation so that many aspects of political opinion are represented.

It has not always been possible to achieve this aim. All the past Conferences were small ones, involving from two to six dozen participants, and since we concentrated on disarmament problems and gradually went into the more sophisticated arguments about disarmament treaties, it was necessary to rely more and more on people who had a professional competence in these matters, or who had been concerned with them in a semi-official capacity on behalf of their governments. For the same reason we included among the participants a few non-scientists. As a result of all this we had to leave out many scientists who, although deeply interested in the problems of disarmament, have not specialized in this field. It will be for you to

Appendix 11   202

comment on this policy and to make recommendations about the method of
selection of participants at future conferences.

Some statistics about the attendance at the past Conferences may be useful
in this respect. The nine Conferences held hitherto had a total of 396
full participants (excluding observers), i.e., an average of 44 per Conference. The actual number of people participating was only 204, because
many scientists came more than once; but 65 per cent of all participants
attended only one Conference. This was not because they did not want to
come again but because the Committee wanted to enable as many scientists
as possible to attend the Conferences.

Although these are Conferences of scientists, it has proved fruitful to
bring in people from other disciplines. Eighteen per cent of all participants were in this category, comprising economists, lawyers, historians,
and politicians. Among the natural sciences there was a strong predominance of the physical sciences--45 per cent of all participants were physicists. Chemistry accounted only for 8 per cent, biology and medicine for
18 per cent, and the remaining 11 per cent were technologists, mainly in
electronics, and mathematicians. At the earlier Conferences the percentage of physicists was even higher, about 65. This is understandable, as
these are the scientists most directly concerned with nuclear weapons,
but the time has probably come for a more balanced distribution of participants among the various branches of science.

The geographic distribution reflected more the expense of travel than the
expanse of science. Twenty-five countries were represented: 54 per cent
from Europe, 36 per cent from North America, 8 per cent from Asia and 1
per cent each from Australia and South America. We are very glad that the
remaining continent, Africa, is for the first time represented at the
present Conference.

Other Activities
Turning from the Conferences to other forms of our activity, it is obvious
that the intermittent effort which the international Conferences represent
is not the most efficient way to make progress. A continuing effort is
needed and statements of general principle are becoming of little value.
Much detailed study on specific topics must take place in study groups,
in which scientists can work either full-time or part-time in the interval
between Conferences. The Conferences themselves should serve as a means
of confrontation and co-ordination of the ideas which have emerged from
these study groups.

The most worth-while are, of course, international study groups. We have
recommended the setting up of such study groups several years ago, but
they did not materialize for financial reasons; such a continuing effort
involves a very great expense. It seems now very likely that one international study group, on arms control and disarmament, will receive financial backing and begin work in the near future; but several other problems
must receive similar intense and urgent attention.

In the meantime we have encouraged the formation of study groups in several countries on a national scale, and you will hear today about their experience. We have also sponsored regional meetings of scientists from countries not too distant geographically. There have been five such meetings in Geneva, with participants from the Western European countries; these will be enlarged in the future to include scientists from Eastern Europe.

The pattern of our future activities is thus gradually beginning to crystallize. We shall have to rely largely on national groups of scientists to organize study groups, meetings, lectures and other activities in the pursuance of our aims. We shall also have to set up international study groups whenever possible, and use the international Conferences as the culminating points of this detailed work.

In the interval between Conferences, a valuable link between the national groups would be a journal and/or a bulletin of limited circulation, containing information about work in progress. One issue of such a Newsletter was prepared and circulated among our Conference participants a few years ago, but preoccupation with other types of publication have put further issues in abeyance. It is becoming clear, however, that the Newsletter would perform a different function from the other publications. With the greater emphasis on national groups, such a Newsletter would become a necessary part of our activities, possibly in conjunction with a central office to act as a clearing house for information for the national groups.

Financial Problems
The limiting factor in our activities, whether on a national, regional, or international level, is finance. Scientists, on the whole, are not rich, and their salaries are not sufficiently high to allow for frequent travelling abroad, even in the economy class. Attendance at international scientific conferences is now accepted as an integral part of one's scientific work, and there are many foundations and government agencies which offer grants for this purpose. This is a relatively recent development and has not yet found general application to conferences of the Pugwash type. The notion that it is as important for the future of mankind to discuss the implications of the progress of science as this progress itself, is far from being generally accepted. This is unfortunate, because it should be clear that scientific research work without regard to its implications will eventually lead to wastage far greater than the expense involved in sponsoring the activities we are advocating. Anyhow, as far as we are concerned, the result has been a continuous struggle to keep going, even on a limited scale. In fact, if it were not for the philanthropic attitude of a few individuals and groups we would not have been able to start.

In this connection I must express our indebtedness to Mr. Cyrus Eaton whose munificence made possible the first few Conferences. We are very grateful to other individuals for their support. Some of them, Mrs. Agnes Meyer, Mr. James Wise, and Mr. Alfred Bingham, we are very pleased to see here as our guests, and I am glad of this opportunity to acknowledge our gratitude. This applies also to several institutions, in particular, the Körner Foundation in Austria, the Soviet Academy of Sciences, and the Ford Foundation in the United States, whose generous grants have made possible the Conferences in Kitzbühel, Moscow and Stowe. For the Cambridge Conference, which was held last week, and for the present Conference, we are indebted mainly to the generosity of many people and firms in Great Britain who have responded to a public appeal.

Unfortunately, the funds collected were not sufficient to enable us to pay travelling expenses and to offer hospitality to participants. This is the reason why, instead of the anticipated 300 people, we have less than 200. Many scientists, particularly from remote countries, were unable to come, although deeply interested and anxious to participate. It is indeed a tribute to the high regard for these Conferences that more than a half of all former participants are here, despite the many other calls on their time and money. All the same, we very much regret the absence of other colleagues. In particular, we miss our colleagues from the People's Republic of China. We have sent an invitation to them and had hoped that they would be able to join us here; but we heard from the Chinese Academy of Sciences that they regret that other duties prevented them from coming; they sent their best wishes for the success of the Conference. We also regret the absence of scientists from the German Democratic Republic, four of whom had accepted our invitation but are not here for a different reason: they were unable to obtain travel permits. This is a reflection of the tense situation which exists about the Berlin issue, and a reminder to us of the urgency of finding means of terminating this absurd state of affairs.

The reason for the absence of another scientist, Professor Jose Teixeira, who would have been the only participant from Portugal, is distressing. I have just heard that he has been arrested by the political police and is kept in prison.

Future Organization
One of the problems which has to be decided by you, and which is related to the scope of future activities, is the form of organization which we should adopt. On several occasions suggestions have been made that we should set ourselves up as a formal organization with a well-defined membership, constitution, subscription, etc. There are several advantages in having such a formal organization: we could register with the United Nations as a Non-Governmental Organization and avail ourselves of the many facilities which this offers; also, many of the national groups would find it convenient to be affiliated formally to an international organization. It may well be that the time has now come for the setting up of such an organization. On the other hand, there are many advantages in the informal way in which we have been conducting our affairs so far. It is certainly more in the spirit of our independence. Also, having no rigid structure, formal constitution or established staff, we depend largely on the enthusiasm of individuals, which makes for a much more lively if somewhat precarious existence. It is indeed remarkable that so much has been achieved with so little organization. At one stage the Committee decided that there

should be a central office in London, but there is not a single full-time officer or employee there; there is in fact no office and no staff. All the work has been done by scientists in their spare time and by part-time secretaries. This is probably one of the reasons why many more people know of Pugwash as a colourful character in a children's comic than as a movement of scientists.

Finally, a few words about the Continuing Committee itself. Apart from the formal appointment of a Secretary-General in 1959, the Committee managed to avoid too much formality in the conduct of its affairs. There have been fifteen meetings of the Committee since 1957, and except for the very first meeting, no vote has been taken on any of the decisions we have made. This does not mean that there were no differences of opinion among members of the Committee. There have been considerable differences, heated arguments and interminable discussions, but in the end we have always managed to talk it out and reach an understanding acceptable to all. This, of course, is true of the Pugwash Conferences in general. We come here because we are anxious to establish a stable world, and in the long run there is no point in the majority imposing its will on the minority. Science is not ruled by a majority vote, but by the acceptance of the soundness of arguments. We apply this principle to our Conferences. It is because of this spirit that we managed to get together people who represent entirely different points of view, as exemplified today by the **presence on this platform of two members of the House of Lords, its Leader** and one of its oldest members, but who do not exactly see eye to eye in many other ways. It is because of this spirit that our Conferences have become a symbol of successful international debate on controversial issues and a model for similar efforts in other fields.

The present Conference differs in magnitude, programme and purpose from the previous ones, and about half of the participants here have never been to a Pugwash Conference, but I am sure that the Pugwash spirit will prevail here. We have behind us five years of efforts to establish international understanding and good will. This was achieved by a very small group of scientists. We now want to extend these ideas to embrace a large part of the scientific community, because we believe that the time is ripe for such an extension. As Lord Russell has just reminded us: "Science has provided the means of mass destruction, and science, therefore, has the responsibility of doing what it can to cause these means to be employed for better ends."

We are all aware of **these** better ends of science. We have before us the vision of a new world in which men of all lands will live together in peace, in friendship and in plenty. We scientists can play an important part in making this vision a practical reality.

12 REPORT FROM THE STANDING COMMITTEE ON FUTURE ACTIVITIES TO THE TENTH PUGWASH CONFERENCE IN LONDON

At the first session of the Tenth Pugwash Conference in London, a standing committee was charged to recommend future activities. The Standing Committee received advice and many excellent proposals from Conference participants. The selection of proposals was governed by the limited financial and staff resources of the Continuing Committee. In addition, there was the requirement that all proposals be faithful to the following principles:

1. The goal of full disarmament and permanent peace is realistic and urgent, and all activities of the Pugwash Movement should be directly related to this goal.

2. Pugwash is an association of scientists, and the criterion of work should be that it is scientific or technical in itself, or represents a problem which can be tackled by the application of the scientific method.

3. Pugwash must not duplicate the work of other international agencies, but this does not exclude examination of questions being considered by these agencies.

4. Pugwash Conferences must be non-governmental, although scientists serving in official capacities are welcome.

5. The Conferences as a general rule should be small.

6. All Conferences should be directly concerned with achievement of disarmament and permanent peace. Subjects less directly relevant to this goal may be included on the Conference agenda. It is recommended that it would be desirable to rotate the participants in order to broaden the representation from various countries.

Future Conferences

1. The International Continuing Committee shall convene conferences at its discretion.

2. It is recommended that, in response to the invitation from our Pugwash colleagues in India, a Conference should be held in that country. The programme would consider the uses of science in assisting developing nations, the possibilities of international collaboration in this endeavour and its significance for the achievement of permanent peace.

3. In response to an invitation from Yugoslavia, it is recommended that a Conference be held in Yugoslavia on the "Role of the Smaller Powers in Achieving the Goal of Disarmament and Permanent Peace." Although participants from the larger powers should be invited, the major working papers should be prepared by the smaller nations.

4. The Committee on Future Activities welcomes the invitation from Czechoslovakia to hold a Conference in Prague on "Friendly Relations and Peaceful Collaboration among States."

5. It is recommended that the Continuing Committee expand its activities so as to include regional conferences. It is proposed that a conference be arranged with the participation of scientists from India and Pakistan in order to promote contacts and co-operation in science between these two countries. The regional conferences should be in accordance with the spirit and organization of the international Pugwash Conferences.

Agenda Items to be Included in Future Conferences
The Committee felt that according to the principles outlined in the introduction to this report the following items did not individually merit the attention of a full Conference, but considered them of sufficient importance to be included as agenda items at other Conferences to be held:

1. An assessment of the biological and environmental consequences of possible nuclear wars and the peacetime releases of radioactive materials.

2. Implementation of the specific proposals made at the Seventh Conference on international collaboration, and any new proposals which might arise. If indicated, either in the working group of a conference, or by other developments, interim study groups should be **arranged to forward specific proposals**.

3. The general problem of keeping the peace in a disarming and disarmed world should be an item on the agenda in future disarmament conferences. Working Group 4 of the Ninth Conference discussed several aspects of this subject.

Pugwash Projects

1. Study Groups.
(a) It was agreed that preliminary discussion under Pugwash auspices among a small group of East and West scholars should begin on the topic "Fear and Mistrust as Barriers to Disarmament and Stable Peace."

(b) National Pugwash study groups should be encouraged to undertake investigations on particular problems and any new approaches which may contribute to disarmament conferences and the maintenance of peace, e.g., the question of whether a nuclear disarmament zone is feasible in Central Europe and what measures of control might be required. A second subject might be the study of a limited zone of disarmament as a test zone for control procedures.

(c) It is suggested that the Continuing Committee encourages the formation of other groups in relation to the Pugwash Movement, based on the same pattern of East-West scientific collaboration, to deal with such subjects as education, aid to developing nations and other matters.

Appendix 12

2. Publications. The International Continuing Committee should fulfil two responsibilities in the area of publications and communications. The first task is to keep Pugwash scientists informed of one another's work and activities. The second task is to inform the public.

To carry out the first task, the Committee recommends a private Pugwash Newsletter to be issued about four times a year. The copyright should be held by the International Committee and the circulation limited to Pugwash participants and supporters. The Secretary-General should be Editor-in-Chief, and should delegate responsibility to an editor. An editorial board should be established under the jurisdiction of the International Committee. The Newsletter should contain, in addition to short reports and articles, a bibliography of all published material which the Editorial Board believes should be brought to the attention of Pugwash scientists. It would be desirable that all publications bearing the Pugwash name should appear simultaneously in English and Russian.

To fulfil the second task of informing the public, the national Pugwash groups should be encouraged to undertake wide distribution of approved material. The Secretary-General should be empowered to give such approval. The Committee recommends that past efforts which included publication of Pugwash Conferences' papers (with the author's permission) in magazines and journals throughout the world should be increased. Every working group from Conferences and all study groups (national or international) should inform the Secretary-General whether they agree to general publication.

3. Fund Raising. The Committee supports the general rule that financial assistance is welcomed from any individual, foundation, or government, provided that no strings are attached. Financial contributions should not imply any right of participation at conferences or other activities.

National groups should explore systematically new sources of funds and continue to support the travel of their members to international conferences. In addition, national groups should assume a share of the operating costs of the international office.

The efficient functioning of Pugwash activities internally requires that a systematic effort be made to acquire adequate finances. The Secretary-General may employ a suitable individual or utilize the services of a small group of interested supporters to undertake work in this connection. It is recommended that the Secretary-General appoints a committee to devise an equitable formula allocating respective national responsibilities necessary for the support of the International Office.

STATEMENT FROM THE TENTH PUGWASH CONFERENCE, HELD IN LONDON, SEPTEMBER 3-7, 1962

We scientists from 36 countries, assembled at the Tenth Pugwash Conference on Science and World Affairs, are united by an awareness that the scientific revolution has created a radically new situation for humanity, endowing man with an unprecedented capacity for creation and destruction. We have come to London to seek the most effective ways to ensure that science shall be a blessing to mankind and not a curse.

Our chief concern is to prevent war and to relieve humanity of the fearful anxieties and the grave economic burdens caused by the arms race. A general war with nuclear weapons would be a disaster of unimaginable magnitude. It would destroy a large fraction of the people now alive and jeopardize the conditions of life of the survivors.

Throughout the world competition in armaments absorbs an immense amount of talent and resources. This is wasted because so far from giving security, it increases the risk of war. Against global rockets with thermonuclear warheads there is no effective defence. In this situation, the traditional view of war, or the threat of war, as an instrument of policy is obsolete. War must be eliminated from the life of mankind. General and complete disarmament, with effective means of preserving international security, is the most urgent issue in world affairs.

Disarmament and a stable peace are essential conditions for making a new society in which poverty could be abolished. The prospect of such a world is no longer Utopian. The technological and scientific triumphs of our own times have already far outstripped the boldest dreams of recent generations and knowledge increases ever more rapidly.

In our Conferences we have, therefore, concentrated attention on the complex problems of disarmament. These have included: the steps by which disarmament could be achieved, and measures to ensure the confidence and security of states during the process; the measures needed to keep the peace in a disarmed world; and the economic problems which might be encountered while disarming. Our discussions have led us to believe that solutions may be found for all these problems.

We have also paid special attention to the problem of stopping nuclear tests, and to proposals on this subject made at Geneva by non-aligned nations. Novel suggestions were made at the Conference for improving the effectiveness of the means of detecting nuclear tests by automatic sealed seismic stations. These would be put in places in agreed numbers by the host nation after being sealed by an international authority and would not, we think, endanger the security of any country.

We have reached the conclusion that in the process of general and complete disarmament, the early elimination, with adequate and effective verification measures, and within a short period of time of the means of delivery of the weapons of mass destruction, would constitute a satisfactory

Appendix 13   210

beginning when linked with substantial reductions of conventional military
forces and armaments and with the solution of the problems arising from
the presence of troops and bases on foreign soil.

The experience of our Conferences leads us to believe that scientists have
a special contribution to make to the solution of these problems. Informal discussions between scientists contribute to the understanding of
different points of view.

We consider that our Conferences have been useful, but we are in a period
of immensely rapid change in which new problems are constantly emerging.
Scientists should, therefore, increase their efforts to bring about disarmament and conditions of lasting peace. Scientists of all nations have
a commanding duty to help their fellow citizens to understand that war is
obsolete and what steps can ensure peace. They should, we believe, recognize their responsibilities to promote disarmament and should invite governments, learned societies and other institutions to support them in
this task.

Increasing confidence between nations is an essential element in progress
towards disarmament and stable peace. As a contribution to mutual understanding we have, therefore, also considered constructive proposals for
many kinds of international collaboration in science. These have included
proposals for large-scale co-operation in pure science and international
efforts for the application of science to the advancement of the newly
developing nations.

We are now at a stage in which general statements of principles are not
enough; action is needed. Some proposals to promote disarmament and human
welfare need detailed study to assess their implications; others could be
implemented immediately. We reassert our conviction that the goal of full
disarmament and permanent peace is realistic and urgent. This work is
truly to be seen as a part of a long struggle for the progress of mankind,
and it is one in which scientists have a responsible part to play. We
call upon scientists everywhere in the world to join us in this task.

This text was agreed *nem. con.*, with the following abstaining:
Dr. D. G. Brennan, Mr. A. H. Katz, Dr. H. A. Kissinger, Prof. L. Lipson
and Mr. W. Young.

Participants

Australia
Dr. John W. Burton, Prof. J. D. B. Miller, Sir Mark Oliphant

Austria
Dr. Manfred Breitenecker, Prof. F. Mainx, Prof. R. Steinmaurer,
Prof. Hans Thirring

Brazil
Prof. C. M. C. Lattes

Bulgaria
Prof. G. Nadjakov

Canada
Dr. N. Z. Alcock, Dr. Brock Chisholm, Prof. J. C. Polanyi

Czechoslovakia
Prof. V. Husa, Acad. Joseph Macek, Acad. Ivan Málek, Mr. T. Němec, Acad. Vladimir Prochazka, Acad. F. Šorm

Denmark
Prof. O. Kofoed-Hansen, Prof. Ole Maaløe

Federal German Republic
Mr. H. Afheldt, Prof. G. Burkhardt, Dr. H. Franz, Prof. H. Friedrich-Freska, Prof. Hanfried Lenz, Prof. E. Menzel, Prof. K. A. Wolf

France
Father Pierre-Leon Dubarle, Prof. B. P. Gregory, Dr. A. Gros, Mr. G. Gueron, Prof. J. Gueron, Prof. Andre Lwoff, Prof. Michel Magat, Dr. H. Marcovich, Prof. P. Piganiol, Prof. Pierre Rosenstiehl

Ghana
Prof. J. A. K. Quartey, Dr. J. Yanney-Wilson

Greece
Dr. S. Vatistas

Hungary
Prof. R. Bognar, Prof. Lenard Pal, Prof. F. B. Straub

Iceland
Dr. O. Gunnarsson

India
Prof. P. C. Mahalanobis

Ireland
Dr. E. J. Conway

Israel
Dr. Hugo Boyko, Prof. M. Sela

Italy
Prof. A. A. Buzzati-Traverso, Prof. G. Favilli, Prof. Lucio Mezzetti

Japan
Prof. S. Kamefuchi, Prof. Iwao Ogawa, Prof. H. Yukawa

Lebanon
Prof. T. Raven

Appendix 13

Malaya
Sir Alexander Oppenheim

Netherlands
Prof. C. J. Gorter, Dr. S. L. Kwee, Prof. B. R. A. Nijboer, Mr. G. H. Slotemaker de Bruine, Prof. H. A. Tolhoek

New Zealand
Dr. J. Read, Prof. D. Walker

Nigeria
Dr. Chike Obi

Norway
Dr. T. Förland, Dr. H. Wergeland

Pakistan
Prof. Abdus Salam

Poland
Prof. M. Danysz, Prof. Leopold Infeld, Prof. Karol Lapter

Rumania
Acad. H. Hulubei

South Africa
Dr. T. E. W. Schumann

Spain
Prof. J. Catala de Alemany

Sweden
Dr. G. W. Funke, Prof. Olov Lindberg, Dr. L. Revesz

Switzerland
Prof. W. Heitler, Prof. F. G. Houtermans

U.A.R.
Dr. S. R. Morcos

U.K.
Mr. F. C. Bawden, Prof. J. D. Bernal, Prof. P. M. S. Blackett, Prof. W. E. Burcham, Prof. E. H. S. Burhop, Prof. R. Calder, Sir John Cockcroft, Prof. J. Cohen, Sir Charles Darwin, Sir Howard Florey, Prof. O. R. Frisch, Prof. A. Haddow, Prof. Dorothy Hodgkin, Sir Julian Huxley, Dr. Patricia Lindop, Sir Ben Lockspeiser, Dame Kathleen Lonsdale, Prof. Gordon Manley, Dr. D. C. Martin, Sir Nevill Mott, Mr. Philip Noel-Baker, Sir Rudolph Peters, Mr. N. W. Pirie, Prof. C. F. Powell, Prof. J. Rotblat, Earl Russell, Prof. M. G. P. Stoker, Sir George Thomson, Prof. C. H. Waddington, Mr. Wayland Young

U.S.A.
Dr. Peter G. Bergmann, Dr. Viola W. Bernard, Prof. Kenneth E. Boulding, Dr. Donald G. Brennan, Prof. Robert B. Brode, Prof. Harrison Brown, Dr. Ralph W. Burhoe, Dr. Barry Commoner, Dr. William V. Consolazio, Prof. William C. Davidon, Prof. Freeman J. Dyson, Dr. John T. Edsall, Prof. Bernard T. Feld, Prof. Jerome D. Frank, Prof. Bentley Glass, Prof. Roger M. Herriott, Dr. Hudson Hoagland, Dr. David R. Inglis, Dr. Marvin Kalkstein, Dr. Martin M. Kaplan, Mr. Amrom H. Katz, Dr. Henry Kissinger, Prof. Otto Klineberg, Mr. Richard S. Leghorn, Prof. Wassily Leontief, Prof. Leon Lipson, Dr. Margaret Mead, Prof. Matthew Meselson, Prof. Jay Orear, Dr. Harry Palevsky, Prof. Linus Pauling, Dr. John B. Phelps, Prof. Eugene Rabinowitch, Prof. Roger Revelle, Prof. Alexander Rich, Prof. Theodor Rosebury, Prof. Albert B. Sabin, Prof. Edward Shils, Dr. John S. Toll, Prof. Victor F. Weisskopf, Dr. Hugh C. Wolfe

U.S.S.R.
Acad. L. A. Artsimovitch, Dr. N. I. Bazanov, Dr. G. P. Besedin, Acad. A. A. Blagonravov, Acad. N. N. Bogolubov, Acad. M. M. Dubinin, Prof. V. S. Emelyanov, Prof. N. N. Inozemtsev, Acad. V. A. Kargin, Prof. V. M. Khvostov, Dr. S. G. T. Korneev, Prof. I. J. Kozhevnikov, Prof. A. M. Kuzin, Prof. O. Leipunski, Mr. V. Pavlichenko, Prof. J. Riznichenko, Prof. M. I. Rubinstein, Prof. N. A. Talensky, Prof. I. E. Tamm, Acad. A. V. Topchiev, Acad. A. N. Tupolev, Prof. A. N. Vernov

Yugoslavia
Dr. D. Calic, Prof. A. Kuhelj, Prof. Ivan Supek

Observers and Scientific Staff

Australia
Prof. P. Fitzgerald, Dr. R. E. B. Makinson

Austria
Dr. Robert Jungk

Canada
Dr. F. R. Joubin

Denmark
Mr. Børge Michelsen, Dr. J. W. Ulrich

Netherlands
Mr. J. Fieyra, Mr. L. O. ten Cate

South Africa
Mr. J. A. King

U.K.
Dr. H. R. Allan, Dr. T. E. Alibone, Mr. Hedley Bull, Sir Anthony Buzzard, Mr. Nigel Calder, Mrs. S. Campbell-Smith, Prof. G. E. G. Catlin, Mr. A. Clow, Dr. R. Fraser, Mr. Maurice Goldsmith, Mr. Arthur Haslett,

Appendix 13   214

U.K. (Continued)
Prof. G. W. Hutchinson, Sir Joseph Hutchinson, Dr. Alick Isaacs,
Sir Stephen King-Hall, Mr. Gerald Leach, Dr. W. Levitt, Mr. John Maddox,
Dr. Tom Margerison, Mr. E. Max Nicholson, Dr. Felix Pirani, Dr. Antoinette
Pirie, Sir Oliver Scott, Miss Esther Simpson, Dr. A. P. Willmore

U.S.A.
Mrs. Ruth Adams, Prof. Walter C. Clemens, Jr., Mr. Robert C. Cowen,
Dr. E. Raymond Platig, Mr. Victor Rabinowitch, Dr. George W. Rathjens,
Prof. F. Reif

UNESCO
Dr. V. A. Kovda, Dr. H. Roderick

14 STATEMENT FROM THE ELEVENTH PUGWASH CONFERENCE, HELD IN DUBROVNIK, SEPTEMBER 20-25, 1963

The 11th Pugwash Conference on Science and World Affairs was held in Dubrovnik from 20 to 25 September 1963. These conferences bring together distinguished scientists from East and West for frank and informal discussions on important problems of common interest; particularly those related to the threat of nuclear war, the problem of achieving general and complete disarmament, and ways of ensuring the widespread application of science for peaceful purposes.

The Dubrovnik Conference was organized by the Continuing Committee of the Pugwash Conferences, of which the Secretary-General is Professor Joseph Rotblat of London, together with a Yugoslav Organizing Committee under the chairmanship of Professor Ivan Supek. The Conference was sponsored by the Council of Yugoslav Academies. Among the 64 participants from 24 countries there were 13 from the U.S.A., 11 from the U.S.S.R., and 7 from the U.K. In addition there were 14 observers.

The main theme of the Conference was "Current Problems of Disarmament and World Security," and five Working Groups were formed to consider the following topics:
1. Problems of General Disarmament.
2. Consequences of the Spread of Nuclear Weapons.
3. Denuclearized zones, especially in Central Europe and the Balkans.
4. Role of Non-Aligned Nations in Disarmament and World Security.
5. The Partial Test-ban, the Problems of Detection, and the Next Steps.

The timing of the meeting, following so closely on the successful negotiation of a Nuclear Test-ban Treaty, was fortunate, and the friendly cooperative and hopeful atmosphere of the discussions was immediately apparent to the participants. The reports of the Working Groups were substantial and showed that much progress had been made in reaching common understanding on important practical issues, in giving consideration to clarifying different points of view, and in raising novel suggestions which can be studied and given further consideration at subsequent conferences.

Prevention of Surprise Attack

In Working Group 1, two important proposals were made relating to the prevention of surprise attack in Central Europe, where NATO and Warsaw Pact countries face each other. It is essential that both sides should assure themselves against surprise attack since this would make possible a mutual reduction of conventional defence forces, and eventually of nuclear forces also. It could thus greatly help in the creation of atom-free zones in Central Europe.

Firstly, it was suggested that rapid agreement might be obtained for establishing control posts at major transportation centres within agreed areas of Central Europe. These posts would give warning of any surprise attack which required the massing and transport of large numbers of conventional arms and forces. The control posts would be equipped with all necessary facilities for access and communication.

Secondly, it was suggested that military officers from each side should be stationed and should reside with the troops of the other side within the agreed areas. These officers would have adequate means of communication with their own governments. It was suggested that the details should be worked out by military experts of the countries concerned.

Minimum Deterrent Force. The Group discussed, as a first step in disarmament, the destruction of all nuclear delivery vehicles whatsoever, except for the creation of a minimum deterrent, or "umbrella," force which would be sufficient to deter, but not sufficient to allow an aggressor to wage a major thermonuclear war. It was thought that a very substantial number of vehicles could be eliminated in less than a year.

The Group agreed that during the period of disarmament, world security would have to be guaranteed by the umbrella forces of the U.S.A. and U.S.S.R. alone. Most participants thought, however, that the adoption of a substantial measure of nuclear disarmament by these two major powers might be sufficient to persuade the other nuclear powers to forego their nuclear forces altogether, and so make it very difficult for any further country to enter the nuclear arms race.

Control and Inspection. The Group agreed that control and inspection of the process of disarmament should be effected by a permanent International Disarmament Organization enjoying all necessary privileges and powers. They state that the possibility that any power could cheat by evading inspection has been grossly exaggerated, but that the inspection system has not only to maintain security and prevent cheating, but also has to alleviate the fears that cheating might occur. Since no inspection system can be perfect, greater efforts might profitably be made to devise machinery to deal openly with the doubts and fears which must inevitably arise from time to time. Inspection would also be eased if short-range tactical weapons could be drawn back from an atom-free zone between East and West.

Limiting the Spread of Nuclear Weapons

In Working Group 2, several valuable contributions were made. First, that since the development of nuclear reactors in many countries might lead to a proliferation of nuclear weapons, control of fissile materials should be made more effective, and the major powers should transfer their fissile materials through the International Atomic Energy Agency rather than, as is often now the case, through bilateral agreements; and that IAEA should assume full control of such transfers. Further, to avoid the waste of man-power and resources by many small nations which would follow from the development of their own nuclear technology, international centres for peaceful nuclear technology, especially power-production, should be set up and should be organized along the lines of the present successful international centres for pure research. In such centres, all nations would be able to contribute and gain experience and skills on a common, open basis. The second contribution was an appraisal of the argument sometimes used to justify atomic bomb construction—that important scientific and technical forces are thus created for the strengthening of the industrial and economic capacity of a country. It was concluded that further bomb-production in our present circumstances, would be a grossly inefficient way of securing such technical and scientific advantages. They can be obtained much more economically by other methods.

As further steps for the prevention of the spread of nuclear weapons, the Group recommended that the security of countries which forego the construction of nuclear weapons should be guaranteed by the strengthening of the system of collective security, and that the Great Powers should accept a special responsibility for this within the framework of the U.N. Such countries should also be supported by making available to them the scientific and technical knowledge which they might have gained from the production of nuclear weapons. The Group also agreed that some form of sanctions should be established against any power which undertakes the testing or production of atomic weapons, after a complete test-ban has been signed and a substantial measure of disarmament achieved.

Atom-Free Zones

In Working Group 3, there was a fruitful discussion about atom-free zones, and two specific recommendations were made. The first, to all Governments directly concerned in Central Europe, suggested that they should enter into negotiations leading to the lessening of tensions in the area and to the establishment of a denuclearized Central Europe. The second proposed that the Governments of the Balkans, Africa and Latin America should conclude a treaty banning nuclear weapons from those parts of the world and conforming to the U.N. Charter, with arrangements for international inspection.

Non-Aligned Nations

Working Group 4 stressed the contribution which could be made by non-aligned nations by their renunciation of nuclear weapons, and by establishing atom-free zones as a contribution towards complete disarmament. The Group also suggested that the non-aligned nations, ether individually or collectively, should set up institutes or groups for the study of the military, strategic and technological problems met in disarmament. Such institutes should maintain close contact with the various disarmament officials of individual states, and with the U.N. and its special agencies. Such action could allow the creation, in good time, of a competent body of personnel for the support of an International Disarmament Organization.

Extending the Test-Ban

Working Group 5 stressed the importance of early progress towards general disarmament in order that the international confidence generated by the Moscow Treaty may be maintained. Even steps with no great military significance should be sympathetically considered since they may help in improving the political climate. The Group suggested that scientists should take every opportunity to influence public opinion so that the Test-ban Treaty shall be adhered to by all nations (including France and the People's Republic of China). It expressed the opinion that any further tests in the atmosphere, water, or outer space would not only increase radioactive fallout, but could also contribute to the breakdown of the Test-ban Treaty and to a further escalatory series of atomic tests.

To assist in extending the test-ban to include underground tests, the Group suggested that not only should the work of individual states on underground explosion and earthquake detection be continued and intensified; but also that international collaboration in this field should be established. A co-ordinated seismological programme, with full interchange of records of explosions and earthquakes, should be begun by the U.S.A., U.S.S.R. and U.K., with other nations contributing later. Improved methods of detection would diminish the ambiguities in the interpretation of the seismic records and increase the precision with which the origins of such events can be established. In addition, an international seismological station, manned by specialists from different nations, could be established in a politically suitable and seismologically quiet area. Another recommended step which would have the effect of increasing international confidence was that a ban on orbiting nuclear weapons should be negotiated between the major powers.

International Scientific Co-operation
Many of the proposals for international scientific co-operation made at the Seventh Pugwash Conference (Stowe, Vermont in September 1961) have already been agreed or formally proposed. They include various forms of co-operation in space, plans for a world medical and biological research centre, a broadening of the U.S.-U.S.S.R. exchange of scientists, and projects to drill deep into the Earth's crust, such as the Mohole project. The Group considers that there are still further projects worthy of serious consideration.

In spite of widespread agreement on many important issues amongst members of the Conference, a number of questions remained unresolved and several novel suggestions require further consideration. These will be taken up at the next Pugwash Conference to be held in Udaipur, India, towards the end of January 1964. The agenda for this Conference will also include discussions on technical, medical and scientific assistance to the development of new nations.

Participants

Australia
Dr. J. W. Burton

Austria
Prof. H. Thirring

Brazil
Dr. W. Kerr

Bulgaria
Acad. G. Nadjakov

Canada
Dr. N. Z. Alcock

Czechoslovakia
Acad. V. Knapp, Acad. I. Málek

Denmark
Prof. O. M. Kofoed-Hansen

Federal German Republic
Mr. H. Afheldt, Prof. H. Rumpf

France
Father Pierre-Leon Dubarle, Dr. H. Marcovich, Mr. J. Moch, Prof. F. Perrin

German Democratic Republic
Prof. H. Barwich, Prof. G. Rienäcker

Ghana
Mr. D. K. Abbiw-Jackson

Greece
Dr. B. Dimissianos

Hungary
Prof. R. Bognar

India
Prof. M. G. K. Menon

Italy
Prof. A. A. Buzzati-Traverso

Netherlands
Prof. H. A. Tolhoek, Dr. P. Valkenburgh

Poland
Prof. L. Infeld, Prof. K. D. Lapter

Rumania
Acad. D. Dumitrescu

Sweden
Prof. A. Engstrom

Appendix 14   220

Switzerland
Prof. K. P. Meyer

U.K.
Prof. P. M. S. Blackett, Sir John Cockcroft, Prof. B. H. Flowers,
Sir Nevill Mott, Rt. Hon. P. J. Noel-Baker, Prof. C. F. Powell, Prof. J. Rotblat

U.S.A.
Prof. H. Brown, Prof. P. Doty, Prof. B. T. Feld, Prof. R. Fisher,
Prof. D. A. Glaser, Prof. H. B. Glass, Prof. F. A. Long, Prof. M. Meselson,
Prof. I. I. Rabi, Prof. E. Rabinowitch, Prof. A. Rich, Prof. M. Shulman,
Prof. L. Szilard

U.S.S.R.
Acad. L. A. Artsimovitch, Acad. A. A. Arzumanjan, Acad. A. A. Blagonravov,
Acad. N. N. Bogolubov, Prof. V. M. Khvostov, Acad. V. A. Kirillin,
Mr. V. P. Pavlichenko, Prof. N. A. Talensky, Acad. A. N. Tupolev,
Acad. A. P. Vinogradov, Prof. B. M. Vul

Yugoslavia
Acad. M. Bartos, Acad. D. Kanazir, Acad. A. Kuhelj, Mr. Leo Mates,
Acad. I. Supek

Observers and Scientific Staff

Czechoslovakia
Mr. T. Němec

Denmark
Prof. O. Maaløe

Federal German Republic
Prof. G. Burkhardt, Dr. E. Heimendahl

France
Mr. P. Genevey

German Democratic Republic
Dr. P. Hess

U.K.
Mr. Gerald Leach, Dr. Patricia Lindop, Mr. B. T. Price

U.S.A.
Mrs. Ruth Adams, Prof. H. Kissinger, Mr. D. Lang, Dr. V. Rabinowitch

Yugoslavia
Dr. V. Knapp, Mr. M. Lazanski, Prof. A. Moljk

UNESCO
Mr. W. A. Mills, Prof. Tha Hla

WHO
Dr. M. Kaplan

15 STATEMENT FROM THE TWELFTH PUGWASH CONFERENCE, HELD IN UDAIPUR, JANUARY 27-FEBRUARY 1, 1964

A. Disarmament and Measures for Collective Security

We have reviewed recent progress in the reduction of tensions and the limitations of armaments. We have noted with satisfaction the agreement between the governments of the U.S.S.R. and the U.S.A. not to orbit objects with nuclear weapons, and the decisions of these governments to reduce their military budgets--events which have occurred since our last meeting. Nevertheless, we are still faced with the central problem of achieving concrete and substantial measures of disarmament by the great powers.

We recognize that the Moscow Test Ban Treaty of 5th August, 1963, is a significant step towards general and complete disarmament and the course of events since then has justified the hopeful expectations it has created.

We believe that the adoption, in particular by the nuclear powers, of balanced measures requiring no control, by way of the policy of mutual example, would make a valuable contribution to the restriction of the arms race, and the improvement of the international atmosphere. Such measures should include the further reduction of military budgets and of armed forces, withdrawals of troops on foreign soil and closing of foreign military bases.

We recommend that an agreement be reached, along the lines of the proposal made in the letter of Chairman Khrushchev of 31st December, 1963 and the response of President Johnson of 20th January, 1964, which would reaffirm the obligations of the U.N. Charter and prohibit the use of force in settling any territorial dispute or question of frontiers.

The Moscow Test Ban Treaty has made the acquisition of nuclear weapons capability by other nations less likely. At the same time it places on the two major nuclear powers, who continue to maintain nuclear weapons, a heavy responsibility to give ever increasing content to the policy of peaceful co-existence so that they may with full effect make their contribution to safeguarding international security. It is, therefore, essential to strengthen the U.N. system for safeguarding the security of weaker nations, by co-operation of the U.S.A. and U.S.S.R. who should assume special responsibility for this purpose within the framework of the U.N.
To the extent that such a guarantee of security and territorial integrity of all nations, particularly of the non-aligned nations, becomes effective, it would stimulate reductions in the armaments of non-nuclear nations, thereby releasing resources for advancing their economic progress. It would also facilitate further steps towards general and complete disarmament.

In view of the continuing dangers of the spread of nuclear weapons and delivery systems, we believe the following additional measures to be necessary: (1) all nations presently possessing nuclear weapons should jointly undertake not to transfer these weapons or technical information relating to them to any other state or group of states; (2) all nations not possessing nuclear weapons should undertake not to produce such weapons, nor to acquire them or the special technical information necessary for their production; (3) the government of each of the nuclear powers should take whatever measures may be open to it to prevent its nationals with experience in the field of nuclear weapons technology from contributing to the development of the nuclear weapons capacity of any foreign power.

The concept of a nuclear umbrella, or minimum deterrent force, which we have been discussing in our Conferences since 1960, to be maintained by the two great nuclear powers during the process of general and complete disarmament, is of major importance in providing the necessary guarantee against aggression by hidden weapons. We welcome the proposal of the U.S.S.R. to extend it to the end of the disarmament process. We regard the possibility of agreement on the principles of a nuclear umbrella, or minimum deterrent force, to offer one of the most helpful avenues to reach agreement on comprehensive disarmament under effective controls.

In the long run we must realize that disarmament will be neither general nor complete unless all nations, including the People's Republic of China, adhere to the agreements. Whole-hearted adherence of the People's Republic of China will be made more likely if she is brought into the disarmament deliberations soon. In view of this, we urge that steps be taken which will make it possible for her to participate in the discussions and to take her place as a member of the United Nations family.

B. The Relation Between the Economic Problems of Developing Nations and World Security

We have also discussed the relation between the economic problems of the developing nations and world security.

The two problems facing mankind today are the achievement of disarmament and the elimination of poverty. Both are of special concern to scientists. It is the advance of science which has opened up the vast possibilities of destruction that lie before us today. Both require for their solution a new sense of international responsibility; members of each nation must acknowledge that their fate is bound up with the security and prosperity of the members of all other nations.

The conclusion of an agreement on general and complete disarmament would make it possible for advanced nations to divert large resources to the development of developing nations. For example, an increase in aid by an amount equivalent to even one-fourth or one-fifth of the total saving in military expenditure, as a consequence of general and complete disarmament, could, if accompanied by good planning and implementation of programmes for development, be expected roughly to double the present rate of economic growth of the underdeveloped countries.

But the promise of more aid at the time of disarmament must not be an excuse for not giving more aid now. In the light of recent events, when some cuts in military expenditure were not accompanied by increased aid, we strongly feel that it would help to remove misapprehensions and provide reassurance, if the leaders of the advanced nations were to reaffirm now their intention to divert to the developing countries as high a proportion as possible of the resources released by disarmament. Economic aid should not be linked to military and political conditions.

Disarmament in the developing countries themselves would release resources for development. The armed forces of the developing nations, like those of the advanced nations, would be reduced to the minimum level necessary to maintain law and order.

There are several ways in which a start might be made upon greater international co-operation now. The advanced nations may contribute jointly to capital funds, they may work jointly on major projects (e.g., dams) in the developing nations, and they may send joint teams of experts. We urge that these teams, wherever practically advisable, should have a truly international composition not only in the top administration, but also in the field.

The trading position of the developing countries has suffered gravely from the deterioration in their terms of trade over the past decade. Moreover, as they develop they will require increasing markets in the advanced countries for semi-manufactures and finished manufactures, which they will be able to supply in addition to primary products. The advanced countries can greatly help the developing countries through trade. We welcome the United Nations Conference on Trade and Development, which is going to tackle these problems, and we hope that participation will be open to all nations regardless whether or not they are members of the United Nations. We particularly welcome any measures which promote trade and economic co-operation between East and West.

C. Science and Technology for Developing Countries

Modern science and technology have provided the instruments that could lead to a brilliant future for mankind. But the brutal fact is that half the human race lives in misery and degradation. The economic gap between the advanced and the developing countries is widening. If this gap is allowed to grow, as it must in the absence of substantial aid, it is bound to threaten world peace and security.

The hope of solving the problems of poverty depends, above all, on men learning to work together. How shall we make wise international investments for the creation of a better world? How can we produce in the poor countries a sufficient and growing number of well qualified scientists and engineers? How can we improve education at all levels? What is the best way to prevent the loss of scientists from the poor countries to the rich ones?

Assistance by the more prosperous countries to the developing nations is an investment in a better world. To be effective, it needs to be long continued and maintained at a much higher level than at present. Allocations for assistance should be independent of any measures of disarmament, but it is manifest that substantial progress in disarmament could release great resources, a considerable fraction of which could be devoted to raising the productive capacities of the newly developing countries. This would be a modern version of beating swords into ploughshares.

Generally, we would like to see an ever widening degree of internationalism in economic relations, including co-operative planning for the development of the world's resources.

In the common interest of all nations, aid to developing countries must be removed from the context of the cold war. There are two principal means of doing this and we urge statesmen to explore both. One is through the multilateral agencies (though we believe both bilateral and multilateral aid will continue to be needed), the other is through common enterprises in which East and West collaborate in carrying out large development projects--for example, a joint attack on the salinity problems in the Punjab.

Advances in science and technology are even now opening up new resources of wealth outside the jurisdiction of national states. We suggest that now, while the situation is still in flux, the question be explored of giving U.N. jurisdiction over outer space, the oceans outside recognized national jurisdiction, and Antarctica; this jurisdiction to include exclusive rights to regulate activities in these areas, for the benefit of the developing countries.

All past experience in the advanced countries shows that the return on investments in research, both pure and applied, can be very high, indeed higher than in almost any other areas.

We believe that similar investments in the developing countries will yield similar returns. Such investments should be limited only by the availability of persons competent to undertake the work, and these investments should be rapidly increased year by year until they reach the order of 2-3 per cent of the gross national product.

Each nation should undertake those kinds of research which are most important for its development and which it can best do. Each region of the world offers particular opportunities and every nation can contribute to world science. For the most part research in developing nations, as in others, should be applied. Local problems involving the economic development of the nation should be identified and explored. These problems will range from those of basic geology and geophysics to plant physiology and genetics, and from the economics of development to the sociology and biology of human reproduction.

Developing nations, like the more advanced ones, are faced with the double task of engaging in research necessary for their economic growth and at the same time of training expanding numbers of competent research workers. Research institutes formed for the purpose of expediting research in specialized areas should be closely connected with the universities. The leading research personnel should teach in the universities, and graduate students should be encouraged to conduct their research in the institutes.

Appendix 15

Universities anywhere, but especially in developing countries, cannot hope to be excellent in all fields. Initially, each university in a developing country should concentrate on a few areas for research, and training in research, which are particularly important to that country. Interchange of staff and research students with universities in the advanced countries should be encouraged by every possible means. To be truly effective, such co-operation between universities must go far beyond what has happened in the past. The developing countries have great opportunities to become leaders in many fields of the social and natural sciences, where they can offer unique facilities for research.

Scientists and engineers of East and West can work together on scientific problems of development. For example, research is required on soil salinity in the Indus plains of India and Pakistan. Soil scientists from the U.S.S.R. and U.S.A. could gain valuable insights and mutual understanding by working together on this critical problem. Means must particularly be sought through the international scientific unions, and in other ways, to help individual scientists from the rich and poor countries to work together.

The formation of international youth teams, possibly under the auspices of the United Nations, in which young specialists and technicians from East and West, North and South, could work together on specific projects under the supervision of senior experts, could also be useful. Possible examples are health teams and geological survey teams.

The disparity in the conditions of work, in status, and in salaries, between scientists in the developing and the advanced countries must be reduced. This would be the best way to avoid the tragic loss of many of the ablest and best trained young men from the poor countries.

A scientific attitude must pervade the whole of the educational process in the schools. The methods of teaching science in the developing countries can be greatly improved by the use of new teaching techniques and by continued research in ways of better teaching.

In the development process, the stage of identifying and analysing the major problems of a country or region will almost always involve a multidisciplinary approach, in which engineers, agronomists, operational analysts, natural scientists, sociologists, economists, specialists in public administration, and humanists concerned with the traditions and the values of the people, must all work together. A good analysis is the least expensive step in the development process; yet it can multiply many-fold the effectiveness of large development expenditures. If the analysis is to be acceptable to the developing country, its representatives must participate in organizing the analysis. For these and other reasons, the stage of analysis is one in which the U.N. agencies can play an essential role.

We recommend the establishment within the United Nations family of a semi-autonomous institute or commission for resource analyses. Its members would be those nations which wish to co-operate in making or using multidisciplinary analyses of development problems. Its programmes would be worked out and approved by conferences of the member states. But the work would be paid for by the countries in which the analytical teams were situated and by other countries interested in the problem. Thus, the budget of the institute itself could be relatively small. One of its essential functions would be the training of teams from the developing countries in the methods of analysis and data interpretation.

We suggest that UNESCO should play an important role in establishing and sponsoring the new organization, but other specialized agencies of the United Nations should also be intimately involved.

To strengthen UNESCO for its newly assumed tasks of helping to apply science and technology for development, the National Commissions for UNESCO in each member country should contain many more natural and social scientists and engineers. National liaison agencies with UNESCO should include those concerned with science and technology as well as the ministries of education.

We believe that a semi-autonomous world health research centre under the sponsorship of the World Health Organization could be useful to the developing countries if its field operations included support of and collaboration with existing research laboratories in those countries, and the establishment of regional laboratories for specific needs such as the study of tropical communicable disease.

The developing countries have experienced great difficulties in obtaining trustworthy and sufficiently complete technical information on industrial processes and the design of machinery and plants for industry. We urge the U.N. and the specialized agencies to do much more towards developing industrial consulting services, reference-collections of technological information, and a central exchange to publicize the needs in the developing countries for specific technical and industrial knowledge.

Studies on an international scale should be undertaken on the problems of population growth and its impact on economic development.

Participants

Australia
Sir Mark Oliphant

Brazil
Dr. O. Ianni

Canada
Prof. J. C. Polanyi

Czechoslovakia
Acad. I. Málek

Appendix 15

Federal German Republic
Prof. E. Menzel

France
Mr. A. Joxe, Prof. M. Magat, Dr. H. Marcovich

German Democratic Republic
Prof. G. Rienäcker

Hungary
Prof. J. Bognar

India
Prof. H. J. Bhabha, Prof. D. S. Kothari, Prof. M. G. K. Menon, Prof. V. A. Sarabhai, Prof. M. S. Thacker, Dr. S. H. Zaheer

Israel
Dr. A. de Shalit

Italy
Prof. B. Bertotti

Japan
Prof. Y. Miyake, Prof. Eiji Yamada

Malaysia
Prof. A. A. Sandosham

Netherlands
Prof. B. Landheer

Norway
Dr. J. Galtung

Pakistan
Prof. A. Salam

Poland
Prof. L. Infeld

Rumania
Prof. C. Dragulescu

Sweden
Dr. G. W. Funke

Thailand
Dr. C. Puranananda

Uganda
Prof. M. Crawford

U.K.
Mr. R. R. Neild, Prof. R. E. Peierls, Dr. F. Pirani, Prof. C. F. Powell, Prof. J. Rotblat, Sir Gordon Sutherland

U.S.A.
Prof. K. Boulding, Prof. H. Brown, Prof. B. T. Feld, Prof. M. Gell-Mann, Prof. C. Kaysen, Prof. R. Revelle, Prof. A. Rich, Prof. J. P. Ruina, Prof. E. Seitz, Prof. E. Staley

U.S.S.R.
Acad. M. M. Dubinin, Prof. V. S. Emelyanov, Prof. V. M. Khvostov, Prof. M. I. Kovalev, Prof. V. V. Lozinski, Acad. M. D. Millionshchikov, Mr. V. P. Pavlichenko, Prof. M. I. Rubinstein, Prof. N. A. Talensky, Prof. B. M. Vul

Yugoslavia
Prof. I. Supek

Observers and Scientific Staff

France
Mr. P. Genevey

India
Dr. P. Pant, Mr. V. C. Trivedi

Sweden
Mr. M. Fehrm

U.K.
Dr. Patricia Lindop

U.S.A.
Prof. E. Erikson, Mr. L. S. Finkelstein, Dr. G. Piel

U.N.
Mr. D. Blickenstaff

UNESCO
Dr. R. Maybury

WHO
Dr. M. Kaplan

STATEMENT FROM THE CONTINUING COMMITTEE ON THE THIRTEENTH PUGWASH CONFERENCE, HELD IN KARLOVY VARY, SEPTEMBER 13-19, 1964

The 13th Pugwash Conference has now concluded. It was attended by 86 scientists and scholars from 19 countries. Our discussions have been frank and co-operative. They have been chiefly concerned with disarmament and related questions, but they have also dealt with matters such as the responsibility of scientists in the modern world. Our confidence in the value of the Pugwash Conferences has been further strengthened.

The discussions have distinguished a great many ways in which prompt action could attain and then consolidate an improvement in the international situation, both military and political. They have also identified some of the more distant targets at which it seems reasonable to aim, and some of the problems raised by the development of science and technology.

This statement has been drawn up by the Continuing Committee on the basis of the reports submitted by the Working Groups to the Conference as a whole.

A. Immediate Steps towards Disarmament

Several means of relaxing the present tensions, of reducing the danger of war, and of paving the way to more lasting agreements, have been identified:

1. It would be valuable if the nations concerned with the German problem, and in particular the former occupying powers together with the Federal German Republic, would promptly recognize and guarantee the existing frontiers of Germany with its neighbouring states.

2. A non-aggression treaty between the North Atlantic and the Warsaw Treaty Organizations would be most valuable. The treaty would require that under no circumstances would the armed forces of one country violate the frontiers of another, or of West Berlin, or the accesses to that city. Access to Berlin shall not be interrupted pending a final agreement upon the complex of problems embracing Berlin and Germany.

3. The idea of a nuclear freeze in Central Europe, applying to an area on each side of the demarcation line in Central Europe, deserves urgent consideration. It would help in the reduction and elimination of nuclear weapons in Europe.

4. Governments concerned with the establishment of the NATO multilateral force should forthwith abandon it. This project adds nothing to military security. It increases political tensions and the danger of the proliferation of nuclear weapons.

5. To avoid nuclear proliferation, a number of inter-related measures are desirable:
(a) International agreements committing the nuclear powers not to give, and the non-nuclear powers not to accept, nuclear weapons, materials for

nuclear weapons, or aid in their development, would contribute substantially to the safety of the world.

(b) Governments should seek means to prevent their nationals from assisting other nations in the development of nuclear weapons and other weapons of mass destruction.

(c) Procedures should be universally adopted for international control of the movement of fissile materials for peaceful purposes from one country to another.

(d) The partial test ban treaty should promptly be extended to cover underground testing, if necessary by a moratorium, pending the final agreement. Technical problems of control should not now be an obstacle. It is very important that ways and means be found to convince the governments and the peoples concerned of the inadvisability of any further atmospheric testing.

(e) A cut-off of further production of fissile materials for weapons use, with a treaty stipulating verification procedures, would also be most desirable.

B. Further Steps towards Disarmament

The steps outlined in the preceding section could be implemented in the near future. Other measures which may need more time include the following:

1. There are a number of regions in which it would be possible to ban the presence of nuclear weapons. Scandinavia, the Balkans, Africa, Latin America, the Middle East, and the South and East of Asia together with Australasia, are all potential nuclear-free zones.

2. In Central Europe there is a strong case for seeking to reduce the risk of surprise attack by the establishment of demilitarized strips on either side of the line dividing the armed forces of NATO and the Warsaw Treaty Organization. There would have to be accompanying agreements on means of detecting violations and on the strengths and characteristics of border police.

3. The current proposals for the elimination or substantial reduction of strategic bomber forces are promising and should be further explored. It was urged that any resources freed by such measures should be balanced by comparable allocations of resources to specified peaceful uses.

In addition,

4. It is proposed that the Pugwash Committee should set up a study group to examine the requirements for an inspection scheme for biological weapons. For trial purposes the inspection scheme would be limited to a small group of Central European countries representative of Eastern, Western, and non-aligned nations.

Appendix 16

C. Collective Security

It is plain that measures will have to be taken to increase the effectiveness of the existing peace-keeping machinery of the U.N. In discussing military measures by the U.N., it was stressed that these were a method of last resort. The U.N. has not yet employed enforcement action under Chapter 7 of the Charter, which requires agreements with member states about the provision of military contingents, and depends on the approval of the Great Powers. In this respect we welcome the memorandum of the U.S.S.R. Government of 10th July 1964 which endorses the implementation of this type of peace-keeping machinery.

There should not for the present be a standing U.N. military force, but instead there should be specially trained contingents in various countries. There should be in addition stand-by police units. Both these would be specially trained to handle the type of situation which the U.N. has frequently faced. It was also thought that wider use of U.N. observers would be helpful.

The possibility of enforcement action by the U.N. is of special importance for the non-aligned nations. It may be an advantage for them to conclude the relevant agreements ahead of other nations. They could thus provide the U.N. with the means to protect non-aligned nations, given the good will of the Great Powers.

The possibility was considered that, instead of financing each peace-keeping operation *ad hoc*, the U.N. might be provided for this purpose with a steady source of income. Several ideas for raising such an income were suggested, such as a levy on member states according to their military budgets, a royalty on mining rights under the high seas, a tax on the use of communications satellites, or even a small tariff on international trade. These and other ideas need further study.

Besides the idea of prohibiting the use of force in the settlement of territorial disputes, which was proposed in the message from Prime Minister Khrushchev of 31st December 1963, and the reply by President Johnson of 20th January 1964, we consider that the cause of collective security would be well served by a more comprehensive agreement or declaration that would ban the use of force by any nation in violation of the territorial integrity of another. This should exclude neither self-defence, nor collective action under the provisions of the U.N. Charter. The right of self-determination in internal affairs is in no way prejudiced by such a ban.

In the context of the U.N. resolution for ending colonialism, it is now appropriate for the U.N. to take measures to implement it.

A study of the security problems of a disarmed world is urgent because, without confidence in the stability of such a world, and in the security of the sovereign states in it, fear of the future would remain an obstacle to disarmament. In the long run, a peaceful world will require the solution of such issues as racial inequalities and economic disparities between nations and peoples.

In the changed circumstances of a disarmed world, new or changed institutions will be required within the framework of the U.N.; for example, permanent machinery for continuous verification of the fact of disarmament.

D. The Responsibilities of Scientists

Though disarmament has been the chief concern of the Pugwash Conferences, it has always been recognized that there is a mutual influence between disarmament and international co-operation. Disarmament can permit the scope of international co-operation to be enormously enlarged, and in its turn international co-operation can increase confidence between nations and thus facilitate disarmament. Consideration has, therefore, been given to a number of measures which would strengthen the international ties between scientists and promote concrete measures of international co-operation in several fields. They include the following:

1. Steps to strengthen international exchanges between scientists. At present the participation of scientists at international conferences is often frustrated by passport or visa difficulties which may prevent them from leaving their own or entering another country. Particular difficulties arise from the operation of the allied travel office in Berlin which issues the travel documents needed by the scientists of the G.D.R. for travel to NATO countries. All such restrictions should be removed.

2. The scope of international exchange arrangements permitting the flow of scientists between countries to work in research centres abroad should be greatly increased. This could be done both through the official exchange programmes and by an increase in the traditional method of individual invitation.

3. The World Health Research Centre, now under discussion, for the study of important medical problems encountered on a world scale, should be established without further delay. It would promote the study on an adequate scale of urgent problems, such as the toxic effects of drugs and various environmental pollutants, epidemiological patterns, and methods of analysis of information and data on health research.

4. Steps should be taken to develop a co-ordinated and unified system of scientific information storage and retrieval. New methods based on modern computer techniques are essential. At the moment in many disciplines new publications accumulate so fast that scientists are not made rapidly aware of much of the published information bearing on their work and there is a resultant duplication of effort in research. The matter is urgent because different systems are being established in different disciplines which are not compatible with one another, like the different systems of weights and measures. It is to be emphasized that such a co-ordinated world-wide system would require the active participation of scientists on a great scale. Appropriate studies should be initiated without delay under the auspices of UNESCO or ICSU.

5. The remarkable progress already made in international scientific co-operation in several areas of research, including space research, was

reviewed. Such co-operation is warmly recommended, as well as the participation in the International Biological Programme which has just started under the auspices of ICSU.

6. The proposal by the Swedish Government to establish and support an institute for research on problems relating to peace was warmly applauded.

Participants

Australia
Dr. K. Fowler

Canada
Mr. W. Boyd

Czechoslovakia
Acad. J. Kožešník, Acad. I. Málek, Mr. T. Němec, Acad. K. Siška, Dr. A. Šnejdárek, Acad. F. Šorm

Denmark
Mr. D. J. Adler, Prof. O. Kofoed-Hansen, Prof. O. Maaløe

Federal German Republic
Mr. H. Afheldt, Prof. G. Burkhardt

France
Monsieur P. Biquard, Monsieur A. Joxe, Monsieur J. Moch

German Democratic Republic
Dr. P. Hess, Prof. J. Kuczynski, Prof. G. Rienäcker

Hungary
Prof. L. Pal, Prof. F. B. Straub

India
Prof. V. Sarabhai

Italy
Prof. A. Buzzati-Traverso, Dr. Laura Forlati, Dr. G. Jona-Lasinio

Netherlands
Prof. B. V. A. Roling, Prof. H. A. Tolhoek

Norway
Dr. T. Forland, Prof. J. Galtung

Poland
Prof. M. Danysz, Prof. L. Infeld, Prof. K. Lapter

Rumania
Prof. I. Agarbiceanu, Acad. C. Dragulescu, Dr. V. Hanga, Acad. M. Nicolescu

Sweden
Prof. H. Alfven

U.K.
Prof. L. R. B. Elton, Prof. B. H. Flowers, Prof. O. R. Frisch, Dr. Patricia Lindop, Mr. P. J. Noel-Baker, Prof. R. E. Peierls, Prof. C. F. Powell, Prof. J. Rotblat

U.S.A.
Mrs. Ruth Adams, Prof. H. Brown, Prof. P. Doty, Prof. B. T. Feld, Prof. D. A. Glaser, Prof. B. Glass, Prof. H. Kissinger, Mrs. Betty Lall, Prof. M. Meselson, Prof. H. Morgenthau, Prof. J. Grear, Prof. E. Rabinowitch, Prof. A. Rich, Prof. J. B. Wiesner

U.S.S.R.
Dr. P. V. Andreyev, Acad. L. A. Artsimovitch, Acad. A. A. Blagonravov, Acad. N. N. Bogolubov, Acad. M. M. Dubinin, Acad. V. M. Khvostov, Prof. A. M. Kuzin, Prof. S. S. Medvedev, Acad. M. D. Millionshchikov, Mr. V. P. Pavlichenko, Prof. M. Rubinstein, Prof. N. A. Talensky, Acad. A. P. Vinogradov

Yugoslavia
Dr. V. Knapp, Acad. L. Vavpetic

Observers and Scientific Staff

India
Mr. V. C. Trivedi

Netherlands
Mr. F. J. A. Terwisscha van Scheltinga

Sweden
Dr. R. Bjornerstedt

U.K.
Mr. J. Maddox, Mr. J. K. Wright

U.S.A.
Dr. V. Rabinowitch

ICSU
Acad. D. Blaskovic

U.N.
Dr. R. J. Bunche, Mr. V. P. Suslov

UNESCO
Dr. J. Hochfeld, Dr. R. Krause

WHO
Dr. M. Kaplan

17 STATEMENT FROM THE CONTINUING COMMITTEE ON THE FOURTEENTH PUGWASH CONFERENCE, HELD IN VENICE, APRIL 11-16, 1965

The 14th Pugwash Conference which was held in Venice from the 11th to 16th April, 1965, was attended by 77 scientists and scholars from 20 countries. The agenda was concerned with two main topics: international co-operation in science, and problems of disarmament. The Conference also considered problems relating to the situation in Vietnam. The discussions have been held in five working groups which submitted their reports to the Conference as a whole. In addition, the Conference received a report from a study group on biological warfare which met in Trieste prior to the Venice meeting.

This statement has been drawn up by the Continuing Committee on the basis of the reports from the above groups.

A. National, Regional and International Institutes

In view of the tremendous advances which have taken place in science and technology it is clear that, even at our present level of knowledge, it is possible to transform radically the standards of living in the developing areas of the world in a few decades. It is of vital importance that there is an understanding of this in the developing nations so as to generate an atmosphere of confidence in the future. It is also **of the greatest importance to create soon an objective approach to all aspects of human endeavour**, an approach which follows immediately from the development of science.

An important component in the growth of science in the developing countries is the creation of national scientific cadres. The immediate task in these areas is the transfer of existing scientific knowledge (with necessary adaptation to local conditions) and its application to ensure rapid economic growth. The major effort of the national cadres should be on task-oriented programmes with defined time scales for their accomplishment. Fundamental research, however, needs to be supported strongly to ensure balanced development; this is true also for the advanced countries.

The limited resources in finance and skilled manpower can be best utilized in a few centres of high quality at national level. Regional and international institutes should have lower priority, wherever the creation of national institutes is feasible.

These few centres for research and development should be strongly associated with teaching, either by being part of existing universities, or by developing into university-like institutions; if for specific reasons centres purely for research have to be set up, very good co-ordination between them and the universities should be ensured. Regional-international-type institutes can be of great value, since they can utilize materials for study and research which are most readily available in their regions; their studies can cater for the scientific objectives of the regions and thus be directly beneficial to them.

International institutes for research should be set up only if they fulfil scientific needs which cannot be catered for by national centres for reasons of cost, skills, location, etc. Such institutes should have only a small permanent staff and establish strong two-way relationships with universities and other national centres, so that scientists can be cycled continuously through the international centres, and large numbers can thus benefit from the excellent facilities set up for all.

These institutes should not develop into centres of attraction to drain away permanently the best brains from universities. This is also true for national centres which are set up to carry out research only. The international institutes should have a simple, flexible organizational and administrative structure and be essentially run by working scientists.

International scientific expeditions, such as the International Indian Ocean Expedition, can serve a very important function and be particularly valuable to the developing areas, since they do not drain away the best scientists from these areas, while contributing to scientific development and economic growth of these regions and to further international co-operation.

B. Problems of International Co-operation in Science

The Working Group welcomed the activities of groups of scientists in several countries in connection with the International Co-operation Year, and appealed to scientists everywhere to expand such efforts.

The Group discussed the state of the International Biological Programme and recommended that the U.N., its agencies and the Expanded Technical Assistance Programme assist scientists from developing countries to increase their participation in the Programme, and that Pugwash National Groups urge their governments to support the I.B.P. projects, including expeditions and the organization of centres for the collection, analysis and publication of the assembled data.

The Group discussed the problem of storage, retrieval and analysis of scientific data, and noted the interest of the International Council of Scientific Unions (ICSU) and UNESCO in the field. It made several recommendations to these groups, including the establishment of an international code of practice for the publication of scientific papers and abstracts, a unified international system for coding the contents of scientific publications, and the elimination of wasteful duplication of abstracting efforts in different countries. The Group hoped that initial co-ordination will pave the way to the creation of an international centre of scientific information. The activities in this field should include not only collection of data, but also their analysis and presentation, much of which can be now done by computers, and the preparation of compendia.

The Group recommended that at the forthcoming Pugwash Conference in Addis Ababa, a Working Group be set up for the study of problems of population growth and of the resources needed to take care of the growing population. The Group suggested that the World Health Organization, Food and Agricultural Organization, and UNESCO, as well as natural and social scientists in both developed and developing countries, increase their concern with the biological (including clinical), social, educational, and economic aspects of the problems of human populations and resources.

Noting that the U.N., its agencies and non-governmental organizations, such as ICSU, are now increasingly concerned with co-operation in science as a contribution to the establishment of stable peace, the Group believes that these activities should be further increased. It recommended the establishment of an International Science Foundation, to help scientists of countries not able to support adequately scientific research. This Foundation should support, on the basis of achievement and promise, individual scientists rather than nations or programmes. The necessary funds might be provided by the International Bank for Reconstruction and Development, as well as by other sources, and the Foundation could be established under the sponsorship of UNESCO.

The Group noted the establishment by the U.N. Economic and Social Council of a Scientific Advisory Committee on the Application of Science and Technology to Development and recommended that the Pugwash Continuing Committee explores (a) the possibilities of better liaison of this Advisory Committee with the scientific communities and (b) the possibility of improving the U.N. machinery for co-operation in science and technology in areas not covered by the ECOSOC Advisory Committee.

The Group recommended that steps be taken by the U.N. to set up an International Institute for Technical Economics; it reaffirmed an earlier Pugwash resolution recommending the establishment by UNESCO of an Institute for Natural Resources Analysis.

The Group welcomed the establishment of an Institute for Peace Research in Sweden and suggested that its programme should be concerned with the pre-conditions for the establishment of stable peace in a society revolutionized by science and technology; and that both social and natural scientists should participate in these studies.

C. International Co-operation in Science Education

In a world of rapidly accelerating change, brought about through science and technology, general education must be concerned with the adjustment of men and of societies to change. It must concern itself, among other things, with the role of science in human life, and also with the nature of scientific investigation itself. Scientific knowledge is now doubling every 10 to 15 years. The useful lifetime of most scientific textbooks is about that of an automobile (5-10 years), and the obsolescence of a teacher of science, lacking renewal of training, covers about the same span of time. Enlightened public policy will, therefore, implement efforts to improve science curricula and extend the training and renewal of training of science teachers.

It follows that the task of revising and reforming our educational programmes and methods is urgent and needs to be continuous. In this task international co-operation is particularly needed.

The future progress of science depends upon effective education in science, fully as much in the secondary and elementary schools as in the universities. More attention must be given by scientists to revising and reforming the science curriculum in order to keep it sound and broadly based, yet flexible and experimental in nature.

The simplest and least expensive form of international co-operation in science education consists of two steps:

1. The development of mechanisms for prompt transmission and free use of the products of curriculum studies prepared in one country by interested groups in other countries; and

2. The payment of expenses to enable experienced personnel from one country to work with active science education groups in other countries in sessions of some weeks to months in duration.

The developing countries have special problems in this area because of their great shortage of trained scientists and science teachers. Regional groups of such countries may profitably unite in developing new science courses for the elementary and secondary schools.

The Group recommended that the pilot projects of UNESCO in Brazil (physics), in India (chemistry) and in Africa (biology) be pushed with speed and urgency, and be extended as soon as possible on a more comprehensive scale, and that further study be devoted to science education in the next and later Pugwash Conferences.

A greatly reformed training of science teachers and their retraining at periodic intervals by means of specially planned institutes, seminars and summer courses, are necessitated by the rapid advances of science itself. We emphasize the great importance of breadth of training, especially for elementary and secondary school teachers; and equally emphasize that the sciences must be integrated in general education. The relations of the sciences to the humanistic and social studies must be stressed.

The Group recommended that UNESCO and other agencies be asked to form a permanent study group to devise such measures and to communicate them to all governments. It also recommended more vigorous action to support joint studies and programmes relating to the training and renewal of training of science teachers.

The recruitment of science teachers is inadequate in all countries, and in some countries is desperately low. In nearly all countries teachers are seriously underpaid. Better salaries, leading to higher social standing, and a reduction in the daily load of classes and subsidiary duties may be recommended. In the developing countries, where science teachers are in very short supply, corps of teachers acquainted with modern methods of science teaching and curricula should be organized on a multinational basis to assist in teaching and in training of teachers.

Human society is based on utilization of a diversity of types of individuals. There will be no peace among nations until we have learned not only to tolerate but in fact to esteem these differences between ourselves and others. The study of science is particularly able to teach the lessons of tolerance. Science itself is international in scope and cannot flourish in secrecy.

The Group believes that in a peaceful, disarmed world, education will have the first priority in the budgets of the nations and first claim on the quality and quantity of manpower.

The Group believes that even now all nations should reconsider their apportionment of funds and manpower and allocate far more to education.

As disarmament proceeds, the liberated funds now devoted to military defence should be shifted with highest priority to the improvement of education. A generation better educated in science and in tolerance will lead mankind toward lasting peace.

D. Current Problems of Arms Control and Disarmament

1. Interim measures towards arms limitation or reduction.

(a) Destruction of bomber aircraft. The Working Group considered some of the suggestions for arms limitation or reduction discussed at previous Pugwash Conferences, and reaffirmed the view that one of the measures to limit the arms race and one of the first steps of actual disarmament might be the destruction of bomber aircraft over the next few years, within an agreed period and without replacement. This could be done by an agreed sequence according to type of aircraft.

Taking into account that bomber aircraft are vital for the national security of some nations which do not possess more advanced military equipment, one could begin with the major powers.

(b) Foreign bases. The Group discussed the problem of military bases and troops on foreign territory. While there were some dissensions, the following represents the views of most members of the Group.

They agreed with the views expressed at previous Conferences that foreign troops and bases contribute to international tension, especially between the major powers, and consider that, as a step towards general and complete disarmament, all such bases should be liquidated and all foreign troops withdrawn as soon as possible.

Having this in mind as an ultimate goal they consider that reduction in the strength and number of military units maintained in foreign bases and territories, as a step towards their gradual elimination, would make an important contribution to the relief of tension. Amongst foreign bases, those maintained against the wishes of the country in whose territory they are located have a special position. It was felt that in the first place one should reduce in strength, or eliminate, the bases in countries whose governments have requested their abolition.

The Group considered that temporary difficulties which might arise in certain circumstances in connection with the elimination of foreign bases and troops, should be solved in accordance with the principles and provisions of the United Nations Charter.

2. Measures to relieve tension. The Group discussed the problem how to prevent small commitments of a major power in a distant area growing into a major involvement which might ultimately escalate into a major conflict, particularly in the event of civil war.

3. Extension of test ban treaty. The Group endorsed the hope expressed at the 13th and previous Pugwash Conferences that the Moscow Test Ban Treaty be extended to underground tests and to all countries, and that there be a moratorium on underground testing pending the conclusion of a treaty covering such tests. This hope has not yet been realized and, since the 13th Conference, underground tests have been carried out.

E. Problems of General and Complete Disarmament

The Working Group considered the difficulties which are standing in the way of further progress towards comprehensive disarmament and measures which should be undertaken to overcome them. The Group recognized that the conclusion of a treaty on general disarmament, under effective controls, would eliminate the problems arising from the large-scale proliferation of weapons of mass destruction, and also create an atmosphere in which it would be much easier to solve many of the political problems which are now impeding progress. On the other hand, the adoption of interim measures of arms control and reduction would not only decrease the dangers of nuclear war, but would also make it easier to arrive at a more comprehensive disarmament agreement. There was, however, a spectrum of opinions regarding the relative emphasis which should be placed at this time on the short-range measures as compared with the ultimate goal.

On the question of further proliferation and dissemination of nuclear weapons and of weapons technology, the Group reaffirmed the conclusions of the Pugwash Conference in Karlovy Vary regarding measures which should be undertaken to prevent proliferation, as well as the dangers of proliferation which arise from various schemes for nuclear sharing (as for instance the M.L.F.). The discussions elaborated on some of the Karlovy Vary proposals, most especially those relating to the guarantees which could be given to the non-nuclear nations on the part of the nuclear powers within the framework of the United Nations, to the control over materials used in peaceful atomic energy applications, and to the types of measures which could prevent the work by experts from one country on weapons programmes in another. The Group also considered schemes for applying and strengthening the peace-keeping procedures provided for in the Charter of the United Nations.

F. Biological Warfare

The Study Group considered the consequences of the possible use of biological and chemical weapons and reiterated its concern about the danger to mankind from the further development and use of these weapons. A total ban on such weapons, as well as of nuclear weapons, must be accomplished in achieving our final aim of complete and general disarmament under strict international verification.

The dangers to world security posed by all classes of biological and chemical weapons are closely interrelated. Both in public opinion and in military practice it does not appear possible to maintain any lasting distinction between incapacitating and lethal weapons, or between biological and chemical warfare. The great variety of possible agents forms a continuous spectrum, starting from those that are temporarily incapacitating and ending with highly lethal ones. If the restraints on the practice of any kind of biological or chemical warfare are broken down, the entire spectrum of these weapons may come into use.

The Geneva Protocol of 1925 banning the first use of biological and chemical weapons was briefly discussed. The Group felt that the effectiveness of this Protocol would be greatly increased if those states which have not yet adhered to it were to do so. However, the Group wishes to emphasize its conviction that arrangements going beyond the Geneva Protocol will be needed if the development and **production** of biological weapons are to be avoided.

Although the problems of preventing the use of biological and chemical weapons are interrelated, the Group confined its discussion to means for preventing the use of biological weapons, because the far greater destructive potential of biological weapons qualifies them for attack on large civilian populations. The Group is of the opinion that the human destructive potential of biological weapons could, with continued research and development, eventually rival that of nuclear weapons. Furthermore, once they are perfected, devastating biological weapons may be far cheaper and easier to produce than nuclear weapons, thus placing a great destructive capability in the hands of many nations.

At present there are reasons to believe that biological weapons have not been brought to a degree of perfection which would make them operational for any but limited military ends. However, a number of states are known to be working in this field. In this situation, it is important to consider means for inhibiting the further development of biological weapons. A variety of proposals for accomplishing this have been discussed.

It is hoped that a series of pilot activities will be implemented in several European countries aimed at minimizing secrecy in biological research, building mutual trust and confidence, and the conclusion of an agreement not to do research and development of biological weapons.

G. The Situation in Vietnam

The participants in the 14th Pugwash Conference considered that the recent aggravation of military action in South-East Asia threatens by escalation the peace of the world, and increases the suffering of the Vietnamese people. They think that reason and humanity should prevail.

Different views were expressed as to the origin of the conflict and the means for its settlement. All participants, however, agreed that means should be sought to achieve the earliest restoration of peace in this area; the United Nations should do everything in their power to achieve this.

It was agreed that the members of each national group will convey the different opinions expressed at the Conference to their governments.

H. The Use of Gas in War

At the instruction of a plenary meeting, a Working Group prepared the following statement:

We have discussed the dangers inherent in the use of unconventional weapons. We condemn the use of gas warfare in any part of the world.

The public response to the recent use by the United States of an agent, known in the United States as a riot-control gas, in combat in South Vietnam shows how deeply this concern is felt by public opinion.

We believe that there is much wisdom in this public reaction against even the most limited use of gas and even when the effects of such use are said to be no more than temporarily incapacitating.

There are two considerations which lead us to this belief:

1. There are gases of all grades of toxicity, running from gases with only brief effects to lethal nerve gases. But that which is only incapacitating for a healthy adult can be deadly for an infant or a weak person. Once gas of any kind is used and the various barriers to the use of gas are broken down, there is no clear line to prevent escalation to the use of the entire range of gas weapons available.

2. If weapons said to be merely temporarily incapacitating come into general use, they would be directed against civilian populations in cases when more destructive weapons would never have been used, thus civilians would become exposed to military action to which they are not now subject.

I. International Year for the Preparation of Disarmament

To focus general attention on the necessity of disarmament and on the ways in which disarmament can be safely carried out under international control, the Conference suggests that an International Year for the Preparation of Disarmament (IYPD) be proclaimed by the United Nations and organized by the methods so successfully used in the International Geophysical Year, the International Years of the Quiet Sun and the Freedom from Hunger Campaign.

Governments should take the initiative in setting up National Committees of Preparation for Disarmament, in which voluntary organizations of all kinds should be invited to join. The Committees should promote lectures in universities, teacher-training colleges and high schools, organize public meetings, prepare suitable literature, and make full use of television, radio and other media.

Appendix 17

The Conference suggests that a representative preparatory Committee for the holding of the IYPD be set up in which the Pugwash Movement will take an active part.

Participants

Australia
Dr. D. F. Martyn

Austria
Prof. H. Thirring

Czechoslovakia
Acad. I. Málek, Mr. T. Němec

Denmark
Mr. D. J. Adler, Prof. O. Maaløe

Federal German Republic
Mr. H. Afheldt, Prof. G. Burkhardt, Prof. J. H. D. Jensen

France
Monsieur J. Lestel, Prof. M. Magat, Dr. H. Marcovich, Monsieur J. Moch, Prof. P. Rosenstiehl

India
Prof. M. G. K. Menon

Indonesia
Dr. S. Prawirohardjo

Israel
Prof. A. Keynan, Prof. G. Stein

Italy
Prof. M. Aloisi, Prof. E. Amaldi, Prof. G. Arangio-Ruiz, Prof. G. Bernardini, Prof. A. Buzzati-Traverso, Prof. F. Calogero, Dr. Laura Forlati

Japan
Dr. M. Konuma

Netherlands
Prof. B. V. A. Röling

Poland
Prof. L. Infeld, Prof. K. Lapter, Prof. I. Malecki

Rumania
Prof. I. Agarbiceanu

Sweden
Prof. H. Alfvén, Dr. R. Björnerstedt, Mr. J. Prawitz

U.A.R.
Dr. Laila Shukry El Hamamsy, Dr. A. R. Abdel Meguid

U.K.
Prof. H. Bondi, Prof. B. H. Flowers, Dr. Patricia Lindop, Dr. D. C. Martin, Mr. P. J. Noel-Baker, Prof. R. E. Peierls, Prof. J. Rotblat, Sir Gordon Sutherland

U.S.A.
Prof. H. Brown, Prof. B. T. Feld, Prof. B. Glass, Prof. W. Leontief, Prof. F. A. Long, Prof. M. Meselson, Prof. E. Rabinowitch, Prof. R. Revelle, Prof. R. Rollefson, Prof. L. Sohn

U.S.S.R.
Dr. P. V. Andreyev, Acad. L. A. Artsimovitch, Acad. M. M. Dubinin, Prof. V. S. Emelyanov, Acad. V. M. Khvostov, Acad. M. D. Millionshchikov, Mr. V. P. Pavlichenko, Prof. M. Rubinstein, Prof. N. A. Talensky, Acad. A. N. Tupolev, Acad. A. P. Vinogradov, Prof. B. M. Vul

Yugoslavia
Dr. M. Markovic, Prof. I. Supek

Observers

Italy
Prof. B. Bertotti, Prof. P. Budini, Prof. G. Giacometti

U.K.
Mr. H. Bull, Mr. J. Davy

U.S.A.
Dr. V. Rabinowitch

U.S.S.R.
Prof. O. A. Griniewsky, Prof. M. S. Voslensky

U.N.
Mr. W. Epstein, Mr. J. H. G. Pierson

UNESCO
Dr. A. Bertrand, Prof. A. Matveyev

WHO
Dr. M. Kaplan

18 STATEMENT FROM THE CONTINUING COMMITTEE ON THE FIFTEENTH PUGWASH CONFERENCE, HELD IN ADDIS ABABA, DECEMBER 29, 1965-JANUARY 3, 1966

The 15th Pugwash Conference was held in Addis Ababa from the 29th December, 1965 to 3rd January, 1966. It was attended by 86 scientists and scholars from 31 countries drawn from all the continents. The theme of the Conference was "Science in Aid of Developing Countries." A mutually stimulating exchange of ideas and information took place between participants from the developed and developing countries. It became abundantly clear in the course of the Conference that Pugwash-type discussions are of great interest to scientists in both the developed and developing countries, and that further meetings dealing with the same or related topics could be very profitable.

The work of the Conference was carried out in five Working Groups. Four of these Groups dealt with a wide range of topics relating to the role of science in development, in Africa, Asia and Latin America. The fifth Working Group dealt with problems of security, including current conflicts. The five Working Groups submitted their reports to the Conference as a whole. This statement has been drawn up by the Continuing Committee on the basis of these reports.

Groups 1 to 4 inclusive were concerned with many aspects of the application of education, science and technology to development. There was a general consensus of opinion among them on the crucial importance of a number of technical and political factors which were inhibiting development.

Building up education, science and technology, all indispensable for development, is an expensive process. It is unrealistic to believe that sufficient resources will be made available for their support in the absence of very substantial measures of disarmament on a world-wide scale. A second crucial factor for a developing country is its economic and political independence, and, for many of them, the introduction of radical socio-economic reforms.

A general agreement was also present in the Groups that scientists should be encouraged to play an active part in the social and political life of a developing country, and in helping to solve the urgent problems facing the nation in the sphere of development. The universities were regarded as particularly important in the early stages of development. They are the primary source of new scientists, teachers and advanced technical personnel; they bring together many disciplines, including the natural and social sciences and humanities; and, given sufficient autonomy, they can provide good conditions for penetrating independent enquiry. The proper support and improvement of existing research institutions relating to the economy, in the early stages of development, was also stressed.

It was generally agreed that support for science and technology in the developing countries by the developed countries is an important contribution to world development. It helps to reduce the political tensions which can result from the growing disparity between standards of living in rich and poor countries. And it enriches world science by bringing to its support the abilities and cultural heritage of many peoples previously alienated from it. It is, therefore, of mutual advantage for rich and poor countries.

1. Education in Developing Countries

To rectify the chronic shortage of school teachers in most developing countries, the Group recommended a massive programme for the training of science teachers, either on a national or regional basis, and with financial help from developed countries, international organizations and foundations.

The Group also stressed the need to improve the salaries and conditions of service of teachers. To meet the crucial role of science for development, there should be a higher proportion of science students among the student population of a developing country, and provision should be made for a rapid growth of science teaching in schools. The Group also stressed the importance of ensuring, as soon as possible, that a large proportion of the teachers, scientists and technologists of a country should be drawn from the indigenous population. The manpower needs of a country in this respect should be estimated both for the short and the long term. For political reasons and on grounds of economy, an increasingly large core of indigenous teachers should be employed as soon as practicable on the staff of training institutions. This will have the additional advantage of increasing the stability of the staff.

It is very important to strengthen the training institutions and universities in developing countries. This may be done by attracting good personnel, by improving the quality of their research, by encouraging exchanges of staff with both developed and developing countries, and by encouraging people from developed countries to undergo postgraduate training at universities in developing countries. When students are educated abroad, it is important that their qualifications should be effectively evaluated on their return home, and steps taken to ensure that they find an appropriate position.

A very important objective of the educational system of a developing country is to inculcate a questioning, critical and experimental attitude to all knowledge, and especially so in the universities. Such an attitude is essential for the generation of new ideas vital for the solution of all the novel problems facing a developing country. In view of their responsibilities, the training of teachers should be very carefully planned to foster the spirit of vigorous independent enquiry.

2. Organization of Scientific Institutions and Research in Developing Countries

The developing countries are at widely differing stages in the advancement of science. They vary, for example, in the availability of scientific manpower and equipment, the degree to which science is organized, and in the size and quality of the supporting educational system. Ready made plans

which would suit all countries cannot, therefore, be provided; they have
to be worked out and fought for in the situation prevailing in each country. In considering the planning and co-ordination of scientific research
in developing countries, the Group considered that some type of advisory
body at the highest level of government, responsible to the Cabinet and
not under any particular minister, was necessary. This body should consist of representatives of government departments, industry, academies
and universities, and research institutes; it should have a high proportion
of active natural scientists and some social scientists.

The organization of research should be designed to liberate the creative
energies of scientists and provide them with what they need for effective
work. A rigid bureaucratic organization which does not sufficiently devolve responsibility on working scientists leads to grave frustrations
among them and should be rigorously avoided. There are great advantages
to be gained by the development of a team spirit, a multidisciplinary approach, the efficient use of equipment and a proper evaluation of research.
In the early stages of development, efforts should commonly be directed
towards the solution of urgent national problems; and they should be selected only after a realistic appraisal of the resources available for
the execution of the work.

The Group emphasized the importance of the integration of science and scientists into governments. A senior scientist should sometimes be prepared
to give up his research work for a period, in order to accept a post in
the appropriate branch of government service. He may thus actively participate in creating a better understanding in high governmental circles
of the role of science, help in formulating national plans, and, in addition, acquire some insight into the problems of government.

The Group also stressed the importance of international collaboration at
all levels, welcomed the action already taken to promote it by international and other agencies, and recommended its extension in a wide variety
of forms.

3. Scientific Approach in Aid to Developing Countries

In discussing the scientific approach to aid, the Group stressed that all
aid should contribute to increasing the self-reliance of the receiving
country and its capacity for independent growth, and that the latest advances in science and technology should be imaginatively employed to promote such a development. Programmes originating from demagogic or narrow
political considerations, or from group interests, ought to be discouraged.

Aid should involve no interference in the internal affairs of the country.
It should not be used for political advantage by the donor nations, nor
should competition in aid be used as a means of exerting political pressure by the receiving nations. If many past failures in aid programmes
are to be avoided it is important to ensure the continuity needed for
their completion. A close correlation should be established between the
training of personnel and technical development programmes, to ensure both
the adequate staffing of new facilities and institutions and the full employment of graduates.

Aid programmes should be planned to safeguard the best aspects of the indigenous culture and technology so that a dull standardization of cultural patterns may be avoided.

In order to implement these principles, the Group made a number of practical recommendations, including greater support for the work of the U.N. and its agencies, particularly ECOSOC's Advisory Committee on the Application of Science and Technology to Development; better organization in developing countries for the scientific survey of their needs; and formulation of requests for aid through a national planning authority and a scientific advisory council. In some areas, particularly Africa, such bodies might be established on a regional or continental basis.

"Twinning" of institutions in developing countries with those in advanced countries, as well as pairing of scientific institutions from East and West in giving assistance to the programmes or to institutes in developing countries, was warmly endorsed.

Scientists in the developed countries should be encouraged to show greater interest in working, at least for limited periods, in developing countries, and procedures should be elaborated to avoid any consequential damage to their scientific careers. The scientific communities of all countries should co-operate to keep aid mechanisms under review, and to assist in finding highly qualified scientists for this work.

4. Specific Problems of Developing Countries

Economic assistance of developed countries to the developing ones, however important, taken alone can have only a marginal effect. Even if relaxation of international tension would release additional resources for this assistance, the rate of economic growth in developing countries will remain largely dependent upon their own determination and effort. Both in planning for economic development and in implementation of the plan, scientists should play a far greater role in the future than they have in the past.

Industrialization is a key factor in development. Increased participation of scientists in industrial planning, concentration of industrial effort, the co-ordination of industrial with agricultural development, and the creation of integrated markets to solve the problems of small countries, are all necessary to accelerate industrial growth.

In the next ten or fifteen years there is a grave danger of a broadening of the gap between the growing population and the production of food in the developing countries. Merely to maintain the present meagre standards of food consumption, a great increase in agricultural production in the developing countries, with better water supplies, fertilizers, pesticides, better seeds, and greater incentives to farmers, will have to take place. It will also be necessary to augment local supplies by food aid from developed countries which have excess capacity in food production.

Shortage of proteins in the diet causes grave diseases and reduces physical and mental activity. It can be mitigated by increasing the productivity of protein-rich crops, by improving the quality of plant proteins by addition of synthetic amino acids, by cultivation of micro-organisms not only in familiar media but also in petroleum and coal products, and by the increased use of fish and of wild animals.

The natural resources of the earth are sufficient to support a very much increased population, but this will only be realized if technology and human effort can be combined with capital investment, greatly to increase agricultural and industrial production. The needed increases in production are severely inhibited by rapid rates of population growth and the imbalance in age groups which results from it. Experience is being gained in several developing countries with new techniques of fertility control, but the Group emphasized that this control alone is not the solution. Continued reliance must be placed on increased production in developing countries, and on aid from developed countries.

The development of water resources is important for agricultural and industrial growth, and for better standards of sanitation and health. Scientists should play an increasing role in the investigation of water supply potentials, and in water management. There is also a great need for increased co-operation among countries sharing riparian rights.

Natural resources must not only be developed but also conserved. Scientific research and assistance in preparing and managing conservation programmes is imperative. This requires a high degree of international co-operation. Active participation of scientists from developing and developed countries in projects such as the International Biological Programme and the International Hydrological Decade is, therefore, of great importance.

5. Security Problems of Developing Countries
Security in the developing countries and regions is an integral and important part of world security.

THE ATTITUDES OF DEVELOPING COUNTRIES TOWARDS SECURITY PROBLEMS

The security of developing nations is gravely endangered by acts of interference, covert or overt, in their internal affairs, as well as by any form of colonialism. Many developing countries have frontier problems as a result of the division of tribes by boundaries drawn by the colonial powers. Every encouragement should be given to the peaceful settlement of such disputes. The appropriate scale of armed forces in a developing country depends upon local circumstances. However, it is clearly necessary for each country to limit armaments and to give economic development first priority.

ECONOMIC BURDEN OF ARMAMENTS ON DEVELOPING COUNTRIES

Even a small defence expenditure is a serious burden on a developing country. It drains financial resources, especially foreign exchange, and makes demands on the limited reservoir of technically trained manpower. Any considerable expenditure on the **armed** forces is liable to threaten national development plans and bring about a risk of inflation.

CURRENT CONFLICTS

(a) Vietnam. The escalation of the war in Vietnam is inflicting terrible suffering on the Vietnamese people, and constitutes a threat to the peace and security of the entire world.

With regard to the nature of the conflict and the ways and means for its settlement, different opinions have been expressed which make it impossible to come out with a general statement on this issue. It is suggested, therefore, that all the participants should inform their respective governments of the views expressed, indicating to them the urgent necessity of taking energetic measures to restore peace in Vietnam. This can be achieved by adhering to the Geneva Agreements of 1954, which would provide the Vietnamese people with the possibility of deciding their own destiny.

(b) Rhodesia. The question of Rhodesia, though of a different nature from that of Vietnam, was considered. It was agreed that the present situation is unjust and oppressive for the majority of the population of Rhodesia and that strong steps should be taken to bring down the illegal Smith regime, with a view to early majority rule.

The Group agreed that the African people of Rhodesia should be given all possible help and support in its just struggle for independence and national rights. Strong support was expressed for the U.N. resolutions adopted by the 20th Session of the General Assembly on the question of Rhodesia.

(c) The Group expressed the hope that the initiative of holding negotiations in Tashkent, between the Prime Minister of India and the President of Pakistan, will be instrumental in bringing about a peaceful settlement of the conflict between the two countries.

ROLE OF THE U.N. IN THE SECURITY OF DEVELOPING COUNTRIES

The big powers, acting in concert with developing nations through the U.N. in conformity with its Charter, can play a crucial role in helping to resolve disputes, in stopping local conflicts, and in the reduction of the burden of armaments in developing countries.

The Group welcomed the Declaration of December 20, 1965, adopted by the 20th Session of the General Assembly of the U.N., which provides a charter for the non-intervention by one state in the affairs of another, and for peaceful co-existence of states. The Group urged the members of the U.N., and particularly the big powers, which have a special role in the Security Council, to activate all provisions of the U.N. Charter, including Chapter VII, designed to provide effective support for the security of countries against whom force is threatened or used by another country.

It was suggested that the cost of peace operations could, among various means, be recovered by U.N. regulation and taxation of the use of oceans, atmosphere and outer space for communications or telecommunications, and of the exploitation of mineral resources under the oceans.

Appendix 18

REGIONAL ORGANIZATIONS AND SECURITY PROBLEMS

The Group recognized the great value of regional organizations for promoting peace, economic and social development, and for aiding the resolution of political questions. It took note of the valuable role played by the Organization of African Unity, for example, by securing recognition of existing boundaries, and mediating in the dispute between Morocco and Algeria.

The Group believed, however, that the U.N., rather than regional organizations, should provide collective security. This is because the positive development role of regional organizations may be impaired and the unity of the organizations subjected to excessive strains if the organizations are called upon to undertake military action.

THE ROLE AND RESPONSIBILITIES OF NATIONS FOR PROMOTING SECURITY

The Working Group firmly believed that all states, both developed and developing, are directly responsible for peace and security in the world, since an armed conflict in one area endangers the security of nations in other areas.

In the long run, the security of all nations requires the achievement of an agreement on general and complete disarmament under strict international control. The Group recommended that the Eighteen Nation Disarmament Committee begin serious and detailed consideration of the G.C.D. treaty, possibly starting from those aspects, in the later stages in both the Soviet and American draft treaties, in which a fair measure of agreement now exists.

In the meanwhile, pending agreement on G.C.D., partial measures should be undertaken for reducing armaments and strengthening the peace.

The Group drew attention to the positive role of co-operation and mutual interdependence of countries in promoting security. Sharing the benefits of common projects, on which the economies of two countries are vitally dependent, may be a strong deterrent to armed conflict between them.

NON-PROLIFERATION OF NUCLEAR WEAPONS

The Working Group discussed various aspects of the problem of preventing further proliferation of nuclear weapons. It agreed that further spread of nuclear weapons is fraught with grave dangers to the security of all nations.

The Group firmly believed that it is high time to take resolute action aimed at concluding a non-proliferation treaty which would have no provisions that could, directly or indirectly, lead to the spread of nuclear weapons. Urgent steps are called for to increase the number of signatories to the Moscow Test Ban Treaty and to extend it to underground testing. Effective measures must also be taken to establish nuclear-free zones.

Participants

Afghanistan
Dr. S. A. S. Ghazanfar

Argentina
Dr. R. V. Garcia

Australia
Dr. Helen Hughes, Mr. F. G. Nicholls

Brazil
Prof. W. E. Kerr

Ceylon
Dr. N. G. Baptist

Colombia
Dr. H. Groot

Czechoslovakia
Acad. I. Málek

Dahomey
Dr. L. Quirino

Ethiopia
Prof. Aklilu Lemma, Dr. Aseffa Tekle, Prof. M. Duri, Prof. P. Gouin, Mr. Kassa Wolde Mariam, Dr. Melak H. Mengesha, Prof. R. O. Whipple

Federal German Republic
Mr. A. von dem Bussche

France
Dr. E. Bauer, Dr. H. Marcovich

German Democratic Republic
Prof. J. Kuczynski

Ghana
Prof. F. G. Torto

India
Prof. M. G. K. Menon, Mr. A. Rahman, Prof. V. A. Sarabhai

Israel
Prof. A. de-Shalit, Dr. Y. Peter

Kenya
Prof. D. P. S. Wasawo

Nigeria
Prof. O. Bassir

Norway
Prof. J. Galtung

Peru
Prof. J. D. Pozo Olano

Poland
Prof. K. Lapter, Prof. I. Malecki

Sierra Leone
Mr. G. E. A. Lardner

Sudan
Prof. M. Hassan Ishag

Sweden
Dr. S. Dedijer

Tanzania
Dr. W. K. Chagula

Thailand
Dr. Panee Chiowanich

U.A.R.
Dr. A. R. Abdel-Meguid, Dr. M. A. Lakany

U.K.
Dr. E. C. Childs, Mr. W. F. Gutteridge, Dr. Patricia J. Lindop,
Prof. C. F. Powell, Prof. J. Rotblat, Sir Gordon Sutherland, Dr. G. E. W. Wolstenholme

U.S.A.
Prof. H. Brown, Prof. J. S. Coleman, Prof. B. T. Feld, Prof. E. S. Munger,
Prof. E. Rabinowitch, Prof. R. Revelle, Prof. A. Rich

U.S.S.R.
Prof. V. Y. Aboltin, Dr. P. V. Andreyev, Prof. B. G. Gafurov, Dr. O. A.
Griniewsky, Acad. V. A. Kargin, Acad. M. D. Millionshchikov, Mr. V. P.
Pavlichenko, Prof. M. Rubinstein

West Indies
Mr. S. L. Martin

Yugoslavia
Prof. I. Supek

Observers

Ethiopia
Mr. Abebe Kebede, Dr. I. Abu Sharr, Mr. Asseffa Seifu, Prof. R. M. Baxter, Dr. R. L. Burling, Prof. E. Dierauf, Mr. Endalkachew Mekonnen, Prof. G. S. Jacobsen, Prof. I. Paz, Mr. E. A. A. Rowse, Mr. Talahun Taye, Dr. E. K. Urban, Prof. B. Winid

U.S.A.
Dr. W. S. Dillon, Dr. E. R. Platig, Mr. J. Stulman

Economic Commission for Africa
Mr. R. K. A. Gardiner, Dr. A. Sundralingam

FAO
Chief G. Akin Deko

U.N.
Dr. J. H. G. Pierson, Mr. M. L. Vejvoda

UNESCO
Mr. F. I. Ajumogobia, Prof. A. Matveyev

19 STATEMENT FROM THE CONTINUING COMMITTEE ON THE SIXTEENTH PUGWASH CONFERENCE, HELD IN SOPOT, SEPTEMBER 11-16, 1966

The 16th Pugwash Conference was held in Sopot from the 11th to 16th September 1966. The theme of the Conference was "Disarmament and World Security, Especially in Europe." Under this heading a number of controversial problems of current interest were discussed, including the situation in Vietnam. As in past Pugwash Conferences the discussions aimed at analysing the problems by the scientific approach rather than at finding complete solutions. The discussions have been frank and stimulating and, despite divergence of opinion on some problems, have resulted in better understanding on many of the complex issues of the day and in a number of specific proposals.

The work of the Conference was carried out in four Working Groups, the membership of each Group consisting of scientists from both East and West. Two of these Working Groups, dealing with problems in Europe, have profited from the work carried out during the past year by the Pugwash Group on European Security. The other two Groups were concerned with various aspects of disarmament.

This statement has been drawn up by the Continuing Committee on the basis of the reports from the Working Groups. In addition, the Conference received a report from the Pugwash Study Group on Biological Warfare, and a summary of this report is included in the statement.

1. Disarmament in Europe

(a) <u>Freeze of Nuclear Weapons</u>. The Group discussed all aspects of the proposed controlled freeze of nuclear weapons in Central Europe, including the freezing of existing stockpiles and of their ownership, as well as the controlled prevention of military application of the nuclear industries in the area under consideration, i.e., the Federal Republic of Germany, the German Democratic Republic, Poland and Czechoslovakia. It was stressed that the freeze, if achieved, could lead to further steps toward reduction of tensions in Europe.

In the discussion on the control and verification of the freeze, the technical difficulties of controlling the movements of small nuclear weapons and smaller components of their delivery systems were stressed.

Some members of the Group pointed to the fact that the current differences between the U.S. and the U.S.S.R. proposals for a world-wide non-proliferation agreement would also be a stumbling-block for agreement on a freeze in Europe, and that the conclusion of a non-proliferation treaty would increase the chances of an agreement on a freeze. Other members of the Group stressed the difference between the freeze and the non-proliferation treaty and suggested independent pursuit of both steps for the reduction of tensions in Europe.

(b) <u>Military Forces and Conventional Weapons</u>. In view of the reduction of tension which has already taken place in Europe in recent years, it was agreed that an appreciable reduction in the number of troops could and should be undertaken--including a substantial withdrawal of foreign troops to their countries and the corresponding dismantling of their bases. It was agreed that the governments concerned are in a position to satisfy themselves regarding the verification of such a withdrawal without any special control machinery.

Measures should be taken to prevent the withdrawal of foreign troops from being accompanied by an increase in the number of national troops on the part of the European nations affected by the withdrawal.

(c) A Non-Aggression Pact. The values of a non-aggression pact between the NATO and the Warsaw Treaty powers were discussed at a joint session of Working Groups 1 and 2.

Most participants stressed the value of a non-aggression or mutual security pact, particularly for progress towards German reunification. They observed that such a pact might develop into part of a wider agreement between East and West. Other participants were of the opinion that a non-aggression pact should be a part of a wider political agreement, including real progress towards German reunification. The view was expressed that the difficulty arising from non-recognition of the G.D.R. by the NATO-states can be overcome in a manner similar to that used at the signing of the Moscow Test Ban Treaty, or even in simpler ways.

(d) Observation Posts. An additional measure, discussed at earlier Conferences, and designed to give a greater sense of confidence, would be to set up some simple inspection procedures based upon mutually agreed observation posts at major transport centres in Europe. Such posts would be of value not only in giving some warning of surprise attack, but also in connection with any substantial troop withdrawals and with the implementation of any non-aggression pact which might follow.

2. Reduction of Tensions and Political Settlements in Europe

The Group considered the reduction of tensions in Europe and the problems of political settlement there. Certain needs for European security can immediately be pointed out, such as recognition of the existing frontiers between the European states; normalization of relations between states with different social systems; peaceful settlement of the German question; and establishment of a lasting system of security based on guarantees by all European countries.

In order to bring about a peaceful settlement of the German question and reunification of that country, in addition to recognition of the existing frontiers between the European states, certain other specific steps should be undertaken:

1. Relations between the states of the Warsaw Treaty and the Federal Republic of Germany should move toward normalization and mutual confidence.

2. Without raising the issues of recognition, the governments of both German states should encourage mutual co-operation in economic, scientific,

Appendix 19

cultural, and religious fields through existing or new methods or organizations, and should examine ways of unofficial co-operation in joint external humanitarian operations and in co-ordinating aid to developing countries. They should also take steps to ease individual contacts between persons living in the separated parts of Germany.

The Group agreed that the eventual reunification of Germany is a necessary part of any lasting system of security in Europe; that it must be achieved by peaceful means and with the full consent of the German people; that a reunified Germany should not represent a threat to European security; and that reunification is likely to be a long and difficult process.

There was also full agreement about the value of larger and freer trade relations between all European states.

Tensions in Europe are related to world tensions, and the war in Vietnam may influence the European situation. Its existence should not prevent continued efforts toward a relaxation of European tensions.

The widening disparity in living standards between the "developed" and the "developing" parts of the world may endanger world security and calls for greatly increased assistance to the developing nations in the technical, educational, and economic fields. Co-operation to this end among all countries, particularly through the United Nations and other international organizations, may contribute substantially to a relaxation of tensions, including those in Europe.

The future organization and development of Europe was a major area of study and discussion. It was recognized that many processes of a scientific, industrial, or technological nature extend across the frontiers of the European nations.

In the areas of economic and industrial co-operation, problems which clearly extend beyond the borders of many European states include: development of natural resources; exchange of technical knowledge on decontamination of water; methods of control of sources of fresh water for international rivers and lakes; flood control; power development; air pollution; energy policy (coal, oil, nuclear energy, natural gas); weather and climate control; technical standardization; patents; science planning (including scientific and technical exchange); industrial co-production; transportation.

Because many of these problems are highly technical and require the close collaboration of engineers, natural and social scientists, it is recommended that one or more permanent European agencies be set up to deal with them, or that existing agencies be extended, with perhaps a European Conference of specialists on these issues.

New projects of European economic planning, and better co-operation among existing organizations, are required. These, however, should avoid creating such barriers as would produce a still greater gap between the prosperity of Europe and of the developing nations.

Specific proposals for scientific, cultural and political co-operation include: greater participation of the smaller European nations in the many existing international non-governmental organizations; co-operation in education extended and directed toward common textbooks in international relations, international law, etc.; co-operation for exchange of scientists and technical information; exchange of newspaper columns among nations (East-West) and exchange of suitable TV-broadcasts; more participation by countries of Eastern and Western Europe in round table discussions, like those recently held by Poland-Britain and Poland-Denmark; co-operation in projects of technical assistance to the developing countries; international co-operative volunteer services; reduction of travel formalities; abolition of visas, at least between many smaller European nations.

3. Main Problems of Progress towards General and Complete Disarmament (G.C.D.)

The Working Group has considered at length the main problems of progress towards G.C.D.; it has examined some of the obstacles which exist and possible constructive approaches towards a solution.

Different means of strengthening the peacekeeping machinery of the U.N. were discussed. There was, however, a general feeling that most plans proposed would be unrealistic unless the problems of strengthening the U.N. organization were themselves tackled, for it was the conferring of real power on that organization which was generally at the root of the matter. Where great powers or non-members of the U.N. are involved, difficulties are at present often intractable within the U.N. framework. A revival of the original spirit of the U.N.--in particular as it affects the Security Council--was advocated.

In the context of obstacles to G.C.D. particular consideration was given to the problem of the liquidation of foreign bases and the withdrawal of foreign troops from the soil of other nations. The problem was felt to be so complex that it may be desirable to set up an international working group to investigate the transitional difficulties between the present situation and the situation when G.C.D. becomes effective. The Group also recognized the need for the ending of colonialism in all its forms. The Group reasserted its belief that G.C.D. is in the interest of all nations and felt that significant obstacles could be overcome if a progressive liquidation of foreign bases could be achieved.

The proposed International Disarmament Conference in 1967 was welcomed by the Group with the hope that it would give impetus to the work of existing U.N. Committees and of the Geneva Disarmament Conference in this field. The Group was unanimous that the entry of the Chinese People's Republic into the United Nations was vital to future developments in all areas, including disarmament discussions.

The Group also discussed the problem of Vietnam. The attitude of the Conference to this problem is indicated in section 5.

4. Measures for Arms Limitation

(a) <u>Extension of the Test Ban Treaty</u>. The Group concerned itself with a number of measures for arms limitation. The first one considered was an extension of the nuclear test ban treaty to cover underground tests, the ultimate objective being a Comprehensive **Test** Ban Treaty. There was general agreement that the status of the technical procedures for detecting, identifying and locating underground seismic events is improving, and general belief that the major obstacles to **an** agreement are political rather than technical.

Since the problem of on-site inspection appears to remain a major one in negotiations, the Group spent much time in considering possible solutions or arrangements which might be more negotiable, and hence lead promptly to an extension of the present partial test ban. In developing possible alternatives it was generally assumed that seismic detection systems would be national with, however, provisions for co-operation and data exchange between **nations**.

Beyond this the variants were:

1. A threshold treaty with provisions for gradually lowering the threshold.

2. A threshold treaty with additional commitments by the signatory state to refrain from **any** testing of nuclear weapons.

3. A threshold treaty with additional commitments by the signatory states:

(a) to refrain from any testing of nuclear weapons,

(b) to co-operate in technical studies aimed at improving the identification capability and at lowering the threshold,

(c) to supply whenever requested by any signatory state all feasible information and explanations on unidentified seismic events occurring in its territory.

4. A comprehensive treaty with a provision for locating unmanned seismic stations in the territory of the two or three largest nations, e.g., the U.S.A. and the U.S.S.R., either for validating data from national networks or for additional help in identifying **earthquakes.**

5. Provision in a comprehensive treaty of procedures for obtaining more information, including possible on-site inspection of unidentified seismic events, utilizing the "request and invitation" procedure of requesting clarification.

6. As a preliminary to a treaty agreement among the nuclear powers, a limited duration trial period of no testing with provision for the above "request and invitation" procedure.

In the view of the Group the most interesting of the above are variants 3 and 4.

The Group was greatly interested in the proposed establishment of a "Detection Club," to make high quality seismic data available on a broad basis, as an item of possible use to several of the alternative proposals. It hopes the establishment of this organization will proceed rapidly, but it also urges that its establishment should not stand in the way of prompt negotiation of an extended treaty; a treaty which, it should be noted, could be of great assistance in preventing the proliferation of nuclear weapons.

(b) Non-proliferation. Non-proliferation of nuclear weapons remains an urgent matter, and there was consensus that it is of the utmost importance to obtain prompt agreement on a treaty to prevent proliferation, as this would be an important step toward nuclear disarmament. A treaty to accomplish this should be a simple one, in which the nuclear nations agree not to transfer nuclear weapons to other states, and the non-nuclear nations agree not to manufacture or acquire them on either an individual or a collective basis. The Group felt that additional steps would be needed, in which the nuclear powers took positive actions of restraint, and toward decreasing their reliance on nuclear weapons. The problem of guarantees to non-nuclear nations was discussed, but no proposals were developed which seemed likely to find the necessary acceptance. However, the suggestion was generally approved that the nuclear powers should formally agree not to use weapons on nations which do not have such weapons, and on whose territory nuclear weapons are not located.

(c) Nuclear-Free Zones and Regional Disarmament Measures. Recognizing that any conflict, however small, contains in it the germs of world-wide war, there was discussion of a number of measures which might help in minimizing or eliminating regional conflicts. One especially useful agreement would be the prompt establishment of nuclear-free zones in different areas of the world. Particular note was taken of the activities of the Polish Government in developing proposals for denuclearization and for a "nuclear freeze" for Central Europe (the Rapacki and Gomulka plans), which could not only be helpful in the development of acceptable plans for Central Europe, but could also be a useful spur to other nations in other areas to develop plans for their own nuclear-free zones, as for example in South America, and in Africa and the Middle East.

In connection with the general problem of arms races among developing nations, the value of limitations on the supplying of arms by industrial nations to others, and the importance of regional arms limitation agreements of various types, in addition to nuclear-free zones, were pointed out by some participants.

(d) Nuclear Freeze Proposals. The topic of possible world-wide freeze agreements was discussed in the particular context of the likely development and deployment of antiballistic missile systems (ABM). At least three types of such freezes were considered:
   (i) a freeze on the deployment of ABM systems;
  (ii) a freeze on the numbers of offensive nuclear delivery systems, especially missiles;
 (iii) a freeze on total number of nuclear delivery systems.

Appendix 19

No general agreement was reached on any one of these.

(e) Peaceful Uses of Atomic Energy. In the context of the clearly desirable expanded development and peaceful utilization of atomic energy, it is very important to have adequate and uniform control arrangements to ensure that fissionable nuclear materials are used as scheduled for peaceful purposes.

A single international system for this control is clearly desirable, and the Group recommended the universal support and use of the currently available international system, that of the International Atomic Energy Agency.

5. Vietnam

The problem of Vietnam was discussed in detail at a plenary session specially devoted to this subject, as well as in Working Group 3. While there was an extensive and frank exchange of views among the participants, the Conference was unable to arrive at any agreed conclusions on the causes and nature of the war and on possible ways for bringing to an end this dangerous and tragic conflict.

6. Problems of Biological Warfare

Progress has been reported by the Pugwash Study Group on Biological Warfare, part of whose work has now been taken over by the Stockholm International Peace Research Institute (SIPRI). At the last meeting of the Study Group, held in Stockholm 4-6 September, attention was given to technical possibilities for the development of rapid detection methods for microbiological agents (including viruses and toxins). Specific research was defined in this field, to be undertaken by a group of scientists from Eastern, Western and non-aligned countries, and to be carried out under the auspices of SIPRI. The meeting in Stockholm also examined the results of four trial inspections of microbiological laboratories in Austria, Sweden, Denmark and Czechoslovakia, carried out during the spring and summer of 1966.

Both these activities of the Biological Warfare Study Group represent a useful contribution to the problem of biological weapons disarmament and their control.

Participants

Austria
Dr. R. Jungk

Belgium
Prof. R. Leclercq

Canada
Dr. N. Z. Alcock

Czechoslovakia
Acad. I. Málek, Mr. T. Němec, Dr. A. Šnejdárek, Acad. F. Šorm

Denmark
Mr. D. J. Adler, Dr. P. L. Ølgaard, Dr. J. Wilhjelm

Federal German Republic
Mr. H. Afheldt, Prof. E. Menzel, Prof. L. Raiser

France
Dr. E. Bauer, Mr. A. Joxe, Dr. H. Marcovich

German Democratic Republic
Dr. A. Kolesnyk, Prof. H. Kröger, Prof. G. Rienäcker

Hungary
Prof. L. Reczei

India
Prof. M. J. Desai, Prof. V. A. Sarabhai

Israel
Dr. S. Freier

Italy
Prof. G. Giacometti

Netherlands
Prof. P. B. Smith, Prof. H. A. Tolhoek

Norway
Dr. S. Cyvin, Prof. J. Galtung

Poland
Prof. I. Adamczewski, Prof. L. Infeld, Prof. A. Klafkowski, Prof. K. Lapter, Prof. I. Malecki

Rumania
Prof. I. Agarbiceanu, Prof. V. Hanga

Sweden
Dr. K. Birnbaum, Dr. R. Björnerstedt, Mr. J. Prawitz

U.A.R.
Dr. M. Lakany

U.K.
Prof. H. Bondi, Dr. L. M. Brown, Prof. B. H. Flowers, Mr. W. F. Gutteridge, Prof. R. E. Peierls, Prof. J. Rotblat

U.S.A.
Prof. K. Boulding, Prof. P. M. Doty, Prof. F. J. Dyson, Prof. B. T. Feld, Prof. Bentley Glass, Prof. H. A. Kissinger, Mrs. Betty G. Lall, Prof. F. A. Long, Prof. S. Muller, Prof. E. Rabinowitch, Prof. A. Rich, Prof. M. D. Shulman

Appendix 19   264

U.S.S.R.
Prof. V. Y. Aboltin, Prof. P. V. Andreyev, Acad. L. A. Artsimovitch,
Acad. M. M. Dubinin, Prof. V. S. Emelyanov, Acad. V. A. Kargin,
Acad. V. M. Khvostov, Acad. M. D. Millionshchikov, Prof. N. A. Talensky,
Acad. A. P. Vinogradov, Prof. B. M. Vul

Yugoslavia
Prof. V. Butozan

Observers and Scientific Staff

Czechoslovakia
Dr. V. Hajdu

Poland
Dr. M. Blusztajn, Prof. J. Bukowski, Prof. K. Kopecki, Dr. A. Kruczkowski,
Mr. J. Lider

U.K.
Mr. Hedley Bull, Mr. J. K. Wright

U.S.A.
Mr. S. Stone

U.S.S.R.
Dr. V. V. Shustov

U.N.
Mr. A. N. Nesterenko, Mr. V. Petrovsky

WHO
Dr. M. Kaplan

20 STATEMENT FROM THE FIRST SOUTH-EAST ASIAN REGIONAL PUGWASH CONFERENCE, HELD IN MELBOURNE, JANUARY 23-27, 1967

The first South-East Asian Regional Pugwash Conference was held at International House, University of Melbourne, from 23rd to 27th January, 1967. It was attended by participants from Australia, Ceylon, India, Indonesia, Japan, Malaysia, New Zealand, Pakistan, Singapore, and observers from the Continuing Committee, the United Nations and the Australian Department of External Affairs.

The Conference concerned itself with the following major areas:

1. Definition of crucial areas in which the application of science and technology will most rapidly improve living standards; pre-requisites for success in these areas.

2. Problems of security and their effect on the development of science and technology.

3. Education and training; role of tertiary institutes; the question of developing a technician force.

The discussions were held in a frank and cordial atmosphere and were most fruitful. This Conference has shown the need for this type of discussion among scientists in the South-East Asian region and it was decided that further regional conferences should be held at regular intervals.

The following is a brief summary of the discussions arranged under the headings of:
1. Regional co-operation in development and education.
2. Food science and technology in developing countries.
3. Problems of security and development.

These categories correspond to the subjects studied by specific working groups in the latter stages of the Conference.

1. Regional Co-operation in Development and Education
The Conference considered that the term "aid" may inhibit responsible requests, and thought it necessary to stress the mutual advantages to be gained by both developed and less developed countries from a co-operative programme of regional development.

To facilitate such co-operation some mechanisms for selection and integration of projects were discussed.

1.1 Mechanisms for administering co-operative programmes.
(a) <u>For large programmes</u> administration should be through existing international organizations, including international finance institutions. To expedite effective administration more support should be given, both financially and in terms of expert scientific and technical manpower, to the United Nations Economic and Social Council's Advisory Committee on the Application of Science and Technology to Development.

(b) <u>For smaller projects</u> bilateral co-operation between governments may be more appropriate.

(c) In order to build up the scientific and technical personnel needed to enable programmes under (a) and (b) to be used more efficiently, an immediate effort should be made to increase contacts and exchanges between scientists and institutions in the region.

1.2 Co-operative programme selection. For the better integration of the development programme on a country and regional basis, the recommendation of the United Nations Committee and ECAFE*, that proposals should be channelled through science research councils or similar bodies where they exist, is supported. Where these do not exist advisory scientific committees should be set up in both recipient and **donor** countries to include, amongst others, scientists involved in government departments, industrial research groups and the universities. Such advisory groups could:

(a) assess the feasibility and priorities of development projects in the light of the country's resources and needs;

(b) advise on the suitability of candidates for service in particular projects overseas;

(c) be used as a communication body to make maximum use of scientists and technicians from overseas visiting the country.

Many of these activities are at present carried out by existing bodies in some countries, but it was felt that the reliance of programme administrators on the advice of such an integrating group would help it to develop and extend its use where these do not yet exist.

1.3 Choice of programmes. The principles governing the choice of programmes should include the following:

(a) Priority should be given to short term projects, which are attractive in achieving a rapid result at a finite cost, only where they are able to initiate a continuing process of development.

(b) Preference should be given to projects which can add to the experience of the region as a whole, where continuous exchange of experience between countries in the region can lead to easy adjustment of the programmes.

(c) In considering suitable projects all phases of the programme must be considered--its integration into the existing local situation, the ancillary services needed by way of initial equipment and personnel, and the introduction of the project into the social system.

---

*Economic Council for Asia and the Far East.

1.4 Supply of scientific and technical personnel.

(a) In order to avoid waste of time by visiting scientists, the host country should make sure that, if possible, it can provide suitable accommodation and facilities. Careful selection of the visiting scientist and his adequate briefing on the country's particular problems is necessary, and could be undertaken by the science research councils or equivalent bodies.

(b) There is a need to encourage scientists to work overseas. Academic and government bodies are asked to facilitate the free movement of scientists and to encourage service overseas as part of a normal career and without prejudice to their professional advancement.
   (i) A specific proposal is made that the Australian Pugwash Group should request the Vice-Chancellors' Committee to initiate discussions with C.S.I.R.O. and the Department of External Affairs on the sending of staff to developing countries for two years, one year to be paid for by the employer, and one year by the Department of External Affairs.
   (ii) It is recommended to the Australian Government that provision be made under the Colombo Plan and other schemes for scientists and technologists, especially those of a more senior level, to study in Australia without the undue financial sacrifice which, in many cases, they have at present to make.

1.5 Education.
The Conference considered some general features of education in the region and emphasized the importance of stressing world-wide human values in education. Past practices have sometimes made it difficult for children to cultivate attitudes appropriate to a shrinking and uniting world.

Technical training. The Conference noted the recommendations for general education and training made by the United Nations Advisory Committee on the Application of Science and Technology to Development. While agreeing with these recommendations, the Conference noted that the training of technicians is not discussed. The rapid creation of a technician cadre, intermediate in skill and function between the tradesman and the professional or technologist, is essential to a country's development and at least four such people are needed for each professionally trained one. In the absence of a developed local industry, adequate technical training cannot be provided and a start must be made by obtaining the necessary skills abroad.

It became apparent that there are many *ad hoc* methods for obtaining this initial stimulus. These can be regarded as training schemes; they must not be regarded as an alternative to this.

2. Food Science and Technology in Developing Countries
The wastage and **spoilage** of food is as important a problem in feeding the world as is the failure to produce high yields per acre. In this context a number of important questions were considered, including:
- the high proportion of the population engaged in food production;
- lack of literacy amongst food producers;

Appendix 20

- the prevalence of subsistence farming;
- ignorance of the relation between health and nutrition;
- inadequate advisory services in agriculture and fisheries;
- ineffectual health inspection services;
- lack of attraction for careers in extension services;
- preference of university and college graduates for urban employment;
- emphasis of developmental projects on industrialization;
- low standards of sanitation and hygiene;
- dietary proscriptions and taboos;
- man's distrust of technological change.

The solution is seen in the establishment of a safe chain in food management from producer to consumer, one which is firmly rooted in the social habits and the cultural pattern of the population. Based on the experience in technologically advanced countries, a solution must be found to incorporate this in the ways of life of developing ones.

We need to measure the magnitude of the problem in each of these developing countries, and then to deal with it by incorporating the necessary knowledge into the educational system at every level from primary education to teacher training. The education of girls and women here is especially important.

3. Problems of Security and Development

The Conference discussed a number of aspects relating to the effect of security arrangements on development. These included the effect of setting up military-science complexes; the "uncertainty" which enters into the making of decisions by individual nations under conditions of military security, and the related questions of the spread of nuclear weapons in South-East Asian countries; the need for establishing institutes for peace research as distinct from those for the study of war; and the refugee problem in South Vietnam.

In the short time available it was not possible to discuss these problems in depth, although it was recognized that they were of vital importance. For this reason the Conference suggests that this topic be discussed further at the next Regional Conference.

3.1 Interaction between Science, National Security and Development within individual countries in South-East Asia. The Conference recommends that the following steps be taken to prepare for the discussion of this item at the next Conference:

A person or persons should be asked to formulate specific queries which might most usefully elicit information of the kind required.

Scientists in each of the participating countries should be asked to provide the information referred to in these queries.

This information should then be collated in the form of a working paper for discussion at the Conference.

The Conference suggests that questions of the following kind should be considered in formulation of the queries referred to above:

(a) What proportion of the national scientific effort in terms of money and manpower, is being specifically directed towards increasing the military potential of the country?

(b) What arguments are used by the government to support this outlay of resources?

(c) Is the true extent of the financial and manpower commitment in this direction ascertainable?

(d) To what extent is scientific research in university or civil research centres financially supported by funds from the defence budget?

(e) To what extent is scientific research in laboratories of all kinds financed by **grants** from overseas funds?

(f) Can any reliable estimate be made of the potential of the country for the production of nuclear weapons, preparations for biological and chemical warfare and **delivery** systems?

(g) Has there been any recent build-up of conventional armaments in the country?

3.2 Regional **co-o**peration in peace research. The Conference endorses the earlier approach to the problem of Regional Co-operation in Research as outlined in Section 4 of the report of Working Group 2 of the Fifteenth Pugwash Conference. In addition to this, and guided by the same principles, the Conference believes that the establishment of an International Institute directed towards peace research, with particular interest in South-East Asia, would be one of the most valuable contributions which could be made to the security and development of the area. In the meantime, the fullest support should be given to research groups within individual countries, which seek answers to such questions as:

(a) What conditions cause nations to initiate wars?

(b) What factors lead a country to believe that its national security is threatened?

(c) Can a stable state of overall security in the area be achieved by the principle of mutual deterrence based on non-nuclear weapons?

3.3 Vietnam. The Conference views with the gravest disquiet the continuing escalation of the war in Vietnam, which may lead to a third world war and has already brought the world into a new phase of the arms race.

The Conference regrets the violent death of so many people, both combatant and **non**-combatant, due mostly to the indiscriminate nature of warfare.

Scientists of the whole world must be concerned about the increasing use of science for the destruction of human lives and vital resources.

Of special and immediate concern is the plight of refugees and the devastation of once-fertile areas. Every effort should be made to extend aid for the rehabilitation and care of the civilian population.

The Conference affirms that the only satisfactory way out of this disastrous situation is a negotiated settlement. There was substantial agreement that conditions must be created in which the Vietnamese people north and south of the provisional demarcation line settle their own affairs without outside interference as stipulated, for example, in the 1954-1962 Geneva Agreements.

The Conference agreed that the countries in this region have a particular contribution to make to this settlement and recommends an appeal to all scientists to make every effort towards this solution of the Vietnam conflict.

The disastrous situation in Vietnam is a reminder that scientists must make greater efforts to bring about conditions in which scientific and technological developments lead to world peace rather than world war.

Participants

Australia
Dr. W. Boas, Prof. T. O. Browning, Sir Macfarlane Burnet, Dr. P. J. Fensham, Dr. K. Fowler, Sir Otto Frankel, Dr. Helen Hughes, Dr. H. G. Higgins, Mr. I. Langlands, Dr. M. R. Lemberg, Dr. D. F. Martyn, Prof. B. Y. Mills, Sir Mark Oliphant, Dr. F. H. Reuter, Sir Frederick White

Ceylon
Dr. J. C. V. Chinnappa

India
Dr. S. Dhawan

Indonesia
Prof. B. Soemantri

Japan
Prof. Y. Miyake, Prof. E. Yamada

Malaysia
Prof. C. J. Eliezer, Dr. A. A. Sandosham

New Zealand
Prof. J. F. Duncan

Pakistan
Mr. M. A. Rana

Singapore
Mr. H. H. Lim, Mr. E. J. Seow

Observers and Scientific Staff

Australia
Dr. J. M. Dickins, Dr. E. K. Inall, Miss Maris King, Mrs. Blanche Merz

Pugwash Continuing Committee
Dr. Patricia J. Lindop, Prof. J. Rotblat

United Nations
Mr. A. C. Tyrrell

21 STATEMENT BY THE PUGWASH CONTINUING COMMITTEE ON THE NON-PROLIFERATION TREATY (MAY, 1967)

At a meeting held in Marianske Lazne on 13-15 May 1967, members of the Pugwash Continuing Committee discussed various aspects of the non-proliferation treaty with scientists from 13 countries, i.e., Belgium, Czechoslovakia, Federal German Republic, France, German Democratic Republic, Hungary, Italy, Netherlands, Poland, Sweden, U.K., U.S.A. and U.S.S.R.

The following statement was agreed unanimously by the members of the Continuing Committee present in Marianske Lazne.

After examining the available information on the proposed non-proliferation treaty, as well as the various objections which have been raised against it, we have arrived at the conclusion that a text of the treaty could be formulated which would satisfy all reasonable objections and which should be acceptable to all nations. We urge the 18-Nations Disarmament Committee of the United Nations to formulate and agree upon such a treaty with all possible haste.

The acceptance of this treaty by a large number of countries is a necessary prerequisite for any further progress towards disarmament, and would represent an essential step towards preventing nuclear war.

Technical Considerations
A careful consideration of the objections of a technical nature which have been advanced against the treaty, as outlined below, has convinced us that these objections have no solid basis.

The treaty will be effective only if it involves some reasonable and appropriate forms of international control.

The dangers, deriving from any such control system, of hindering the industrial development of the non-nuclear countries, can be eliminated by a carefully designed system of safeguards.

An appropriate design of such a control system would also solve the problem of possible industrial espionage. In any case, the very concept of industrial espionage appears obsolete and inappropriate when considered in the light of the present rapid pace of development of industrial technology.

The safeguards already contained in the control system of the International Atomic Energy Agency of Vienna, approved unanimously by its Assembly, appear to satisfy the conditions outlined above. Where necessary, they could eventually be further improved by relatively minor amendments.

It is clear that the development of a military nuclear programme is of only moderate advantage for the development of a parallel industrial programme. In monetary terms alone, the benefit to the latter from the former is certainly less than one-fifth of the investment involved in a military programme. Furthermore, the initiation of such programmes will unavoidably entail enormous economic stresses for the country involved, which could be disastrous in the case of developing countries.

At the present time there are no useful applications of nuclear explosions for peaceful purposes. If and when they do materialize, their use should be assigned to an International Agency, which would obtain materials and information from the nuclear powers. Such a system would be far more advantageous to the developing countries.

Political Considerations
The main objection of a political nature, that the treaty would maintain the distinction between militarily nuclear and militarily non-nuclear countries, appears very weak. This distinction is today a simple matter of fact. Its alternative is a large number of nuclear powers. For the future, it is in the best interests of the non-nuclear countries to take all steps which favour the evolution of the present situation towards a reduction of the armaments of the nuclear powers. The non-proliferation treaty will represent an important step in this direction.

The objection, that the treaty would crystallize the existing division of the world into two opposing blocs, appears irrelevant, especially if the current situation is compared with that of a world in which many countries independently deploy national nuclear arms.

We wish to emphasize that along with the treaty, the nuclear powers must accept the responsibility, through appropriate and carefully prepared international arrangements to guarantee that the security of the non-nuclear, non-aligned countries will not be jeopardized by their adherence to it.

For all these reasons we consider the non-proliferation treaty as a fundamental step towards a safer and more stable world, and we, therefore, strongly recommend to the governments of the non-nuclear powers that they work for wide adherence to the treaty. We wish to express our conviction that the nuclear powers must at the same time assume specific and meaningful commitments to halt the arms race.

Among many such possible measures of arms control and reduction, at least some of which should be adopted within a specified time, we urge the governments of the U.S.A. and U.S.S.R. to consider seriously: an extension of the nuclear test ban to include underground testing; a cut off of production of fissile materials for weapons use; a freeze of nuclear delivery systems, and of the deployment of possibly destabilizing new systems of a defensive or offensive nature; a further reduction of armaments and troops in Europe, etc.

In particular, it is clear that the non-proliferation treaty would command a larger acceptance if the U.S.A. and the U.S.S.R. would unilaterally submit a significantly larger number of their civilian power reactors to the controls of the IAEA.

We further urge the governments of all the nuclear powers, in particular those of Great Britain, France and China, not just to refrain from further increasing or improving their arsenals of nuclear weapons as well as their systems of delivery, but, rather, to take steps gradually to reduce them.

We urge all the members of the 18-Nations Disarmament Committee, and in particular the U.S.A. and U.S.S.R. Co-Chairmen, to renew in a **spirit of** friendly and conscientious co-operation, and as soon as possible, the discussions at Geneva aimed at reaching further agreements on the reduction of their armaments in general and their nuclear arms in particular.

We urge all scientists throughout the world to take all possible steps to convince their own governments to move rapidly along the lines outlined above.

22 THE WORK OF THE CONTINUING COMMITTEE SINCE 1962 (REPORT TO THE SEVENTEENTH PUGWASH CONFERENCE IN RONNEBY)

J. Rotblat

1. Introduction

It was exactly five years ago, on the 3rd September 1962, that I reported to the Tenth Pugwash Conference in London on the first five years of Pugwash activities. There was then a general feeling that such reports should be given about every four or five years to a large gathering, representative of the whole Pugwash Movement. It is my honour to present to you, on behalf of the Continuing Committee, the report of our activities during the past five years.

In presenting this report, I shall assume that the members of the Conference have looked at the book *Pugwash: A History of the Conferences on Science and World Affairs*, copies of which have been sent to all Pugwashites. The book brings the history of Pugwash up to April of this year, and as such it may be regarded as a report of our activities during the ten years since Pugwash came into being. I do not want to waste your time by repeating the account given in the book. I propose, therefore, to give a general summary of our activities, to draw attention to some conclusions and, in particular, to compare our achievements during the two quinquennia as a basis for our thoughts on the future.

2. International Conferences

The main guide-lines for our work were laid down by the London Conference, and although that Conference gave the Continuing Committee full discretion in directing and carrying our Pugwash activities, the Committee followed closely these guide-lines, and most of the programme laid down in London has been carried out.

The main activity was the organizing of the international conferences. Six such conferences were held since the London meeting in 1962, until the present meeting. Although we aimed at alternating the site of the conferences between Eastern and Western countries, it so happened that in this quinquennium three conferences were held in Eastern Europe, and one each in Western Europe, Africa and Asia.

Among the participants in these six conferences there were 140 newcomers to Pugwash. It is worth noting (Table 1) that among the newcomers there were very few from the three countries, the U.S.A., U.S.S.R. and U.K., which previously accounted for more than half of all Pugwashites; the fresh blood came from other countries, particularly from Asia and Africa.

The six conferences were roughly of the same size, the average number of participants being 66, with a standard deviation of 6. This compares with an average of 43, with a standard deviation of 22 for the first nine conferences. Similarly the number of countries from which the participants came averaged 23 ± 4, compared with 12 ± 5 during the first five years. These differences, on the one hand reflect the growth and spread of the Pugwash Movement, and on the other hand, they show evidence of our settling down to a more steady routine.

Appendix 22

Table 1. Participants in Pugwash Conferences

	First Quinquennium (10 Conferences)	Second Quinquennium (6 Conferences)
Total number of first attendances:	287	140

	Percentages	
U.S.A.	28	10
U.S.S.R.	13	7
U.K.	13	7
Europe	32	41
America (other than U.S.A.)	4	5
Asia and Australasia	9	17
Africa	1	13

Table 2. Newcomers to Pugwash Conferences

	First Quinquennium %	Second Quinquennium %
Philosophy, Education, etc.	4	11
Physical Sciences	56	38
Biological Sciences	22	16
Social Sciences	18	35

An interesting trend is seen when participants are grouped according to their profession or field of study. Figure 2 in the *History* (p. 64) shows the percentage of participants from the different disciplines in successive conferences. A gradual increase in the proportion of social scientists is seen, with a corresponding decrease in the proportion of physical scientists. The proportion of biological scientists, philosophers and educators remained practically unchanged, and quite low. The increase in the proportion of social scientists was particularly high among the newcomers to Pugwash (Table 2). Thus, in the first quinquennium, social scientists represented 18% of the total, while of those who joined us in the second quinquennium 35% were social scientists. Various factors may have contributed to this change in composition, but the most important is probably the greater emphasis on political aspects of the problems on our agenda, which requires the presence of, what we call, social scientists: economists, lawyers, sociologists and experts in international relations.

The Continuing Committee since 1962

This brings me to the next point--the topics of discussion at our conferences. In accordance with the decisions of the London Conference, disarmament has been our main theme. In five of the six conferences under review the term "disarmament" figured specifically in the title of the conference; only one, the Fifteenth Conference at Addis Ababa, was entirely devoted to problems of developing nations, but even there, one of the five Working Groups dealt with problems of security. Significantly, this working group had by far the smallest number of participants from the developing nations, thus showing that problems other than disarmament are considered to be of greater importance to the scientists from these countries. Various aspects of science and technology in developing nations were also discussed in working groups in Udaipur and Venice.

Under the heading "Disarmament and World Security" some topics were discussed repeatedly at several conferences. These include: progress toward general and complete disarmament, reduction of tensions, collective security, spread of nuclear weapons, comprehensive test ban, and nuclear-free zones. Security in Europe was also a recurrent topic, and it figured specifically in the title of the last conference at Sopot.

Apart from disarmament and the problems of developing nations, there were two other main topics: international co-operation in science and technology, and the responsibilities of scientists. Various aspects of these problems were discussed at several conferences.

The present procedure for summarizing the discussions and conclusions of Pugwash Conferences has been adopted as a result of trial and error. The main work of the conference is usually carried out in four or five working groups, each tackling some specific aspect of the main theme of the conference. Members of the other working groups are given an opportunity to comment on the draft reports from each working group, but ultimately each report is issued as a document from the working group, rather than from the conference as a whole. Although we aim at reaching agreement on the topics discussed, it is now our practice to include in the report important and original suggestions, even if they failed to gain full support of the working group. In this way ideas are recorded which the group felt merit further consideration and development. The final draft of the report is published in the Pugwash Newsletter, as well as in the Proceedings of the Conferences, and distributed to former Pugwashites, heads of government, and various international institutions.

The reports from the working groups also serve as basic material for the Continuing Committee in preparing the public statement which has been issued after each conference. At the earlier conferences, the statement used to be discussed and drafted by the conference as a whole, but after the Twelfth Conference in Udaipur, when it took a seven-hour session to agree on the statement, it was thought impracticable to work on a draft in a large gathering, and henceforth the Continuing Committee drafted and issued the statement as a document of its own. Even so, it takes the Committee about ten hours to prepare and agree on the draft. The statement is handed out to the Press at a press conference held the day after the conclusion of the conference. Usually, the publicity given to the statement is very good in the country in which the conference is held, but press coverage in other countries has, on the whole, been very poor. Perhaps the Committee should have paid more attention to publicity arrangements and to our public image. As it is, even after ten years of existence and some very significant achievements, many more people have heard of Captain Pugwash, the pirate, than of a Movement of eminent scientists aiming at the preservation of peace on land and the seas.

I have just referred to our achievements. It is not easy to measure them because no numerical data are available. We have good reason to believe that the conferences have made important contributions towards greater understanding and convergence of views between East and West on disarmament problems. It was very gratifying to hear from U Thant that our deliberations receive careful attention at the United Nations and national governments. There were also specific items to our credit, for example, our contribution to the test ban treaty. However, on the whole, the progress made was much slower, and the tangible achievements fewer, than in the first quinquennium. Some reasons for this apparent decline are obvious. In the early years, there were very few ideas about disarmament and few people were thinking about them. Moreover, there were practically no contacts between East and West on these problems. Pugwash represented the first serious attempt to establish such contacts and to inject novel ideas about disarmament. Since that time, and largely stimulated by the success of Pugwash, many other bodies became concerned with these problems; a number of institutes, both national and international, have been set up in which studies are carried out on disarmament, arms control, and on peace; there are now many people engaged full-time in research on these problems. Another possible reason is that in the early days many of the disarmament problems were primarily of a technical nature, in which Pugwashites had a special competence, and on which agreement could be reached fairly easily among scientists. Although there are still many technical problems to be solved, even in the first steps towards disarmament, the emphasis in recent years has shifted towards political issues, in which we have no special expertise, and which are much more difficult to solve. A third reason is that when Pugwash started, the cold war was at its height. Now we are in a period of so-called co-existence, and although the threat of a nuclear war is just as great, the whole problem of East-West relations has taken on a different aspect. Moreover, there is the growing threat arising from the disparity in standards of living between the developed and developing countries, and on this we have been spending far too little time. It may well be that an entirely new approach to the disarmament problem is now necessary, as well as a reappraisal of its relative position in our programme.

3. Regional and Special Conferences

I have dwelt at some length on the subject of the international conferences, since these constitute our major and most conspicuous activity. But the Continuing Committee is involved in a variety of other functions, including other types of conferences.

One of these, is the regional conference. The dilemma of maintaining the international character of the Pugwash Conferences without further increasing their size, combined with the problem of the very considerable travelling expenses from distant countries, can be partially solved by organizing regional conferences in different parts of the world, and which, in addition to our usual topics, would also deal with issues of specific interest to the region. The first regional conference in South-East Asian countries was held in January this year in Australia; its theme was "Scientific, Technical and Industrial Development in South-East Asia." Despite the absence of scientists from a number of countries in the region, the Conference was very successful, and has stimulated many scientists to take an active part in Pugwash. This prompted the Committee to encourage further regional meetings. Another conference in South-East Asia is planned for next year in Ceylon. Preparations are also afoot for a regional conference to be held in Latin America.

Another type of conference organized by the Continuing Committee are small meetings to discuss more specific problems, and whose success depends on their being completely private. During the past five years, three such meetings were held: in March 1963 in London on the technical and political aspects of a nuclear test ban; in August 1965 in London, on the Vietnam problem; and in June 1967 in Paris, on the Middle East crisis. No reports are issued from these meetings and their main purpose is to provide an opportunity for an absolutely free and frank exchange of opinion, and to help in the understanding of the thinking on the particular problem; any consensus reached is conveyed directly by the participants to the governments concerned.

4. Study Groups

Apart from conferences a great deal of work has been going on in the Study Groups. At the present time we have two permanent Study Groups; on Biological Warfare, and on European Security. We shall receive reports from them this afternoon, and therefore, I shall limit myself to general remarks. The Study Groups are international in composition, and the main difference between the Pugwash conferences and the Study Groups is that the latter represent a continuing effort, each meeting of a Study Group being a continuation of the previous meeting and planning the programme for the following meeting. In practice, it has not always worked out in this way, and occasionally the meetings of the Study Groups tended to become too much like the ordinary Pugwash conferences.

Both Study Groups did valuable work. The one on Biological Warfare was particularly successful. There are several reasons for this. One was that its problem is fairly precise, mostly technical and not very controversial. Another important reason was that it worked in close association with SIPRI, which provided financial backing for some projects and commissioned special papers. As you will hear in the afternoon, this Study Group has carried out a model experiment on inspection, has made definite proposals concerning detection of biological weapons, and has worked out a concise programme for the future work of the Group.

In the case of the Study Group on European Security, the subject is very diffuse, mostly political and highly controversial. Despite these difficulties some very useful contributions towards understanding of the European problem have been made by the Group, a notable feature of its work being the close collaboration between scientists from both parts of Germany.

Summing up, our experience with both Study Groups has shown that if the subject of discussion is well defined and within the competence of the members, and if the homework is done properly, very good results may be expected. We should keep in mind these lessons when planning our future activities.

5. Liaison with Other Institutions

I shall now describe briefly some of the other activities, regular and *ad hoc*, on which the Continuing Committee has been engaged, either as a body or through its Officers. To the regular activities belong the liaison with the National Pugwash Groups, about which I shall have more to say in a moment, and with other organizations, which share common interests with Pugwash.

Foremost among these is SIPRI, or, to give it its full name, the "International Institute for Peace and Conflict Research," which, as we all know, was conceived by the Prime Minister and endorsed by the Swedish Government and parliament. This Institute promotes research into many of the problems in which we have always been greatly interested. We are particularly grateful to SIPRI for financial support in organizing this Conference. We maintain close contact with SIPRI; several Pugwashites serve on its Governing Board and Council, and the Director himself is an old Pugwashite. We hope to hear a report of the work of SIPRI in the afternoon.

Another body with which we maintain contact is IPRA, the International Peace Research Association; its Executive Committee has an observer on our Continuing Committee, and we have one on their Executive Committee.

We collaborated with UNESCO in sponsoring a Study Group on the Long Term Consequences of Disarmament. We have a keen interest in the East-West Study Group on disarmament and arms control which we fathered. We held a joint meeting with the United Nations Committee on the Application of Science and Technology to Development. We maintain contact with the Universities and the Quest for Peace, which is planning a World Congress of university representatives and scholars on the inclusion of the concept of peace into university curricula. We have also had observers at a meeting of the International Association of University Teachers and the recent Conference on International Penal Law.

Of the *ad hoc* activities, I have mentioned in the *History* our intervention during the Cuban crisis, the sponsoring of talks between Indian and Pakistani scientists, and the letter to the President of Argentina. We have also taken an active part in the International Co-operation Year in 1965, and we had extensive discussion on the needs to set up a World Health Centre.

Two recent events were the sending of letters to the Presidents of Israel and the U.A.R. suggesting to arrange a meeting between scientists from these two countries in connection with the Middle East crisis, and a public statement on the non-proliferation treaty.

6. Organization of Pugwash

Since one of the tasks before this Conference is to elect a new governing body for Pugwash, I ought to say something about the present organizational set-up. The Continuing Committee, as elected in London, consisted of two *ex officio* members, the Chairman and the Secretary-General, and twelve members representing certain geographical areas; namely, three each from the U.S.A. and U.S.S.R., two each from the U.K. and Western Europe, and one each from Eastern Europe and Asia. Subsequently, the Continuing Committee decided that there should be two representatives from Eastern Europe. Since our Chairman, Lord Russell, was not able to participate in our work, and Professor Powell chaired the meetings of the Continuing Committee when present, he was appointed as Vice-Chairman. To ease the work of the Secretary-General, Dr. Patricia Lindop was appointed Assistant Secretary-General. Apart from these, there were some individual changes in the representations from the U.S.A., U.S.S.R. and U.K.

The whole Continuing Committee meets about twice a year. The average attendance during the twelve meetings held since 1962 was 70%. Members unable to come may send deputies, and sometimes other persons are invited to attend for some items on the agenda, so that the average number attending the meetings was sixteen persons. Each of the meetings usually lasts about three days, and the business includes planning of international conferences, preparing of statements from the conferences, and dealing with the various other activities.

In between meetings, the day-to-day affairs of the Continuing Committee are carried out by the Central Office in London, that is by the Secretary-General, Assistant Secretary-General and one full-time secretary. There also exists a small executive committee, with whom the Secretary-General can consult in an emergency.

The present set-up of the Central Office, with only one person receiving a salary and no rent to pay for an office, is, of course, very economical; the average expenditure of the Central Office, including postage, cables and telephone was about $3,000 p.a. The cost of the publications issued by the Central Office, the Proceedings of the Conferences and the quarterly Pugwash Newsletter, was on the average $3,500 p.a.; travelling expenses for some participants and staff to conferences and committee meetings amounted to about $4,500 p.a. The total budget comes to less than $12,000 p.a. Considering the multitude of activities carried out by the Central Office this is a very modest budget indeed. It is about half of the budget which had been agreed by the Continuing Committee after the London Conference, but it had to be cut to the available income, which comes mostly from contributions from three countries, the United States, the Soviet Union and the United Kingdom.

This budget does not, of course, include the expenditure incurred in organizing the conferences themselves, such as hospitality offered to participants, secretariat, simultaneous translation, etc., and travelling expenses. Contributions towards the latter have been received from UNESCO, the Carnegie Endowment and from private sources, but the main cost of organizing the conference is usually borne by the Pugwash Group in the host country. This brings me to the work of the National Pugwash Groups.

7. National Groups

National Groups form a very important aspect of Pugwash work, because they enable a large number of scientists to become involved in our activities, without making the conferences too large and unwieldy. Among the tasks of the National Groups is to prepare papers for conferences, and to recommend to the Continuing Committee names of their nationals to be invited to the conferences. In addition, National Groups may carry out a variety of other activities, e.g., organizing lectures and discussions, issuing pamphlets and regular publications, studying special problems. By 1962 ten National Groups were in existence; since then twelve more came into being, so that we now have National Groups in Australia, Austria, Canada, Czechoslovakia, Denmark, Federal German Republic, France, German Democratic Republic, Ghana, Hungary, India, Israel, Italy, Japan, Netherlands, Norway, Poland, Sweden, U.K., U.S.A., U.S.S.R. and Yugoslavia.

The various Groups differ greatly in their size, organization and programme. There are no rules or restrictions in this respect, and every Group can decide on its own method of work. Very often the liveliness of a Group depends on having a specific task to perform, for example, the organization of an international conference. Often, it depends on the type of relationship with the academies of science or other scientific bodies.

As a result of all this, there is an enormous variability in the achievements of and state of vigour among the various Groups. Some of them are dormant, and they only spring to life when the Committee asks them to nominate participants to the international conferences. Other Groups have a very lively programme. Most of the National Groups have sent in reports of their work during the last five years, and these reports will be distributed to you. I should like to draw attention to a few high-lights of these activities, omitting the countries which send the largest contingents to our conferences since their activities are well known.

The Australian Group organized the first South-East Asian Regional Conference; it also issues a newsletter, which comes out every few months. The Canadian Group collaborates closely with the Canadian Peace Research Association, and has completed a study on the economics of disarmament in Canada. The Danish Group was co-initiator of the Study Group on European Security and host to a meeting of this group; it also participated actively in the work of the Study Group on Biological Warfare. The West German

Group works through the "Vereinigung Deutscher Wissenschaftler," holds regular seminars, organizes meetings on a variety of topics, and has set up a small research institute in Hamburg for the study of problems of arms control, disarmament and security. The East German Group, working closely with the Academy of Sciences in Berlin, holds regular meetings, discussions and seminars. The Italian Group, apart from organizing the Fourteenth Conference in Venice, has held in 1966 a very successful international summer school on disarmament and arms control, and is planning another one for next year; it has also made an extensive study of the non-proliferation problem, with an effective impact on public opinion. The Japanese Group, working through "The Kyoto Conference of Scientists," has held several seminars, and published the findings in the form of statements. The Netherlands Group has also published a number of brochures dealing with various aspects of nuclear disarmament; it has a sister organization "Friends of Pugwash," with a membership of about 1,000. The Polish Group organized the Sixteenth Pugwash Conference in Sopot, and was very active in the work of the Study Group on European Security. The Yugoslav Group has organized the Eleventh Conference in Dubrovnik, and was host to a meeting of the Study Group on European Security; it also issues a periodical "Encyclopaedia Moderna."

The achievements of two of the National Groups deserves special mention. The Czechoslovak Group has carried out an amazing number of activities. The list includes the following: (i) organizing the Thirteenth Conference in Karlovy Vary; (ii) commissioning a documentary film on Pugwash under the title "To Be or Not To Be," and presenting copies of the film to other Pugwash Groups; (iii) co-initiating the Study Group on European Security, and being hosts to two meetings of this Group; (iv) taking an active part in the work of the Study Group on Biological Warfare and being hosts to a meeting of this Group in Marianske Lazne; (v) arranging, through the Academy of Sciences, the printing of the "History of Pugwash"; distributing 1,000 copies to Pugwashites, and providing another 1,000 copies to be available for sale to the public by a commercial publisher; (vi) last, but not least, offering, through the Academy, hospitality to a Pugwash meeting to be held every year in Czechoslovakia.

And finally, our hosts, the Swedish Pugwash Group. This Group has taken a very active part in the work of the Study Group on Biological Warfare; it organized a pilot scheme for inspection of micro-biological laboratories in four countries, and has been hosts to several meetings of the Study Group; it has played an important role in setting up SIPRI; and now--the most tangible evidence of their efforts--the organization of this, the largest of our Conferences. The best evidence of the high standing of Pugwash in Sweden is, of course, the presence of the Prime Minister. We are most grateful to you, Sir, for being with us, for delivering such a stirring message and for giving our Conference such a propitious start.

8. Pugwashites
In summing up the work of the National Pugwash Groups two conclusions may be drawn. One is that the best way to activate a Group is to entrust it with a well-defined, concrete task. The other is that the success of a

Appendix 22   284

Group depends enormously on there being one or two enthusiastic people, who are prepared to make an extra effort and who often, by their example, trigger the interest of others.

This dependence on enthusiasms of individuals applies, of course, to all Pugwash activities. Pugwash is a Movement of scientists. It is said to express the realization by scientists of their social responsibility. The majority of scientists have a social conscience, but this is often suppressed by the day-to-day worries, professional duties, absorbing research work, or the many other calls for administrative or national consultative functions which are made on such people. In the absence of a trigger, the needs to discharge one's obligation to society, to help to avert war and strife, are often pushed aside. Yet, scientists could make most valuable contributions to these issues, even if they devoted only 5 to 10% of their time. We are rightly proud in Pugwash of having among us the most eminent scientists of the world, but quality alone is not sufficient; it needs to be supplemented by quantity. The more people think of a problem, the greater is the likelihood of something new emerging, either through original ideas from individuals, or by mutual stimulation and cross-fertilization.

Although we often discuss in Pugwash the need to bring in more people, we have not done very much about it. In the sixteen Conferences held over ten years, a total of 427 scientists took part. Even if we add the 50 newcomers to this Conference, observers and members of the Study Groups and National Groups, the total number of Pugwashites is still less than one in a thousand of the scientific manpower. Even among the Pugwash participants the burden was not shared equally; half of all attendances at the Conferences was by one-fifth of our members.

There are also other anomalies in our membership. Among the 427 Conference participants, there were only 11 women, that is 2.6%, which is by an order of magnitude less than the proportion of women in science. Perhaps the more worrying is the age distribution. I do not have the exact data for all participants, but the British Pugwashites represent a fair sample, and their mean age is 59 years, which is at least 15 years higher than the average age of scientists. This is, of course, partly explained by the eminence of our members; wisdom is supposed to come with age; but old-age is not conducive to new ideas and this is what we need most.

Another disadvantage of the high mean age is that many of our colleagues go into retirement and cease to be active scientists; and we have always emphasized the need of our Movement being based on active scientists. And of course we lose members by death.

9. Obituary
During the last quinquennium 14 Pugwashites have died. Some of these have been very active in the Movement, and it is appropriate that we should pay tribute to them in this gathering.

Alexander Vassilievich Topchiev played a major role in the establishing of the Pugwash Movement. He attended almost every Pugwash Conference until his death, and was a member of the Continuing Committee until 1958. He was Chairman of the Soviet Pugwash Group and has made lasting contributions towards East-West understanding and co-operation.

Leo Szilard was one of our most remarkable personalities. Always ahead of others in his thinking, he enlivened and stimulated Pugwash Conferences with the originality of his ideas, good humour and tremendous drive. Although highly individualistic and unconventional, he has helped enormously in getting the Pugwash Movement going and making the Conferences successful from the beginning.

Morton Grodzins, one of the earliest social scientists in Pugwash, did a great deal to set up and strengthen the Pugwash Group in the United States. His incisive comments and commonsense interventions at Conferences did much to emphasize the useful role which social scientists could play in Pugwash.

Herman Muller was one of the signatories of the Russell-Einstein Manifesto of 1955, which gave rise to the Pugwash Movement; he was also a participant of the first Conference in Pugwash.

Homi J. Bhabha was a member of the Organizing Committee for the Twelfth Conference in Udaipur, and as Chairman of the Indian Atomic Commission was host to the participants of that Conference.

Norayr Martirosovich Sisakyan took an active part in several of the earlier Pugwash Conferences as well as in the work of the Soviet Pugwash Group.

Sir Charles Darwin took a lively part in the Second Conference in Lac Beauport and in the London Conference. He was also very active in the British Pugwash Group.

Other deaths during that period were of Academician Anushavan Agafonovich Arzumanyan and Professor E. A. Korovin of the U.S.S.R., Dr. Trevor Gardner of the U.S.A., Professor Vaclav Husa of Czechoslovakia, Professor Heinz Barwich of Germany and Professor F. G. Houtermanns of Switzerland. Very recently we recorded the death of Professor Nikolai A. Talensky, an ardent Pugwashite who attended eleven out of the sixteen Pugwash Conferences, in each of which he was a very active participant.

(The audience stood in silence in tribute to the departed Pugwashites.)

10. Tasks Ahead
We must now turn our attention to the living, since it is our aim and purpose to ensure a lasting future for mankind. Even when presenting a report of the past activities, we should remember that its main purpose is to show the way ahead. It is for this reason that I have pointed out our successes as well as failures, and that I have not confined myself

merely to give facts and figures, but have also drawn attention to the lessons we can learn from our past experiences.

It is the task of this Conference to make decisions about the future, and to outline the scope of our activities for the next five years. We have had some remarkable achievements in the past, and were highly successful in bringing about greater understanding between East and West, and perhaps in reducing tension among nations. But our task has hardly begun. As we have just heard from the Prime Minister, the world is still in a turmoil, and mankind in danger. There is as yet no sign of a disarmament treaty being agreed to; the number of nuclear powers is growing, and biological and chemical weapons are being developed. The war in Vietnam is continuing with mounting ferocity and terrible suffering, and with the growing danger of escalation. There is misery and hatred in the Middle East, and civil war in Africa. There is increasing hunger in the world and greater disparity between the rich and poor peoples. Our premise, that in the atomic age disputes should be solved by means other than war, is far from being accepted; nor is there any realization among the general public of the implications of the tremendous advances of science and technology. And, as far as participation in Pugwash is concerned, our main weakness is the lack of contact with China, our inability to renew the links with our colleagues from the country with the largest population in the world.

All this means that the objects which we set before us when Pugwash was founded ten years ago have still to be achieved. We may have to change our methods and organization, but our goal remains the same; it is the same as expressed in the Russell-Einstein Manifesto and in the statements from our Conferences. Five years ago we concluded the statement from the London Conference with the following: "We re-assert our conviction that the goal of full disarmament and permanent peace is realistic and urgent. This work is truly to be seen as a part of a long struggle for the progress of mankind, and it is one in which scientists have a responsible part to play. We call upon scientists everywhere in the world to join us in this task." I submit, that the struggle is still on, and the call is more urgent than ever.

23 REPORT OF THE STANDING COMMITTEE ON FUTURE ACTIVITIES TO THE SEVENTEENTH PUGWASH CONFERENCE IN RONNEBY

Introduction

This Committee was formally appointed on 3rd September 1967 in order to lay down guide-lines for the future activities of Pugwash, which, for the past five years, has operated on certain principles agreed to by the London Conference of 1962. Some members of the Committee held three informal meetings in Stockholm on 1st and 2nd September in order to give preliminary consideration to these problems. The Committee has held two meetings jointly with the Standing Committee on Future Organization. Throughout the discussions in Stockholm and Ronneby, many of the members of the present Continuing Committee attended one or more of its meetings. In particular, the Secretary-General has been in almost continuous attendance; his ideas on future activities and his vast experience have been invaluable to the Committee in its deliberations.

The Committee considered that it had three functions:

(1) to re-define briefly the raison d'etre of the Pugwash Conferences, and the fields which these should cover;

(2) to lay down some general rules for the organization of conferences and meetings of various types;

(3) to consider the problems of publicity, publication and the issuing of statements in the name of Pugwash and to make proposals concerning these matters.

Problems of central organization, of the constitution and powers of the Continuing Committee, and of finance, were discussed and suggestions on these made to the standing Committee on Future Organization.

Our conclusions and recommendations are as follows:

1. Continuance of Pugwash

It was our unanimous view that the Pugwash Conferences on Science and World Affairs should continue. Pugwash has considerable accomplishments to its credit in the past ten years, but its original task is far from completed. Although new organizations with closely related objectives have come into being since 1957 (many of them stimulated by Pugwash) the contributions which Pugwash can make to the solution of problems of world security and international co-operation are unique, since scientists through their training and objective approach to problems should not only have a more detached outlook but a greater appreciation of the international possibilities (both dangers and opportunities) arising from scientific and technological developments.

2. Scope of the Pugwash Activities

The ultimate goal of Pugwash was and still is the establishment of lasting world peace. In order to achieve this goal Pugwash will be concerned with two main problems:

(a) The prevention and cessation of wars through various means, with special emphasis on disarmament.

(b) Acceleration of the improvement in the state of the less developed countries. This implies not only an absolute improvement but the elimination of the gap between standards in the developed and less developed countries of the world.

There are unique contributions which Pugwash can make in the field because of its non-governmental and unofficial status as an international group of scientists of some repute. However, care must be taken not to duplicate activities of other organizations working in the field, e.g., U.N. agencies such as FAO, WHO, etc.

In dealing with these two main problems Pugwash must devote considerable attention to two related and very important problems:

(c) International co-operation, i.e., science should have no national boundaries and Pugwash should continue to take the initiative in promoting new international projects in science, relevant to its two main problems.

(d) Pugwash should try and promote a greater sense of social responsibility among all scientists regarding the political and social consequences of their scientific work, i.e., their loyalty should not be merely to themselves nor to pure science, but to mankind.

In order to achieve its objectives, it is essential to draw up a framework within which Pugwash will operate. We believe it is wise that this framework should not be too rigid nor defined in too great detail. The following general guide-lines are proposed for the next quinquennium.

3. Types of Future Meetings

(a) There should be an Annual Pugwash Conference covering the main activities of the Pugwash Movement. At this conference, the topics and approximate dates of Pugwash meetings which might take place in the next 18 months or so should be discussed. The Continuing Committee should make the final choice about the future programme at the conclusion of this conference.

(b) There should be several Pugwash Symposia every year, each with a different and specific topic. In general, these should be limited to 30-50 participants in order to allow a professional treatment of the topic, i.e., following the pattern of a small specialized scientific conference. All papers should be pre-circulated and some would be specially commissioned. Possible topics are anti-ballistic missiles, chemical warfare, food from the oceans, nuclear and non-nuclear proliferation.

(c) In addition there would be meetings of Study Groups and Regional Conferences. The utilization of these and the procedures for their operation should be in the hands of the Continuing Committee, essentially as at present.

4. Organization of Conferences and Statements

(a) All Conferences and Meetings must have received the prior approval of the Continuing Committee. This does not apply to purely national meetings organized by the National Groups.

Formal openings and reading of messages at the start of conferences or meetings should be abolished or kept to an absolute minimum.

(b) The Annual Pugwash Conference would continue to be organized and financed as hitherto, by the Continuing Committee in conjunction with the host country.

(c) For Pugwash Symposia, the local arrangements and the financing would be the responsibility of the host country. With regard to the invitation list, main speakers and other matters of policy, these would be best done by agreement between the host country and the Continuing Committee. Any national Pugwash Group should feel free to take the initiative over the proposal for a Pugwash Symposium.

It is hoped that about six National Groups will contract to act as host once a year (if requested) for such a symposium. This would considerably ease the financial problems involved in holding symposia. It would not preclude other National Groups acting as hosts at less frequent intervals.

(d) The problems of organization and financing of other international Pugwash meetings, e.g., Study Groups and Regional Conferences, are left in the hands of the Continuing Committee.

5. Publication, Publicity and Statements

(a) Notes and brief reports of all conferences and meetings should continue to be published in the Newsletter.

(b) For the Symposia, publication, if considered desirable by the Continuing Committee, would probably be best done in the form of a monograph.

(c) All conferences and meetings should continue to be held in private (i.e., Press and public not admitted). The issuing of statements in the name of Pugwash must remain entirely in the control of the Continuing Committee. Press Conferences should be discouraged, except at the Annual Conference, but if considered essential by the host country, then it must be made clear that statements made to the Press are those of individuals and are not authorized by Pugwash.

(d) It was considered most important to get greater recognition of the work of Pugwash by scientists through the publication of reports of meetings and of important individual papers by existing journals widely read by scientists, e.g., *Nature, Science, New Scientist, Nauka I Zhisn*, etc.

6. Increase of the Activities of National Groups and in the Number of Participants

In order to carry out the tasks outlined above it will be necessary to increase the activities of the existing National Groups, to multiply considerably the number of scientists participating in the activities of Pugwash and to organize new National Groups in countries where they do not now exist, and Regional Groups in areas where the organization of National Groups would be impracticable because of the small number of scientists. It is particularly important that a large fraction of new recruits should be young scientists.

The members of the committee were:

Sir Gordon Sutherland (U.K.) Chairman
Dr. Aklilu Lemma (Ethiopia)
Dr. R. Björnerstedt (Sweden)
Professor H. Brown (U.S.A.)
Academician M. M. Dubinin (U.S.S.R.)
Dr. R. V. Garcia (Argentina)
Academician P. L. Kapitza (U.S.S.R.)
Dr. M. M. Kaplan (U.S.A.)
Professor M. Magat (France)
Professor L. Mates (Yugoslavia)
Mr. T. Němec (Czechoslovakia)
Dr. S. H. Zaheer (India)

STATEMENT FROM THE CONTINUING COMMITTEE ON THE SEVENTEENTH PUGWASH CONFERENCE, HELD IN RONNEBY, SEPTEMBER 3-8, 1967

The Seventeenth Pugwash Conference on Science and World Affairs, marking the 10th Anniversary of the foundation of the Conferences, met in Ronneby, Sweden, from 3rd to 8th September, 1967. It was attended by nearly 200 participants from more than 40 countries.

The discussions showed that there was a broad and deep concern among the participants at the gravity of the world situation. Armaments multiply and their destructive power increases. There is no progress in disarmament and nuclear weapons are spreading. Radical new weapons are continually developed. Local wars break out, devastating the populations involved, and threatening escalation into major conflicts. The gap between the rich and poor countries grows wider, in nutrition, in industry, in science. Urgent and sustained efforts are necessary to avoid an impending crisis and to create the prosperous, stable and peaceful world which science has made possible.

Science and technology have brought many benefits to the world and can continue to do so in the future. But scientists must increasingly broaden their activities into still wider fields. They must put all their strength into helping to solve the many problems involved in ensuring a peaceful future. The reputation of scientists, of science itself, the future directions of our civilization, all are at stake.

It was under the spur of this sense of urgency that the 17th Pugwash Conference went about its work. To accomplish its studies the Conference divided into seven working groups and in what follows the findings of these working groups are summarized.

Problems of Disarmament

Texts of the drafts on the nuclear non-proliferation treaty submitted by the U.S.A. and U.S.S.R. to the 18-Nations Disarmament Conference were examined by one of the working groups. It was concluded that acceptance of a treaty based on these drafts would be a major step in preventing further proliferation of nuclear weapons and in reducing the threat of nuclear war. Completion of negotiations on the treaty, in particular, the resolution of differences arising with respect to Article III, dealing with the control system, and the acceptance of the treaty by all states, should be accomplished at the earliest possible date.

The working group examined objections to the treaty. Although it regarded objections relating to the control system as exaggerated, it believed that it would be useful to allay such fears, as far as possible, by minimizing the intrusiveness of the inspection. For the same reason, it was suggested that it would be desirable eventually to subject the peaceful nuclear facilities of the nuclear-weapons states to the same inspection as is required of the non-nuclear states. The control system of the International Atomic Energy Agency, which has already been accepted by more than 90 countries, appears to be entirely adequate for the required inspection.

Appendix 24

Because of the very great importance of early agreement on the non-proliferation treaty, it would be a mistake to make acceptance contingent on any other specific arms control or disarmament measures. It can be expected that agreement on the non-proliferation treaty would have such a profound effect on the political climate in the world that the prospects for other arms control and disarmament measures involving the nuclear powers would be improved. It would also be very helpful if, at this time, nuclear-weapons states would express their willingness at least to initiate discussions and studies of other disarmament measures that might be implemented following negotiation of the nuclear non-proliferation treaty. Some examples suggested include the following: an extension of the nuclear test ban to cover underground tests; early discussion of measures to limit and reverse the arms race in both strategic offensive and ABM defence systems; a cut-off of production and reduction of stocks of fissile materials for weapons use; the establishment of nuclear free zones; and limitations on the traffic in conventional arms.

It was suggested that a useful mechanism for moving in this direction would be the undertaking of obligations by the nuclear-weapons states not to use nuclear weapons against those states which accede to the treaty, which do not possess nuclear weapons, and which give assurance that no nuclear weapons are located on their territories.

Other Measures towards Disarmament
In considering the problem of limiting levels of strategic nuclear weapons, it was concluded that the possibility of coupling limitations on ballistic missile defences with limitations on strategic offensive systems, should be thoroughly explored with high priority.

In considering a comprehensive test ban it was agreed that technical capabilities now exist for extending the test ban to include testing underground; the nuclear powers should be urged to undertake negotiations to this end at the earliest possible date.

Turning from the problems of arms limitation to those of disarmament, it was noted that there has been no progress toward substantial world disarmament in recent years. A serious complication has been the repeated outbreak of local wars—often fearfully damaging in themselves. Moreover, by increasing international tension and weakening international security arrangements, they make negotiations towards disarmament much more difficult. An additional serious complicating factor is that military research continues to produce new or greatly improved weapons systems. These new weapons tend to accelerate the arms race and seriously complicate the search and negotiation for agreed measures of disarmament.

A treaty to ban further research on weapons of mass destruction was proposed as meriting further study even though the problems of negotiating and monitoring such a treaty appear formidable.

It is particularly important to take all possible measures to avoid further militarization of the oceans and outer space. Internationalization of the ocean floor, with a prohibition of all military use, is an interesting possibility. A specific suggestion was to establish, under U.N. auspices, a sonar detection network to permit world-wide monitoring of all submarines capable of launching nuclear weapons.

The development and use of new and more dangerous chemical and biological weapons is one of the major problems of the coming years. Scientific and technical analyses of these weapons could increase public awareness of the dangers inherent in them.

It is extremely important that all nations adhere strictly to the Geneva Protocol of 1925, which was unanimously endorsed by the U.N. in 1966. All nations are, therefore, called upon to refrain, in any conflict between nations, from the use of any chemical and biological weapons whatsoever. It is also urged that vigorous efforts be made towards a formal treaty, to be signed by all nations, which would prohibit both the use of, and the transfer to, other nations of all chemical and biological weapons.

Prevention and Resolution of Conflicts

The working groups which considered these issues arrived at the following conclusions. International conflicts, even of a local character, are aggravated by the sharp division of the world into military blocs, leading to the danger of world-wide escalation of conflicts when these blocs become involved. It is, therefore, more and more important to stop existing conflicts and to find methods of preventing future ones. Even de-escalation of existing conflicts would be a step towards creating a better atmosphere in international relations. The United Nations should be universal and should be given an increasing role in settling and preventing international conflicts.

In Europe, in particular, all existing frontiers should be recognized. It would help European security if all states were to recognize the German Democratic Republic, with its present borders, and if both German states were admitted to the U.N., all this without prejudice to their possible future re-unification. The armaments and military budgets of both German states should be substantially reduced. All European states should sign a treaty forbidding the use of force in international relations, and should establish means for settling disputes. It is in the interests of European security that, as soon as a non-proliferation treaty is agreed upon, all European states, including both German states, ratify it.

Current conflicts in Vietnam, the Near East and Africa are causes of terrible suffering and can at any moment evolve into a world-wide thermonuclear war.

As regards Vietnam, it is necessary:

(a) that the bombing of North Vietnam be stopped immediately and unconditionally;

(b) that following that cessation, negotiations for a peaceful settlement begin without delay;

(c) that subsequently a conference be convened to establish a stable peace in all of South-East Asia.

The Middle-East conflict was the object of a long discussion, but no general agreement was reached.

In the southern part of the African continent, the movement towards national independence and democratic government has been retarded and has even retrogressed. While, understandably, calls at the United Nations for action are becoming more and more impassioned, there is no sign of effective action through the United Nations, or even of full implementation of U.N. resolutions. All great powers should do much more to implement U.N. principles in Africa.

Serious concern was expressed about the tragic events in Nigeria which caused thousands of deaths and millions of refugees.

International Scientific Projects

In the discussion on international scientific projects, particular attention was directed to an earlier Pugwash proposal to establish an International Science Foundation. This would permit young scientists in the developing countries to undertake research programmes for which their countries are not able to provide. Such a Foundation would help to reduce the loss of scientists from countries for which the retention of their scientifically trained youth is vital.

An appropriate U.N. organization should consider the feasibility of establishing the International Science Foundation within the framework of the U.N.

In reviewing progress of the International Biological Programme, attention was directed to its satisfactory progress in the richer countries but the failure to develop it in the poorer countries, due largely to shortage of funds. Yet, for such countries, the implementation of the Programme is particularly important; and ways to obtain the necessary support must be found.

There has been important progress in international co-operation in space research, in the development of global communications by use of satellites, in planning for a global atmospheric research programme. It was recommended that the Meteorological Programme should be developed through a co-operative organization of several autonomous centres, one of which should be located in the Southern hemisphere.

Previous recommendations were endorsed that efforts must be made to facilitate the travel of scientists to international conferences and to increase the opportunities for scientists to work temporarily in other countries.

Development, Education and Technology

The Problem of World Food Supply was discussed. More than a fifth of the poorer countries of the world is living on a near starvation diet, well below their physiological needs. Limitation of the growth of populations is essential, but will be of little help in the short run. If disaster is to be avoided, immediate action is necessary to increase food supply, primarily by improvement of crop yields.

Relatively little is known about the production of essential food stuffs in the tropics. The problem is not simply one of transferring technology, nor in itself exclusively technological: there are religious, economic and social factors.

Intimately linked to the problem of increased food supply is that of rapid economic development. The developed nations can greatly help here, utilizing a combination of multilateral and bilateral modes of technical assistance. There should also be a study of methods for facilitating a transfer of technology from industrial enterprises in developed countries to similar organizations in developing countries. Intimate collaboration between scientists of developing and developed countries is essential for the success of all these programmes.

An example of a feasible and potentially very useful technical project is the creation of agro-industrial power complexes in coastal deserts or semi-desert fertile areas. These could boost regional food supplies in an unprecedented fashion and create a breakthrough in industrialization. They would be based on large nuclear reactor systems producing cheap heat, energy and electric power for desalination of water and for fertilizer production. The economies of entire regions could be profoundly transformed by large projects of this sort.

The total supply of scientists and engineers is barely adequate for the needs. Furthermore, there is a large-scale migration of scientists, engineers, and physicians, especially from the developing to the developed countries. Forms of legal control or restriction of this migration are conceivable but were considered generally objectionable. The developing countries have a responsibility to match output of trained manpower more nearly to the needs of local development, and to make attractive working opportunities for their scientists and technologists. The developed countries ought to aim to produce more scientists than they need, so that some could be available to work in other parts of the world.

A possible immediate step, to help increase numbers of scientists and engineers in developing countries, is to create a massive scholarship programme for students from these areas to be trained in developed countries, and ultimately to be available for the many technical organizations and other tasks in their home countries.

Further recommendations include: aid in the world development of technology; a study of the application of technology (satellite communications, new methods, aids, etc.) to education; and consideration of means of assisting developing countries to establish well equipped international centres of research.

Social Responsibilities of Scientists and the Future of Pugwash
In the face of the dangerous conflicts now raging, and the many hard long-range problems facing mankind, scientists must increase their efforts to help in the creation of a peaceful and increasingly prosperous world. Many of the dangers facing mankind are associated with the advancement of science, and their resolution depends critically on a constructive application of science and technology. In this situation, it is an evasion of responsibility when scientists withdraw complacently into their laboratories, and are indifferent to the consequences of their discoveries and the fate of mankind.

The scientists involved in the Pugwash Movement accept these responsibilities. At this 17th Conference the participants agreed to expand the Pugwash activities, by involving more scientists, engineers, and scholars, particularly those of the younger generation, in this work. It is planned to arrange, in addition to annual general conferences, symposia for a more thorough exploration of such difficult problems as disarmament, education for life in the scientific age, and development of the technologically underdeveloped parts of the world.

Participants

Argentina
Dr. R. V. Garcia

Australia
Dr. H. D. Rathgeber

Austria
Dr. R. Jungk

Belgium
Prof. R. Leclercq

Brazil
Prof. J. Leite Lopes

Bulgaria
Prof. K. Bratanov, Prof. G. Nadjakov

Canada
Dr. N. Z. Alcock, Mr. W. Boyd

Ceylon
Dr. N. G. Baptist

Czechoslovakia
Prof. V. Filkorn, Dr. V. Hajdu, Acad. J. Kožešník, Dr. L. Liska,
Acad. I. Málek, Mr. T. Němec, Prof. A. Šnejdárek

Denmark
Mr. D. J. Adler, Mr. A. Boserup, Prof. O. Maaløe, Dr. J. N. K. Wilhjelm

Ethiopia
Dr. Aklilu Lemma, Dr. Assefa Tekle, Prof. R. O. Whipple

Federal German Republic
Mr. H. Afheldt, Dr. J. Delbrück, Prof. H. Friedrich-Freska,
Prof. W. Kliefoth, Prof. E. Menzel, Prof. L. Raiser

Finland
Prof. J. J. Saukkonen

France
Dr. E. Bauer, Mr. G. Gueron, Mr. B. Laponche, Prof. M. Magat, Dr. H.
Meyrowitz, Mr. J. Moch, Prof. F. Perrin, Prof. E. Roth

German Democratic Republic
Prof. P. Hess, Dr. A. Kolesynk, Prof. H. Kröger, Prof. A. Lösche,
Prof. H. Wünsche

Ghana
Prof. F. G. T. Torto

Hungary
Prof. R. Bognar, Dr. I. Kende, Prof. L. Pal, Prof. L. Reczei

Iceland
Prof. O. Gunnarsson

India
Prof. M. G. K. Menon, Dr. S. H. Zaheer

Ireland
Dr. C. O'Ceallaigh

Israel
Prof. M. Feldman, Prof. G. Stein

Italy
Prof. E. Amaldi, Prof. G. L. Bassini, Prof. F. Calogero

Japan
Prof. Y. Miyake, Prof. I. Ogawa, Prof. T. Toyoda, Prof. E. Yamada

Kenya
Prof. D. P. S. Wasawo

Appendix 24

Malaysia
Prof. A. A. Sandosham

Netherlands
Dr. S. L. Kwee, Prof. B. Landheer, Prof. P. B. Smith

Nigeria
Prof. O. Bassir

Norway
Dr. S. Cyvin, Dr. K. Evang, Prof. J. Galtung

Pakistan
Prof. A. Salam

Peru
Prof. J. Pozo-Olano

Poland
Prof. I. Adamczewski, Prof. J. Bukowski, Prof. M. Dobrosielski, Prof. I. Malecki

Romania
Prof. V. Hanga

Spain
Prof. J. Catala de Alemany

Sudan
Dr. K. E. Nagger

Sweden
Dr. Katarina Ahnlund, Prof. H. Alfven, Dr. R. Björnerstedt, Prof. A. Engström, Mr. M. Fehrm, Prof. C-G. Hedén, Dr. S. Nilsson, Mr. J. Prawitz, Dr. L. Revesz, Prof. A. Sparring, Dr. L-E. Tammelin, Prof. A. Tiselius

Switzerland
Dr. Y. Goldschmidt-Clermont, Prof. K. P. Meyer

Tanzania
Dr. W. K. Chagula

Thailand
Dr. Panee Chiowanich

Togo
Dr. N. Agblemagnon

U.A.R.
Prof. S. El-Bedewi, Dr. M. A. Lakany

U.K.
Dr. C. F. Barnaby, Mr. N. Calder, Prof. E. B. Chain, Sir John Cockcroft, Prof. J. Cohen, Dr. M. Davies, Prof. R. W. Ditchburn, Prof. L. R. B. Elton, Mr. W. F. Gutteridge, Prof. Dorothy Hodgkin, Dr. P. E. Hodgson, Prof. G. O. Jones, Prof. A. Martin, Mr. R. R. Neild, Dr. C. H. G. Oldham, Prof. R. E. Peierls, Prof. C. F. Powell, Prof. J. Rotblat, Sir Gordon Sutherland

U.S.A.
Mrs. Ruth Adams, Prof. P. G. Bergmann, Prof. H. S. Brown, Prof. W. C. Davidon, Mr. W. S. Dillon, Prof. C. Djerassi, Prof. B. T. Feld, Prof. J. D. Frank, Prof. R. L. Garwin, Prof. B. T. Glass, Prof. R. M. Herriott, Prof. G. Holton, Dr. D. R. Inglis, Dr. M. Kalstein, Dr. A. H. Katz, Prof. C. D. Leake, Prof. F. A. Long, Prof. R. Marshak, Prof. J. Mayer, Prof. H. J. Morgenthau, Prof. S. Muller, Prof. E. S. Munger, Dr. H. Palevsky, Prof. T. Parsons, Dr. J. B. Phelps, Prof. I. I. Rabi, Prof. E. Rabinowitch, Dr. V. Rabinowitch, Dr. G. Rathjens, Prof. R. Revelle, Prof. A. Rich, Prof. R. Rollefson, Prof. J. P. Ruina, Dr. E. Skolnikoff, Prof. L. B. Sohn, Mr. J. Voss, Dr. A. M. Weinberg

U.S.S.R.
Prof. V. Y. Aboltin, Acad. L. A. Artsimovitch, Acad. M. M. Dubinin, Prof. V. Emelyanov, Acad. V. A. Engelhardt, Acad. S. E. Esenov, Prof. A. A. Gryzlov, Acad. A. A. Imshenetsky, Acad. P. L. Kapitza, Acad. V. A. Kargin, Acad. M. A. Kashkai, Acad. Y. Matulis, Acad. S. S. Medvedev, Acad. M. D. Millionshchikov, Dr. Y. P. Platanov, Acad. K. K. Plaude, Mr. I. G. Pochitalin, Prof. M. Rubinstein, Prof. M. Shelepin, Prof. I. A. Sokolov, Acad. A. P. Vinogradov, Prof. M. S. Voslensky

Yugoslavia
Prof. M. Markovic, Prof. L. Mates, Acad. L. Vavpetic

Observers

Federal German Republic
Prof. W. Häfele

Sweden
Mrs. Alva Myrdal, Dr. Inger Paulsson

U.S.A.
Dr. H. Scoville, Mr. W. Swartz, Dr. Gertrud W. Szilard

FAO
Mr. T. E. Richie

IAEA
Dr. H. Seligman

SIPRI
Mr. O. Berner

Appendix 24   300

U.N.
Mr. G. B. Gresford, Mr. A. E. Nesterenko

UNESCO
Prof. G. Burkhardt

UQP
Dr. R. S. Elim

WHO
Dr. M. M. Kaplan

25 STATEMENT FROM THE CONTINUING COMMITTEE ON THE EIGHTEENTH PUGWASH CONFERENCE, HELD IN NICE, SEPTEMBER 11-16, 1968

The Eighteenth Pugwash Conference on Science and World Affairs was held in Nice from 11th to 16th September 1968, at the invitation of the French National Pugwash Group. It was attended by 81 scientists from 28 different countries including some from each of the five continents. In addition 12 observers and 8 science writers were present.

As is customary at these Conferences, the meeting divided into Working Groups which discussed, and prepared reports on, the following four topics: "Arms Control and Disarmament," "Regional Arms Control," "Current Problems," and "Scientific and Technological Manpower Problems in Developing Countries."

Lively debate took place on the most burning issues, with the expression of strongly opposing views, and this was particularly true of the discussions on "Current Problems," Nigeria, the Middle East, Vietnam and Czechoslovakia, where the report shows the limits of the agreement which the Working Group found it possible to reach.

The reports were presented and discussed at Plenary Sessions of the Conference, but as is customary at Pugwash Conferences the conclusions and wording remain the responsibility of the respective Working Groups alone. The reports are appended to this statement.

1. ARMS CONTROL AND DISARMAMENT

Preamble
The Working Group believes it necessary to resume as soon as possible, and notwithstanding the present political situation, the negotiations on a comprehensive Treaty of General and Complete Disarmament, which is the hope of all men and a vital necessity for their future.

The Working Group underlines the aims of such a Treaty, whose objectives in earlier negotiations always were, and must remain, to stop the armaments race, to eliminate all the weapons of mass destruction, and to reduce progressively the military manpower and expenditure, and the conventional armaments. In the end of the process of execution of the Treaty, each State will only keep the limited military forces and the light armaments necessary for its internal security and its international obligations.

The same Treaty must foresee and put into action a permanent international control organization, and a peacekeeping machinery allowing the peaceful settlement of all international disputes.

1. Current Developments
Since the negotiation of a general treaty will presumably continue to be delayed for some time and will, in any event, require a long period of

negotiation, there must be an active concern with partial measures of arms control and disarmament.

Fortunately, there has been progress in two directions during the past year: the negotiations and signing by many powers of the Non-Proliferation Treaty and the agreement of the U.S.A. and the U.S.S.R. to hold talks on the limitation of offensive and defensive missiles.

With regard to the signing and ratification of the Non-Proliferation Treaty, most of the Working Group think it essential to recognize that the benefits of this Treaty are world-wide and that it now represents the next stage in the evolution of international agreements leading to disarmament. However, the Working Group notes the risk that current political crises appear to threaten its prompt ratification by several important powers. The withholding of ratification should not be an instrument of expression for or against political developments outside the scope of the Treaty. Instead, just as the Treaty was negotiated in a period of conflicts and world tension, so its ratification and its coming into effect should proceed independently of the state of world tension. Its conclusion would clearly contribute to the relaxation of these tensions.

It is also possible that the present political turmoil may delay the governmental discussions on limiting missile deployment. The Working Group urges instead that these discussions begin as soon as possible. The arms race is now, more than ever, in a critical phase and time lost at this juncture may make more difficult and costly agreements that are now quite feasible.

2. Generalities on Partial Measures

The Working Group thinks that as the negotiation of a general disarmament treaty may be delayed in the present circumstances and will, in any case, be a long one, it is of urgent necessity to negotiate some practical and immediately realisable measures of arms control or limitations, which can be immediately applied, without endangering the military situation of any nation, and which would help to create a better international atmosphere and therefore help to attain as quickly as possible the permanent goal of disarmament.

Such measures are varied and numerous. Without excluding any of them, the Working Group underlines the possibility of the following measures.

3. Nuclear Weapons Limitations

The partial steps which seem most appropriate for serious discussion at the ENDC and between the U.S.A. and the U.S.S.R. consist not only in limitations on offensive and defensive missiles but also in a cut-off in the production of weapons-grade fissile materials and in the prohibition of all nuclear explosions. Indeed, these three items are logically related, entailing a freeze on deployment, on production, and on development of nuclear warheads; they should reinforce each other; and it would probably take considerably less total time to negotiate the three in parallel.

With regard to the problems associated with the limitation of strategic missiles and anti-missile systems the Working Group recommends consideration of the Third Pugwash Symposium held in Krogerup, Denmark in July 1963, which is summarized in a separate report to this Conference. While this Working Group recognizes that difficult problems intimately connected with national security will confront the two governments in their discussions, it urges that the improvements now available in verification be fully utilized so that some agreements may be promptly reached.

With regard to the examination of the requirements of a comprehensive test ban the Working Group recommends due consideration of the Report of the Study Group on Seismic Detection held recently at SIPRI. There too, modern advances should ease the reaching of an acceptable treaty.

With regard to the cut-off of production of fissile material, it is important to appreciate the very considerable knowledge available on plutonium plants and the absence of such knowledge on uranium plants. The Working Group urges that the nuclear powers co-operate with the International Atomic Energy Agency in providing the basis on which verification procedures for the stopping of production of weapons-grade U-235 can be developed.

Another important measure in the same field is an agreement on non-use of nuclear weapons.

The nuclear states should recognize the urgent duty of negotiating an agreement on general prohibition of use of nuclear weapons. This obligation appears to the Working Group to require the participation of all the five nuclear powers.

If those states are not agreed in banning such use, as many nuclear states as possible should sign an agreement prohibiting the use of nuclear weapons against non-nuclear states which do not have nuclear armaments on their territory. Some members, however, proposed extending this guarantee to all non-nuclear nations.

4. Limitation of Trade of Armaments
The limitation of trade of armaments is an important and difficult question. It is soluble because, even in the Western world, this trade though made by private enterprises, is now under control of the governments.

Therefore the Working Group, thanking SIPRI for their studies, asks the Continuing Committee of the Pugwash Conference to recommend that the Secretary-General of the United Nations convene a committee of experts to examine the collection and verification of information on this transfer of conventional weapons in excess of a certain weight, which the Working Group suggests as a start may be two tons per item, so that practical measures of limitation could be proposed for the most important types of war materials like heavy guns and rockets, tanks, airplanes, ships, etc., excluding, at least temporarily, the light weapons, more difficult to control.

5. Military Manpower and Conventional Armaments

A freezing, in 1969, of the military manpower and of the conventional armaments at their present levels, followed, in 1970, by a token reduction, of 5% for example, which could be realized without endangering the military position of any state, and without necessitating an on-the-spot control, would greatly contribute to alleviate the international tensions and to make possible other progresses on the road to disarmament.

Therefore, the Working Group recommends that all governments take such a measure unilaterally.

6. Military Expenditure

In the same feeling as the symbolic freezing and reductions of manpower and conventional armaments, it would be highly desirable that a freezing of military budgets, at least of the major powers, be agreed to in 1969. Moreover, a U.N. Conference should be called to examine the means of assessing and verifying total military expenditure of nations. When this Conference is concluded it is urged that a 5% reduction in military budgets be agreed to so that the opportunity will be provided to test experimentally the ability of nations to satisfy themselves that such reductions can be verified. If successful, this should provide a new dimension for disarmament procedures and for budgetary limitations from which a portion could be available for developing countries.

7. Chemical and Biological Weapons

It is once more recommended that all countries should be urged to adhere to and, where necessary, to ratify the Geneva Protocol of 1925.

The Working Group welcomed the attention now being given to chemical and biological warfare at the Eighteen Nation Disarmament Conference in Geneva. It was noted that some of the considerations which had in the past led Pugwash discussions to the conclusion that it might be easier _technically_ to enforce a ban on production and stock-piling of biological weapons than a ban on production and stock-piling of chemical weapons had now been cast in some doubt. SIPRI has recently extended its studies to cover chemical weapons as well as biological weapons and is planning to produce a general report early next year. This should help to clarify the problem.

The Working Group warmly welcomed the proposal of the ENDC that the Secretary-General of the U.N. should appoint a group of experts to study the implication and effects of biological and chemical warfare. The advantages of more public knowledge of the dangers of biological and chemical weapons outweigh its disadvantages; and the subject is in a state where an exploration of the facts is a necessary prelude to the formulation of new policies and is best conducted separately.

2. REGIONAL ARMS CONTROL

1. The Working Group began with discussion of the nature of an international dispute. No comprehensive definition was formulated but it was generally agreed that there were various types of dispute. The Group then

considered some examples of the operation of different kinds of regional grouping to see in what ways these promoted local stability by encouraging such conditions as symmetry, a higher degree of equality and inter-action between states on various levels. There were the regional defence pacts like NATO, and the Warsaw Pact, which included the U.S. and U.S.S.R., as well as other powers and which were intended essentially to provide security against outside aggression. There were also other, primarily inner directed associations, such as the Organization of African Unity or the Arab League. The danger was that all such pacts might in the event be used to encourage conformity or prevent the withdrawal of one of their members. The second category had not always succeeded in preventing conflicts between members and in both cases quoted have as one of their purposes action against the "outsider" state in their geographical area, i.e., South Africa and Israel respectively.

2. Due to these and other considerations, the Group agreed on the importance of having regional organizations so structured as to enhance peaceful relations among all the states in any given region. This suggested the merit of regional organizations, whose membership included all the states in a given geographical region, combining non-intervention, non-aggression and arms control elements in agreements. Under these circumstances, however, precautions should be taken against the building-up, the consolidation or the perpetuation of the power of a particularly strong nation in that region. The Group agreed that some safeguards against such dangers might be achieved through an overall supervisory role of the U.N. in relation to these organizations, as further discussed below.

2.1 The Group were agreed that if any measure of disarmament or arms control were to be effective within a regional grouping, restraints on the part of the major powers who were the arms suppliers, in the shape of formal agreements, were an essential prerequisite. While the Non-Proliferation Treaty was highly desirable for its purpose, it had nevertheless consolidated the position of the existing nuclear powers. Such a privileged position should not be allowed in the case of the control of conventional arms.

2.2 While the Group recognized the limited role of regional pacts in relation, for instance, to local boundary disputes and especially attempts at secession, it was felt that the regional arrangements not dominated by a major power were to be encouraged as having the potential to provide the conditions in which positive peace, as opposed simply to a state of "no-war," could develop.

2.3 The great powers could assist a commencement of this process by providing guarantees of neutralization beginning with those regions in which tension is at a low level because they are not important enough to interest the powers and, thereby, become the subject of a major conflict. The case of Antarctica was cited and the hope expressed that eventually tropical Africa and perhaps even the Middle East and South-East Asia, after the resolution of current conflicts, would prove areas where this could be achieved.

Appendix 25

2.4 The question of the relationship between such pacts and the United Nations was discussed. It was not felt that there was a very serious danger of their undermining the effectiveness of the parent international organization, always bearing in mind the role of the U.N., particularly under Chapter VIII of the Charter. It was felt that only through development of this kind could the notion of major power spheres of influence, which has at best been a tenuous means of maintaining world order, be replaced by a less fragile system.

3. The Working Group considered the concept of regional security commissions for various parts of the world, under the jurisdiction of the U.N. Security Council. The commissions might be modelled on the analogy of the various regional economic commissions and their relationship to the U.N. Economic and Social Council. Such a commission would pay special attention to non-military as well as military aspects of security and would promote and facilitate a diversity of interests which cut across the lines of national division. In particular, the Working Group studied a paper by J. Galtung entitled "A Security Commission for Europe," which took as its basis a discussion of the Economic Commission for Europe. The ECE provided an umbrella for discussions between the economic power blocs in such a way as to allow for the presence of national representatives on an egalitarian basis. A Security Commission would require a secretariat and the co-operation of specialists with both expertise and imagination. It should be situated in some conveniently accessible place such as Geneva and would embrace not only the members of NATO and the Warsaw Pact but would also be open to non-aligned countries. The possibility of being a member of a Commission without being a member of the U.N. was stressed, as well as the relative lack of success on the part of the U.N. in dealing with European security questions. It would be likely to make attainable a European Security Conference of the kind at one time suggested in that it might enable the achievement of some agreements in advance and would provide a mutually acceptable secretariat. Arrangements would need to be made for some kind of associate membership for states with defence and related interests there, but not actually located in each area.

3.1 This proposal was felt by the Working Group to have merits and to be worthy of further study. It, therefore, recommends that Pugwash and its member groups urgently seek to promote discussion of it both within the Movement and outside it, if possible in Government circles.

3.2 The Working Group also discussed at some length the threat to European security arising from the German question. The Group wished to endorse the view of Working Group 2 at the Ronneby Conference on "Peacekeeping and Security" "that all existing European borders, including the borders between the two German States and West Berlin should be recognized; that both German States should be admitted to the United Nations; and that it would be important for European security if all states would recognize the German Democratic Republic, without prejudice to the possible future unification of the two German States. The co-operation of the two German States should be encouraged." The Working Group also suggested that other Governments should bear in mind the possible reaction to their policies of different political groups within Germany. The Group was of the opinion that the aim of all-European security, including the solution of the German problem, would be more easily achieved if considerably more support was given to economic, technical and cultural co-operation leading to a higher degree of interaction at a number of different levels.

4. A number of suggestions were made and discussed which were calculated to assist the establishment on a regional basis of areas of stability. Several of these were felt to be matters in which Pugwash could take the initiative in constructive discussion.

4.1 There was a clear need for greater justice to the small powers. While the balance of nuclear power gave them some opportunities to be influential, e.g., in the U.N., more effective regional groupings could help to counteract the overwhelming influence and pressure of major powers. Such organizations as O.A.U. needed to be strengthened in terms of planning secretariats and so on and there might then be organized more readily a movement towards rationalization of the armaments supply situation by regional agreement. This, however, would need the co-operation of the supplying powers. An agreement restricting the supply of especially sophisticated conventional weapons to a small local group of states might make a useful beginning for a widespread movement to arms control. There were recipient states who might be well disposed to such a proposition which would have to be based on agreement about the restriction of local production as well as supply, and which might be facilitated by incentives in the shape of economic aid.

4.2 The possibility of a pilot scheme for a Traffic in Arms Year Book in a particular region, in which arms transactions within, and to or from the area should be published was mentioned as a possible means of improving the psychological climate and reducing suspicion and over-reaction to moves of rival states. This would probably best be linked with some agreement on the non-proliferation of conventional weapons.

4.3 The lack of U.N. sponsored research on security matters was noted and it was suggested that a useful area for initiative would be towards the development of devices which might assist the effectiveness of U.N. observer and policing operations in the case of regional disputes.

5. The Working Group considered the question of nuclear-free zones in relation to the provisions of the Non-Proliferation Treaty. The Treaty provides for no production and no sale of nuclear weapons but does not deal with the matters of stationing and use of such weapons. The case of the Latin American Agreement for a nuclear-free zone was cited as embodying all four and thus helping towards a possible general treaty on non-use of nuclear weapons. The arguments in favour of a nuclear-free zone in Europe from Scandinavia to the Mediterranean were strong and would have implications for the German situation in that such a zone would not be possible without the acceptance by the Government of the German Federal Republic of the provisions of the Non-Proliferation Treaty. It was felt that with regard to the Latin American Agreement, Soviet support might be secured

Appendix 25   308

if the problems connected with the U.S. Government's Cuban base were to
be solved.

The general importance of the ratification and reinforcing by all possible
means of the conditions of the Non-Proliferation Treaty were stressed.
This, though a remarkable step forward in international relations, should
be seen as a basis for further disarmament measures and not as an end.

6. Though it was recognized that the U.N. is dependent to a considerable
extent on the support of the U.S.A. and U.S.S.R. in any specific matter,
considerable concern was expressed at the frequent inability to resolve
conflicts, as opposed to checking them at a particular point in development. The speed of U.N. action was regarded as too slow, whereas it should
be able to some extent to anticipate a crisis.

A number of suggestions were made for the improvement of U.N. efficiency;
these involved primarily building on existing provisions and proceeding
further by informal as well as formal methods. It was, for instance,
hoped that member countries--under the terms of Article 43 of the Charter--
seek to make bilateral arrangements with the Security Council for the ear-
marking of military forces.

There were, it was generally agreed, possibilities under Article 99 for
informal talks between the Secretary-General and senior advisers on the
avoidance of crises and thus the promotion of peaceful change. Too often
U.N. action, as in Kashmir or Cyprus, has contributed to the freezing of
a dispute without being able to resolve the situation.

Some members of the Working Group felt that there was a role for a Human
Rights Council on the lines of the Trusteeship Council, but others doubted
the practicability of providing for the protection of allegedly aggrieved
minorities in this way in view of the existing powers of the Economic and
Social Council. All were agreed on the necessity for the early mobilization of informed public opinion on critical issues to enable representatives at the U.N. to act in support of the Secretary-General who must not
be put into the position of too frequently having to take an individual
initiative. Informal discussions outside the Security Council and the
General Assembly were to be encouraged. There was general support for the
view that Pugwash should uphold the principle of the Charter as stated in,
for example, Articles 11, 34 and 39 by which no international dispute is
beyond the purview of the United Nations.

3. CURRENT PROBLEMS

Preamble
Recent events in all parts of the world have demonstrated that there are
many problems of great significance and urgency. In the report which follows we discuss four of these, but we wish to preface their discussion by
some remarks of general relevance.

We emphasize our belief that all nations must abide by the United Nations
Charter, particularly by the clause that all members shall refrain in their

international relations from the threat or use of force against the territorial integrity or political independence of any state, or in any other manner inconsistent with the purposes of the United Nations.

In addition, we appeal to the industrialized nations to avoid endangering the peaceful existence of the economically underdeveloped nations by using or encouraging internal conflicts for selfish political and/or economic purposes.

1. Nigeria

The members of the Working Group are appalled by the violence and suffering which have characterized the civil war in Nigeria, and wish to express profound sympathy with all those who have been affected by these tragic events. While we urge the quickest possible end to the fighting, we know that the cessation of hostilities will not end the suffering. We, therefore, wish to emphasize the urgent need for massive amounts of food, medical supplies, and technical assistance both now and in the post-war period of national reconstruction. We appeal to all concerned to do all in their power to facilitate the speedy flow of these supplies.

As scientists, we are particularly aware of the grave biological consequences of malnutrition, especially in children. Nothing less than an immediate, massive programme of relief can alleviate this dreadful situation. We appeal for international support.

It is also suggested that the Nigerian Government might wish to invite an international observer corps to be present during the initial period of rehabilitation.

2. Middle East

The Working Group has considered the Middle East question and taking into account the need to eliminate acts of war and to secure a just and lasting peace:

(1) urges speedy implementation of Security Council Resolution No. 242 of 22 November 1967;

(2) urges the parties to co-operate fully with the Jarring mission to obtain this implementation;

(3) suggests, as a guarantee of a peaceful settlement under the auspices of the United Nations, the temporary demilitarization of certain sensitive zones along the borders following the withdrawal of Israeli troops in implementation of the Security Council resolution;

(4) suggests that restrictions on the supply of arms to contending parties, following the implementation of the resolution, should be considered.

3. Vietnam

The situation in Vietnam remains of grave concern. Some progress has been made in that the U.S. has stopped the bombing of the northern regions of North Vietnam and, even though the minimum requirement of full cessation of bombardment has not been acceded to, North Vietnam agreed to commence talks with the U.S. in Paris and these talks are continuing. However, the Working Group wishes to state with utmost emphasis that this degree of progress falls far short of that which the 17th Pugwash Conference called for a year ago.

The war continues fiercely, destruction and death of population remains high. It is vital that prompt and effective steps be made toward peace.

As a precondition for peace, it is of the first importance that there be a full and unconditional stoppage of the bombing of North Vietnam. It is increasingly clear that only this will lead to progress in the talks in Paris. Once the bombing of North Vietnam has stopped, it is urgent that serious negotiations commence for a peaceful settlement.

4. Czechoslovakia

The Working Group discussed the events in Czechoslovakia. Different, and often conflicting, views were expressed on the reasons and the justification for the presence of foreign troops in Czechoslovakia.

We were unanimous in the belief that the situation should be resolved as rapidly as possible by the efforts of the governments concerned with the adoption of measures which would include the withdrawal of foreign troops from Czechoslovak territory and would let the Czechoslovak people, with whom we all feel great sympathy, continue to run their own affairs.

The view was stressed by some participants that the tensions resulting from these recent events have caused a setback to the prospects of peaceful co-existence and to the progress of negotiations for disarmament and arms control. Some speakers stressed that these events were being exploited by circles opposed to the cause of peace. The members of the Working Group unanimously reaffirmed their determination to continue to work for peaceful and stable settlements, as has always been the aim of Pugwash. We urge all governments to follow this course.

4. SCIENTIFIC AND TECHNOLOGICAL MANPOWER PROBLEMS IN DEVELOPING COUNTRIES

Preamble

The primary subject to which the Working Group addressed itself was that of Scientific and Technological Manpower Problems in Developing Countries with special emphasis on international co-operation. The questions asked were:

(i) What is the best way in which the developing areas of the world can produce rapidly a sufficient and growing number of well-qualified scientists and technologists to meet the demands of development?

(ii) What is the best way in which education can be improved at all levels; and in particular, how does one ensure that the educational system can assimilate the rapid developments that are taking place in scientific knowledge and in the methods of teaching?

(iii) How is it possible to match the educational pattern, in quality and quantity, and the output of scientific and technological manpower, to the national needs as planned and as they arise in agriculture, health, industry, etc.?

1. Science Education and Manpower Utilization

The Working Group agreed that it was essential to ensure that the science curricula used in schools and colleges take into account the explosive increase in scientific knowledge that we have been witnessing; it is important both that the curricula be modernized and constantly updated and that they be suitably adapted to the local background of the country and its educational system. It was emphasized that there was a real need to evaluate correctly the magnitude of the problem involved in training a sufficient number of science teachers in order to design a suitable system to meet this need. The system of education has to be a balanced one at all levels, if scientific research, industry, agriculture and the like are to be provided adequate numbers of trained personnel.

The Working Group considered the view that permanent continuous study groups should be formed to correlate the ideas now being generated in different countries in regard to science education, and to inform and advise all countries of the best new plans and programmes. It felt that UNESCO should be stirred to more vigorous action in these matters, along the lines of its praiseworthy support of special training programmes in Asia, Africa and Latin America, but less through sporadic conferences and local curriculum projects than by establishing and supporting international study groups and clearing houses so that successful development anywhere may become rapidly utilizeable for adaptation everywhere.

The Working Group felt that a special Symposium might be organized to study aspects relating to educational TV programmes, particularly through the increasing use of communication satellites, and also audiovisual methods appropriately adapted for local use, both of which offer the possibility of obtaining the large multiplicative factors, both in quantity and quality, that are needed for rapid growth in education in the developing countries.

It was generally agreed that students should study in their own countries in all the areas and up to the highest levels catered for by the country's educational system. Only beyond this level or for fields in which the developing country had not set up training facilities of its own should the students be sent out to the advanced countries for study. This step is essential to ensure that the students have the maximum opportunity to develop cultural roots and interests for work in their own countries.

It was also felt that developing countries should attempt to provide a sufficient number of posts at appropriate level and also adequate research facilities to ensure that the scientists trained at home and abroad can be utilized effectively.

It is clear that the problem of training must be considered in the context of utilization. The first involves educational policy in all its aspects whilst the second involves the political framework and development strategy laid down in science, industry, agriculture, etc.

With regard to utilization, special attention was given to the obstacles which exist in the effective utilization of trained scientific and technical personnel. It was pointed out that ignorance of what is attainable through science and technology, coupled with insufficient decolonization of the mind, an uncritical adulation of foreign experts, obscure attitudes on the part of even some scientists in the developing areas, and the fact that industry is often in the hands of non-nationals or based on foreign collaboration, leads to a lack of or insufficient demand for research by industry, agriculture and other sectors of the economy in the developing country and this militates against the effective use of the limited human resources.

Large defence expenditures in the developing countries reduce considerably the resources for education and development.

In the initial discussion it turned out that whilst the problems of education and utilization of scientific and technological manpower are important topics for discussion, the subject as a whole is connected intimately with the whole process of development and cannot be discussed in isolation. The report of this Working Group will, therefore, in many places, refer to problems of development as a whole.

2. Implementation of Recommendations

The Working Group was of the view that at several Pugwash Conferences in the past, important and useful suggestions had been made in the Working Group dealing with the problems of development concerning: education, manpower, technical assistance, etc. Many of these recommendations have unfortunately remained on paper and this Working Group urges the Continuing Committee to take note of this. In particular, it recommends that a committee be set up by the Continuing Committee, which would itemize the recommendations that have been made and will continue to be made, and attempt to follow these up with appropriate agencies. A report on the extent of implementation could be a regular feature of Pugwash Conferences. A suggestion made in this regard was that each National Pugwash Group should nominate one individual for this task, who would look into aspects of implementation within his own country and also into his country's effort in this regard in international agencies; such a group of individuals would constitute a world-wide network. The members so nominated would also correspond among themselves. For countries or regions of the world, in which Pugwash Committees do not exist, the Continuing Committee could nominate appropriate scientists for this purpose.

3. University Graduates from Advanced Countries in the Developing Countries

The Working Group considers that the assistance to developing countries that young University graduates can give, if they are prepared to work for extended periods of time, of a year or more, as doctors, engineers, scientists, technologists and teachers, can be of real value.

The attention of the Working Group was drawn to the practice of the French Government in permitting young University graduates to substitute their compulsory military service by service in the developing countries. The Working Group was of the view that this substitution by social service on an international basis, for national military service, conforms to the spirit of the Pugwash Movement, and would constitute a good step towards international understanding and world peace. The Working Group recommends the adoption of similar enlightened measures by other nations in the world where such compulsory military service exists.

Members of the Working Group pointed out that there is today, amongst University students in the world a great deal of unrest, and there is dissatisfaction with the existing social system and the opportunities for work; many students feel that they would like to contribute to the much wider world interests and are unable to do so. The Working Group felt that this intellectual ferment, and desire on the part of the young educated classes, to contribute to the creation of a more equitable world system should be recognized and usefully channelled. A possibility would be to provide these young University graduates with challenging opportunities to work in the developing areas of the world. This could be worked out bilaterally amongst the nations; but a centralized multilateral agency acting as a clearing house in this regard could be of great value to keep a record of personnel available, requests from scientific personnel to work in developing areas, etc.

4. Multinational Science Corps

It was suggested in the discussions that one might also consider the possibility of something like an "International Science Corps" at higher (say post-doctoral) levels. With such a multinational Science Corps it would be possible to set up, in specific developing regions of the world, centres devoted to research in defined areas of science that are of interest to these regions, and to train cadres of personnel at the highest levels on problems which have deep roots and relevance to these regions. For specific programmes of this nature it might be possible to obtain the support and co-operation of learned and scientific Societies in various parts of the world, such as the Royal Society, London, the National Academy of Sciences of the U.S.A., the U.S.S.R. Academy of Sciences, etc., and from Foundations. The Pugwash Central Office may be able to play a direct or indirect role in acting as a clearing house.

5. Self Reliance

It was repeatedly emphasized in the Working Group that assistance from the advanced countries of the world to the developing regions has thus far been quite limited; and given the present state of international affairs it will be difficult to obtain a substantial increase in this already small effort. What has been provided has often had strings attached, being aimed to provide advantages for the donor countries in the political, commercial or defence areas. Even assistance provided with wholly benevolent intentions can create in the recipient countries, amongst leaders in politics, administration and industry, an increasing feeling of

Appendix 25   314

dependence; and correspondingly create among these a lack of confidence
and esteem in the national scientists and technologists.

It is thus becoming increasingly clear that the developing nations will,
to a great extent, have to depend on their own resources and abilities,
and will have to lift themselves up through their own efforts. It is essential for the developing nations rapidly to build up self-confidence
for this purpose. They should learn to find the wherewithal for development within themselves and not to depend substantially on outside assistance from the advanced nations. The education and training of scientific
and technological manpower has to be examined with this as the prime objective.

In the development process the stage of identifying and analysing the
major problems of the country or region will almost always involve a multidisciplinary approach; and it is also important that this analysis should
take into account the traditions and values of the people concerned. A
good analysis is the least expensive step in the development process and
yet can increase manifold the effectiveness of large development expenditure. Scientists and technologists have an important role to play in this
process of analysis and decision making. An appropriate group of scientists and technologists could also play a very useful role by keeping under
continuous review advances in their fields and their possible application
to local needs and conditions. The establishment in the developing countries of a scientific community which has self-confidence and self-esteem
is thus a matter of the greatest importance.

6. Regional Symposia
The Working Group recommends strongly that Regional Symposia of the following two types be organized in different regions of the developing world.

(A) To consider the principles relating to the process of development which
can lead to self-confidence and self-reliance. These Symposia would also
examine the important question: what are the objectives the people of a
region have for the development of the region? For example, it may be inappropriate for a particular developing region to adopt in detail or to
imitate the methods, values and patterns for life as seen in many of the
present advanced countries, and it may be far better for them to work out
structures for themselves, consonant with their local heritage and resources. The strategy of development can be defined only after the objectives of development have been defined. The Working Group recognizes that
there are common human goals for all nations, in terms of food and nutrition, health, shelter, etc. that have to be achieved everywhere as rapidly
as possible.

(B) The second type of Symposia would deal with specific concrete objectives. Specific proposals for Regional Symposia put forward to this Working Group, which can be commended are: (i) in New Guinea, to consider aspects of agriculture, nutrition and health; (ii) in Ceylon, to discuss aspects of education and development for the South and South East Asian region; (iii) in Africa, to discuss the possibilities of a co-operative analysis study relating to the development of the Nile river system. Participation in these Symposia should, as far as possible, be confined to scientists of the regions concerned; there could additionally be some recognized specialists in the areas under discussion and some persons long active in the Pugwash Movement to convey the spirit of Pugwash to these Symposia.

It was felt that a Pugwash Conference primarily devoted to the problems of "Development" should be organized reasonably soon after some of the Symposia described under (A) and (B) above had been held, to see what common features emerge when one considers development in a world-wide context.

7. Research in Developing Countries

There was discussion on the research activities that should be undertaken in the developing countries. Each nation or region should undertake research of the type that would prove to be important and relevant for its development, and in areas in which it possesses natural advantages. It was recognized that each region of the world has special advantages for research in certain areas and can thus contribute significantly to developments in world science, even in pure science. In fact, in these areas, scientists from advanced nations would find it profitable to work in the developing regions because of these existing national advantages. Any such participation on the part of scientists from the advanced countries should be only on the basis of mutuality, in collaboration with scientists of the region.

The Working Group noted that over the past decades many basic studies and surveys relating to data collection or in applied areas, such as meteorology, hydrology, soil science, crops, etc. had been carried out in the developing countries. Many of these have not been published and, being dispersed, run the risk of being lost; this is in contrast to work in pure science which generally gets recorded because of the many recognized channels that exist for publication. It would be in the interest of these countries and of other countries which could make use of this information if these studies could be suitably collected to permit retrieval of the data contained in them.

This would mean the setting up, or reinforcement and ensuring the proper utilization of national documentation centres; this might be done with assistance from U.N. agencies. Powers which possess material relating to colonies currently or previously in their possession should be invited to make available whatever documentation in this regard that they have.

It was pointed out that in many areas research work of a similar nature in applied areas such as agriculture, food processing, etc. was being carried out in different developing countries. Whilst it is recognized that there is considerable scope for duplication in research work, it was felt that information on what was going on at other places would be of value to each group. This information could be made available in simply devised forms that could be circulated. The Working Group noted that the reports of an investigation may contain both scientific data which could be of general value and advice or recommendations to a Government, involving aspects of Government policy, which should remain confidential; in such cases the report should be made in two parts to facilitate release of the scientific data independent of material that needs to be kept confidential.

8. Co-operation between Developing Countries

The Working Group felt that too often consideration was given only to relationships between developed nations and developing nations and to aspects of aid, technical assistance, etc. that could be provided by the former to the latter. It would like to emphasize, however, that every country in the world can in some respects be in the position of a donor country. It is clear that much closer ties should be established among the developing nations themselves, who are faced with similar situations and problems and are attempting to reach similar goals. International co-operation for peaceful purposes among the developing nations can be an important factor for development. It cannot be over-emphasized that the misery and degradation associated with a stage of under-development constitute an important factor threatening world peace and security. It was felt that many detailed aspects of such co-operation could be worked out in the Regional Symposia that we have recommended earlier. It was considered that exchange of scientists in various fields, at governmental and non-governmental levels, should be initiated and encouraged. Scientific institutions, organizations and academies in developing nations should be particularly requested to bear this in mind.

Participants

Argentina
Prof. C. M. Varsavsky

Australia
Prof. S. Encel

Belgium
Prof. P. Baudoux

Bulgaria
Acad. G. Nadjakov

Ceylon
Prof. N. Baptist

Czechoslovakia
Mr. T. Němec

Federal German Republic
Mr. H. Afheldt

Finland
Prof. J. M. Jansson

France
Prof. P. V. Auger, Mr. E. Bauer, Dr. J. Bussac, Dr. J. Klein, Dr. B. Laponche, Prof. M. Magat, Prof. H. Marcovich, Mr. J. Moch, Prof. F. Perrin, Prof. A. M. Rodriques, Prof. P. Rosenstiehl, Prof. E. Roth

Ghana
Prof. F. G. Torto

Hungary
Prof. L. Reczei

India
Prof. P. C. Mahalanobis, Prof. M. G. K. Menon, Prof. V. A. Sarabhai, Prof. S. H. Zaheer

Israel
Mr. S. Freier

Italy
Prof. E. Amaldi, Prof. G. Giacometti, Prof. C. Shaerf

Japan
Prof. K. Matumoto, Prof. S. Tanaka

Madagascar
Dr. A. Ramiadrasoa

Netherlands
Dr. P. Boskma, Prof. P. B. Smith

Nigeria
Prof. O. Bassir

Norway
Prof. A. Eide, Prof. J. Galtung

Poland
Prof. I. Adamczewski, Prof. J. Bukowski, Prof. M. Dobrosielski

Romania
Prof. V. Hanga

Sweden
Prof. N. Herlofson, Dr. S. Nilsson

U.A.R.
Prof. F. El Bedewi

U.K.
Dr. C. F. Barnaby, Prof. F. C. Frank, Mr. W. F. Gutteridge, Dr. Patricia J. Lindop, Dr. N. Lipman, Prof. Sir Rudolf Peierls, Prof. C. F. Powell, Prof. J. Rotblat

Appendix 25

U.S.A.
Dr. D. G. Brennan, Prof. H. Brown, Prof. C. Djerassi, Prof. P. Doty, Prof. B. T. Feld, Prof. B. Glass, Mr. R. Kleiman, Prof. Betty Lall, Prof. F. A. Long, Prof. S. Muller, Prof. T. Parsons, Prof. E. Rabinowitch

U.S.S.R.
Prof. V. Y. Aboltin, Acad. L. A. Artsimovitch, Acad. M. M. Dubinin, Prof. V. S. Emelyanov, Acad. V. A. Engelhardt, Prof. I. G. Gverdziteli, Acad. P. L. Kapitza, Acad. V. M. Khvostov, Acad. M. D. Millionshchikov, Dr. I. G. Pochitalin, Acad. A. M. Prokhorov, Prof. I. A. Sokolov, Acad. A. P. Vinogradov

Yugoslavia
Prof. M. Osredkar, Acad. I. Supek

Zambia
Prof. L. K. H. Goma

Observers

France
Mr. G. Scalabre

U.S.A.
Mr. W. Swartz

FAO
Mr. R. Aubrac

IAEA
Mr. A. D. McKnight

SIPRI
Mr. F. Blackaby, Mr. R. Neild, Mr. J. Perry-Robinson

U.N.
Dr. R. Björnerstedt, Mr. G. B. Gresford, Dr. L. N. Kutakov

UNESCO
Dr. M. Makagiansar

WHO
Dr. M. M. Kaplan

Science Writers

Mr. S. Berg (France)
Mr. R. Clarke (U.K.)
Mr. P. Fisson (France)
Dr. P. Stubbs (U.K.)

Science Writers (Continued)

Prof. P. Thuillier (France)
Dr. J. Tooze (U.K.)
Mr. M. Ullmann (France)
Mr. N. Vichney (France)

STATEMENT FROM THE CONTINUING COMMITTEE ON THE NINETEENTH PUGWASH CONFERENCE, HELD IN SOCHI, OCTOBER 22-27, 1969

The Nineteenth Pugwash Conference on Science and World Affairs met in Sochi from the 22nd to 27th October, 1969, at the invitation of the Pugwash Group of the U.S.S.R. The Conference was attended by 101 scientists from 29 countries; in addition there were 10 observers from international organizations and 8 science writers.

The Conference took place at a time when the world situation remains very serious. The arms race is increasing in intensity; weapons of mass destruction multiply and new weapons systems are being introduced. Most countries are increasing their arms expenditures not only without adding to their security but also to the detriment of badly needed investment to raise their standards of life, particularly in the developing parts of the world. Armed conflicts are actually going on in several areas of the world; in addition to the suffering that they bring to the peoples involved, they present serious dangers of escalation into a global conflagration.

Under the title "World Security, Disarmament and Development" all these problems have been discussed at the Conference.

Most of the work of the Conference took place in five Working Groups which discussed the following topics: (1) Measures for terminating current military conflicts and keeping the peace; (2) European security; (3) Reduction and elimination of nuclear weapons and delivery systems; (4) Biological and chemical weapons; (5) Science and developing countries.

The reports of the Working Groups were presented and discussed at plenary sessions of the Conference. The statement that follows has been prepared by the Continuing Committee on the basis of these reports.

1. Measures for Terminating Current Military Conflicts and Keeping the Peace

Since the Eighteenth Pugwash Conference in Nice, in 1968, the state of the local armed conflicts in Vietnam, Nigeria, and the Middle East has become even more dangerous and tragic. Regarding Vietnam, even though the Paris talks continue, and even though the military operations during the past few months have been at a relatively lower level, no significant results towards a peaceful settlement seem to have been achieved. In Nigeria, the conflict still continues. No agreement has been achieved for relief of the millions of innocent people who suffer and die of malnutrition and disease. In the Middle East the cease-fire has become an undeclared but growing war.

Vietnam. The Group discussing these problems considered that complete withdrawal, as quickly as possible, of American troops from South Vietnam is a necessary condition for the establishment of peace in that country. It also felt that a very substantial and very rapid reduction in the strength of American forces would facilitate achieving a cease-fire, and aid in the negotiations for a political agreement among the parties in South Vietnam. To facilitate a settlement of the Vietnam conflict, it is necessary to promote the setting up of a coalition government in the South.

It was stressed that the goal must be an end to the war, and not the so-called "Vietnamization" of the war. Only when this senseless and tragic conflict comes to an end will it be possible to devote attention to the necessary and pressing tasks of political, social and material reconstruction.

Nigeria. It was agreed that an immediate cease-fire without prejudice to the military position on either side could and should be achieved. This cease-fire ought to be internationally supervised by a group of countries or body acceptable to both sides.

It was felt that this cease-fire would create an atmosphere in which meaningful discussions for a political settlement could take place; it is important that such a political settlement should be achieved at the earliest possible date.

It was emphasized that such a cease-fire would greatly facilitate agreement for bringing medicine and food in to relieve the widespread suffering now going on.

Middle East. The Group noted the fact that the resolution of the Security Council of 22nd November, 1967, has been accepted as a whole, without modification, by most Arab countries and by Israel. The Group urges the remaining Arab countries to declare their acceptance of this resolution. Discussions took place on the ways by which this resolution could be unambiguously interpreted and effectively implemented.

In considering the grave situation in the Middle East, the Working Group proceeded from the statement adopted in the Eighteenth Pugwash Conference in Nice: "The Working Group has considered the Middle East question and taking into account the need to eliminate acts of war and to secure a just and lasting peace:

(1) urges speedy implementation of Security Council Resolution No. 242 of 22nd November, 1967;

(2) urges the parties to co-operate fully with the Jarring mission to obtain this implementation;

(3) suggests, as a guarantee of a peaceful settlement under the auspices of the United Nations, the temporary demilitarization of certain sensitive zones along the borders following the withdrawal of Israeli troops in implementation of the Security Council resolution;

(4) suggests that restrictions on the supply of arms to contending parties, following the implementation of the resolution, should be considered."

The Group emphasizes its deep regret at the delay in implementing the U.N. resolution and urges fast action toward its complete implementation.

On this problem, as well as on the problem of Nigeria, the frank exchange of views which took place was made more fruitful by the presence of scientists from the two sides of the conflicts.

2. European Security

The present situation in Europe, characterized by the existence of two military blocs, is highly unsatisfactory because of the danger of military conflict and the political tensions involved. The aim must be the creation of a system for European security and the dissolution of the military blocs. The creation of such a system is not an easy task which could be realized in a short time. However, meanwhile many important steps can be taken which would reduce the danger of conflict and lessen mutual fear and suspicion. Such measures might include the conclusion of agreements banning the use of force, and mutual reduction of the levels of military forces and weapons in Europe. Thus the problem is two-fold: to search for, and work towards a system for European security without military blocs, and meanwhile to take all possible steps to improve the situation in the short term.

The Group supported the idea of a European security conference between governments and welcomes initiatives for such a conference by any government. Such a conference could contribute to the solution of both problems. Some members felt that this conference should lead to the establishment of a permanent body, which might possibly take the form of a regional security Commission for Europe, perhaps under the United Nations. It was stressed by some participants that in their opinion such a conference could be held only with the full participation of the U.S.A. and Canada. Others stressed that the question of the participation of the U.S. or Canada was a matter for decision by the participating European states. The Group also supported the idea of a non-governmental conference on European security and co-operation.

The Group reaffirmed the statement made at the Pugwash Conference in Ronneby in 1967 that all existing European borders, including the borders between the two German states and West Berlin should be recognized; that both German states should be admitted to the United Nations; and that it would be important for European security if all states would recognize the German Democratic Republic, without prejudice to the possible future unification of the two German states. The Group further declared itself in favour of the initiation of negotiations between the governments of the Federal German Republic and the German Democratic Republic to establish normal and equitable relations between those two states.

As has been stressed repeatedly by Pugwash, friendly contacts between East and West in different fields should be encouraged and developed.

One aspect of such contacts is the movement of people, goods and information. Some participants strongly felt that total abolition of censorship would considerably decrease the tension in Europe and help to promote mutual understanding. More particularly, when there is an international conflict all countries should make the views of the other parties fully known to their citizens through the media of mass communication. Others, while fully agreeing with the principle of expanding in every way the exchange of information contributing to the mutual understanding among the peoples of Europe, do not share, at the same time, the view that the principle should apply to propaganda for war, racism, fascism, and other concepts undermining the foundation of peace, international security, and cooperation among nations.

The Group pointed to the need for abolishing discrimination in trade practiced by some states in relation to others.

If contacts between East and West are to contribute to peace and co-operation they should take into account the existing realities, social, political and ideological, in countries belonging to different systems, otherwise they may create additional tension and arouse suspicion.

There are many ways of developing fruitful co-operation on an all-European scale. One proposal which found general support was to expand the agenda of the European Security Conference to include the elaboration of arrangements for European co-operation in all fields. A suggestion was made that consultation on economic policy may forestall economic crises whose repercussions could extend through the whole of Europe. Co-operation might be useful on such problems as pollution, not only by exchange of information and techniques, but also joint action in such case as water-pollution in which the effects can transcend national boundaries.

For co-operation in these and many other fields it may be desirable to set up European regional organizations either *ad hoc* or under the existing U.N. agencies. Moreover, the Group felt that such agencies could not be developed as extensions of the existing Western European agencies such as OECD.

At the request of the Czechoslovak Pugwash Committee the Group unanimously deleted "Czechoslovakia and European Security" as a separate item from the agenda. References to this topic, expressing very conflicting views, were made in the discussion on some other items of European security.

3. Reduction and Elimination of Nuclear Weapons and Delivery Systems

The prospect of another escalation in the strategic armaments levels of the U.S. and the U.S.S.R. is now a particularly acute problem because of the possibility of Anti-Ballistic Missile (ABM) and Multiple Independently Targetable Re-Entry Vehicles (MIRV) deployment, which will lead to a new and very dangerous stage in the steeply ascending spiral of the strategic arms race. Deployment of either of these weapons systems would almost certainly have the effect of introducing large uncertainties into the calculations made by both sides of the level of strategic armaments required to deter a nuclear attack. It would seem virtually certain that strategic force levels would be greatly expanded; this is due to the combination of

Appendix 26

the assumption by each side that the capabilities of the other would be at the highest possible level, with the assumption that its own capabilities are at the lowest level of the range of uncertainty. Such an approach has been used in the past as a pretext to justify very great arms increases. Experience shows that this approach, instead of making the world safer, has resulted in a diminution of the security of all nations. An expansion of armaments will not only increase the waste of resources and the danger of accidental or unauthorized launching of nuclear-armed missiles, but will also increase the probability of nuclear war, since one or another of the major nuclear powers might conclude that there are advantages to be gained by striking first rather than accepting the risk of a first blow by its adversary.

With these considerations in mind, the Group concluded that early negotiation of an agreement to limit strategic armaments was a matter of highest priority, and that indeed the urgency was particularly great with respect to the deployment of ABMs and MIRVs and the testing of the latter. Action on this problem should be at the top of the agenda of the Soviet-American Strategic Arms Limitation Talks (SALT). The Group heartily welcomed the announcement that these talks are to begin on 17th November in Helsinki.

Effective deterrence can be obtained with a drastically reduced level of nuclear stockpiles. Movement towards such reduced levels would provide opportunities for making progress toward general and complete disarmament.

Recognizing the danger of further proliferation of nuclear weapons capabilities, the Group believes that early ratification and implementation of the Non-Proliferation Treaty, with the participation of the greatest number of states, including all the nuclear and potential nuclear weapons states, is a matter of great urgency. Hope was expressed that progress in the Strategic Arms Limitation Talks will encourage adherence to the Non-Proliferation Treaty by all nations.

The possibility of preventing the placement of weapons of mass destruction on the seabed, and extending the Nuclear Test-Ban Treaty to cover all environments, were discussed, and the Group favoured the implementation of treaties to achieve these purposes.

It was urged that countries that have not yet subscribed to the partial Test-Ban Treaty should do so now. Concern was expressed about the extent of present underground nuclear testing. There was a consensus that difficulties in detection of underground tests have been reduced to the point where they are no longer a serious impediment to extending the Test-Ban to include underground testing.

It was felt that there is considerable and unwarranted complacency on the part of the general public and among many officials about the seriousness of the present situation in the nuclear arms race. The enormity of the destruction that would result from a full-scale nuclear war with present stockpiles of nuclear weapons is simply not comprehended by the general public. Scientists have a great responsibility to help educate the public about this.

4. Biological and Chemical Weapons

The Group reviewed the data now available in relation to means of eliminating the use of chemical and biological (CB) weapons.

The U.N. report on the possible effects of the use of CB weapons, emphasizing the need for an effective international ban on the development, production and stockpiling of these weapons adopted by delegates from 14 nations seemed to hold great promise for the negotiation of such a ban. The technical reports on CB weapons from the Stockholm International Peace Research Institute (SIPRI) and WHO will also help in preparing an effective ban.

The Geneva Protocol of 1925 has been an effective instrument of conventional law, and all nations should be urged to ratify it. Steps beyond the Protocol, which only bans first use of CB weapons, are urgently needed. Dangers of weakening the Protocol can be foreseen if new adherents were to interpret it as permitting the use of chemical agents in war of which the customary peace-time use is restricted to riot control, and use in agriculture. In war-time, for example, riot control agents can be used to increase the lethality of conventional weapons. Ways of defining acceptable peace-time uses of chemical and biological agents therefore need careful study.

In addition to the Protocol, efforts must be made to ban development, production, stockpiling on home or foreign territories, and transfer of technical expertise on weapons development between nations. Since biological weapons are not now used, it may be possible to outlaw them completely, but separating biological from chemical weapons might outweigh the advantages of this partial measure. Efforts might better be concentrated on banning simultaneously further development of both types of agents. In the meantime, any unilateral action by a nation to ban production and, where relevant, eliminate stockpiles of any of these weapons would be a positive contribution towards a total ban.

The Group considered the two CBW-disarmament-related topics that SIPRI had undertaken on the recommendation of Pugwash. A progress report was heard on the BW inspection experiment. It was felt that this experiment had yielded fruitful results both as regards the technical problems of verifying observance of non-production agreements, and as regards arousing the interest and active participation of several countries, both East and West. The Group recommended that Pugwash/SIPRI convene an international symposium to consider how the experiment might most usefully be extended (a) to include an evasion exercise, and (b) to explore the problems of verifying observance of agreements outlawing chemical weapons.

A progress report was made on the work in Sweden on rapid detection and identification methods for BW agents. The Group felt that this work, which was still in its early stages, was potentially very useful, and reiterated the recommendation of the Pugwash CBW Study Group that a workshop be convened to discuss the results to date, and to explore further the technical problems involved. It was felt to be essential that experts from national CBW defence laboratories should participate in the workshop.

5. Science and Developing Countries

The Group concerned with this subject expressed the belief that Pugwash should be deeply concerned with the ways in which science and technology may help to narrow the gap between the more developed and the less developed countries, since this gap is as much a threat to peace as the arms race between the developed countries. Attention was called to the increasing expenditures on arms by the developing countries, detrimental to their economic and social betterment. Three problems, felt to be of extreme interest for the developing countries, but also affecting developed countries, were discussed in some detail: inadequate food supplies and malnutrition; population growth; and water supply, particularly in arid lands.

Food Supplies. The relative roles of protein deficiency and calorie deficiency in the developing countries were discussed; the interdependence and importance of both of them was recognized. The possibility of irreversible damage to children's mental development caused by protein deficiency in early age, even after the first six months of their lives, was considered as calling for further study. The favourable result of the introduction of new high-yield strains of cereals was noted, but so were the complex problems that have to be solved to make proper use of the potentialities of these crops, such as fertilizer supply, pest control, marketing distribution, etc. It was pointed out that all these techniques will have to be developed in the country itself and could not be imported.

Population. The problems of developing contraceptive methods adequate for use in developing countries were discussed. The slowness with which this development can proceed in advanced countries because of stringent regulations imposed on clinical experimentation was pointed out, and the need in the developing countries for testing procedures fast enough to permit application in the next decade was stressed. The possibility of transferring the control of clinical testing--as distinct from that of actual distribution--to an international agency was discussed.

Water. The problem of water supplies is already being considered by many international agencies. One point that seems to have been overlooked is the need of the developing countries to acquire the technical infrastructure necessary to take utmost advantage of the programmes on development of water resources prepared by the international agencies, and the possibilities of Pugwash playing a role in this field were discussed.

International Foundation for Scientific and Technical Development. With the aim of supporting research by scientists and technologists of developing countries in their own academic institutions and laboratories, the Working Group suggested as worthy of study the proposal of an International Foundation (or Fund) for Scientific and Technical Development, already recommended in two previous Pugwash Conferences. A rather detailed outline of the structure of this Foundation and of the types of research to be supported by it, was proposed. The Group suggested that funds should come to this Foundation not only from governments and inter-governmental agencies, but also industries, foundations and individuals. The legal structure of the Foundation should be such as to ensure a highly competent governing body, and review committees of respected scientists from both developed and developing countries.

Finally, the Group made recommendations tending to ensure the continuity of the action of Pugwash in the field of development.

In the discussions, both in the plenary sessions and in the Working Groups, the urgent need for all scientists to concern themselves with these life-or-death problems has been repeatedly stressed. The importance of reaffirming the original goals of Pugwash—as expressed in the Russell-Einstein Manifesto, issued in 1955—was emphasized, and the need was expressed to expand these to include problems which have since arisen, particularly in relation to the developing nations. It is no longer sufficient, as has mainly been the case until now in Pugwash, to bring in senior scientists; involvement of the younger generation of scientists and students is vital for the attainment of our aims. It is, after all, the young who will have the task of preserving and securing our heritage.

Participants

Argentina
Prof. C. M. Varsavsky

Australia
Dr. E. K. Inall

Austria
Prof. P. Weinzierl

Belgium
Prof. E. Coppetiers

Bulgaria
Acad. K. Bratanov, Acad. G. Nadjakov

Canada
Mr. P. C. Dobell

Ceylon
Prof. N. G. Baptist

Czechoslovakia
Prof. V. Hacik, Acad. I. Málek, Dr. J. Moravec, Mr. T. Němec

Denmark
Mr. A. Boserup, Prof. O. Maaløe

Federal German Republic
Mr. H. Afheldt, Prof. H. Glubrecht, Prof. E. Menzel

Appendix 26 328

France
Mr. E. Bauer, Prof. M. Magat, Prof. H. Marcovich, Mr. J. Moch,
Prof. F. Perrin

German Democratic Republic
Prof. W. Ersil, Dr. A. Kolesnyk, Prof. H. Kröger

Hungary
Acad. M. Szabolcsi, Acad. K. Vas

India
Mr. A. Parthasarathi, Prof. S. H. Zaheer

Israel
Prof. S. Z. Lifson, Prof. G. Stein

Italy
Prof. E. Amaldi, Prof. F. Calogero, Prof. C. Schaerf

Mongolia
Prof. N. Sodnom

Netherlands
Dr. P. Boskma, Prof. P. B. Smith, Dr. A. van der Woude

Nigeria
Prof. O. Awe, Prof. J. O. C. Ezeilo, Prof. C. A. Onwumechilli

Norway
Prof. J. Galtung

Poland
Prof. I. Malecki, Prof. K. Popiolek, Dr. W. Wieczorek, Dr. E. Wotjaszek

Romania
Prof. C. I. Foias, Prof. C. Penescu

Spain
Mr. J. L. Leal

Sweden
Prof. N. Herlofson, Mr. J. Prawitz

U.A.R.
Dr. N. Eissa, Prof. F. El-Bedewi

U.K.
Dr. C. F. Barnaby, Mr. W. F. Gutteridge, Prof. M. Howard, Dr. Patricia J.
Lindop, Dr. W. Mendl, Mr. P. Noel-Baker, Prof. Sir Rudolf Peierls,
Mr. N. W. Pirie, Prof. J. Rotblat, Dr. C. J. H. Watson

U.S.A.
Prof. C. Djerassi, Prof. P. Doty, Prof. B. T. Feld, Prof. R. L. Garwin, Prof. D. A. Glaser, Prof. K. Hansen, Prof. W. Leontief, Prof. H. Morgenthau, Prof. E. Rabinowitch, Prof. G. Rathjens, Prof. R. Revelle, Prof. A. Rich, Prof. J. Ruina, Prof. M. D. Shulman, Dr. H. York

U.S.S.R.
Prof. V. Y. Aboltin, Prof. G. A. Arbatov, Acad. L. A. Artsimovitch, Acad. M. M. Dubinin, Prof. V. S. Emelyanov, Acad. V. A. Engelhardt, Dr. Ludmila A. Gvishiani, Acad. A. A. Imshenetsky, Prof. R. V. Khohlov, Acad. V. M. Khvostov, Dr. V. F. Kuleshov, Acad. M. D. Millionshchikov, Prof. D. P. Novikov, Mr. I. G. Pochitalin, Acad. O. Reutov, Dr. V. A. Shustov, Dr. I. A. Sokolov, Prof. V. G. Solodovnikcv, Acad. A. P. Vinogradov, Prof. M. S. Voslensky, Prof. B. M. Vul

Yugoslavia
Prof. V. Benko, Prof. A. Tanovic

Observers

FAO
Mr. R. Aubrac

IAEA
Mr. I. S. Zheludev

SIPRI
Mr. R. Neild, Mr. J. Perry-Robinson, Dr. K. Sinyak

U.N.
Dr. R. J. Bunche, Dr. E. Y. Kutovoj

UNESCO
Dr. H. Alpert, Mr. S. O. Awokoya

WHO
Dr. M. M. Kaplan

Science Writers

Mr. O. N. Anichkin (U.S.S.R.)
Dr. I. S. Bengelsdorf (U.S.A.)
Mr. R. Clarke (U.K.)
Mr. R. Kleiman (U.S.A.)
Mr. V. F. Liustiberg (U.S.S.R.)
Mr. W. S. Sullivan (U.S.A.)
Mr. O. S. Vasiliev (U.S.S.R.)
Mr. N. Vichney (France)

27 STATEMENT FROM THE CONTINUING COMMITTEE ON THE TWENTIETH PUGWASH CONFERENCE, HELD IN FONTANA, SEPTEMBER 9-15, 1970

The Twentieth Pugwash Conference on Science and World Affairs, held from the 9th to 15th September 1970 in Fontana, Wisconsin, was attended by 109 scientists and scholars from 31 countries, and from 5 international organizations. Under the theme "Peace and International Co-operation: A Programme for the Seventies," and following the pattern of informal and lively exchange of views that has characterized these unofficial conferences since their inception in 1957, the participants discussed a variety of international problems in five Working Groups on the following topics: International Security Problems (General Aspects); European Security Arrangements; Disarmament and Arms Limitation; International Co-operation in Science and Technology; and Science, Technology and Development. In addition, plenary sessions were held on International Aspects of Environmental Pollution and the Depletion of Natural Resources, and on Problems of Population and Economic Growth.

The reports of the Working Groups, submitted to the Continuing Committee, are felt by us to be of broad general interest, and are attached herewith. It should be emphasized that the contents of these reports represent a broad consensus of the respective Working Groups and not necessarily of the Conference as a whole.

It will be noted that these reports contain a number of recommendations on future activities; these proposals will be considered by the Continuing Committee.

The 20th Pugwash Conference was organized under the auspices of the Committee on Pugwash Conferences of the American Academy of Arts and Sciences with the co-operation of the National Academy of Sciences of the U.S. Our host was the Adlai Stevenson Institute of International Affairs.

One new arrangement tried at this conference was the invitation of a group of student aide-participants. This group included 24 students of science, international relations, and science policy from 10 countries. A special session was arranged at which students and other participants exchanged views about Pugwash. It is expected that this experiment will be repeated at future conferences.

At the final session of the conference, the Continuing Committee announced the election of Professor Hannes Alfvén of Sweden, distinguished physicist, as President of Pugwash.

The 21st Pugwash Conference will be held in Sinaia, Romania, from the 26th to 31st August, 1971. The Continuing Committee has elected Professor Corneliu Penescu to be President of this Conference.

1. INTERNATIONAL SECURITY PROBLEMS

1. General Aspects of Security

The Group considers the world situation to remain very serious despite some favourable trends in international politics. The threat of a nuclear conflagration still exists, the intensity of the arms race is growing, and armed conflicts are going on in different places of the world. In the light of these developments Pugwash cannot and should not weaken its efforts to secure universal peace.

Therefore, the Group considered it important to move away from traditional strategic thinking where states are seen as pieces on a chessboard. A conceptual framework should be adopted in which the aim was not only to achieve and maintain peace, in the sense of absence of violence--which may or may not be protected through a balance of terror--but where security and peace include also disarmament, co-operation, material progress and national self-determination. Measures to be taken to promote these aims could include the following:

- promoting universal application of the principles of peaceful co-existence between states irrespective of their political, social and economic systems;

- avoiding interference by all states in the domestic affairs of other states, so that any state may change its social and political system without the fear of interference from outside states;

- facilitating support, by non-violent means, to national liberation movements which are seeking to unseat regimes condemned by the United Nations for violations of human rights;

- increasing economic, technical and scientific co-operation between all nations, emphasizing in particular the need for such co-operation with different economic and political systems;

- promoting comprehensive disarmament and demilitarization in the developed world;

- implementing fully the U.N. resolutions on decolonization;

- attempting to dissuade the developing countries from the build-up of military forces;

- increasing substantially economic, technological and scientific assistance to help these countries develop themselves;

- encouraging personal contacts in various fields between nationals, including in particular those countries between which there exist conflicts. Such action would be consonant with the aims and within the potential of Pugwash;

- specifically taking serious steps to bring China back into international organizations, particularly to take her seat in the Security Council, and to intensify the efforts to re-establish Chinese participation in the Pugwash Movement;

- improving regional and universal security arrangements. In this connection, it was considered important to discuss in more depth, at the next Pugwash Conference, measures to increase the capability of the U.N. to handle local conflicts.

2. Current Conflicts
A. The Middle East. The Group welcomed the acceptance by the parties of the Rogers plan and the establishment of a cease-fire, but deplored the fact that the peace negotiations had not yet commenced. The Group re-endorsed the statement on the Middle East originally adopted in the 18th Pugwash Conference in Nice (see Appendix I) and then noted in the 19th Conference in Sochi. While considering it probable that the present cease-fire has brought the U.N. resolution closer to its implementation, the Group urges that all parties should avoid any action which could further increase the mistrust now prevailing between them. The Group calls for a speedy resumption of negotiations through the Jarring mission, in an atmosphere of scrupulous observance of the cease-fire conditions and credibility of intentions.

The Group examined various proposals for steps that could be taken to bring peace to the Middle East, and to provide for a humane settlement for all living in the area. The Group holds that all people in the area should enjoy their human rights and live in peace, and that all states in the region should have the right to exist. In this context, the Palestinian refugee problem has to be solved according to the principles of the U.N. Charter (see 4 below).

B. Indo-China. The Group considered it a matter of grave concern that since the last Pugwash Conference, the armed conflict, far from being stopped, has spread to Cambodia. The Group, proceeding from the statement adopted at the 19th Conference in Sochi (Appendix II), stresses that for Laos and Cambodia as well as South Vietnam, the aim must be to achieve peace, not to equip or support the local parties to continue the conflict.

3. Arms Trade Involving Developing Countries
This question was seen as virtually important, and various proposals were put forward. The Group agreed that arms trade must be seen in connection with issues of disarmament and security concerns in both the developing and developed countries. Differences of opinion were expressed, and the Group agreed that the question needs further study (see 4 below).

4. Proposals for Further Study
The Group felt that the Pugwash Movement, because of its unique network of contact and interaction between scientists devoted to peace and development, can play an increasingly important role in matters of political importance. In some cases Pugwash-sponsored studies, particularly in areas

where governmental organizations may be disinclined to do so, would help disseminate facts, clarify problems and elucidate the positions of the parties involved.

Middle East. The Group recommends that the Continuing Committee establish a working group to help to find ways to implement the United Nations Security Council Resolution 242.

Indo-China. The Group suggests that the Continuing Committee constitute a study group on Indo-China and request a suitable institution to provide facilities for the collection and distribution of information to the participants in the study group. The group should report at the next Pugwash Conference, but should be free at any time to present its proposals to the parties.

Arms Trade Involving Developing Countries. At the 19th Conference in Sochi, it had been recommended that the United Nations convene a committee of experts to examine certain aspects of arms trade. Since the United Nations has not adopted this proposal, and because of the complexity of the problem, the Group recommends the following steps:

a. That the Continuing Committee propose to one of the institutes presently engaged in research in this field that it convene a group of experts to examine the collection and verification of information on this issue.

b. That the Continuing Committee organize a symposium with participants from both developed and developing nations, to discuss the economic, technical, political, social and military problems related to arms trade to, and production of arms in, the developing countries.

c. That this symposium report to the next Pugwash Conference, so that the Conference can consider the possibility of drawing up a draft convention on the limitations of such arms trade.

Appendix I
Middle East.* The Working Group has considered the Middle East question and taking into account the need to eliminate acts of war and to secure a just and lasting peace:

(1) urges speedy implementation of Security Council Resolution No. 242 of 22 November 1967;

(2) urges the parties to co-operate fully with the Jarring Mission to obtain this implementation;

(3) suggests, as a guarantee of a peaceful settlement under the auspices of the United Nations, the temporary de-militarization of certain sensitive zones along the borders following the withdrawal of Israeli troops in implementation of the Security Council resolution;

---

*Proceedings of the 18th Pugwash Conference in Nice, 1968, p. 309.

Appendix 27

(4) suggests that restrictions on the supply of arms to contending parties, following the implementation of the resolution, should be considered.

Appendix II
The following statement was made at the 19th Pugwash Conference:*

"The Group considered that complete withdrawal, as quickly as possible, of American troops from South Vietnam is a necessary condition for the establishment of peace in that country. It also felt that a very substantial and very rapid reduction in the strength of American forces would facilitate achieving a cease-fire, and aid in the negotiations for a political agreement among the parties in South Vietnam. To facilitate settlement of the Vietnam conflict, it is necessary to promote the setting up of a coalition government in the South.

It is stressed that the goal must be an end to the war, and not the so-called 'Vietnamization' of the war. Only when this senseless and tragic conflict comes to an end will it be possible to devote attention to the necessary and pressing tasks of political, social and material reconstruction."

2. EUROPEAN SECURITY ARRANGEMENTS

1. Assessment of the Situation in Europe as a Result of Recent Developments
Since the 19th Conference in Sochi there has been a marked change in the atmosphere of international relations in Europe, characterized and largely brought about by the conclusion of the treaty between the Soviet Union and the Federal German Republic. This new situation opens up possibilities of further development of co-operation and improvement in the relations between the signatories, improved relations of the F.G.R. with other East European states, and greater security for Europe.

The conclusion of the treaty represents determined efforts by both sides to reach agreement, but it was also facilitated by the general lessening of cold-war tensions, which until recently were rather intense.

While this treaty represents a major advance, it is only one step in the right direction, which, one hopes, will soon be followed by others.

The reports of the Ronneby and Sochi Conferences drew attention to the desirability of admitting both German states to the United Nations, of recognition of all existing European borders, and of recognition of the G.D.R. by all states without prejudice to possible future unification of the two German states. These aims have not yet been fully achieved.

Up to the present the treaty has been signed but has yet to be ratified. Public opinion in the F.G.R. is not unanimous, and there are sections opposing ratification. Early ratification of the treaty is of great importance, and its prospects can be greatly assisted by co-operative attitudes

---
*Proceedings of the 19th Pugwash Conference in Sochi, 1969, p. 320.

by all concerned over practical matters, such as the handling of border procedures and of other day-to-day transactions. Such signs of good will, which in some measure are taking place, can help to create confidence that the treaty is bringing tangible and immediate benefits.

Apart from this treaty, other recent moves are the direct negotiations between the governments of the G.D.R. and the F.G.R., although these have not yet led to agreement, and direct negotiations between the F.G.R. and Poland. Similarly, there are negotiations in progress between the four occupying powers concerning West Berlin.

2. Recommendations for Further Action

In this situation the prospects of an early implementation of the proposal for a European Security Conference appear good, particularly since neither the question of the participation of the G.D.R. and the F.G.R. with full and equal status, nor that of the participation of the U.S.A. and Canada seem to be any longer matters of controversy. Pugwash should urge all governments concerned to initiate steps towards convening such a conference. The conference should consider a treaty to be signed by the states of Europe that would obligate them:

(a) to solve their disputes exclusively by peaceful means and to assume the obligation to refrain, pursuant to Article 2 of the Charter of the United Nations, from the threat of force or the use of force in questions which affect security in Europe and international security;

(b) to respect unreservedly the territorial integrity of all states in Europe in their present frontiers; and

(c) to conduct their mutual relations according to the principles of sovereign equality and to assume the obligation to refrain from intervention in each other's internal affairs.

The conference should also consider the problem of the high level of armaments and armed forces in Europe and means of their reduction. It cannot be expected that this complex problem can be disposed of at a conference, but it may be possible to set up a continuing body for the purpose of studying the problem of arms reduction. It may also prove possible and desirable to have this or some other organization concern itself on a continuing basis with European security.

The conference should not, however, be restricted to security, but should concern itself with the improvement and expansion of all forms of co-operation within Europe which may have become possible or easier as a result of improved relations, and which can in turn contribute to a consolidation and further improvement of these relations. This includes economic relations as well as scientific, technical and cultural ties. It is important to eliminate, to the maximum possible extent, restrictions on trade, travel and the free movements of persons.

In the field of economic co-operation, there already exist many examples
of joint economic and industrial projects, including countries of East
and West Europe jointly, usually on a bilateral basis. Their total scale
is, however, still small, and much more can be done. The Group noticed
that in this field, as in scientific and technical exchanges, there was
much emphasis on the field of highest prestige, probably because these
most easily attracted the attention of the few national organizations that
now function as the channels for such co-operation. To widen the scope
of collaboration it would be useful to decentralize the initiative, so
that suggestions for binational or multinational ventures could arise
from many channels.

Regional multilateral arrangements function now, for example, in the management of the Danube, and similar arrangements might now be workable in
the Baltic. There are other subjects suitable for multilateral arrangements for the preservation of the environment. In the fields of scientific and cultural co-operation there also exist already many working arrangements, some bilateral, some multinational but relating to special
fields, and all of these are worth extending. Here again any possible
decentralization of initiative would be beneficial.

The Group considered, but did not favour, the idea of some institution
responsible for cultural exchanges throughout Europe, but a body which
would look at possible additional forms of cultural collaboration and
would encourage these where appropriate might be profitable.

Mutual understanding would be greatly assisted by measures to ensure that
school textbooks, particularly of history and geography, used in each
European country were based on well-informed and objective understanding
of the situation in other countries to which they refer.

3. The Place of Europe in the World
The Group felt that it was premature to express any definite view or suggestions concerning the means and ways of integrating the current efforts
in Europe into a wider endeavour to create a world-wide system of security
and co-operation as envisaged in the Charter of the United Nations. It
was, however, agreed that the security of Europe and the prosperity of the
nations of Europe are not possible without the further development of the
ties which link the nations of Europe with nations on other continents.

In this respect the Group emphasized the possible role of Europe as a factor influencing international relations in general, and particularly those
between the superpowers, and the role of Europe in the developing areas of
the world.

The view was expressed that these problems could be further studied and
elucidated at some future Pugwash meeting.

3. DISARMAMENT AND ARMS LIMITATION

With grave concern the Group has to record that the year which has elapsed
since our Conference at Sochi, despite some positive events (the beginning

of the Soviet-American strategic arms limitation talks and the coming into force of the non-proliferation treaty), has brought no significant decrease in the threats inherent in the arms race. In the view of some, hopes of controlling the arms race to any truly significant extent, by means of partial measures, are receding rather than becoming brighter. In this situation the Group is convinced that it would be the missing of an historic opportunity if the Resolution of the U.N. General Assembly adopted on 16 December 1969 A/RES/2602E (xxiv), declaring the Decade of the 1970's as a Disarmament Decade, were allowed to remain yet another cry in the desert. The Group can see no lack of realism in the General Assembly's request to the Conference of the Committee on Disarmament (CCD) that, while continuing intensive negotiations with a view to reaching the widest possible agreement on collateral measures, it should work out, at the same time, "a comprehensive programme dealing with all aspects of the problem of the arms race and general and complete disarmament." The easing of tensions in Europe, the achievement of near-parity in the "strategic" capabilities of the principal nuclear powers, the vast potentials of satellite reconnaissance as an instrument of verification, these are some, but by no means the only factors, which would tend to make the resumption of negotiations on complete and general disarmament a meaningful endeavour. In the unanimous view of this Group the starting point of this great enterprise should be a critical review by the U.S. and Soviet Governments, in the perspective of those changes and developments which have supervened during the past eight years, of the plans they had respectively put forward in 1962 in the shape of the Revised Soviet Draft Treaty on General and Complete Disarmament (September 24, 1962) and the United States Outline of Basic Provisions of a Treaty on General and Complete Disarmament in a Peaceful World (April 18, 1962, as amended on August 6, 1962 and August 8, 1962).

Practically all that is stated and argued in the next following sections of this Report tends to show that any attempt to buy national security by further military build-up is self-defeating. The Group is anxious that it should be fully realized by governments and public opinion all over the world that the superficial quiescence of major conflicts is deceptive and that complacency at the present time is pregnant with massive dangers. It is the duty of Pugwash to bring these dangers to the urgent attention of all those who are actively concerned with problems of arms control, disarmament and international security.

Problems of Strategic Arms Limitation

The strategic arms limitation talks and the approaches of the major nuclear powers to strategic policy appear to be based largely on the idea of maintaining a capability to inflict unacceptable damage on each other in the event of nuclear war, i.e., on "deterrence."

The concept of deterrence was extensively discussed and the following criticisms were voiced. First, there is the fact that requirements for deterrence have been used as a rationale for a continuing growth in nuclear weapons stockpiles. Second, the idea of one of the major powers deterring a deliberate calculated nuclear attack by the other seems of limited utility because the most real threat of nuclear war is not in such an attack but rather in accidents, miscalculation or in an uncontrolled escalation of an international crisis. For these and other reasons the final objective of arms control and disarmament negotiations must be general and complete disarmament. Prevention of further growth in "strategic" armaments and even substantial reductions must be regarded as at best interim measures.

Despite these reservations, realistically, efforts at arms control and disarmament will, in the present situation, probably continue to be related to the concept of nuclear deterrence. In that context, present stockpiles of nuclear weapons and delivery systems seem grossly excessive. This seems particularly so when it is recognized that many nucelar weapons and delivery systems which are often characterized as "tactical" could in fact be used to destroy not just military objectives but the population, industry and fabric of society in many countries; and when it is recognized that the damage-inflicting capabilities of nuclear weapons are generally and notoriously under-estimated primarily because only immediate fatalities and direct effects are considered. Actually, each of the major components of "strategic" force, such as the ICBM's or the missile launching submarine forces alone would have a more-than-adequate capability for deterrence.

Despite the enormous "overkill" inherent in present "strategic" forces, we are now threatened with a further multiplication in numbers of "strategic" nuclear warheads, principally because of the development of MIRV's (multiple independently targeted re-entry vehicles). When coupled with improvements in missile accuracy, which seem entirely feasible and very probable, there is basis for serious concern.

First there is the possibility of an attempt by one or both of the superpowers to develop a "first-strike" capability against its adversary's fixed land-based missiles. Were such a capability developed, a "first-strike" would seem extremely improbable considering that, even if successful, it would not prevent a devastating retaliatory blow by other forces--submarine based missiles and bombers. Nevertheless, efforts to develop a "first-strike" capability would be very undesirable for several reasons:

in a time of severe crisis the incentives to strike first would be increased;

ICBM's might be launched in an almost automatic way, based on a warning of attack, in order to prevent their destruction; and reliance of such automatic response might result in erroneous launching of missiles with catastrophic results;

there would be an adverse effect on the arms race. With the perception that ICBM's might be vulnerable to pre-emptive attack, there would be incentives to build new delivery systems to replace them, or to increase the number that might survive attack by defending them or by increasing their number.

The development of highly accurate MIRV's is also dangerous because it may play into the hands of those who would argue in favour of using nuclear weapons not only for deterrence, but for actual war-fighting. There will be those who will claim that with large numbers of highly accurate, relatively low-yield nuclear weapons, it will be possible to execute "surgical" type attacks against adversary military targets with their being a minimum of collateral damage to civilian population and other targets. The concept is wrong because of the aforementioned under-estimation of the effects of nuclear weapons, and it is dangerous in the extreme because of the probability of uncontrolled escalation. It is, therefore, important to warn the public and political leadership about such dangers and if possible to prevent the further development and deployment of highly accurate MIRV's.

Last year at Sochi we warned of the adverse consequences of further development of MIRV capability. Regrettably the testing of MIRV's has proceeded much further, and recently deployment has begun. That being the case, limitations of MIRV's would now be much more difficult than one year ago. However, the Group expressed the hope that it might not be too late to negotiate limitations and urges that it be an urgent objective of SALT.

In any case, considering how far the programmes have gone, serious consideration should be given, in both the SALT negotiations and in unilateral national decisions, to minimizing the adverse implications of MIRV development. This might be accomplished by reducing the main rationalizations for their deployment; namely, by limiting ABM defences; and by reducing reliance on fixed land based ICBM's for deterrence. Because of their vulnerability to attack by highly accurate MIRV's, fixed land based ICBM's seem likely to be obsolete (unless a launch-on-warning doctrine is adopted for them) within the next decade. Phasing them out of inventories very rapidly seems preferable to attempting to extend their operational life by a few years through proliferation or active defence (and also much to be preferred to the adoption of a launch-on-warning doctrine).

We would generalize and urge that in both the SALT negotiations and unilaterally, the superpowers make a special effort to eliminate those strategic systems which are particularly likely to lead to increased risks of nuclear war or to an acceleration of the arms race.

In this connection limitations on anti-submarine warfare would seem highly desirable. As long as the superpowers insist on maintaining deterrent forces, there is great advantage in their being as invulnerable as possible, since any suggestion of vulnerability seems almost certain to lead to an effort to compensate for that real or imagined vulnerability with the result being an expanded arms race. The Group was of the opinion that at present missile launching submarines are highly invulnerable. To allay concern about future vulnerability, inhibiting or preventing development and deployment of improved anti-submarine warfare capabilities would be desirable. This would increase the acceptability of greater reliance on missile launching submarines and a more drastic and rapid phase-out of some other "strategic" delivery systems. An agreement to prohibit deployment of large active sonar systems seems particularly desirable. There are no compelling arguments for deploying such systems for purposes other than to attempt to locate missile launching submarines. Furthermore, there would be no problems in verifying compliance with such an agreement. Other measures for limiting anti-submarine warfare were discussed (limiting numbers of hunter-killer submarines and geographical limitations on deployment of certain naval forces). Consideration of such measures merits serious attention in SALT.

Severe limitations on ABM deployment are likely to be essential to any significant limitations on strategic armaments. Any ABM deployment is likely to stimulate a race in ABM technology, and to make limitations of strategic offensive forces more difficult. In particular, even a very limited ABM deployment would make more difficult drastic reductions in strategic missiles. From this, the desirability of a total prohibition on ABM is apparent, and the Group would hope that an agreement on such a prohibition could be negotiated very quickly. However, negotiation of an agreement limiting ABM to very low levels and limited geographic areas would also be of the greatest importance, especially if it opened the way to early agreement on a total prohibition.

Negotiation of limitations on bomber defences is likely to be much more difficult. That being the case, the best hope of preventing a bomber–anti-bomber arms race would be in the exercise of restraint with respect to construction and reliance on bombers. The Group would urge that in the event of a lessening of reliance on ICBM's for deterrence there not be an effort to compensate for this by increased reliance on bombers, either short or long range.

The preferred reliance on certain components of the "strategic" forces—that appears to be suggested by the above arguments—will appear objectionable to military and other groups that have a vested interest in the preservation, and expansion, of other sectors of the strategic forces. Firm control over all decisions relevant to the strategic postures of the major nuclear powers by the civilian political authorities within them is, therefore, essential if there is to be optimum progress towards arms limitations and disarmament.

The Group recognized that there are a number of military systems with multipurpose capabilities: "tactical" nuclear weapons, aircraft carriers, "tactical" aircraft and shorter range missiles. Some of these can be dealt with in the SALT negotiations, the others in the context of general and complete disarmament and in negotiations on European and other regional security measures.

Despite some complications arising because of the present political and military situation in Europe and in the increase in the number of nuclear powers there are very substantial areas of potential SALT agreements.

While there was a consensus within the Group that the SALT efforts should be encouraged, there were expressions of serious concern.

First, the fact that the SALT negotiations have been in prospect for three years and in progress for almost one has resulted in a diminution of serious arms control efforts in other fora where more nations are represented. In particular, measures that might normally have been considered in the CCD have been put aside in the hope that they would be dealt with in SALT or on the grounds that consideration of them should be deferred pending a SALT agreement.

Second, there is a very real danger in an unproductive prolongation of SALT negotiations, of the major nuclear powers going ahead with weapons programmes, that would otherwise not be undertaken, in the hope of strengthening their bargaining positions. Indeed, this may already have happened.

If no significant agreement is reached in SALT, we could well be worse off than if the negotiations had never been undertaken. Aside from the possible adverse consequences mentioned above, a failure of SALT is likely to result in a worsening of Soviet-American relations, an increase in military influence, a disillusionment on the part of the rest of the world in the sincerity and capability of the superpowers to act responsibly, an adverse impact on the containment of nuclear proliferation, and a long interval before there would again be a prospect for making major progress on arms control and disarmament.

With these considerations in mind, it is of the greatest importance that (1) the SALT negotiations proceed expeditiously; (2) that the United States and the Soviet Union exercise great restraint in acquiring additional strategic systems during the negotiations; and (3) that concurrently with the SALT negotiations, there be vigorous efforts in the CCD and elsewhere to move forward with general and complete disarmament and with other partial measures.

Nuclear Test Ban Treaty
The Partial Test Ban Treaty has greatly reduced atmospheric contamination from nuclear tests, but it has not put an end to the development of nuclear weapons. The rate of nuclear testing has been higher since the Partial Test Ban came into force in 1963 than it was before (an average of 48 reported tests a year compared with 40 previously). Moreover, there has been a continuing trend towards increasing the maximum yield of the weapons being tested underground.

There was consensus within the Group on the fundamental point that the problems of extending the Moscow Treaty to underground testing are essentially political and that the technical problems of verification are not the real stumbling block.

Such difficulties as existed previously in the detection and identification of underground tests have been reduced to such an extent that, in the Group's unanimous opinion, Pugwash is now fully justified in pressing for the immediate negotiation of a ban on tests above a certain threshold as a strict minimum requirement. This would raise no problems of verification, even without on-the-spot observation. The Group was also unanimous

Appendix 27   342

in strongly recommending the adoption, ultimately, of a complete ban on
tests whether or not a foolproof verification system by on-the-spot inspection can be devised and accepted. Such a ban, in the view of the
Group, would not present any risk to the national security of either of
the superpowers.

Excessive claims have been made regarding the importance of nuclear explosions for peaceful purposes. Whatever short-term economic advantage
there may be in the use of such explosions is likely to be more than offset by the risks of nuclear proliferation implicit in such explosions.
If they continue to be permitted, it is quite possible that they will be
conducted by non-nuclear weapons states despite the inclusion in the non-
proliferation treaty of provisions for such explosions to be carried out
by the nuclear weapons powers. Moreover, there is the risk that the weapons technology of the nuclear weapons powers would be advanced as a result of explosions for peaceful purposes. Accordingly, inclusion in a
comprehensive test ban treaty of provisions permitting explosions for
peaceful purposes would seem to be undesirable.

Nuclear Proliferation
The Non-Proliferation Treaty entered into force on March 5, 1970. A number
of technologically advanced non-nuclear weapons countries have not so far
signed, let alone ratified, the treaty. Ratification by the majority of
those 42 non-nuclear-weapons countries which have signed the treaty but
not ratified it yet, depends upon the negotiation of safeguards. The
first phase of the safeguard negotiations at Vienna yielded agreed general
principles to be incorporated into safeguard agreements; and there is
reason to hope that the second phase, concerned with the formulation of
general regulations, and the third phase concerned with the adaptation of
these to individual projects, will yield equally positive results.

While the prospects of the Non-Proliferation Treaty being universally
adopted depend on resolution of the aforementioned safeguards problems
and on progress being made in SALT, other factors of importance are the
development of nuclear armament by China, and the continuing existence of
the British and French deterrent nuclear forces. Whatever the military
relevance of these so-called independent deterrents may be, they provide
an incentive and also a measure of political justification for the aspiration of a certain number of other countries to the acquisition of a nuclear
weapon capability.

Nuclear and Other Weapons of Mass Destruction on the Seabed and the Ocean
Floor and the Subsoil thereof
The Group considered the latest joint draft dated September 1, 1970, tabled
by the U.S. and the U.S.S.R. Some of the ambiguities and inadequacies of
the previous drafts have been removed; but even with these improvements
the draft treaty would be limited in its effect to a ban on the emplanting
or emplacing on the ocean bottom of weapons of mass destruction, as well
as of launching installations or other facilities for storing, testing or
using such weapons. The draft also includes a new article imposing upon
the contracting parties the obligation to continue negotiations for further

measures calculated to prevent an arms race on the seabed, the ocean floor and their subsoil.

Although the majority of the Group was prepared to concede that a treaty on the lines of the present draft might do some good in forestalling the future development and deployment of the prohibited weapons, some members deplored the amount of time and energy which had gone into the preparation of its successive drafts to the detriment of projects deserving of a higher priority. It was, however, agreed that this treaty, as well as another treaty calculated to demilitarize the ocean floor, may contribute not only to disarmament but also to the project of creating an international regime for the exploitation of that part of the wealth of the seabed, the ocean floor and their subsoil, which is in process of being recognized as a common heritage of mankind.

Chemical and Biological Weapons
The Group noted with satisfaction that during the past year the Geneva Protocol of 1925 had been ratified by Japan and Morocco; that ratification by Brazil was a foregone conclusions; and that in August 1970 President Nixon had re-submitted the Protocol to the U.S. Senate for ratification. These four ratifications would bring the total number of parties to the Protocol to almost 90 and these parties would include all the major powers in the world. In the view of the Group it can be forcefully argued that the fundamental prohibitions embodied in the Protocol, even in its present state, qualify as rules of customary international law, binding on all states regardless of ratification; nonetheless, it is desirable that the reservations or interpretations which purport to exclude certain agents from the ambit of the prohibition should be avoided. In this context some members of the Group suggested that the validity or otherwise of certain controversial interpretations (e.g., the U.S. interpretation of the applicability of the Protocol to herbicides and the U.K. position on CS gas) should be submitted through the U.N. General Assembly to the International Court of Justice at the Hague for an advisory opinion.

In the unanimous view of the Group even the universal acceptance of the Geneva Protocol would not reduce the urgent need for an international convention prohibiting not only the use in war but also the development, production and possession of all chemical and bacteriological (biological) weapons. The Group gave careful consideration to the British argument that priority should be given to a convention prohibiting the development, production and possession of bacteriological (biological) weapons under any circumstances, but it took the view that the considerations in support of a single convention prohibiting both bacteriological (biological) and chemical weapons were much weightier.

The Group examined in some detail the various proposals for verification of production and possession made partly in the relevant Soviet and United Kingdom drafts and partly in a number of other documents submitted to CCD. It has taken the view that whereas some system of international verification was inevitably necessary in order to overcome categorical opposition from military authorities, an excessively intrusive system, such as might

Appendix 27   344

endanger agreement on a treaty, was not called for. It was suggested by
some members that a relatively thin system operating with e.g., "challenge
inspections" might be sufficient, by others, that national means alone
would suffice.

There was consensus on the point that pending the entry into force of a
convention prohibiting the development, production and possession of C & B
weapons there should be no procurement in any country of weapons of this
kind.

The Group agreed that every encouragement should be given to unilateral
disarmament in this field.

Secrecy should be eliminated even from defensive bacteriological (biological) research, and the Pugwash Symposium on rapid detection and identification of biological agents, to be held in Switzerland early in 1971,
should contribute significantly to this end.

The Group attached great importance to SIPRI's programme of feasibility
studies and experiments in the field of verifying the observance of agreed
prohibitions relating to C & B weapons, and noted with satisfaction that
U.S. and Soviet scientists will participate in the planning and evaluation
of these studies and experiments.

The Group recommended that when chemical agents or weapons are disposed of,
the most careful measures should be taken to avoid contamination of the environment; and that the fullest international consultation and co-operation
should take place if the effect of disposal might affect foreign countries.

4.   INTERNATIONAL CO-OPERATION IN SCIENCE AND TECHNOLOGY

1. Co-operation to Preserve and Maintain the Integrity of the Environment
Recent years have seen wide public recognition of the dangers of severe and
irreparable damage to the ecological balance of man's habitat on earth, not
merely on a local but potentially on a planetary scale arising from

(a) the explosive growth of human population;

(b) the reckless and wasteful use of scarce material resources;

(c) the polluting effects of modern industrial processes on a vast scale.

We recognize that, while some expression of such concern may be exaggerated, real and urgent dangers exist.

The Working Group began by agreeing that efforts should be directed not to
stabilizing the environment, since it would be neither possible nor desirable to arrest the process of technological development on earth, but to
preventing widespread irreversible changes from occurring in the plasticity
of the biosphere. The aim should be to preserve the variety and resilience
of the various ecological regimes and the ability of the habitat to recover

from the ecological insults inevitably offered to it by the manifold technological and industrial activities of man in which the use of fertilizers and pesticides should be included.

It must be recognized that any effort to maintain the integrity of man's environment will necessarily involve considerable expenditures of resources, not only of technical skills but also of energy. The value of such efforts compared to their costs may, therefore, present very different aspects to developed and to developing societies, and it is recognized that whilst development is in itself an improvement in the human environment, in some areas where the motives are largely aesthetic, environmental conservation may be a luxury that some non-industrialized countries cannot at present afford. Nevertheless, the need to safeguard our habitat for future generations is shared by all mankind, and since the problem is essentially indivisible, its solution calls for universal collaboration in which no doubt the richer communities will have to be prepared to shoulder a substantial proportion of the cost. Some statements of interest at the U.N. and other international fora have paid lip service to this necessity without always resulting in positive action.

Our present situation may be regarded as a transition phase between two limiting cases. On the one hand, the activities of stone-age men offered relatively slight perturbation of his habitat, from which it was capable of recovering fully. On the other hand, another type of stable and balanced habitat might in future be created in a controlled technological environment in which all resources are so far as possible conserved and re-cycled for future use. The concept of Spaceship Earth in which all resources would eventually be conserved and controlled might be regarded a limiting state towards which mankind may aspire. The present situation represents a difficult phase of transition in which the rates of wastage and pollution exceed the capacity of the biosphere to repair. Grave risks of irreversible damage to man's environment will persist until these deleterious processes are brought under control.

Unfortunately, ecology is still an infant science and the extremely complex processes involved are at present scarcely understood. All too frequently science policy encourages research toward immediate economic benefits, and neglects the long-term gains to be derived from basic research into the fundamental processes of nature. The solution of the problems of environmental control will undoubtedly involve an enormous research effort, not only in the field of ecology but also in the economic sciences in relation to the question of so-called "external costs" and disutilities, which might be felt to fall outside the present competence of Pugwash. It may be envisaged that in the long term research will have to be directed to:

(a) regulating the incidence of external monetary costs and external non-monetary disutilities arising out of industrial and agricultural practices; and also

(b) sharing by all peoples in the regulation of the use of limited fishery and forest resources on a global basis.

Appendix 27 346

Additions may be needed to international law comparable to the Test Ban Treaty or to existing international fisheries agreements.

The problem is many-sided, therefore, having social, economic and legal aspects outside the competence of the Working Group. On the purely technical side, however, we wish to emphasize that the following measures should be implemented as a matter of urgency.

(a) Basic ecological research should be strengthened on the basis of international collaboration not only of the institutional kind foreshadowed, for example, at the International Centre of Insect Physiology and Ecology at Nairobi, but also on the level of individual and institutional exchanges.

(b) There is an urgent need for continuous international collaboration in the task of forming independent estimates of scarce resources on a global scale--including sources of energy, of materials, of fresh water, and fertility levels, both terrestrial and marine.

Appropriate specialized agencies of the U.N. should also be charged with the duty of estimating and projecting levels of demands for these resources in relation to developing patterns of economic growth in various parts of the world. In addition, they should keep under review and make recommendations concerning levels of efficiency in utilization of these resources with a view to discouraging wasteful practices, on the one hand, and encouraging economy in recycling waste and fully utilizing by-products, on the other hand. Prevention is better than cure.

In this connection, the information and data retrieval system (technical and scientific, economic and social) should, as was recommended in the U.N. report on "The Capacity of the U.N. Development System," be so organized that its component parts would be mutually compatible and that it can be integrated into a future world-wide system.

(c) The creation of an international commission--or its equivalent--to link the ongoing work of the ICSU Special Committee on the problems of the environment with that of the U.N. agencies in reviewing, not only hazards to human health and genotype, but also hazards to the viability of the habitat, and to recommend minimal standards in relation to biological, chemical and radioactive contamination of the environment. Attention should also be paid to noise pollution, particularly in relation to the proposed development of supersonic transport aircraft.

(d) The development of an international network of environmental monitoring stations to report continuously on a global basis on the state of the atmospheric, terrestrial and marine environments, including:

(i) the gaseous and particulate compositions of the air, together with observations of secular changes in the albedo, cloudiness, turbidity and circulation patterns of the earth's atmosphere;

(ii) the chemical and particulate composition of the oceans and inland seas and on ecological changes in these waters, whether these changes be due to surface oil, or chemical or thermal pollution, or to biological waste;

(iii) the pollution of soil and underground waters throughout the world by pesticides, toxic wastes and other products of human activity, and also soil erosion, in particular relating to the fertility of both cultivated and uncultivated land and the potability of freshwater supplies; and

(iv) to provide an early warning system on adverse health and ecological effects.

(e) The creation after appropriate research and discussion, of a mechanism through which, once a serious level of environmental damage is established or (better) foreseen, actions can be proposed to remove the causes and ameliorate the damage.

In this connection attention is drawn to the possibility of using satellite monitoring devices on the one hand, and on the other hand to use new techniques of assaying micro-organisms as indicators of changes in biological niches.

With reference to levels of man-made radioactivity, it was suggested that Pugwash could set up an international and independent group of specialists in relevant disciplines to assess and interpret the physical and biological data on this problem being collated by UNSCEAR and ICRP. This group could also be instrumental in studying the possibility of a reduction to 10% of the planned radioactivity release limits in the nuclear power industry, and should consider the question of power reactor siting and the rate of development of the nuclear power programme in the light of its interpretation of available data.

2. International Scientific Co-operation

The Working Group then turned its attention to the promotion of international co-operation in science and technology.

The number, variety, importance and scope of international co-operative ventures expand continuously. If Pugwash is to make a unique contribution in this field (as it has in the development of the concepts underlying the International Science Foundation and the International Centre of Insect Physiology and Ecology) it seems essential that:

(a) Pugwash should have a small standing group of regular participants interested in international co-operation to provide a memory and continuity for Pugwash efforts in this field, and that

(b) the international co-operation group should be linked systematically with the other elements of Pugwash (arms control, international security, and most importantly, development) because international co-operation is an abstract concept that becomes operative only in specific concrete situations.

Future Pugwash Conferences may well wish to avoid consideration of international co-operation in the abstract, in favour of a closer analysis of how Pugwash can facilitate the development of new strategies and mechanisms for co-operation using concrete cases and stimulate fresh initiatives.

As a concrete proposal we suggest that the following step be taken:

An *ad hoc* international co-operation committee of correspondence be formed. Besides the standing members, the group should have at its disposal a number of associated members to provide by correspondence materials concerning individual disciplines. The committee of correspondence should serve as a collecting and collating body, to prepare a comprehensive report for each Pugwash Conference, with a view of recommending positive international collaborative projects on a disciplinary or interdisciplinary basis.

3. The Role of Pugwash in Promoting International Co-operation

For years Pugwash scientists have viewed international co-operation in research and teaching not only as valuable in itself, but also as a means of improving the relationships between nations and promoting development. This view has led to a series of proposals to create specific centres or organizations, some regional and others global. Among these are ICIPE in Nairobi, SIPRI in Stockholm, and the proposed International Science Foundation, whose origins may be traced back to earlier Pugwash proposals.

Reviewing this situation, the Group tried to define the conditions under which new programmes for international scientific co-operation would have the best chances of success in terms of such different criteria as: (a) the advancement of the disciplines they serve; (b) the educational functions they perform; (c) their roles as integrating or divisive factors among the countries or regions they serve; (d) any responsibility they might bear toward developing countries. It was agreed that effective co-operation can often best be based on existing universities and research institutions which individually or in groups can promote joint research and training programmes. Success obviously requires a high professional standard in the area chosen, but also the political will to share costs and facilities. Among factors influencing the willingness of governments to invest research resources, whether of men or money, in an international organization, will be the benefits accruing to the participating countries, both in terms of scientific or technological results and, in some cases (such as CERN or ESRO), in terms of industrial contracts.

The Group felt that the creation of new international scientific centres or organizations is not advisable unless a feasible objective can be clearly seen which is sufficiently challenging to attract good scientists, and which would be difficult or impossible to achieve within or between existing universities or research institutions. It was also realized, however, that international programmes largely involving routine monitoring of the environment (such as we advocated above) would not be likely to succeed unless it were given such a research content as would attract gifted research workers.

4. Population Growth and Human Reproduction

The very rapid increase in population throughout the world involves profound effects on human society, and these will become increasingly serious during the next several decades. It is clear that unless intensive analyses and efforts are greatly augmented in the near future, critical situations will arise in many areas of the world that will affect the health and well-being of thousands of millions of people, not to speak of the social instability and threat to world peace that will result.

There are many facets to the problem which must be attacked simultaneously because of their interlocking nature. Previous Pugwash meetings have stressed the necessity of giving first priority to the need for increasing food production--both natural and synthetic. Great differences exist between cultural and national needs and values, and population regulation must at present remain the choice of individuals in a particular cultural setting. Motivations vary widely, and unless there is a clear understanding among peoples and their leaders of choices and consequences with respect to population growth in particular contexts, as well as in relation to the world as a whole, motivation--the necessary basis of influencing individual and social practices--will probably not be modified to any great degree. Motivation itself, and the means of changing it, is a poorly understood factor and much more research is required in this field.

Experience to date has shown that economic improvement has an appreciable impact on lowering the rate of population growth, and in many instances provides the single most rapid and effective condition for slowing population increase.

These are complex considerations and the Working Group could only touch briefly upon them. Two technical aspects of the problems, however, were given particular attention. These concerned the need to expand considerably research and development of more adequate contraceptive devices, and research on the biology of human reproduction.

These two sets of problems, and their potential solutions vary for different regions and cultures. It is suggested that Pugwash, in consultation with WHO, could usefully promote specific studies to determine, firstly which population regulation devices and procedures would be acceptable to particular regions and groups, and secondly to help mount the necessary scientific research and development aimed to meet these needs. Since there is usually a lapse of 10 to 15 years with present practices from the start of research and development to the application of new birth-regulation procedures, and the procedures at present available are markedly inadequate, it is urgent that greatly augmented research efforts, funds and international co-operative effort be undertaken as soon as possible in these and other areas so that the problem of population growth might be dealt with more effectively, hopefully in the near future, but especially towards the latter part of this century, when the problem will inevitably have assumed even more serious proportions.

5. Education for a Changing World

One of the most outstanding characteristics of our times is the rate of change now imposed upon all human society by the exponentially rising increase of science and technology. Education must change with equal rapidity, or it cannot aid our youth to live in such a world and to adjust to such incredible changes.

Science education must include the study of science as a social process, resulting in our altered human circumstances, and must be extended to everyone. For such education neither the natural scientist nor the social scientist can properly function alone. For example, the problems of pollution or other challenges to a healthful environment require both scientific and social analysis and remedy.

The effective collaboration of teams of one natural and one social scientist in the development of teaching materials and courses suggests that the Pugwash Conferences could well initiate teams of natural and social scientists representing different political and social systems or different degrees of economic and industrial development.

The Group noted, however, that international programmes which include studies of the sociological or economic aspects of the impact of science and technology on society may be biased by ideological considerations. It was realized that an unbiased and analytical approach to such problems is often difficult and that it is particularly important that studies in these and similar areas remain objective.

In addition, we should at long last, as a tribute to C. F. Powell, hold the four Pugwash science education conferences recommended by him and others at the London Pugwash Conference in 1962, on the following subjects:

(1) education and human ecology;

(2) the evolution of education;

(3) education for society; and

(4) education and world development.

5. SCIENCE, TECHNOLOGY, AND DEVELOPMENT

1. Preamble

The Group is convinced that the economic and social development of the poor countries is one of the most important problems of our time.

We deplore the decrease in the development* effort of most developed nations, right through the U.N. "Development Decade" and welcome the steps

---

*Except where it is used in the obvious context of R & D, the word "development" in the Report refers to the development of the poorer countries of the world.

taken by Canada to raise substantially its contribution to development
and, in particular, to stimulate and support scientific research and development in areas relevant to the development of the poorer countries.
We hope that this example will be followed by other nations. We heard
with dismay that, according to available U.N. statistical data, only 2
percent of the total research and development effort in the world is at
present devoted to development problems.

While social, cultural, political, and economic considerations are of key
importance for development, we believe that natural scientists and technologists can and must make a substantial contribution towards the solution of the problems standing in the way of economic and human progress.
We welcome the plan, discussed in section 5 below, to stimulate the thinking and action of scientists all over the world in the area of development
by creating an association of "scientists for development" and believe that
this effort deserves the full support of the Pugwash Movement. The success
of this effort requires that scientists display as much objectivity, dedication and unity of purpose in tackling development problems, as they have
done in the furtherance of their own professional interests, both within
and across national frontiers. It also requires them to seek collaboration
with social scientists, humanists and others in a unified, multidisciplinary effort of wide proportions.

2. The Goals and Strategy of Development

The question was raised in the Working Group as to the general definition,
aims and strategy of development. The Group recognized the virtual impossibility of arriving at any generally acceptable definition. It also recognized that in such a task scientists had no __special__ competence by virtue
of their training. The Group felt, nevertheless, that in thinking about
science and technology as a means to further the developmental process,
there was need to have a general philosophical framework within which to
work. A question raised in this connection was whether this was not the
appropriate time for the developing countries to examine the qualitative
and quantitative aspects of their development strategy. Such timeliness,
it was felt, arose from two considerations; firstly, the fact that we are
now more aware of the fundamentally different social, economic and political predicament from which the poor countries of today are trying to advance, and secondly, the environmental and spiritual crisis apparent in
the highly industrialized countries. It was suggested that it would be
proper for Pugwash to initiate, in collaboration with concerned social
and political scientists, a panel or symposium dealing with the quantitative aims and desirable levels and directions of advance, for both the
more and the less developed countries.

While there was partial agreement that development is far more complex than
"mere" economic growth, little agreement could be reached in the Group on
its precise nature and aims. Three views, it was felt, merited further
consideration. A first suggestion was that development was primarily an
augmentation of all those resources—natural, human, mechanical—which are
scarce in a given society and which, therefore, constrain its advance.
Attention was focused on the fact that maximal exploitation of the total

Appendix 27

resources of a society included satisfaction of "rational," material, and of "value-derived" preferences. A second point of view focused on "real" political, economic and cultural independence of a society, implying its ability of working with more affluent nations on the basis of mutual respect and understanding. A third suggestion was couched in more ethical terms, and stressed as the primary development goal the acquisition of freedom and justice by all the individuals in the society. The Group was, however, reminded by several participants that in many developing countries the immediate provision of minimum physical needs must have absolute priority. The concern of scientists must be not only with the ultimate goals of development, but, most urgently, with its immediate needs.

3. Contributions which Science and Technology Can Make to Development

The Group considered at considerable length how scientists could contribute most effectively to development. The Group agreed on the necessity of promoting the scientific and technological capacities of a developing society by improving and spreading education and research. Some members suggested that the resulting development of an infrastructure would by itself serve not only to generate a "microclimate" conducive to the promotion of science as such, but also to support its application to economic and social needs. Others stressed the danger of creating "outward-looking" scientific communities oriented from the socio-economic goals of the developing country and looking to the scientific communities of the world for topics of their research and recognition of their work.

The creation of scientific and technological infrastructures should be used to link scientific communities of different nations with one another. It should enable decision-makers to call on a body of specialists able to make meaningful technical judgments on task-oriented ventures, such as industrial, agricultural and medical projects.

It was suggested that structures should be developed which would give stimulation and provide recognition for research in development areas, both for indigenous scientists and for scientists from developed countries, devoting several years of their careers to problems of development, at home or in developing countries.

4. The Contribution of Pugwash

In considering how Pugwash could contribute to development, the Group felt that one question to ask is: what is unique about Pugwash? A welter of organizations exists, both national and international, governmental, intergovernmental and private, concerned either with development, with science or technology, or their application to development. The uniqueness of Pugwash consists in a combination of characteristics. It is widely interdisciplinary (though primarily scientific), broadly international, fiercely individualistic, and, we may say, indelicate. Few private organizations include members from such a broad range of disciplines, and from so many countries, both East and West and North and South. Few official national or international organizations have such tenuous ties to governments, or such a tendency to talk freely even on delicate and sensitive subjects. The Working Group discussed at length a summary of the discussion at the

Pugwash Symposium on "Science and Development--What can scientists do about it?" held on September 1-4, 1970 at Stanford, California, outlining the character and purposes of Pugwash involvement in the development area. This was accepted by the Working Group as the basis of plans for future activities.

In the light of the above propositions concerning the unique characteristics of Pugwash the Group felt that Pugwash could attempt:

1. To propose and develop new ideas for international and regional scientific and technical institutions, as exemplified by the International Science Foundation and the International Centre of Insect Physiology and Ecology in Nairobi, both initiated at Pugwash and now in development or active discussion in broader scientific circles. Among such proposals may be the creation of an international Technical and Scientific Volunteer Corps; establishment of an international Institute of Development Sciences; introduction of development curricula in universities; the creation of clearing organizations for directing the study and research of students from developing countries, in educational institutions in developed countries or in developing countries other than their own, towards preparation for development-oriented education and research work at home.

2. To increase the understanding among scientists and the general public of the problems of development, and enhance the exchange of ideas and experiences among representatives of different cultures and of different economic systems. It was agreed in this connection that much more significant contributions could be made if representatives of China and Cuba could be involved.

3. To stimulate the study from different viewpoints of questions, such as the long-range impact of the present unprecedented increase in life expectancy in most less-developed countries. Other subjects for such study are adverse consequences on development of military expenditures in both the more and the less developed countries; comparative experiences of different countries in urbanization; and problems of labour-intensive technology. The inter-relationships among rapid population growth, employment and under-employment, agricultural evolution, electric power development, trade, transportation, and access to resources, exemplified by the situation in the Ganga-Brahmaputra Basin, and the effects of synthetic primary products on development of countries whose economy depends on the export of corresponding natural products, are possible examples.

4. To foster co-operative research on development problems by scientists and technologists from the more and the less developed countries, particularly the younger ones, as well as co-operation among scientists from different less developed countries to exchange information on their experiences in promoting science and technology and applying them to development.

5. To help develop a climate of opinion among scientists and the general public, both national and international, in support of a higher level of

Appendix 27   354

government commitment to:

(a) a large increase in the magnitude of capital and technical assistance from the developed countries to the developing ones; and

(b) the allocation of a part of the R and D resources of the developed countries to work in their own institutions on the problems of development.

6. To help in moulding opinion in both the scientific community and the general population of developing countries against the diversion of scarce material resources to unproductive purposes, in particular, to armaments.

7. To help in the application of new methods of assessment in appraising the social and economic benefits and costs of the use of different technologies in the developing countries, and of the wide consequences of construction of large projects--for example, dams for electric power generation and water storage.

8. To help develop standards for international scientific behaviour, in which equal co-operation and self-disciplined restraint would replace what has been described as "scientific colonialism." In this spirit, Pugwash could also study and make suggestions concerning fields of science and technology which should be fostered in the developing countries. Environmental sciences--meteorology, oceanography, geology, geophysics, geochemistry, hydrology, ecology, forestry and their associated technologies of weather forecasting, fisheries, natural resources development, forest industries, and environmental protection--are examples of such development-related scientific areas.

9. To organize "travelling symposia" on scientific and technical problems related to development which could give stimulus and support to scientific and technical communities in several countries.

10. To promote the revision, among educational institutions, scientific societies and individual senior scientists, in both developed and developing countries, of currently accepted incentives and rewards in favour of research and teaching in developing countries and on topics of importance for development.

11. To evaluate the efforts of the United Nations and its family of specialized agencies and other multilateral institutions, related to the advancement of science, technology and economy in developing nations, and perhaps also in the wider area of assistance to science and technology.

12. To help to develop better understanding between younger and older generations, in recognition that the concern of young people over existing conditions, and their search for better solutions to the problems of poverty and inequality on the national and international scales, is also a concern of the scientific communities, aware of the need to direct the powers given to man by science and technology towards benevolent objectives, particularly the satisfaction of human needs.

13. To help study the possibility of suggesting that governments of developed countries allow university graduates to carry out duties in developing countries in substitution for military service, as is practised by France. In conjunction with this, the panel should study how young men with little experience but much interest in working in developing countries might form a useful "International Science Corps."

5. Future Organizations and Activities

At the Ronneby, Nice, and Sochi Conferences, working groups on science and development expressed concern about the lack of continuity, of adequate preparation for discussions, and of follow-up action, in respect of Pugwash's important and useful recommendations.

The Group felt that the problems raised could best be tackled by the setting up of a Study Group on Science and Development within the Pugwash Movement. The task of the Study Group will include preparation of material for discussions at the Annual Conferences, organization of Symposia, and setting up of panels to consider specific problems in greater depth than is feasible in short conferences.

The Group has compiled a list of topics to which the Study Group could turn its early attention. Among ones considered particularly urgent were:

(a) A panel on ways of increasing the viability of natural product industries likely to be threatened by the development of synthetics.

(b) A travelling symposium on the search for new and more suitable contraceptive procedures for specific developing countries.

(c) Collaboration with the group engaged in preparing an appeal to scientists to organize an Association of "Scientists for Development." The Group endorsed in principle the views expressed in the Draft of a Manifesto prepared by this group (see Appendix). It felt, however, that reference to a specific institution (ISF) and appeals for contributions to it should be omitted.

The Group was informed of the plans of Working Group 4 (on International Co-operation) to establish an *ad hoc* Committee of Correspondence. In view of the common interest of this Group with that of the Study Group on Science and Development, it was recommended that close co-operation be established, possibly in the form of some overlapping membership.

The report of the Symposium on Protein Deficiency, organized by the F.G.R. Pugwash Group*, was received with great interest. The Working Group urges the Continuing Committee to support rapid implementation of the recommendations of this Symposium.

The Working Group avoided in its report duplication of recommendations made by Working Group 4, whose scope overlapped in part with its own.

---
*Pugwash Newsletter, vol. 8, p. 3-17, 1970.

However, the Group wishes to emphasize the special appropriateness of the recommendation that substantial co-ordination with the U.N. Stockholm Conference on the Human Environment is desirable since the subject is so closely interwoven with development.

APPENDIX

Manifesto--Drafted by Buzzati Traverso and Abdus Salam

We live in an age in which the development of countries--human, social and economic--is closely correlated with their strength in science and technology. Indeed, the influence of science and technology on a country's development has become so great that the gap between the rich and the poor countries is actually increasing.

This widening disparity between the wealthy and the impoverished nations has become a matter of the utmost concern, since in the long run, political stability, economic equilibrium and the fulfilment of human aspirations on a global scale cannot be achieved until this gap is substantially reduced. And it should be self-evident that science and its applications must become the chief instrument for achieving a balanced human and economic development of countries of the third world, through the realization of their human potentialities and increased productivity from their available resources.

The dimensions of the problems at hand--70 percent of the world's population live in the developing countries, while 86 percent of the world's intelligentsia and production are to be found in the industrialized countries--represent one of the major challenges of today.

The concern and the contributions of the world scientific community to meet such a challenge have so far been sporadic and limited. At a time when the thinkers of the world are faced with the problems of the misuse of science and its products--which is bringing about a panic-stricken flight from reason--the world scientific community should stand united in reasserting its confidence in the scientific approach to solve the major problems confronting mankind and to concentrate our efforts to help the growth of the countries that have recently become independent.

We summon you, individual scientists and scientific academies and societies, to join us in the establishment of the world-wide movement "Scientists for development" (or "Scientists for human development"), the purpose of which is the mobilization of the world's intellectual-scientific potential for meeting the challenge created by the present world situation.

We think that, united, we could effectively lighten the task ahead of us in several ways:

- by devoting an appreciable part of our thoughts and abilities to the study of the innumerable problems facing the developing countries--and subsequently proposing solutions to those problems;

- by reasserting at the international and national levels the need for a scientific, i.e., rational and detached, approach in the attempt to solve not only strictly scientific problems but also those at stake--internationally and nationally--in political, social and economic circles. workers in the developing nations;

- by reasserting at the international and national levels the need for a scientific, i.e., rational and detached, approach in the attempt to solve not only strictly scientific problems but also those at stake--internationally and nationally--in political, social and economic circles.

Participants

Argentina
Dr. C. M. Varsavsky

Belgium
Prof. R. Leclercq

Bulgaria
Acad. A. T. Balevski, Acad. K. Bratanov, Acad. G. Nadjakov

Canada
Mr. E. L. M. Burns, Mr. J. W. Holmes

Czechoslovakia
Acad. K. Šiška, Acad. V. Zoubek

Denmark
Mr. A. Boserup, Prof. O. Maaløe

Federal German Republic
Dr. U. Albrecht, Prof. H. Glubrecht

Finland
Prof. J. K. Miettinen

France
Mr. E. Bauer, Dr. B. Laponche, Dr. H. Marcovich, Prof. F. Perrin

German Democratic Republic
Prof. H. Kröger, Prof. H. Wünsche

Ghana
Prof. F. G. Torto

Hungary
Prof. F. Csáki, Acad. M. Szabolcsi

India
Prof. S. Bhagavantam, Mr. A. Parthasarathi, Prof. V. A. Sarabhai

Appendix 27   358

Indonesia
Dr. S. Soedjatmoko

Israel
Mr. S. Freier, Prof. S. Friedlander, Prof. A. Keynan

Italy
Prof. F. Calogero, Prof. G. Giacometti, Dr. A. Pascolini

Japan
Prof. Y. Sakamoto, Prof. S. Sawada, Prof. T. Toyoda

Kenya
Prof. T. R. Odhiambo

Netherlands
Dr. P. Boskma, Dr. A. van der Woude

Nigeria
Dr. O. J. Fagbemi

Norway
Mr. A. Eide, Prof. T. Forland

Poland
Mr. B. Lewandowski, Dr. J. Šach, Prof. M. Śmialowski

Romania
Prof. C. Penescu

Senegal
Dr. B. Faye

Sweden
Prof. H. Alfvén, Mr. B. E. Eriksson

Switzerland
Prof. C. Dominicé

U.A.R.
Dr. N. A. H. Eissa, Prof. F. A. El Bedewi, Prof. M. M. Mahfouz

U.K.
Lady Jackson, Prof. Patricia J. Lindop, Prof. A. Martin, Mr. P. Noel-Baker
Prof. Sir Rudolf Peierls, Mr. A. de Reuck, Prof. J. Rotblat

U.S.A.
Prof. H. Brown, Mr. G. Bunn, Prof. C. Djerassi, Prof. P. Doty, Prof. B. T.
Feld, Prof. H. B. Glass, Mr. K. R. Hansen, Dr. G. B. Kistiakowsky,
Prof. F. A. Long, Prof. M. Meselson, Prof. S. Muller, Prof. W. R. Polk,
Prof. E. Rabinowitch, Dr. V. Rabinowitch, Prof. G. W. Rathjens,

U.S.A. (Continued)
Prof. R. Revelle, Prof. T. W. Schultz, Prof. M. D. Shulman, Mr. W. Swartz, Mr. W. M. Todd, Prof. S. Weinberg, Dr. R. R. Wilson, Mr. J. Voss

U.S.S.R.
Prof. G. A. Arbatov, Acad. L. A. Artsimovitch, Prof. V. S. Emelyanov, Acad. V. A. Engelhardt, Prof. A. N. Ermakov, Dr. Ludmila Gvishiani, Dr. V. F. Kuleshov, Acad. M. D. Millionshchikov, Mr. I. G. Pochitalin, Dr. E. M. Primakov, Acad. O. Reutov, Dr. I. A. Sokolov

Yugoslavia
Mr. L. Mates, Dr. M. Sahovic, Acad. I. Supek

Observers

FAO
Mr. R. Aubrac

SIPRI
Mr. R. Neild, Mr. T. Nemec

U.N.
Dr. R. G. Björnerstedt, Dr. R. C. Desai, Prof. Z. Kutakov, Mr. J. A. Mussard

UNESCO
Prof. I. Malecki

WHO
Dr. M. M. Kaplan

Science Writers
Mr. T. A. Kolesnichenko (U.S.S.R.)
Mr. N. M. L. Wade (U.K.)

Students
A-W. I. Allam (U.A.R.)
M. Ansari (Iran)
P. C. Bloch (U.S.A.)
G. Da F. C. Branco (Portugal)
Anne Cahn (U.S.A.)
P. Conway (U.S.A.)
J. C. Davis (U.S.A.)
D. Djerassi (U.S.A.)
Elizabeth Feld (U.S.A.)
J. R. Fjellander (Sweden)
T. Greenwood (Canada)
R. L. Hagengruber (U.S.A.)
A. Hammond (U.S.A.)
B. H. Hardy (U.S.A.)
F. M. Macaranas (Philippines)

Appendix 27

Students (Continued)
J. L. P. de Melo (Brazil)
B. Parekh (India)
C. Plougonven (Netherlands)
M. Rosenthal (U.S.A.)
T. Schaich (U.S.A.)
G. R. Stephenson (U.S.A.)
R. Swartz (U.S.A.)
J. Timbie (U.S.A.)
B. Walton (U.S.A.)

STATEMENT FROM THE CONTINUING COMMITTEE ON THE TWENTY-FIRST PUGWASH CONFERENCE, HELD IN SINAIA, AUGUST 26-31, 1971

The Twenty-first Pugwash Conference on Science and World Affairs was held in Sinaia from the 26th to 31st August 1971, at the invitation of the Romanian Pugwash National Committee.

The Conference was attended by 97 scientists from 31 countries; in addition there were 9 observers from 5 international organizations.

The theme of the Conference was "Problems of World Security, Environment, and Development," and under this title participants discussed the following topics in five Working Groups: (1) European Security Problems, (2) Current Conflicts, (3) International Security and Further Steps towards Disarmament, (4) Environmental Pollution, (5) Economic and Technological Co-operation amongst Nations, in particular for Development.

The reports of the Working Groups were presented and discussed at plenary sessions of the Conference. The statement that follows has been prepared by the Continuing Committee on the basis of these reports.

In addition, there were plenary sessions on "Water Pollution," "General Consequences of the Green Revolution," and on "The Human Problems of East Pakistan and the Refugees." Taking into account the views expressed at this last session the Continuing Committee issued an appeal which is appended.

1. European Security Problems

It was felt that the time was now favourable for taking practical political steps towards an All-European Conference on Security and Co-operation on a multilateral basis and along the lines on which the Finnish Government has been working. This conviction was largely based on recent events—particularly the effects on the political climate of the treaties of the Federal German Republic with the U.S.S.R. and with Poland, the talks between the two German states and the agreements reached on the West Berlin question. These events underline the urgency of admitting the G.D.R. and the F.G.R. to the U.N., establishing normal diplomatic relations between the G.D.R. and all European states, and normal international relations between the two German states. The apparent and growing public desire for holding a European Security Conference was also noted.

Some members felt that the objectives of the desired European Security Conference (ESC) should be further clarified to avoid overloading its agenda, and to guard against the ESC resulting in a consolidation and not a loosening of the power blocs. It was agreed, however, to urge the convocation of such a Conference without preconditions. It now seems to be generally accepted to hold this Conference in Helsinki and to invite all European states plus the U.S.A. and Canada.

The prime objective of the ESC would be to negotiate an agreement between all member states under which:

Appendix 28   362

1. All states in Europe agree to conduct their relations according to the following principles:

(a) renunciation of the use or threat of force for the settlement of disputes, and acceptances of the obligation to settle all such disputes by peaceful means;

(b) non-interference in the internal affairs of any state, and express recognition of the right of any state to choose without external interference its own social and political system;

(c) recognition of the inviolability of existing borders and renunciation of territorial claims.

2. Steps would be taken to encourage co-operation on an equal basis between the European states in the field of trade, economics, science, technology, culture, information and travel aiming at the development of further political co-operation between the states.

3. There would be established a standing body or agency aiming at the development of further political co-operation between the states, which would provide, amongst other things, means for the peaceful settlement of disputes.

Considerable optimism was expressed regarding an early settlement of the following outstanding matters: (a) the ratification and implementation of the treaties between the F.G.R. and the U.S.S.R. and the F.G.R. and the People's Republic of Poland; (b) further steps towards the settlement of the West Berlin question on the basis of the recent agreement between the ambassadors, and (c) the recognition of the invalidity of the Munich agreement of 1938 from the start.

Beyond these steps progress may be expected in the following areas:

(a) On the problem of security the long term goal must be to eliminate military blocs and alliances in Europe and to create an effective security system. Towards this goal, the following steps ought to be taken: a drastic reduction of nuclear and conventional forces without unilateral advantages—possibly accompanied by the establishment of nuclear-free zones; to be followed by the dissolution of the international military organizations of the blocs, the elimination of the remaining forces, bases, armaments and military manoeuvres on foreign soil. It was generally felt that conditions are ripe for dismantling the military build-up in Europe. The obsolescence of the views based on the balance of terror was stressed.

(b) Europe's contribution to world economic and technological progress could be greatly increased by all-European co-operation which would assist in eliminating the technological gap between the U.S.A. and some European countries. A new institutional framework should be developed to facilitate co-operation in this area. Restrictions on trade in Europe, originating from the "cold war" situation should be eliminated, and the system of economic exchange between East and West Europe should be modernized through encouraging industrial and technological co-operation.

(c) It was felt that there is a primary need for International Agreements to permit effective measures to be taken against many forms of pollution.

(d) It was stressed that non-governmental forums, on a broad basis, for discussions of European security and co-operation would be desirable.

2. Current Conflicts

In the second Working Group some current conflicts were discussed. On Indochina they confirmed previous statements urging the withdrawal of all U.S.A. troops, and an end to the war rather than its "Vietnamization." It was noted that there had been a reduction in American ground forces, but the Group deplored the continued intense bombing. It was felt that the seven-points proposals submitted to the Paris Peace Talks by the Provisional Revolutionary Government of South Vietnam constitute a new positive element; it was urged that they be taken seriously.

The Group also endorsed the suggestion by the International Peace Research Institute, Oslo, that an international and inter-disciplinary group should make a study of the history and causes of the war in Indochina.

On the Middle East, it was noted that four years after the resolution by the Security Council, which was aimed at securing a just and lasting peace in the area, the conflict continues and while, fortunately, the parties continue to observe a cease-fire, the situation remains highly explosive. The Group appreciated the fact that Egypt made a proposal to re-open the Suez Canal to free navigation by all nations, including Israel, following a partial withdrawal of the Israeli troops in the region, and welcomed the fact that Israel accepted the principle of an interim arrangement for the re-opening of the canal. It urged that the remaining gap be closed in the direction of a speedy and full implementation of the Security Council resolution referred to. The Group drew attention to the Palestine refugee problem which the violent events in Jordan in 1971 had shown to be not only a tragic humanitarian problem, but also a threat to peace. The settlement of this problem must be regarded by all nations as a matter of high priority.

On the problem of Korea, the Group discussed the danger of a renewed arms conflict. It has been officially stated that foreign troops have been withdrawn from North Korea, and many members felt therefore that all foreign troops should be withdrawn from South Korea; but this view was not endorsed by all.

Twenty-five years after the Nürnberg Trials, crimes against humanity and war crimes are still being committed in many areas and often on a large scale, including mass murder and torture of civilians and of prisoners of war. Since most of these crimes remained unpunished, many members of the Group supported the idea of an International Criminal Court, under U.N. auspices, to try war crimes and crimes against humanity.

Appendix 28   364

3. International Security and Further Steps Towards Disarmament

Because of the importance of progress in disarmament and of the complexity of many of the issues, we have felt it appropriate to present the arguments on these issues in greater detail than we have done for some of the other Groups.

The past year has seen some positive developments--an encouraging statement by the U.S.S.R. and the U.S.A. on the further programme of SALT talks and the successful elaboration of a draft treaty banning Biological Weapons (BW). But the arms race continues to outpace by far the progress in arms limitation and disarmament.

There is an urgent need for measures, partial or general, which will be more effective than those taken hitherto in slowing down the arms race and achieving disarmament.

The Group's considerations reflected its agenda, with emphasis on the limitation and elimination of mass destruction weapons. The discussants were fully aware, however, of the dangers inherent in the conventional arms race, the existence of military blocs not only in Europe but also in other parts of the world, arms traffic, etc. and considered it important that due attention be paid to all these problems.

1. Matters Related to SALT. It is hoped that the SALT Conference will bring some significant results before the end of this year. Prompt and substantial results in this area are a pre-requisite for progress in other areas of disarmament, especially the further expansion in the number of adherents to the NPT and its effectiveness. Such progress will also have beneficial effects on other disarmament measures, such as on European Security, limitations of conventional forces and weapons, and other measures leading towards the final goal of general and complete disarmament.

Specifically, the negotiating parties at SALT are urged to achieve an agreement which would severely limit the deployment of anti-ballistic missiles (ABMs), preferably at the zero level. The zero level was considered to be far preferable to any other because it avoids any questions about qualitative differences and hidden growth potentials and thus removes the last vestige of any stimulus for further arms race not only in ABMs, but to a substantial degree in the field of offensive weapons also. Any possible advantages of a severely limited ABM over a zero ABM do not seem to outweigh the dangers of a continuing arms race.

The negotiating parties at SALT were also urged to achieve a meaningful limitation on offensive weapons in order to stop the arms race immediately and to make it possible to begin the process of substantial arms reduction soon after. Such substantial arms reductions may be more difficult to negotiate, but they are absolutely essential if real world security is to be accomplished. It was emphasized that, in addition to limiting and reducing numbers, it will also be important to make provision for controlling and limiting qualitative features of weapons so that the arms race cannot be simply shifted in this direction. Qualitative features include size, multiple warheads, accuracy, etc. It was suggested that one good means for accomplishing this last objective would be a severe limitation on the rate of missile test launches, including confidence launchings.

This process can and must proceed on the premise that equal consideration is given to the security interests of each party and that neither seeks to obtain unilateral advantages.

Disarmament negotiations also must give attention to limiting or, better, avoiding an arms race in new areas. In this connection the problem of anti-submarine warfare (ASW) was discussed, and it was pointed out that ASW research and development aimed against missile-bearing submarines is research and development on counterforce techniques. Such efforts could be taken by either party as indicating preparation for a pre-emptive attack by the other, and thus can be very destabilizing and can stimulate further arms races in unpredictable directions. An ASW limitation would, therefore, greatly facilitate the achievement of agreements to reduce substantially the numbers of long-range delivery vehicles.

2. Comprehensive Test Ban. Preventing further vertical and horizontal proliferation of nuclear weapons remains extremely important, and the achievement of a Comprehensive Test Ban Treaty will make a major contribution to that end. Fortunately, progress in the development of the means for detecting possible violations has effectively removed the obstacles which once blocked the achievement of such a treaty. These means include not only seismic methods for detection and identification of nuclear explosions but also satellites and other unilateral means for collecting information. The combination of all these techniques now makes it practically impossible to conduct meaningful nuclear testing without detection.

In the process of preparation and putting into effect of such a treaty, it is most important to include at an early stage all the nuclear nations; it is also important to involve other nations, especially those that have the capability of becoming nuclear powers in the near future.

In this connection the problem of so-called Peaceful Nuclear Explosions was also discussed. The conclusions reached at the last Pugwash Conference were re-affirmed: "Excessive claims have been made regarding the importance of nuclear explosions for peaceful purposes. Whatever short term economic advantage there may be in the use of such explosions is likely to be more than offset by the risks of nuclear proliferation implicit in such explosions."

3. Non-Proliferation Treaty. It was noted with satisfaction there has been no nuclear weapon proliferation for the 2 1/2 years since the Non-Proliferation Treaty was first signed. Even so, the great importance of formal accession to the Non-Proliferation Treaty was affirmed and all nations that have not yet done so were urged to sign and ratify it at the earliest possible date.

At the same time, there was an awareness that the continuing effectiveness and durability of the treaty demand substantial progress in inhibiting vertical proliferation by real progress at SALT, adoption of other measures of self-restraint by all the nuclear powers, and agreement on the Comprehensive Test Ban Treaty.

4. Chemical and Bacteriological (Biological) Warfare (CBW).
(a) <u>Geneva Protocol</u>. It was noted with satisfaction that there are now 96 parties to the 1925 "Protocol for the Prohibution of the Use in War of Asphyxiating, Poisonous or Other Gases and of Bacteriological Methods of Warfare." The United States is the last militarily important country which is not a party to it.

In the U.S.A. the Protocol was recently re-submitted to the U.S. Senate for its consent to ratification. It was re-submitted with a letter stating the United States' interpretation that the Protocol did not apply to the use of tear gas and herbicides in war. The Chairman of the Senate Committee responsible for the treaty replied with a letter asking for re-consideration of this interpretation, and it appears that such a re-consideration is now going on. It was urged that the United States withdraw its interpretation excepting tear gases and herbicides and become a party to the Protocol. The U.K. was urged to withdraw its interpretation excepting CS tear gas from the prohibitions of the Protocol.

(b) <u>CB Disarmament</u>. A major issue in the field of CB disarmament has for a long time been whether C- and B-weapons should be got rid of together, or whether a treaty outlawing possession of B-weapons only would be a productive first step to the eventual elimination of both. During the past year the issue was settled in favour of action on B-weapons only.

President Nixon unilaterally renounced development and production of B-weapons and toxins and undertook to destroy the U.S. stocks of these weapons. The Socialist countries, which previously had tabled a draft treaty on C+B, tabled a draft on B-weapons only. After a relatively short period of negotiation, a revised draft has now been agreed and submitted to the CCD by the Socialist countries and the U.S.A.

The draft treaty would not prohibit research to improve defences against B-weapons, such as the preparation of vaccines for innoculation against germs which might be carried by such weapons. It was recommended that secrecy be eliminated from research of this kind as a protection against its being carried further than the production of vaccines, and to minimize the suspicion that may be provoked by this kind of work.

(c) <u>C-Weapon Disarmament</u>. There is a grave risk that the achievement of a B-weapons treaty will lead to a relaxation of efforts to achieve a C-weapons disarmament treaty and thus leave untouched what is undoubtedly from a military point of view the most important part of the CB-weapons field. The draft B-weapons treaty explicitly provides that negotiation of a C-weapons treaty should be pursued, and the non-aligned nations have been trying to strengthen this obligation. Progress to a C-weapons treaty is imperative if C-weapons are not to become a tacitly endorsed item in national armouries.

The obstacle to C-weapons disarmament has been disagreement whether international verification of non-possession of C-weapons is needed and is possible.

The suggestions made at the Conference of the Committee on Disarmament, for a verification procedure not unlike that provided by IAEA safeguards, were noted. Such a procedure would combine a national chemical safeguards system with international audit and spot checks. The objective should be to achieve an overall system which would deter significant violations with as little intrusion as possible.

There were different views in the Group on the need for international verification rather than reliance on national means. There were also differing views as to whether verification was the real point of disagreement.

5. Tactical Arms Limitation. The reduction of nuclear arms in Europe is of very great importance, both from the point of view of European Security and as a substantial step in the general efforts for disarmament. To that end, the following was offered:

A Specific Proposal for Tactical Nuclear Arms Limitation in Europe, designed to serve as a first approximation for further discussion

a. No foreign nuclear weapons in any European country. Delivery systems which are useful only when outfitted with nuclear warheads should be similarly prohibited. This in effect means denuclearization of Europe from the Rhine to the Soviet border.

b. United Kingdom and French nuclear weapons should be limited to those now deployed, or currently in the process of being deployed. No distinction between "tactical" and "strategic" deployments or uses should be made in this case.

c. Soviet MRBM's and IRBM's which are located so as to be capable of striking Europe should be limited to a number equal to the total number of British and French weapons deployed on long range missiles. Similar arrangements for medium range aircraft should also be made.

d. The Non-Proliferation Treaty and the Partial Nuclear Test Ban should be continued in force and expanded to the extent possible. All possible political means should be used to reinforce the treaties so as to prevent any further spread of nuclear arms in Europe.

e. If these radical reductions are to be achieved, there must also be a substantial and simultaneous reduction of conventional armed forces and armaments.

The simultaneous elimination of both military blocs—NATO and the Warsaw Treaty—or, as a preliminary step, the dissolution of their military organizations, thus putting an end to the stationing of troops on foreign territory and their manoeuvres, the existence of foreign military bases, etc.—would be of great importance for European security and disarmament in Europe.

It should be understood that these proposals are not a final blueprint but show only the main direction which could lead to significant results in disarmament in Europe and improvement of the political situation in that continent.

It should also be understood that many particular items which have been ignored or overlooked here will become of importance during possible actual negotiations. These include the disposition of nuclear-capable naval forces and other similar questions. But it is hoped such further details could be readily solved if the negotiations are in the spirit and scope of the above proposals.

It was felt that this radical approach may have a better chance of working than the traditional piecemeal attempts to ensure precise balance in every field each time a small disarmament proposal is made. Bold actions seemed to be the only practical way out of the present impasse.

However, it was felt by some that the proposal is not a realistic one. The question was also raised as to whether entirely new standards and approaches, substituting for the concepts of military balance and deterrence, should be considered. It was emphasized by some that these traditional concepts have led only to an arms race.

6. Organization of Disarmament Negotiations. There are important flaws in the present method of negotiating disarmament agreements. Some of these, and possible corrections for them are discussed in the following paragraphs.

Two nuclear powers, China and France, are not now participating in any negotiating forum. Without them any real major disarmament is very difficult and General and Complete Disarmament is obviously impossible.

France should take her seat at the Conference of the Committee on Disarmament (CCD) and contribute to disarmament again as she did so positively in the past.

China should participate in disarmament negotiations. States having formal diplomatic or informal political relations with China should urge her to do so.

Those countries which could achieve nuclear weapon capability in less than five years have insufficient opportunity to discuss the limitation and reduction of strategic nuclear delivery vehicles with the U.S.A. and the U.S.S.R., who are talking about these matters alone in SALT. Also there is no link between the discussions of strategic nuclear delivery vehicles in SALT and the discussion of other kinds of weapons, both nuclear and conventional, in other forums.

In any case, since progress in other disarmament negotiations depends on progress at Salt, a close link is required between SALT and the other disarmament negotiations. Some of the discussants believed that SALT should become a sub-committee of the CCD. Some others suggested that the U.S.A. and the U.S.S.R. should make periodic reports to the CCD on progress made at SALT. Still others believed that the present system should not be disturbed at such a crucial time.

Some people believe that too much power has been exercised by the U.S.A. and the U.S.S.R. as Co-Chairmen of the Conference of the Committee on Disarmament. They argue that a condition for the entry of France, and possibly China, into this Conference is the abolition of this co-chairmanship. Others feel that this Conference has been productive of a number of agreements and that the work of the Co-Chairmen has really facilitated this progress. They urge that an institution that has worked well in the past should not be abolished hastily or prematurely.

Finally, there was general agreement that a general disarmament conference should be convened in which all interested states could participate and express their points of view.

Successful progress towards disarmament, considering not only interim measures but also general and complete disarmament, requires a radical improvement of the international situation, the elimination of all hotbeds of war and sources of tension, the renunciation by all states of the use of force or threats to use it to resolve international disputes, and the strengthening of international machinery for the resolution of conflicts and keeping the peace.

The 1970s pose a great challenge. They will either see a further, even more dangerous escalation of the arms race, or a turn of the tide towards arms limitation and disarmament. The future of the world depends to a considerable extent on a certain psychological re-orientation involving the fact that in our time war can no longer be regarded as acceptable.

4. Environmental Pollution
The current degradation of the environment is in substantial part a side effect of technology applied to meet the demands of a rapidly increasing population for improving living conditions. There are also economic reasons which are often used as an excuse for the failure to amend technology so as to reduce pollution. This is due in part to the fact that, while some damaging effects of pollution on the biosphere are already widely recognized, others are at present only conjectural. From this combination of knowledge and ignorance concerning the environmental effects of technological progress, there emerges a sequence of actions which should be taken immediately to reduce pollution to more acceptable levels. These measures should lead to larger-scale, and ultimately even more essential, long-term programmes.

1. __Radioactive Pollution.__ This field offers an example of international progress accruing from data collection and research on national scales. Substantial problems remain in connection with disposal of radio-nuclides. In this field, intensive research into new techniques is of prime importance, if the now projected expansion of nuclear power generation is to be safely realized. The programme of nuclear power production for the common benefit should be considered quite separately from that of underground explosions, which offer only limited special advantages. If any such explosions are considered necessary, they should be carried out under international control.

2. __Conventional Pollution.__ Car exhausts and oil spillage at sea are well known toxic pollutants. Relatively simple technologies exist, adequate for reducing significantly or altogether removing their dangers. The use of these technologies should be universally enforced.

3. __Stratospheric Pollution.__ Aeronautical technology has led to development of supersonic transport, with possible adverse effects of its exhausts on the composition of the stratosphere, particularly on its ozone layer, and consequent danger of increased transparency of the atmosphere to ultraviolet light. It would be proper to question the wisdom of large-scale deployment of supersonic transport before scientifically based agreement can be reached on the reality and extent of such hazards.

4. __Pesticides.__ Application of chemical pesticides and related agents offers essential advantages for improvement of agricultural yields and combatting epidemic diseases. However, the hazard for the biosphere, associated with unplanned and unrestrained use of such agents, calls for more intensive research on more specific and less toxic biological or chemical agents of pest control. In the meantime, educational programmes should be initiated to convey to all potential users knowledge of the best agents (or their combination) to be used for a particular purpose with minimum damage to the biosphere.

5. __Data Collection and Centralization.__ Pollution hazards can only be reliably estimated if adequate background data exist, on which environmental monitoring can be based. Therefore, our recommendations depend largely on the establishment of national monitoring systems, using well-defined standards and thus able to convey to an International Centre precisely comparable data.

5. __Economic and Technological Co-operation amongst Nations, in Particular for Development__

There was general agreement on the crucial importance of economic and technical co-operation among developed countries (DCs) and less developed countries (LDCs) and on the necessity of avoiding that such co-operation be accompanied by domination or the exertion of pressure by the DCs.

Steps should be taken to increase the involvement by scientists from the LDCs in the Pugwash Movement, including the activation or formation of Pugwash groups in Latin America, Africa and South East Asia.

Among the Group's specific recommendations, the following merit special emphasis:

(a) Population Growth. Although the rate of population growth differs widely among countries, the rapid increase in world population poses a very serious problem to the future of mankind. In many LDCs the annual increase in population is now virtually as large as the annual increase in production, so that the increase in standard of living is small, if any.

In many technologically developed countries, the depletion of natural resources and pollution will eventually cause difficult problems if these countries delay too long taking steps to limit the increase in their populations.

In discussing population growth, the Group did not discuss the broad socio-economic aspects of the problem. It restricted itself to a discussion of practical aspects of fertility control, which are, or will become, an essential aspect of the problem in all countries even if, as we desire and hope, accelerated increase in agricultural and industrial productivity could be achieved in all parts of the world.

Biological and medical research on newer contraceptive methods should, therefore, be intensified in DCs as well as in LDCs. Since higher apes are the only relevant experimental animals for such work, the establishment of an international centre for primate breeding and primate reproductive biology in the Congo should be explored.

Already with the contraceptive methods now available, a significant decrease in unwanted births can be achieved. Knowledge of these methods should be spread and their use made available without cost. However, as these measures necessarily take time, abortion should be legalized as an ancillary procedure.

(b) Environmental Problems and Development. The present concern with the quality of the environment will have desirable, as well as undesirable, effects on the LDCs. Some of these effects are likely to be the movement of polluting industries from developed to developing countries, the raising of barriers to agricultural and food products of developing countries, the increased costs of production to these countries resulting from efforts to meet environmental standards set by more developed countries, the higher capital cost of industrial equipment manufactured in developed countries, and the diversion of resources from aid to LDCs into expenditure on the environment in the DCs.

Moreover, extension to LDCs of some environmental standards appropriate to DCs may lead to deplorable consequences; for example the prohibition of the use of DDT has led to the violent flare-up of malaria in certain countries where it had previously been virtually eradicated.

It is desirable to promote the formation of an independent institute, on the lines of SIPRI, to carry out objective studies on environmental problems, especially as they impinge on the LDCs.

(c) **Review of Effectiveness and of Programmes of International Organizations**. It is recommended that a study group is appointed to review the continuing effectiveness of established international governmental organizations and agencies dealing with science and technology in development. Pugwash is one of the few forums that can make an independent review of such world problems.

(d) **Priorities in Research.** Different kinds of research have different rates of return. LDCs particularly should determine carefully their research priorities, taking into account their social and economic needs and objectives. For example, in many LDCs research related to agriculture, food processing and public health is likely to yield the highest rates of return. It is urged that there should be a shift of significant material and manpower resources, at present devoted to military research and technological research of benefit only to DCs, to research with a bearing on development.

6. The Problem of East Pakistan Refugees

Recent events in East Pakistan have caused unprecedented human suffering and created a grave situation on the Sub-continent. There has been loss of life on a mass scale and millions of people have been forced to abandon their homes and seek refuge in India. The resulting tensions in the region threaten international peace and therefore demand the urgent attention of the United Nations. We appeal:

- to the Government of Pakistan to promote speedily a peaceful political settlement, refrain from actions which can make such settlement more difficult to achieve, create conditions for the safe return of the refugees to their homes and lands, and make possible the effective operation of international relief agencies among the affected population;

- to all governments to exert their influence on Pakistan to advance towards a peaceful political settlement;

- to all governments, United Nations and other international organizations to recognize that the relief and welfare of the **refugees** in India is an international responsibility, and that they should, therefore, assume immediately the bulk of the financial burden; and

- to all outside countries to avoid any steps which might further aggravate the situation and, in particular, to refrain from supplying arms to Pakistan.

Participants

Austria
Prof. F. Kohler

Belgium
Prof. P. Baudoux

Bulgaria
Acad. A. T. Balevski, Prof. K. Bratanov, Acad. G. Nadjakov

Canada
Prof. A. Legault

Chile
Dr. J. Barzelatto

Czechoslovakia
Dr. J. Moravec

Denmark
Mr. A. Boserup, Prof. O. Maaløe

Egypt
Prof. F. A. El Bedewi, Prof. M. Mahfouz

F.G.R.
Mr. H. Afheldt, Dr. H. U. Albrecht, Prof. H. Glubrecht

Finland
Prof. B. Broms, Prof. J. K. Miettinen

France
Mr. P. Genevey, Dr. H. Marcovich, Mr. J. Moch, Dr. G. Rudali, Dr. D. Thorner

G.D.R.
Prof. H. Kröger, Prof. P. W. Steinbrück, Mr. H. B. Zorn

Ghana
Prof. F. G. Torto

Hungary
Prof. G. Haraszti, Dr. I. Lang, Acad. K. Vas

India
Prof. S. K. Gupta, Prof. V. A. Sarabhai, Prof. S. H. Zaheer

Israel
Prof. S. Friedlander, Prof. S. Lifson

Italy
Prof. E. Amaldi, Dr. A. Pascolini, Prof. C. Schaerf

Japan
Prof. Y. Fukushima

Netherlands
Prof. B. R. A. Nijboer, Prof. P. B. Smith

Appendix 28

Nigeria
Prof. O. Bassir

Norway
Dr. T. Höivik, Dr. M. Thee

Poland
Prof. I. Adamczewski, Prof. P. J. Nowacki, Dr. J. Sach

Romania
Dr. V. Ceoceonica, Prof. I. Curievici, Acad. C. Dragulescu, Prof. O. Gherman, Prof. T. Ionescu, Dr. V. Ionescu, Prof. A. Negucioiu, Prof. C. Penescu, Prof. A. Tanase, Acad. N. Teodorescu, Prof. I. Tripsa, Prof. A. Trutia

Senegal
Dr. B. Faye

Spain
Prof. J. L. Sampedro

Sweden
Prof. H. Alfvén, Prof. N. Herlofson, Dr. A. Sparring

Switzerland
Prof. J. Freymond

U.K.
Dr. J. E. Beckman, Dr. D. Carlton, Mr. W. F. Gutteridge, Prof. Patricia J. Lindop, Dr. C. H. G. Oldham, Prof. Sir Rudolf Peierls, Mr. N. W. Pirie, Prof. M. R. Pollock, Prof. J. Rotblat

U.S.A.
Prof. G. Bunn, Prof. C. Djerassi, Prof. B. T. Feld, Dr. R. L. Garwin, Prof. S. Hoffmann, Prof. H. Morgenthau, Prof. E. Rabinowitch, Dr. V. Rabinowitch, Prof. R. N. Rosecrance, Prof. T. W. Schultz, Mr. W. Swartz, Prof. H. F. York, Dr. A. Zucker

U.S.S.R.
Prof. G. A. Arbatov, Acad. V. A. Engelhardt, Dr. Ludmila Gvishiani, Mr. I. G. Pochitalin, Acad. O. Reutov, Dr. I. Sokolov, Prof. T. Timofeev, Acad. A. P. Vinogradov, Prof. M. S. Voslensky

Yugoslavia
Prof. L. Berberovic, Dr. M. Sahovic

Observers

FAO
Mr. R. Aubrac

IAEA
Dr. E. Lopez-Menchero, Mr. B. Sanders

SIPRI
Prof. R. R. Neild, Mr. T. Němec

U.N.
Mr. P. B. W. Gollong, Mr. I. Pastinen

UNESCO
Acad. I. Malecki, Dr. T. Uchida

Students

Romania
Liana Bologa, Mihaela Cornea, M. Cosma, A. Durobantu, Balasa Ene, M. Mihailescu, M. Mindra, D. Nicuta, D. Popa, M. Popov, G. C. Roman, Denisa M. Sanda, Mioara Stane, Cristina Vulcan, Elena Zamfirescu

U.S.A.
D. Djerassi, Elizabeth Feld, R. Harriman, R. Swartz

Name Index

Abbiw-Jackson, D. K., 95, 219
Abdel-Meguid, A. R., 93, 132, 244, 254
Abebe Kebede, 110, 255
Aboltin, V. Y., 99, 127, 254, 264, 299, 318, 329
Abu Sharr, I., 110, 255
Acimovic, L., 130
Adamczewski, I., 98, 126, 263, 298, 317, 374
Adams, Ruth, 4, 103, 129, 147, 160, 169, 184, 187, 198, 212, 214, 220, 235, 299
Adler, David J., 29, 93, 234, 244, 263, 297
Afhelut, H. H., 94, 125, 211, 219, 234, 244, 263, 297, 317, 328, 373
Agarbiceanu, I., 98, 234, 244, 263
Agblemagnon, N., 101, 298
Ahnlund, Katarina, 101, 298
Ahuja, M. L., 95, 165
Ajumogobia, F. I., 114, 255
Akin Deko, G., 113, 255
Aklilu Lemma, 93, 253, 290, 297
Alaga, G., 130
Albrecht, U., 94, 125, 357, 373
Alcock, N. Z., 92, 110, 197, 211, 219, 262, 296
Alexander, B., 129
Alexandrov, A. P., 99, 168
Alferov, V. V., 127, 133
Alfvén, Hannes, 13, 22, 70, 81, 82, 101, 127, 235, 244, 298, 330, 358, 374
Allam, A-W. I., 116, 359
Allan, H. R., 111, 213
Allibone, T. E., 111, 213
Aloisi, M., 96, 244
Alpert, H., 114, 329
Alting van Geusau, F. A. M., 126
Amaldi, Eduardo, 32, 55, 88, 96, 125, 157, 244, 297, 317, 328, 373
Amati, D., 131
Amati, P., 125
Anderson, V. C., 129
Andrassy, J., 130
Andreyev, P. V., 99, 235, 245, 254, 264
Anichkin, O. N., 115, 329

Ansari, M., 116, 359
Arangio-Ruiz, G., 96, 244
Arbatov, Georgi W., 77, 99, 329, 359, 374
Arnaudi, Carlo, 64, 72
Artsimovitch, Lev A., 72, 88, 99, 197, 213, 220, 235, 245, 264, 299, 318, 329, 359
Arzumanjan, Anushavan A., 99, 168, 220, 285
Aseffa Tekle, 93, 253, 297
Asseffa Seifu, 110, 255
Astor, David, 128
Aubrac, R., 113, 131, 318, 329, 359, 374
Auger, P. V., 93, 316
Awe, O., 97, 328
Awokoya, S. O., 114, 329

Bacigalupo, A., 126
Backstränd, G., 127
Baker, F. G. W., 131
Bakotio, B., 130
Balevski, Anguel T., 88, 91, 357, 373
Balogh, Lord, 128
Bannier, J. H., 126
Baptist, N. G., 92, 123, 253, 296, 316, 327
Barnaby, C. Frank, 14, 22, 101, 128, 299, 317, 328
Bartlema, H. C., 126
Bartos, M., 106, 220
Barwich, Heinz, 94, 168, 219, 285
Barzelatto, J., 92, 123, 373
Bassini, G. L., 96, 297
Bassir, O., 97, 254, 298, 317, 374
Bati, L., 125
Baudoux, P., 91, 123, 316, 372
Bauer, Etienne, 74, 93, 124, 253, 263, 297, 316, 327, 357
Bawden, Frederick C., 101, 165, 212
Baxter, R. M., 110, 255
Bazanov, N. I., 99, 111, 184, 187, 198, 213
Beamish, Crooke J., 128
Beckman, J., 101, 128, 374
Belikov, V. M., 127
Bengelsdorf, I. S., 115, 329
Benko, V., 106, 329

Name Index

Bennett, I., 134
Berberovic, L., 106, 374
Berg, S., 115, 318
Bergmann, Peter G., 103, 213, 299
Bernal, J. D., 7, 101, 212
Bernard, Viola W., 103, 213
Bernardini, Gilberto, 63, 96, 244
Berner, O., 113, 134, 299
Bertotti, Bruno, 64, 96, 111, 126, 228, 245
Bertrand, A., 114, 245
Besedin, G. P., 99, 111, 198, 213
Bethe, Hans A., 103, 186
Bhabha, Homi J., 58, 59, 95, 157, 228, 285
Bhagavantam, S., 95, 357
Bingham, Alfred, 203
Biquard, P., 93, 234
Birnbaum, K. E., 101, 127, 263
Biro, A., 131
Bjol, E., 124
Björnerstedt, Rolf, 11, 70, 88, 101, 111, 113, 131, 134, 235, 244, 263, 290, 298, 318, 359
Blackaby, F., 113, 131, 318
Blackett, P. M. S., 7, 101, 159, 186, 189-190, 197, 212, 220
Blagonravov, A. A., 99, 168, 184, 186, 197, 213, 220, 235
Blaskovic, D., 113, 133, 235
Blickenstaff, D., 113, 229
Bloch, F., 129
Bloch, H., 128
Bloch, P. C., 116, 359
Blusztajn, M., 111, 264
Boas, W., 270
Boeri, E., 96, 157
Bognar, J., 95, 228
Bognar, R., 95, 211, 219, 297
Bogolubov, N. N., 99, 157, 160, 168, 184, 186, 197, 213, 220, 235
Bollinger, K., 124
Bologa, Liana, 116, 375
Bondi, H., 101, 128, 245, 263
Bonifas, V., 128
Born, Max, 2, 53, 94, 139, 157
Boserup, A., 93, 124, 297, 327, 357, 373
Boskma, P., 97, 126, 317, 328, 358
Boulding, K. E., 103, 129, 213, 229, 263

Bowie, R. R., 103, 186, 187
Boyd, W., 92, 234, 296
Boyd-Orr, Lord, 101, 157
Boyko, Hugo, 96, 211
Branco, G. da F. C., 116, 359
Brandt, Willi, 71
Bratanov, K., 91, 296, 327, 357, 373
Brdička, R., 92, 168
Bredow, W. F., 125
Breitenecker, Manfred, 91, 123, 210
Brennan, Donald G., 103, 168, 169, 186, 187, 197, 210, 213, 318
Bridgman, Percy W., 2, 139
Brode, Robert B., 103, 213
Broms, B., 93, 124, 373
Bronk, D., 45, 112, 184
Bronowski, Jacob, 1
Brown, Harrison, 49, 57, 72, 88, 103, 157, 159, 168, 184, 188, 197, 199, 213, 220, 229, 235, 245, 254, 290, 299, 318, 358
Brown, L. M., 101, 263
Browning, T. O., 270
Brunelli, B., 126
Bucek, J., 123
Buchan, Alastair, 101, 168, 197
Budini, Paolo, 63, 111, 126, 245
Bukowski, J., 98, 111, 126, 264, 298, 317
Bull, Hedley, 111, 213, 245, 264
Bullard, Sir Edward, 88, 101, 184, 186, 197
von Bülow, H., 124
Bunche, Ralph J., 77, 113, 235, 329
Bunn, G., 103, 129, 358, 374
Burcham, W. E., 101, 212
Burhoe, Ralph W., 103, 213
Burhop, Eric H., 3, 4, 101, 111, 147, 158, 212
Burkhardt, Gerd, 31, 94, 110, 114, 133, 157, 168, 183, 186, 196, 211, 220, 234, 244, 300
Burling, R. L., 110, 255
Burnet, Sir Macfarlane, 31, 270
Burns, E. L. M., 92, 357
Burton, John W., 91, 110, 167, 197, 210, 218
Bussac, J., 93, 124, 316
Bussche, A. von dem, 94, 253
Butozan, V., 106, 264
Buzzard, Sir Anthony, 111, 213

Name Index

Buzzati-Traverso, A. A., 96, 131, 133, 211, 219, 234, 244, 356
Buzina, R., 130

Cade, J., 131
Cahn, Anne, 116, 359
Calder, Nigel, 14, 71, 102, 111, 213, 299
Calder, R., 102, 212
Calic, D., 106, 213
Calogero, F., 96, 126, 244, 297, 328, 358
Calogero, Louisa, 126
Campbell, J. C., 129
Campbell-Smith, Mrs. S., 111, 213
Carlton, D., 102, 128, 374
Casey, Lord, 71
Caspersson, T., 134
Catala de Alemany, J., 100, 212, 298
Catlin, Sir George, 111, 213
Cavers, David F., 103, 147, 157
Ceausescu, Nicolae, 82
Ceoceonica, V., 98, 374
Chadha, M. S., 125
Chagula, Wilbert, 89, 101, 254, 298
Chain, E. B., 102, 299
Chang-Wei, 92, 168
Chapdelaine, M., 131
Charpak, G., 131
Chayes, A., 129
Chike Obi, 212
Childs, E. C., 102, 254
Chinnappa, J. C. V., 270
Chiowanich, Panee, 101, 254, 298
Chisholm, Brock, 92, 147, 156, 165, 211
Chou Pei-Yuan, 92, 147, 149, 159, 168
Cini, M., 126
Clarke, R., 115, 131, 318, 329
Clemens, Walter C., Jr., 112, 214
Clow, A., 111, 213
Cobos, F., 123
Cockcroft, Sir John, 13, 71, 74, 102, 186, 197, 212, 220, 299
Cohen, J., 102, 212, 299
Coleman, J. M., 103, 129, 254
Collen, B., 127
Commoner, Barry, 103, 112, 158, 213
Consolazio, William V., 103, 184, 213

Conway, E. J., 95, 211
Conway, P., 116, 359
Copeland, B. K. W., 129
Coppieters, E., 91, 123, 327
Cornea, Mihaela, 116, 375
Coryell, Charles, 103, 157
Cosma, M., 116, 375
Cowen, Robert C., 112, 214
Cremer, H. D., 125
Crawford, Sir John, 91, 183
Crawford, M., 101, 228
Csáki, F., 95, 357
Curievici, I., 98, 374
Cyrankiewicz, Jozef, 59, 62
Cyvin, S., 97, 263, 298

Danysz, M., 98, 147, 212, 234
Darwin, Sir Charles, 102, 149, 212, 285
Davidon, William C., 103, 129, 157, 213, 299
Davidson, W. D., 129
Davies, M., 102, 299
Davis, J. C., 116, 359
Davy, John, 14, 111, 245
de Bernard, B., 133
de Charro, F. Th., 126
Dedijer, S., 101, 254
Delbrecht, H., 125
Delbrück, J., 94, 297
Denchev, A., 123
Desai, M. J., 95, 263
Desai, R. C., 113, 359
Devadas, R. P., 125
de Shalit, A., 96, 228, 253
De Wilde, J., 126
Dhawan, S., 270
Dickens, J. M., 271
Diczfalusy, E. F., 127
Diefenbaker, John G., 38
Dierauf, E., 110, 255
Dillon, W. S., 103, 112, 255, 299
Dimissianos, B., 95, 219
Ditchburn, R. W., 102, 299
Djerassi, Carl, 72, 88, 103, 116, 129, 299, 318, 329, 358, 359, 374, 375
Dobell, P. C., 92, 327
Dobrosielski, M., 98, 298, 317
Dobrotin, N. A., 99, 157
Dolman, Claude E., 92, 165
Dominicé, C., 101, 358

Name Index

Doty, Paul, 29, 49, 103, 129, 134, 147, 168, 184, 186, 197, 220, 235, 263, 318, 329, 358
Douglas-Home, Sir Alec, 62
Dragulescu, C., 98, 127, 228, 234, 374
Dubarle, Father Pierre-Leon, 93, 157, 211, 219
Dubinin, Mikhail M., 99, 133, 165, 168, 184, 186, 197, 213, 229, 235, 245, 264, 290, 299, 318, 329
Dumitrescu, D., 98, 219
Duncan, J. F., 270
Duri, M., 93, 253
Durobantu, A., 116, 375
Dyson, Freeman J., 103, 197, 213, 263

Eaton, Anne, 6, 39, 59, 78, 148
Eaton, Cyrus, 10, 14, 20, 36, 39, 43, 59, 78, 141, 148, 161, 203
Eden, M., 129
Edsall, G., 134
Edsall, John T., 103, 150, 168, 213
Eicher, C. K., 129
Eide, A., 97, 317, 358
Eide, Mrs. W. B., 126
Einstein, Albert, 2, 139, 148
Eisenhower, Dwight D., 38
Eissa, N. A. H., 93, 328, 358
El Bedewi, F. A., 93, 298, 317, 328, 358, 373
El Hamamsy, L. S., 93, 244
Eliezer, C. J., 270
Elim, R. S., 114, 300
Elliott, G., 128
Elton, L. R. B., 102, 235, 299
Emelyanov, V. S., 99, 127, 168, 197, 213, 229, 245, 264, 299, 318, 329, 359
Encel, S., 91, 316
Endalkachew Mekonnen, 110, 255
Ene, Balasa, 116, 375
Engel, J., 129
Engelhardt, V. A., 99, 127, 299, 318, 329, 359, 374
Engström, Arne, 70, 71, 101, 219, 298
Epstein, W., 113, 245

Erhard, Ludwig, 59
Erikson, E., 112, 229
Eriksson, B. E., 101, 358
Erlander, Tage, 62, 68, 71
Ermakov, A. N., 99, 359
Ernst, K-D., 124
Ersil, W., 94, 124, 328
Esche, H., 125
Esdale, M., 53
Essenov, S. E., 99, 299
Evang, K., 97, 298
Ezeilo, J. O. C., 97, 328

Fagbemi, O. J., 97, 358
Faulk, W. P., 132
Faulstich, H., 124
Favilli, G., 96, 211
Faye, B., 98, 358, 374
Fedorov, Evginiy K., 88, 99, 157, 160, 168, 199
Fehrm, Martin, 22, 70, 101, 111, 134, 229, 298
Feld, Bernard T., 12, 57, 68, 77, 78, 88, 103, 129, 134, 157, 159, 168, 186, 197, 213, 220, 229, 235, 245, 254, 263, 299, 318, 329, 358, 374
Feld, Elizabeth, 116, 359, 375
Feldman, M., 96, 297
Feng Ping-Fu, 92, 168
Fensham, P. J., 270
Ferreira, W., 132
Fey, H., 128
Fielding, R. J., 128
Fieyra, J., 111, 213
Filkorn, V., 92, 297
Finkelstein, L. S., 112, 229
Fischer, G., 103, 168
Fisher, R., 103, 220
Fisson, P., 115, 318
Fitzgerald, P., 110, 213
Fjellander, Jan R., 80, 116, 359
Florey, Lord Howard, 13, 54, 74, 102, 212
Flowers, Sir Brian H., 102, 111, 197, 220, 235, 245, 263
Foias, C. I., 98, 328
Fono, A., 125
Förland, T., 97, 212, 234, 358
Forlati, Laura, 96, 234, 244

Name Index

Forssell, O. G., 124
Foster, John S., 5, 92, 147
Fowler, K., 91, 234, 270
Franek, J., 133
Frank, C. R., 129
Frank, F. C., 102, 317
Frank, Jerome D., 103, 159, 213, 299
Frankel, Sir Otto, 270
Franz, H., 94, 211
Fraser, R. G. J., 111, 213
Freier, S., 96, 125, 263, 317, 358
Freymond, J., 101, 374
Friedlander, S., 96, 358, 373
Friedrich-Freska, H., 94, 211, 297
Frisch, D., 103, 168
Frisch, O. R., 102, 111, 168, 189, 197, 212, 235
Frisch, Rose, 129
Fubini, E., 129
Fukushima, Y., 96, 373
Funke, G. W., 101, 212, 228

Gafurov, B. J., 99, 254
Gallino, L., 126
Galtung, J., 97, 228, 234, 254, 263, 298, 306, 317, 328
Gamulin, T., 130
Gandhi, Indira, 59, 71
Garcia, Rolando V., 72, 91, 253, 290, 296
Gard, Sven, 101, 134, 165
Gardiner, R. K. A., 113, 255
Gardner, Trevor, 103, 186, 187, 285
Garwin, R. L., 103, 299, 329, 374
Gell-Mann, M., 104, 229
Genevey, Pierre, 93, 110, 197, 220, 229, 373
Geyer, H. M., 124
Ghazanfar, S. A. S., 91, 253
Gherman, O., 98, 127, 374
Giacometti, Giovanni, 64, 96, 111, 245, 263, 317, 358
Gilinsky, V., 129
Glaser, D. A., 104, 134, 220, 235, 329

Glass, Bentley, 12, 49, 52, 88, 104, 134, 157, 165, 168, 184, 186, 197, 199, 213, 220, 235, 245, 263, 299, 318, 358
Gleditsch, N. P., 126
Glubrecht, H., 94, 125, 328, 357, 373
Goldberg, L. J., 129
Goldschmidt-Clermont, Y., 101, 131, 298
Goldsmith, Maurice, 111, 213
Goldwasser, R., 133
Gollong, P. B. W., 113, 375
Goma, L. K. H., 106, 318
Gomer, Robert, 104, 197
Goodman, Rita, 129
Gopalan, C., 125
Gorter, C. J., 97, 212
Goss, C., 129
Gott, H., 123
Gottlieb, H., 124
Gouin, P., 93, 253
Greenwood, T., 116, 123, 359
Gregory, Bernard P., 93, 149, 157, 168, 211
Gresford, G., 113, 300, 318
Grigorieff, W. W., 113, 158
Griniewsky, O. A., 99, 111, 245, 254
Grodzins, Morton, 104, 150, 157, 168, 285
Groom, A. J. R., 128
Groot, H., 92, 253
Gros, A., 21, 93
Gryzlov, A. A., 99, 299
Gueron, G., 93, 211, 297
Gueron, J., 93, 124, 157, 211
Gunnarsson, O., 95, 211, 297
Gupta, S., 95, 373
Gutteridge, W. F., 102, 128, 254, 263, 299, 317, 328, 374
Gverdziteli, I. G., 99, 318
Gvishiani, Ludmila, 99, 127, 329, 359, 374
Gyllenberg, H. G., 124

Hacik, V., 92, 327
Haddow, Alexander, 1, 5, 7, 102, 168, 184, 212
Häfele, W., 110, 125, 299

Name Index

Hagengruber, R. L., 116, 359
Hahn, G., 124
Haigh, C. P., 128
Haile Sellassie, 66
Hailsham, Lord, 53
Hajdu, V., 92, 110, 123, 264, 297
Hajek, J., 123
Hall, W., 129
Hammond, A., 116, 359
Hammond, R. P., 129
Handler, J., 132
Hanga, V., 98, 127, 234, 263, 298, 317
Hansen, K. R., 104, 129, 329, 358
Haraszti, G., 95, 373
Hardy, B. H., 116, 359
Harriman, R. L., 116, 375
Haslett, Arthur W., 112, 213
Hassan Ishag, M., 110, 254
Hassner, P., 124
Hedén, Carl, 28, 70, 101, 128, 134, 298
Heggie, R. G., 129
Heimendahl, E., 94, 110, 168, 220
Heinrichs, J., 125
Heitler, W., 101, 212
de Hemptinne, Y., 131
Herlofson, N., 101, 128, 317, 328, 374
Herriott, Roger M., 104, 213, 299
Hers, I. F. Ph., 133
Hess, P., 22, 94, 110, 124, 234, 297
Hibbs, Albert R., 112, 198
Higgins, Charles C., 104, 165
Higgins, H. G., 270
Higgins, R., 128
Higinbotham, William A., 104, 150, 168
Hill, David L., 104, 157
Hirschman, A. O., 129
Hoag, D. G., 129
Hoagland, Hudson, 104, 112, 184, 213
Hochfeld, J., 114, 235
Hodgkin, Dorothy, 102, 212, 128, 299
Hodgson, Peter E., 1, 102, 299
Hoffmann, S., 104, 374
Höivik, T., 97, 374
Holmes, J. W., 92, 357

Holmes, R., 128
Holst, J. J., 126
Holton, G., 104, 299
Hönl, Helmut, 94, 157
Hoogland, W., 126
Hopper, W. D., 123
Houtermans, F. G., 101, 212, 285
Howard, Michael E., 102, 186, 197, 328
Hughes, Helen, 91, 253, 270
Hulubei, H., 98, 197, 212
Humphrey, J. H., 134
Husa, Vaclav, 92, 168, 211, 285
Hutchinson, G. W., 112, 214
Hutchinson, Sir Joseph, 214
Huxley, Sir Julian, 102, 212

Ianni, O., 91, 227
Imshenetsky, Alexander A., 99, 133, 165, 168, 299, 329
Inall, E. K., 91, 271, 327
Indik, B., 129
Infeld, Leopold, 2, 53, 55, 67, 88, 98, 139, 157, 196, 212, 219, 228, 234, 244, 263
Inglis, David R., 104, 129, 168, 213, 299
Inozemtsev, N. N., 99, 197, 213
Ionescu, T., 98, 374
Ionescu, V., 98, 374
Ipsen, K., 125
Isaacs, Alick, 112, 214
Isakov, I. S., 99, 168
Iselin, C. O'D., 104, 184

Jackson, Lady, 102, 358
Jacobsen, G. S., 110, 255
Janossy, Lajos, 95, 157
Jansson, J. M., 93, 124, 316
Jaquet, L. G. M., 126
Jauho, P., 124
Jeljaszewicz, J., 133
Jelliffe, D., 130
Jelliffe, Mrs. E. F. P., 130
Jensen, J. H. D., 94, 244
Johnson, Lyndon, 59, 222, 232
Joliot-Curie, J. Frederic, 2, 3, 138, 139
Jonas, Franz, 71
Jona-Lasinio, G., 96, 234
Jones, G. O., 102, 299

Name Index

Joos, H., 125
Joubin, F. R., 110, 213
Joxe, A., 93, 124, 228, 234, 263
Jungk, Robert, 91, 110, 158, 213, 262, 296

Kalkstein, M., 104, 213, 299
Kamefuchi, S., 96, 211
Kanazir, D., 106, 220
Kapitza, Peter L., 46, 99, 168, 290, 299, 318
Kaplan, Martin M., 28, 31, 43, 104, 157, 165, 184, 213, 221, 229, 235, 245, 264, 290, 300, 318, 329, 359
Kargin, V. A., 99, 197, 213, 254, 264, 299
Kashkai, M. A., 99, 299
Kassa Wolde Mariam, 66, 93, 253
Katili, John, 30
Katz, Amrom H., 104, 112, 168, 187, 198, 213, 299
Kaysen, C., 104, 229
Kende, I., 95, 297
Kendrew, J. C., 112, 197
Kennedy, John, 46, 48, 54, 55, 57
Kennet, Lord. See Young, Wayland
Kirn, A., 133
Kerr, Donald, 92, 165
Kerr, W. E., 91, 219, 253
Keynan, A., 96, 244, 358
Khan, Ayub, 35, 54, 59, 71
Khohlov, R. V., 99, 329
Khrushchev, Nikita, 38, 45, 54, 59, 62
Khvostov, Vladimir M., 88, 99, 168, 184, 186, 197, 213, 220, 229, 235, 245, 264, 318, 329
Kinf, Maris, 271
King, J. A., 213
King-Hall, Lord, 112, 214
Kirillin, Vladimir A., 57, 59, 88, 99, 220
Kissinger, Henry A., 49, 104, 112, 186, 197, 213, 220, 235, 263
Kistiakowsky, G. B., 104, 186, 358
Klafkowski, A., 98, 263
Kleiman, R., 104, 318, 329
Klein, J., 93, 316
Kliefoth, W., 94, 157, 297
Klineberg, Otto, 104, 213
Knapp, Viktor, 92, 156, 219
Knapp, V., 106, 113, 220

Kofoed-Hansen, O. M., 93, 196, 211, 219, 234
Kohler, F., 91, 372
Kolesnichenko, T. A., 359
Kolesnyk, A., 94, 263, 297, 328
Konuma, M., 96, 244
Kopal, V., 92, 168
Kopecki, K., 111, 264
Korneev, S. G. T., 99, 111, 184, 187, 198, 213
Korovin, E. A., 99, 157, 168
Kosygin, Alexei, 35, 77
Kothari, D. S., 95, 228
Kovalev, M. I., 99, 229
Kovda, V. A., 114, 214
Koževník, J., 92, 156, 234, 297
Kozhevnikov, I. J., 99, 197, 213
Krause, R., 114, 235
Kreisky, Bruno, 39, 80
Krishnan, Sir K. S., 95, 157
Kröger, H., 94, 263, 297, 328, 357, 373
Kruczkowski, A., 111, 264
Kuczynski, J., 94, 234, 253
Kuhelj, A., 106, 213, 220
Kuleshov, V. F., 99, 329, 359
Kumaniecki, K., 98, 168
Kutakov, L. N., 113, 318, 359
Kutovoj, E. Y., 113, 329
Kuzin, A. M., 99, 150, 157, 197, 213, 235
Kwee, S. L., 97, 212, 298
Kybal, D., 104, 168

Lacassagne, Antoine M. B., 93, 147, 157
Lakany, M. A., 93, 254, 263, 298
Lall, Betty G., 104, 235, 263, 318
Landheer, B., 97, 126, 228, 298
Landsberg, H., 129
Lang, D., 112, 220
Lang, I., 95, 373
Langlands, I., 270
Laponche, Bernard, 30, 93, 297, 316, 357
Lapter, Karol D., 67, 98, 133, 212, 219, 234, 244, 254, 263
Lardner, G. E. A., 98, 254
Lattes, C. M. C., 91, 210
Lauritsen, Charles C., 104, 186, 187
Lazanski, M., 113, 220
Leach, Gerald, 14, 53, 112, 197, 214, 220

Name Index

Leake, Chauncey D., 104, 165, 184, 299
Leal, J. L., 100, 328
Leclercq, Robert, 29, 91, 262, 296, 357
Leerhøy, J., 133
Legault, A., 92, 373
Leghorn, Richard S., 49, 104, 150, 159, 168, 197, 213
Leibnitz, E., 124
Leipunski, O., 99, 197, 213
Leite Lopes, J., 91, 296
Leitenberg, M., 131
Lemberg, M. R., 270
Lengyel, S., 125
Lennette, E., 129
Lenz, Hanfried, 94, 157, 211
Leontief, Wassily, 104, 197, 213, 245, 329
Leon-Betancourt, A., 123
Lestel, J., 93, 244
Levai, A., 125
Levitt, W., 112, 214
Lewandowski, B., 98, 358
Lewis, Howard, 14, 79
Lewis, W. B., 123
Lider, J., 111, 264
Lifson, S. Z., 96, 328, 373
Lim, H. H., 271
Lindberg, Olov, 101, 212
Lindop, Patricia J., 14, 37, 43, 73, 88, 102, 112, 128, 134, 150, 158, 165, 169, 184, 187, 197, 212, 220, 229, 235, 245, 254, 271, 281, 317, 328, 358, 374
Lipman, N., 102, 128, 317
Lipson, Leon, 104, 186, 187, 210, 213
Liska, L., 92, 297
Liustiberg, V. F., 329
Ljunggren, A. M. O., 128, 134
Lloyd, B. D., 128
Lockspeiser, Sir Ben, 102, 112, 168, 184, 187, 212
Lofo, J. M., 131
Long, F. A., 72, 88, 104, 129, 220, 245, 263, 299, 318, 358
Lonsdale, Kathleen, 7, 102, 128, 157, 212
Lopez-Menchero, E., 113, 375
Lösche, A., 94, 297

Lozinski, V. V., 99, 229
Ludwiczak, Z., 126
Luistiberg, V. F., 115
Luse, R., 131
Lwoff, Andre, 93, 133, 165, 211

Maaløe, Ole, 88, 93, 110, 124, 133, 211, 220, 234, 244, 297, 327, 357, 373
Macaranas, F. M., 116, 359
Maccacaro, G. A., 133
McCorkle, T., 129
Macek, Joseph, 92, 211
Mach, B., 128
Macioti, M., 131
McKenzie, J., 129
McKnight, A. D., 113, 318
Macmillan, Harold, 54, 57
McNamara, Robert, 190
Maddox, John, 14, 53, 112, 128, 197, 214, 235
Magat, Michel, 93, 124, 211, 228, 244, 290, 297, 316, 327
Magnus, Preben von, 93, 124, 165
Magnusson, G. L., 128
Mahalanobis, P. C., 95, 157, 211, 317
Mahfouz, M. M., 93, 358, 373
Mainx, F., 91, 133, 210
Makagiansar, M., 114, 318
Makinson, R. E. B., 110, 213
Malecki, Ignacy, 11, 30, 67, 68, 88, 98, 114, 127, 131, 244, 254, 263, 298, 328, 359, 375
Málek, Ivan, 22, 61, 72, 88, 92, 123, 133, 211, 219, 227, 234, 244, 253, 262, 297, 327
Manley, Gordon, 102, 165, 212
Marcovich, Herbert, 12, 55, 74, 88, 94, 124, 133, 168, 211, 219, 228, 244, 253, 263, 316, 327, 357, 373
Margerison, Tom, 112, 214
Mark, J. C., 130
Markovic, M., 106, 245, 299
Markvart, J., 123
Marshak, R., 104, 299
Martin, A., 102, 128, 299, 358
Martin, Sir David, 102, 212, 245
Martin S. L., 106, 254
Martyn, D. F., 91, 244, 270
Mates, Leo, 106, 220, 290, 299, 359

Name Index

Matulis, Y., 99, 299
Matumoto, K., 96, 317
Matveyev, A., 114, 245, 255
Maybury, R., 114, 229
Maydl, P., 123
Mayer, J., 104, 299
Mazza, M., 126
Mead, Margaret, 104, 213
Medvedev, S. S., 99, 235, 299
Melman, S., 130
Melnikov, L., 133
de Melo, J. L. P., 116, 360
Mende, T., 128
Mendl, W., 102, 128, 328
Mengesha, Melak H., 93, 253
Menon, M. G. K., 95, 125, 219, 228, 244, 253, 297, 317
Menzel, E., 94, 196, 211, 228, 263, 297, 328
Merz, Blanche, 271
Meselson, Matthew, 104, 134, 213, 220, 235, 245, 358
Meyer, Agnes, 20, 41, 203
Meyer, K. P., 101, 220, 298
Meyrowitz, H., 94, 133, 297
Mezerik, A. G., 112, 158
Mezzetti, Lucio, 96, 211
Michelsen, Børge, 110, 213
Miettinen, J. K., 93, 124, 357, 373
Mihailescu, M., 116, 375
Mikhaltsev, I., 127
Miller, J. D. B., 91, 210
Millionshchikov, Mikhail, 12, 13, 29, 59, 68, 72, 76, 77, 88, 99, 127, 229, 235, 245, 254, 264, 299, 318, 329, 359
Mills, B. Y., 270
Mills, W. A., 114, 221
Milovidov, I. V., 127
Mindra, M., 116, 375
Mitz, M., 130
Miyake, Yasuo, 96, 228, 157, 270, 297
Moch, J., 94, 124, 219, 234, 244, 297, 316, 327, 373
Mojeiko, Igor, 30
Moljk, A., 113, 220
Moravec, J., 92, 133, 327, 373
Morcos, S. R., 93, 212
Morgenthau, H. J., 104, 130, 235, 299, 329, 374

Mortensen, K., 124
Mostacci, E., 134
Mott, Sir Nevill, 51, 53, 88, 102, 197, 199, 212, 220
Muench, Hugo, 104, 165
Muller, Herman, 2, 53, 104, 138, 139, 147, 157, 285, 299
Muller, S., 104, 263, 318, 358
Munger, E. S., 104, 254, 299
Munk, W., 104, 197
Mussard, J. A., 113, 359
Myrdal, Alva, 22, 72, 111, 299

Nadjakov, G., 91, 156, 167, 183, 186, 196, 211, 219, 296, 316, 327, 357, 373
Nag Chaudhuri, B. D., 125
Nagelstein, E. W., 131
Nagger, K. E., 100, 298
Nairn, R. C., 133
Nash, M., 130
Nasser, Gamul Abdel, 35
Negucioiu, A., 98, 374
Nehru, Jawaharlal, 1, 3, 35, 38, 54, 59
Neild, Robert, 22, 52, 70, 102, 112, 113, 131, 197, 229, 299, 318, 329, 359, 375
Němec, Theodor, 61, 92, 110, 113, 123, 134, 196, 211, 220, 234, 244, 262, 290, 297, 316, 327, 359, 375
Nerlich, U., 110, 197
Nesmeyanov, Alexander N., 45, 111, 169
Nesterenko, A. N., 113, 264, 300
Nicholls, F. G., 91, 253
Nicholson, E. Max, 112, 214
Nicolescu, M., 98, 234
Nicuta, D., 116, 375
Nijboer, B. R. A., 97, 157, 212, 373
Nilsson, S., 101, 298, 317
Nita, M., 127
Nixon, Richard, 343, 366
Nkrumah, Kwame, 54, 64, 65
Noel-Baker, Philip J., 78, 102, 112, 158, 168, 186, 197, 212, 220, 235, 245, 328, 358
Novikov, D. P., 100, 329
Novotny, Antonin, 54, 57, 62, 71
Nowacki, P. J., 98, 126, 374

Name Index

Obi, C., 97
O'Ceallaigh, C., 95, 297
Odhiambo, Thomas, 30, 72, 96, 126, 358
Ogawa, Iwao, 96, 147, 157, 211, 297
Okita, S., 126
Oldham, C. H. Geoffrey, 30, 102, 128, 299, 374
Ølgaard, P. L., 93, 124, 263
Oliphant, Sir Mark, 91, 147, 149, 156, 186, 196, 210, 227, 270
Olszewski, E., 127
Omland, T., 126
Onassis, Aristotle, 3
Onwumechili, C. A., 97, 328
Oppenheim, Sir Alexander, 97, 212
Orear, Jay, 104, 112, 157, 168, 184, 187, 197, 213, 235
Osredkar, M., 106, 318
Ouellet, Cyrias, 92, 149

Paffrath, L., 130
Pal, Lenard, 95, 125, 211, 234, 297
Palevsky, Harry, 104, 157, 213, 299
Panofsky, W. K. H., 104, 186
Pant, P., 111, 229
Parekh, B., 116, 360
Parpia, H. A. B., 125
Parsons, T., 104, 299, 318
Parthasarathi, Ashok, 30, 95, 125, 328, 357
Pascolini, A., 96, 126, 358, 373
Pastinen, I., 113, 375
Pauling, Linus, 2, 53, 104, 139, 150, 157, 184, 213
Paulsson, Inger, 111, 299
Pavan, C., 91, 183
Pavelescu, D., 127
Pavlichenko, Vladimir, 4, 45, 100, 111, 147, 150, 157, 160, 165, 169, 184, 187, 198, 213, 220, 229, 235, 245, 254
Paz, I., 110, 255
Peierls, Sir Rudolf, 12, 69, 88, 102, 128, 168, 197, 229, 235, 245, 299, 317, 328, 358, 263, 374
Penescu, Corneliu, 81, 82, 98, 127, 328, 330, 358, 374
Penney, Lord, 102, 186, 197
Perrin, Francis, 13, 74, 94, 124, 186, 196, 219, 297, 316, 327, 357
Perry-Robinson, J., 113, 134, 318, 329
Peter, Y., 96, 253
Peters, Sir Rudolph, 102, 212
Petersen, N., 124
Petrovsky, V., 113, 131, 264
Phelps, John B., 104, 168, 213, 299
Pickering, W. H., 105, 184
Piel, Gerard, 105, 112, 184, 229
Pierson, J. H. G., 113, 245, 255
Piganiol, P., 94, 211
Pihl, Mogens, 93, 156
Pirani, Felix, 102, 112, 214, 229
Pirie, Antoinette, 112, 214
Pirie, N. W., 102, 128, 212, 328, 374
Platanov, Y. P., 100, 299
Platig, E. Raymond, 112, 214, 255
Plaude, K. K., 100, 299
Plougonven, C., 116, 360
Pochitalin, I. G., 100, 127, 299, 318, 329, 359, 374
Polanyi, J. C., 92, 168, 186, 211, 227
Polk, William R., 79, 105, 358
Pollock, M. R., 102, 374
Pomerance, Josephine, 130
Ponnamperuma, C., 130
Popa, D., 116, 375
Popiolek, K., 98, 328
Popkiewicz, J., 127
Popov, M., 116, 375
Popovic, D., 130
Pose, H., 94, 168
Powell, Cecil F., 2, 6, 12, 35, 53, 73, 88, 102, 128, 139, 147, 149, 157, 159, 168, 197, 199, 212, 220, 229, 235, 254, 291, 299, 317, 350
Pozo-Olano, J. D., 97, 254, 298
Prawirohardjo, S., 95, 244
Prawitz, Jan, 70, 101, 128, 244, 263, 298, 328
Preston, T., 123
Price, B. T., 112, 128, 197, 220
Priestley, J. B., 7
Primakov, E. M., 100, 359
Procházka, Vladimir, 92, 196, 211
Prokhorov, A. M., 100, 318
Pryce, M. H. L., 102, 157
Puranananda, C., 101, 228
Purcell, E. M., 105, 186

Name Index

Quaix, H., 131
Quartey, J. A. K., 95, 211
Quik, H. B., 126
Quirino, L., 92, 253

Rabi, Isidor I., 105, 130, 184, 187, 197, 220
Rabinowitch, Eugene, 1, 13, 18, 47, 49, 67, 79, 80, 88, 105, 130, 147, 150, 157, 159, 165, 168, 184, 186, 197, 199, 213, 220, 235, 245, 254, 263, 299, 318, 329, 358, 374
Rabinowitch, Victor, 30, 105, 112, 130, 198, 214, 220, 235, 245, 299, 358, 374
Rachwartono, R., 130
Radhakrishnan, S., 59
Rahman, A., 95, 253
Raiser, L., 94, 263, 297
Rajh, Z., 131
Ramanna, R., 125
Ramiadrasoa, A., 97, 317
Rana, M. A., 270
Randers, Gunnar, 97, 157
Rapacki, Adam, 71
Raska, K., 133
Rathgeber, H. D., 91, 296
Rathjens, George W., 77, 105, 112, 130, 214, 299, 329, 358
Raven, T., 96, 211
Read, J., 97, 130, 212
Reczei, L., 95, 263, 297, 317
Rehberg, P. K. B., 124
Reich, U. P., 125
Reif, F., 112, 214
Resnick, J., 130
Reuck, A. de, 102, 358
Reuter, F. H., 270
Reutov, O., 100, 329, 359, 374
Revelle, Roger, 105, 130, 159, 184, 213, 229, 245, 254, 299, 329, 359
Revesz, L., 101, 212, 298
Rice, H. L., 130
Rich, Alexander, 105, 130, 134, 165, 168, 184, 213, 220, 229, 235, 254, 263, 299, 329
Richie, T. E., 113, 299
Rienäcker, Gunther, 94, 157, 219, 228, 234, 263
Riha, J., 133

Ritchie-Calder, Lord, 102, 212
Ritzen, M., 134
Riznichenko, J., 100, 197, 213
Rochlin, R. S., 130
Roderick, H., 114, 214
Rodriques, A. M., 94, 316
Röling, Bert V. A., 23, 97, 168, 184, 186, 196, 234, 244
Rollefson, R., 105, 245, 299
Roman, G. C., 116, 375
Rorsh, A., 126
Rosenblith, Walter, 105, 184
Rosebury, Theodor, 105, 165, 213
Rosecrance, R., 105, 130, 374
Rosenquist, I. T., 126
Rosenstiehl, Pierre, 94, 186, 196, 211, 244, 316
Rosenthal, M., 116, 360
Rostow, W. W., 46, 105, 168
Rotblat, Joseph, 1-23, 36, 53, 55, 73, 103, 129, 134, 139, 147, 149, 157, 159, 165, 168, 184, 186, 197, 199, 212, 215, 220, 229, 235, 245, 254, 263, 271, 275, 299, 317, 328, 358, 374
Roth, E., 94, 297, 316
Rothschild, K. W., 123
Royon, Betty, 37, 43
Rowse, E. A. A., 110, 255
Rubinstein, M. I., 100, 168, 197, 213, 229, 235, 245, 254, 299
Rudali, G., 94, 373
Ruina, J. P., 105, 130, 229, 299, 329
Rumpf, H., 94, 219
Russell, Bertrand, 2, 13, 37, 41, 44, 45, 53, 55, 80, 103, 140, 141, 148, 157, 199, 205, 212, 281
Rusznyak, I., 95, 168
Rybicki, Z., 127

Sabin, Albert B., 105, 213
Šach, J., 98, 127, 358, 374
Sadovsky, M. A., 100, 168
Sagdeyev, Dr. R., 127
Sahovic, M., 106, 131, 359, 374
Sailor, V. L., 112, 158
Sajovic, D., 131
Sakamoto, Y., 96, 358
Sakata, Schoichi, 96, 157
Sala, Oscar, 91, 196

Name Index

Salam, Abdus, 63, 97, 196, 212, 228, 298, 356
Sampedro, J., 100, 374
Sanda, Denisa M., 374
Sanders, B., 113, 131, 375
Sandosham, A. A., 97, 228, 270, 298
Sands, Matthew, 112, 187
Sannes, J., 126
Saragat, Giuseppe, 64, 71
Sarabhai, Vikram, 55, 58, 72, 89, 95, 125, 196, 228, 234, 253, 263, 317, 357, 373
Saukkonen, J. J., 93, 124, 297
Savic, Paul, 106, 158
Sawada, S., 96, 358
Scalabre, G., 110, 318
Schaerf, Carlo, 32, 96, 126, 317, 328, 373
Schaich, T., 116, 360
Scharf, Adolf, 41
Schelling, T. C., 105, 168, 169
Schlesinger, H., 124
Schultz, T. W., 105, 359, 374
Schumann, T. E. W., 100, 212
Schwarcz, E., 110, 158
Schwarz, U., 128
Scossiroli, R. E., 126
Scott, Sir Oliver, 112, 214
Scoville, H., 112, 299
Searby, P. J., 129
Sedlak, J., 123
Seidenfaden, G., 124
Seitz, Frederick, 54, 105, 157, 197, 229
Sela, M., 96, 211
Seligman, H., 113, 299
Selove, Walter, 105, 147, 157
Semenov, N. N., 100, 168
Seow, E. J., 271
Shazar, Zalman, 35
Shelepin, M., 100, 299
Shils, Edward, 105, 213
Shimonaka, Y., 141
Shmelev, V., 131
Shulman, M. D., 105, 220, 263, 329, 359
Shustov, V. V., 100, 111, 264, 329
Silin, V., 127
Simpson, Esther, 112, 214
Singer, J. D., 130
Sinyak, K. M., 113, 127, 134, 329

Sisakyan, Norayr Martirosovich, 100, 160, 184, 186, 285
Šiška, K., 92, 123, 234, 357
Skobeltzyn, Dmitri, 6, 12, 88, 100, 147, 150, 157, 168, 199
Skolnikoff, E., 105, 130, 299
Skowronski, A., 127
Skryabin, G., 127
Slotemaker de Bruine, G. H., 97, 212
Smart, I., 129
Smialowski, M., 98, 358
Smith, P. B., 97, 126, 263, 298, 317, 328, 373
Smorodintsev, A. A., 100, 165
Šnejdárek, Antonin, 29, 92, 234, 262, 297
Sodnom, N., 97, 328
Soedjatmoko, S., 95, 358
Soemantri, B., 270
Sohn, Louis B., 105, 168, 186, 189, 197, 245, 299
Sohns, E. R., 130
Sojak, V., 123
Sokolov, I. A., 100, 299, 318, 329, 359, 374
Solodovnikov, V. G., 100, 329
Šorm, Frantisek, 61, 62, 92, 123, 211, 234, 262
Sparring, A., 101, 298, 374
Spingarn, J., 105, 159
Spinrad, B., 131
Sproull, R., 130
Staley, Eugene, 105, 184, 229
Standa, Denisa M., 116
Stane, Micara, 116, 375
Steenbeck, Max, 31
Stefański, W., 98, 168
Stein, G., 96, 244, 297, 328
Steinbrück, P. W., 94, 373
Steinmaurer, R., 91, 210
Stephenson, G. R., 117, 360
Sternglass, E., 78
Sterzl, M. J., 133
Stone, J. J., 130
Stone, S., 113, 264
Stocker, M. G. P., 103, 165, 212
Straub, F. B., 95, 133, 183, 186, 196, 211, 234
Stroot, J. P., 123
Stubbs, P., 115, 318
Stulman, J., 113, 255

Name Index

Sullivan, W. S., 115, 329
Sundralingan, A., 113, 255
Supek, Ivan, 56, 88, 106, 131, 197, 213, 215, 220, 229, 245, 254, 318, 359
Supek, R., 131
Suslov, V. P., 113, 235
Sutherland, Sir Gordon, 71, 103, 229, 245, 254, 299
Swartz, R., 117, 360, 375
Swartz, William, 15, 20, 39, 105, 113, 299, 318, 359, 374
Sychev, V., 127
Szabolcsi, M., 95, 328, 357
Szendy, K., 125
Szilard, Gertrud W., 113, 130, 299
Szilard, Leo, 4, 5, 7, 40, 105, 147, 150, 157, 159, 168, 169, 186, 197, 220, 285
Szulkin, P., 98, 168
Szyr, Eugeniusz, 68

Talensky, Nikolai A., 100, 133, 160, 168, 184, 186, 197, 213, 220, 229, 235, 245, 264, 285
Tamm, Igor E., 54, 100, 168, 184, 186, 197, 213
Tammelin, L-E., 101, 128, 134, 298
Tanaka, S., 96, 317
Tanase, A., 98, 374
Tanovic, A., 106, 329
Taye, Talahun, 110, 255
Taylor, C. E. D., 129, 134
Teixeira, Jose, 204
ten Cate, L. O., 111, 213
Teodorescu, N., 98, 374
Terwisscha van Scheltinga, F. J. A., 111, 197, 235
Thacker, M. S., 95, 228
Tha Hla, 114, 221
Thee, M., 97, 126, 374
Thibault, Pierre, 94, 165
Thirring, Hans, 41, 91, 110, 147, 156, 159, 167, 183, 187, 210, 218, 244
Thomson, Sir George, 103, 157, 212
Thore, A., 128
Thorner, D., 94, 373
Thuillier, P., 115, 319
Timbie, J., 117, 360

Timofeev, T., 100, 127, 374
Tiselius, A., 101, 134, 298
Tito, Josip, 38, 54, 57
Todd, W. M., 105, 359
Tolhoek, H. A., 97, 212, 219, 234, 263
Toll, John S., 105, 213
Tomonaga, S., 96, 147, 157
Tondl, L., 123
Tooze, J., 115, 319
Topchiev, Alexander Vassilievich, 1, 33, 44, 88, 100, 147, 150, 157, 168, 199, 213, 285
Torto, Frank G., 30, 89, 95, 125, 253, 297, 317, 357, 373
Townes, Charles H., 105, 113, 184, 186, 197
Towpik, A., 127
Toyoda, Toshiyuki, 96, 184, 186, 297, 358
Tripsa, I., 98, 374
Trivedi, V. C., 111, 229, 235
Trutia, A., 98, 374
Tupolev, A. N., 100, 168, 197, 213, 220, 245
Tyrrell, A. C., 271

Uchida, T., 114, 375
Udis, B., 130
Ulbricht, Walter, 57, 68, 71
Ullmann, M., 115, 319
Ulrich, J. W., 110, 213
Ungar, J., 128, 134
Urban, E. K., 110, 255
Urban, Ludek, 92, 196
U Thant, 29, 35, 54, 62, 82, 278

Valkenburgh, P., 97, 219
Valtanen, J., 124
Varsavsky, Carlos M., 30, 89, 91, 123, 316, 327, 357
Varyrynen, R., 124
Vas, K., 95, 328, 373
Vasiliev, O. S., 115, 329
Vatistas, S., 95, 211
Vavilov, V. S., 100, 157
Vavpetic, L., 106, 235, 299
Vejvoda, M. L., 113, 255
Vernov, A. N., 100, 197, 213
Vichney, N., 115, 319, 329
Vietmeyer, N. D., 130

Name Index

Vinogradov, A. P., 100, 127, 133, 150, 157, 160, 168, 220, 235, 245, 264, 299, 318, 329, 374
Vital, D., 125
Voslensky, M. S., 100, 111, 127, 245, 299, 329, 374
Voss, J., 105, 130, 299, 359
Vries, C. de, 126
Vul, B. M., 100, 220, 229, 245, 264, 329
Vulcan, Cristina, 116, 375

Waddington, C. H., 103, 149, 212
Wade, N. M. L., 115, 359
Walker, D., 97, 212
Walton, B., 117, 360
Wasawo, D. P. S., 96, 253, 297
Watson, C. J. H., 103, 328
Watson-Watt, Sir Robert, 92, 149, 156, 159, 165, 168
Weckstrom, P. M. J., 124
Weinberg, Alvin M., 105, 157, 184, 299, 359
Weinberg, S., 105, 130
Weinzierl, P., 91, 327
Weiss, C., Jr., 130
Weisskopf, Victor F., 88, 105, 130, 147, 157, 159, 199, 213
Weizsäcker, Carl von, 7, 94, 149, 159
Weizsacker, E. von, 125, 133
Wergeland, H., 97, 212
Whipple, R. O., 93, 253, 297
White, Sir Frederick, 270
Wieczorek, W., 98, 127, 328
Wierda, W., 126
Wiesmann, E., 128
Wiesner, Jerome B., 46, 72, 105, 130, 150, 159, 168, 235
Wigner, Eugene P., 105, 157, 159, 184
Wilbrandt, H., 125
Wilhjelm, J., 93, 263, 297
Willmore, A. P., 112, 214
Wilson, Harold, 64
Wilson, R. R., 105, 359
Winid, B., 110, 255
Wise, James, 20, 31, 203
Wojtaszek, E., 98, 328
Wolf, K. A., 94, 211
Wolfe, Hugh C., 105, 213

Wolstenholme, Gordon E. W., 65, 103, 254
Woude, A. Van der, 97, 328, 358
Wouthuysen, S., 126
Wright, J. K., 112, 235, 264
Wrigley, J., 131
Wünsche, H., 94, 297, 357

Yamada, Eiji, 96, 228, 270, 297
Yanney-Wilson, J., 95, 211
Yiftah, S., 125
York, H., 105, 130, 329, 374
Young, Wayland (Lord Kennet), 14, 103, 112, 128, 169, 184, 187, 197, 210, 212
Yukawa, Hideki, 2, 53, 96, 140, 147, 157, 196, 211
Yu Kwang-Yuan, 92, 168

Zacharias, B., 134
Zacharias, J. R., 105, 184
Zachariev, I., 123
Zagari, Mario, 64
Zaheer, S. H., 95, 228, 290, 297, 317, 328, 373
Zamfirescu, Elena, 116, 375
Zelenin, A. V., 127
Zeleny, I., 123
Zhdanov, V., 133
Zheludev, I. S., 113, 329
Zorn, B., 94, 124, 373
Zoubek, V., 92, 357
Zucker, A., 105, 374
Zuckerman, Sir Solly, 112, 187, 197

Subject Index

ABM (anti-ballistic missile), 30, 77, 261, 292, 323-324, 340, 364
Academy of Science of the USSR. See Soviet Academy of Sciences
Accademia Nazionale dei Lincei, 63
Accademia Sinica, 39, 52, 60, 204
Addis Ababa Conference. See Pugwash Conference, Fifteenth
Adlai Stevenson Institute of International Affairs, 79, 80
Afghanistan, 91, 107, 253
Africa, 55, 89, 193, 217, 231, 239, 286, 293, 294, 305
African Pugwash Group, 32
All-European Conference on Security and Co-operation, 361
American Academy of Arts and Sciences, 15, 29, 47, 49, 71, 79, 80
Antarctica, 225, 305
Argentina
  discussed, 35, 280
  represented, 89, 91, 107, 123, 253, 290, 296, 316, 327, 357
Arms
  control, 29-30, 52, 64, 69, 72, 75, 159
  conventional, 191, 256-257, 292, 303-304
  race, 46, 151, 166
  trade, 75, 118, 303, 307, 332, 333
Asia, 55, 89, 281
Association of Parliamentarians for World Government, 1, 5
Atom-free zones. See Nuclear-free zones
Atomic energy, peacetime uses of, 141, 143-144, 146, 155
Atomic Scientists' Association (ASA), 1
Australia, represented, 4, 37, 91, 107, 110, 133, 147, 149, 156, 167, 183, 186, 196, 197, 210, 213, 218, 227, 234, 244, 253, 270, 271, 296, 316, 327
Australian Academy of Sciences, 71
Australian Pugwash Group, 267, 282
Austria
  discussed, 28, 262

Austria (continued)
  represented, 4, 8, 38-39, 41, 91, 107, 110, 123, 133, 147, 156, 158, 159, 167, 183, 187, 210, 213, 218, 244, 262, 296, 327, 372
Austrian Pugwash Group, 282

Balkans, 193, 217, 231
Baden Conference. See Pugwash Conference, Fourth
Bangladesh, discussed, 83
Belgium, represented, 91, 107, 123, 262, 272, 296, 316, 327, 357, 372
Berlin. See German Federal Republic
Biological and chemical warfare and weapons, 42-44, 62, 76, 78, 81, 119, 161-165, 191, 231, 236, 241-242, 262, 269, 286, 293, 304, 325, 343-344, 366-367
Black boxes, 33, 55, 209
Brazil
  discussed, 35, 239
  represented, 91, 107, 116, 123, 183, 196, 210, 219, 227, 253, 296, 360
British Pugwash Group, 15, 27, 32-33, 282
British Royal Society, 53, 54
Bulgaria, represented, 88, 91, 107, 123, 156, 167, 183, 186, 196, 211, 219, 296, 316, 327, 357, 373
Bulletin of the Atomic Scientists, 1

Cambodia, discussed, 332
Cambridge Conference. See Pugwash Conferences, Ninth
Canada
  discussed, 351, 361
  represented, 3, 4, 7, 37, 92, 107, 110, 116, 123, 147, 149, 159, 165, 168, 186, 197, 211, 213, 219, 227, 234, 262, 296, 327, 357, 359, 373
Canadian Peace Research Association, 282
Canadian Pugwash Group, 282
Carnegie Endowment, 66, 282
Ceylon, represented, 92, 107, 123, 253, 270, 296, 316, 327

Chemical warfare and weapons, 42, 74, 76, 78, 81, 118, 243, 366-367. See also Biological and chemical warfare and weapons
Chile, represented, 92, 107, 373
China, People's Republic of
 discussed, 32, 55, 60, 69, 85, 191, 204, 218, 223, 259, 274, 286, 332, 342, 368, 369
 represented, 4, 7, 18, 37, 39, 45, 47, 52, 92, 107, 123, 147, 149, 159, 168
Ciba Foundation, 12, 65
Colombia, represented, 92, 107, 123, 253
Colombo Plan, 267
Committee on Space Research (COSPAR), 175, 178
Conference of the Committee on Disarmament (CCD), 337, 343, 368, 369
Conferences on Science and World Affairs (COSWA), 10, 78, 282
Continuing Committee. See Pugwash movement
Cuba, discussed, 34, 118, 123, 280
Current conflicts. See Local conflicts
Czechoslovak Academy of Sciences, 15, 61, 71
Czechoslovak Pugwash Group, 15, 29, 282, 283
Czechoslovakia
 discussed, 28, 75, 78, 193, 256, 262, 310
 represented, 61, 88, 92, 107, 110, 123, 133, 156, 168, 196, 211, 219, 220, 227, 234, 244, 253, 262, 264, 272, 290, 297, 316, 327, 357, 373

Dahomey, represented, 92, 107, 253
Danish Pugwash Group, 29, 73, 282
Denmark
 discussed, 28, 262
 represented, 93, 107, 110, 124, 133, 156, 165, 196, 211, 213, 219, 220, 234, 244, 263, 297, 327, 357, 373
Developing nations, 26, 31, 48, 49, 54, 58-86, 119, 155, 176, 180-181, 195, 200, 223-227, 236, 239, 246-255, 258, 265-270, 278,

Developing nations (continued), 286-296, 310-316, 326-327, 332, 333, 350-357, 370-372
Disarmament, 1, 5, 26, 29-30, 38, 39, 46, 49-52, 62, 69, 72-75, 77, 81-85, 118, 149-152, 190-191, 195, 195, 200, 206, 209, 222-224, 230-231, 236, 240-242, 256-262, 286-304, 336-344, 364-369
 and control and inspection, 5, 38, 42, 46, 57, 142-152, 166, 185, 189, 216, 257, 260, 272, 291
 general and complete, 62-69, 77, 166-167, 188, 241, 259, 277, 301, 337
Disarmament Decade, 337
Dubrovnik Conference. See Pugwash Conference, Eleventh

Earth sciences, 48, 170-174, 218
East African Academy of Sciences, 72
Economic Commission for Africa (ECA), represented, 113, 255
Economic Commission for Europe (ECE), discussed, 306
Economic Council for Asia and the Far East (ECAFE), discussed, 266
Education, 54, 59, 64-65, 67, 109, 146, 238-240, 246, 247, 265-267, 295-296, 311-312
Egypt. See also United Arab Republic
 discussed, 363
 represented, 93, 107, 116, 373
Eighteen Nation Disarmament Conference (ENDC). See United Nations Eighteen Nation Disarmament Conference
Environmental problems, 26, 67, 82-83, 172-174, 177, 344-347, 371. See also Pollution; Population growth
Ethiopia, represented, 65, 93, 107, 110, 253, 255, 290, 297
Europe, discussed, 29, 42, 67-69, 81, 118, 256-264, 273, 277, 293, 306, 307
 Central, 62, 193, 215, 217, 230, 231, 256
 Eastern, 55, 88, 281
 security of, 76-78, 81, 83, 322-323, 334-336, 361-363

Europe (continued)
  Western, 55, 88, 281
European Security Conference (ESC),
  discussed, 335, 361-362
Expanded Technical Assistance
  Programme, 237

Fallout. See Nuclear tests
Federation of American Scientists
  (FAS), 1
Finland
  discussed, 361
  represented, 93, 107, 124, 297,
    316, 357, 373
Fissile materials, 50, 57, 69,
  185, 231, 273, 292, 302, 303
Fontana Conference. See Pugwash
  Conference, Twentieth
Food and Agricultural Organization
  (FAO)
  discussed, 173, 237
  represented, 113, 131, 255, 299,
    318, 329, 374
Food sciences and technology, 31,
  82, 175-176, 267-268, 295, 326,
  361
Ford Foundation, 29-30, 49, 204
Foreign bases, 38, 148, 189, 210,
  240-241, 259, 362, 367
France
  discussed, 37, 75-76, 218, 274,
    342, 367, 368-369
  represented, 4, 88, 93-94, 110,
    115, 124, 125, 133, 147, 149,
    156, 165, 168, 186, 196, 197,
    211, 219, 220, 228, 229, 234,
    244, 253, 263, 272, 290, 297,
    316, 318, 327, 357, 373
French Pugwash Group, 73-74, 283

Geneva Disarmament Conference, 259
Geneva Protocol of 1925, 164, 242,
  293, 304, 325, 343
German Democratic Republic
  discussed, 29, 31, 48, 57, 63,
    118, 193, 204, 230, 256-258,
    293, 306-307, 322, 334-335
  represented, 52, 94, 107, 110,
    124, 157, 168, 219, 220, 228,
    234, 253, 263, 272, 297, 328,
    357, 373

German Democratic Republic Academy
  of Sciences, 71
German Democratic Republic Pugwash
  Group, 282, 283
German Federal Republic
  discussed, 29, 31, 48, 57, 63, 118,
    193, 204, 230, 256-258, 293, 306-
    307, 322, 334-335, 361, 362
  represented, 37, 94, 107, 110, 125,
    133, 149, 157, 159, 168, 183, 186,
    196, 197, 211, 219, 220, 228, 234,
    244, 253, 263, 272, 297, 299, 317,
    328, 357, 373
German Federal Republic Pugwash
  Group, 282-283, 355
Ghana, represented, 89, 95, 107, 125,
  211, 219, 253, 297, 317, 357, 373
Ghana Pugwash Group, 282
Greece, represented, 95, 107, 211,
  219
Green Revolution, 82, 361

Haile Sellassie I Foundation, 65
Health, 155, 176-177, 218, 227
Hungarian Academy of Sciences, 71
Hungarian Pugwash Group, 282
Hungary, represented, 95, 107, 125,
  133, 157, 168, 183, 186, 196, 211,
  219, 228, 234, 263, 272, 297, 317,
  328, 357, 373

ICBM (inter-continental ballistic
  missiles), 333-340
Iceland, represented, 95, 107, 211,
  297
India
  discussed, 34-35, 83, 239, 251, 280
  represented, 2-3, 58, 89, 95, 107,
    111, 116, 125, 157, 165, 196, 211,
    219, 228, 229, 234, 235, 244, 253,
    263, 270, 290, 297, 317, 328, 357,
    360, 373
Indian Pugwash Group, 282
Indochina, discussed, 323-333, 363
Indonesia, represented, 95, 107, 125,
  244, 270, 358
Institutes, 64, 236-237, 353, 372
Inter-continental science centre,
  48, 180
International Antarctic Treaty, 175

Subject Index 394

International Atomic Energy Agency (IAEA)
 discussed, 29, 57, 158, 216, 262, 271, 272, 273, 303
 represented, 113, 130, 299, 318, 329, 375
International Bank for Reconstruction and Development (World Bank)
 discussed, 238
 represented, 132
International Biological Programme, discussed, 65, 178, 234, 237, 294
International Centre for Insect Physiology and Ecology (ICIPE), discussed, 72, 347, 348
International Conference on Science and Society, 1
International Congress for Microbiology, discussed, 29
International Control Organ, discussed, 191
International Co-operation Year, 63, 237, 280
International Council of Scientific Unions (ICSU),
 discussed, 48, 177, 178, 233-234, 237, 346
 represented, 113, 131, 235
International Court of Justice, discussed, 363
International Disarmament Conference, 259
International Disarmament Organization, discussed, 216, 217
International Foundation for Scientific and Technical Development, discussed, 78, 326
International Hydrologic Decade, 172
International Institute for Peace and Conflict Research. See SIPRI
International Institute for Technical Economics, discussed, 238
International Oceanographic Commission (IOC), discussed, 171, 173
International Peace Research Association (IPRA), discussed, 23, 71, 280, 363
International police force, 185, 189, 194
International research centre, 65

International Science Foundation (ISF), discussed, 65, 118, 238, 294, 347
International scientific co-operation, 29, 39, 54, 57, 64, 72, 81, 119, 146, 149, 154-155, 170-183, 200, 207, 210, 218, 224-227, 236-240, 258-259, 265-270, 277, 288, 294, 312-313, 316, 344-357, 362, 370-372
International Summer School of Disarmament and Arms Control, 16, 32, 36, 283
International Telecommunications Union (ITU), discussed, 174
International Union of Biological Sciences, discussed, 176
International Year for the Preparation of Disarmament, 65, 189, 243
International Youth Science Fortnight, 32-33
Iran, represented, 116, 359
IRBM (intermediate range ballistic missile), 367
Ireland, represented, 95, 107, 211, 297
Israel
 discussed, 281, 305, 321, 363
 represented, 96, 107, 125, 133, 211, 228, 244, 253, 263, 297, 317, 328, 358, 372
Israeli Academy of Sciences, 71
Italian Physical Society, 63
Italian Pugwash Group, 16, 32, 282, 283
Italy, represented, 88, 96, 107, 111, 125-126, 133, 157, 184, 211, 219, 228, 234, 244, 245, 263, 272, 297, 317, 328, 358, 373

Japan, represented, 4, 96, 107, 126, 147, 157, 183, 186, 196, 211, 228, 244, 270, 297, 317, 358, 373
Japan, Science Council of, 71
Japanese Pugwash Group, 282, 283
Jarring Mission, 332, 333
Jordan, discussed, 363

Karlovy Vary Conference. See Pugwash Conference, Thirteenth

Subject Index

Kenya, represented, 96, 107, 126, 253
Kitzbühel Conference. See Pugwash Conference, Third
Körner Foundation, 39, 41, 204

Lac Beauport Conference. See Pugwash Conference, Second
Laos, discussed, 332
Latin America, discussed, 55, 89, 217, 231
Lebanon, represented, 96, 107, 211
Life sciences, 4, 48, 109, 175-178, 276
Local conflicts, 72-75, 77, 83, 151, 292-292, 293, 320-322, 332, 363
London Conference. See Pugwash Conference, Tenth

McCloy-Zorin agreement, 189
Madagascar, represented, 97, 107, 317
Malaysia, represented, 97, 107, 212, 228, 270, 298
Mathematicians, 109
Middle-East conflict, 34, 35, 72, 75, 78, 118, 231, 279, 286, 293, 294, 305, 309, 321-322, 332-333
Military expenditures, 75, 304
Minimum deterrent, 30, 38, 118, 216, 223
MIRV (multiple independently-targetable re-entry vehicle), 323-324, 338-339
Mohole Project, 171, 218
Mongolia, represented, 97, 107, 328
Moscow Conference. See Pugwash Conference, Sixth
Moscow Test-Ban Treaty. See Nuclear Test-Ban Treaty
MRBM (medium range ballistic missile), 367
Multilateral Nuclear Force. See Non-proliferation

National Academy of Sciences of the USA. See United States National Academy of Sciences
National Pugwash Groups, 15-16, 21, 27, 73, 90, 203, 280, 282, 289-290, 370

Natural resources, 250, 258, 344, 347
Netherlands, represented, 97, 107, 111, 116, 126, 133, 157, 168, 184, 186, 196, 197, 212, 213, 219, 228, 234, 235, 244, 263, 272, 298, 317, 328, 358, 360, 373
Netherlands Pugwash Group, 282, 283
New Hope Foundation, 39
New Zealand, represented, 97, 107, 212, 270
Nice Conference. See Pugwash Conference, Eighteenth
Nigeria
  discussed, 72, 75, 78, 294, 309, 321
  represented, 97, 107, 212, 254, 298, 317, 328, 358, 374
Non-aggression pact, 230, 257
Non-aligned nations, 217, 222, 273, 306
Non-proliferation, 29, 30, 38, 42, 57, 62, 69, 81, 148, 216, 222-223, 230-231, 252, 261, 277, 342
Non-proliferation Treaty, 35, 59, 118, 256, 272-274, 281, 291-292, 302, 305, 307-308, 337-341, 364, 365-366, 367
North American Treaty Organization (NATO), discussed, 215, 230, 257, 305, 306, 367
Norway, represented, 97, 107, 126, 157, 212, 228, 234, 254, 263, 298, 317, 328, 358, 374
Norwegian Pugwash Group, 282
Nuclear-free zones, 29, 57, 58, 69, 118, 185, 217, 231, 261, 272, 277, 307, 362
Nuclear test ban, 35, 38, 46, 52, 118, 148, 166-167, 192, 209, 217-218, 231, 252, 260-262, 273, 277, 279, 292, 324, 341
  underground testing, 75, 218, 231, 252, 260, 273, 292, 324, 341
Nuclear Test-Ban Treaty, 33, 42, 56, 57, 64, 69, 81, 188, 215, 218, 222-223, 231, 252, 260-261, 278, 324, 341, 367
Nuclear tests, 49, 78, 141-145, 185, 342
Nuclear umbrella. See Minimum deterrent

Subject Index

Nuclear war, 39, 141-154
  surprise attack, 42, 46, 57, 167,
    215-216, 231, 257
Nuclear weapons, 1, 2, 75, 77, 269.
  See also Non-proliferation; Radiation hazards
  delivery systems, 50, 57, 77, 185,
    269, 273
  freeze, 230, 256, 261, 302
  stockpiles of, 152, 185, 324
  strategic, 231, 292, 323-332
  submarine, 118, 338, 339, 365
  tactical, 367-368
Nutrition, 67, 249-250, 267-268

Ocean, 81, 118, 119, 171-174, 225,
  292-293, 342-343, 368
Organization of African Unity (OAU),
  252, 305, 307
Organization for Economic Co-
  operation and Development (OECD)
  discussed, 323
  represented, 131

Pakistan
  discussed, 34-35, 83, 251, 280,
    361, 372
  represented, 97, 107, 196, 228,
    270, 298
Peaceful Uses of Atomic Energy, 8
Peru, represented, 97, 107, 126,
  254, 298
Philippines, represented, 116, 359
Philosophers, 109
Physical sciences, 4, 18, 48, 109,
  178-180, 276
Poland
  discussed, 193, 256, 361, 362
  represented, 4, 67, 88, 98, 107,
    111, 126-127, 133, 147, 157,
    168, 196, 212, 219, 228, 234,
    244, 254, 263, 264, 272, 298,
    317, 328, 358, 374
Polish Academy of Sciences, 67,
  68, 71
Polish Pugwash Group, 282, 283
Pollution, 80-81, 82, 86, 258,
  344-347, 361, 369-370.
  See also Environmental problems
Population growth, 26, 38, 49, 80,
  83, 119, 177, 237, 326, 344-347,
  349, 371

Portugal
  discussed, 204
  represented, 116, 359
Press, 2, 7, 14, 42, 53, 54, 71,
  278. See also Science writers
Proceedings of the Pugwash Confer-
  ences, 36, 208, 277, 288
Pugwash Conference
  First, 4-7, 141-147
  Second, 7-8, 37-38, 148-150
  Third, 8, 11, 38-41, 151-158
  Fourth, 41-42, 159-160
  Fifth, 42-44, 161-165
  Sixth, 44-46, 166-169
  Seventh, 25, 47-49, 170-184
  Eighth, 49-51, 185-187
  Ninth, 51-52, 188-198
  Tenth, 11, 12, 52-56, 209-214
  Eleventh, 28, 56-58, 215-221
  Twelfth, 35, 58-60, 222-229
  Thirteenth, 28, 29, 60-63, 230-235
  Fourteenth, 63-65, 239-245
  Fifteenth, 65-67, 246-255
  Sixteenth, 29, 67-69, 256-264
  Seventeenth, 11-14, 21, 27, 29,
    70-73, 291-300
  Eighteenth, 20, 73-76, 301-319
  Nineteenth, 12, 20, 76-78, 320-329
  Twentieth, 21, 30, 78-81, 330-360
  Twenty-first, 21, 81-83, 361-375
Pugwash Monographs, 27, 36
Pugwash movement
  Continuing Committee, 6-12, 16, 21,
    34-35, 40-41, 55, 70, 88-89, 148,
    199-205, 271, 275-286, 350
  financing, 3-4, 14-15, 203, 208,
    281-282
  organization of, 16-17, 204-205, 281
  Standing Committee on Future Activi-
    ties, 71, 73, 206-208, 287-290
  Symposia, 12, 21-22, 25-28, 70-82,
    118-122, 288, 289, 314-315
  Working Groups, 16, 25, 48
Pugwash Newsletter, 36, 203, 208,
  277, 281
Pugwash regional conferences, 16,
  30-32, 207, 278-279, 288
  African, 32
  Geneva, 16
  of South-East Asian countries, 16,
    31-32, 265-271, 282

Subject Index   397

Pugwash Study Groups, 28-30, 42,
  71, 202, 207, 279-280, 288
  on Biological Warfare, 28-29, 35,
    62-68, 70, 77, 133-134, 256, 262,
    279, 282, 283
  on European Security, 16, 29, 68,
    256, 279-283
  on Science and Development, 30,
    81, 355
Pugwash--The First Ten Years
  (Joseph Rotblat), 15, 36

Quiet Sun Year, 174

Radiation hazards, 5, 38, 141-154,
  207, 347, 370
Rhodesia, discussed, 67, 251
Romania, represented, 81-82, 98,
  107, 116, 127, 197, 212, 219,
  228, 234, 244, 263, 298, 317,
  328, 358, 374, 375
Romanian Academy of Sciences, 82
Ronneby Conference. See Pugwash
  Conference, Seventeenth
Royal Society. See British Royal
  Society
Russell-Einstein Manifesto, 1, 2,
  86, 141, 286, 327
  reproduced, 137-140

Scandinavia, discussed, 231
Science and World Affairs
  (Joseph Rotblat), 36
Science writers, 20-21, 74, 76,
  79, 115, 318-319, 329, 359
Scientific Commission for Oceanographic Research (SCOR),
  discussed, 173
Scientific information, 48, 65,
  181-183, 192-193, 233, 237
Scientists
  exchange of, 38, 48, 49, 149,
    154, 181-182, 218, 233
  social responsibility of, 1, 5,
    6, 26, 39, 42, 46, 54, 62, 72,
    86, 118, 119, 142, 145-146, 156,
    167, 200, 233-234, 277, 288,
    296, 324
Security, collective, 31, 52, 59,
  62, 81, 193, 222-223, 232-233,
  250, 268-270, 277, 312, 331-334,
  364-369

Senegal, represented, 98, 107,
  358, 374
Sierra Leone, represented, 98, 107,
  254
Singapore, represented, 271
Sinaia Conference. See Pugwash
  Conference, Twenty-first
SIPRI (Stockholm International
  Peace Research Institute)
  discussed, 22-23, 28, 62, 65, 70,
    71, 75, 81, 234, 238, 262, 279,
    283, 303, 304, 325, 344, 348, 359
  represented, 113, 131, 134, 299,
    318, 329, 375
  Study Group on Seismic Detection,
    303
Sochi Conference. See Pugwash Con-
  ference, Nineteenth
Social scientists, 4, 18, 29, 41,
  45, 109, 276
Sopot Conference. See Pugwash Con-
  ference, Sixteenth
South Africa
  discussed, 305
  represented, 100, 107, 111, 212,
    213
South-East Asia, 118, 231, 305
Soviet Academy of Sciences, 7, 9,
  15, 29-30, 39, 45, 47, 54, 71, 76,
  77, 80, 204
Space, 42, 48, 52, 57, 119, 174-175,
  178, 185, 192, 218, 225, 292, 294
Spain, represented, 100, 107, 212,
  298, 328, 374
Special Committee on Antarctic Research (SCAR), discussed, 173
Stockholm International Peach Research Institute. See SIPRI
Stowe Conference. See Pugwash Conference, Seventh and Eighth
Strategic Arms Limitations Talks
  (SALT), 77, 81, 83, 302, 324, 337-
  341, 364-369
Students, 21, 32-33, 38, 75, 79-80,
  116-117, 149, 330, 359-360, 375
Study Group on the Long Term Conse-
  quences of Disarmament, 280
Sudan, represented, 100, 107, 254,
  298
Suez, 3, 118

Sweden
  discussed, 28, 234, 238, 262
  represented, 62, 70, 88, 101, 107,
    111, 116, 127-128, 134, 165, 212,
    219, 228, 229, 235, 244, 254, 263,
    272, 290, 298, 299, 317, 328, 358,
    359, 374
Swedish Pugwash Group, 70, 283
Swedish Royal Academy of Engineering Sciences, 71
Switzerland, represented, 101, 107,
  128, 134, 212, 220, 298, 358, 374

Tanzania, represented, 89, 101,
  107, 254, 298
Thailand, represented, 101, 107,
  228, 254, 298
To Be or Not To Be (film), 15
Togo, represented, 101, 107, 298
Traffic in Arms Year Book, 307

Udaipur Conference. See Pugwash
  Conference, Twelfth
Uganda, represented, 101, 107, 228
UNESCO
  discussed, 66, 172, 173, 214,
    227, 229, 233, 237, 239, 255,
    280, 282, 311
  represented, 114, 131, 221, 235,
    245, 300, 318, 329, 359, 375
Union of Soviet Socialist Republics
  discussed, 143, 152, 174, 175,
    188-190, 216, 218, 222, 223,
    232, 256, 273, 274, 291, 302,
    305, 308, 323, 337, 342, 343,
    361, 364, 367-369
  represented, 1, 4, 7, 11, 18, 39,
    45, 47, 55, 76, 88, 99-100, 107,
    111, 115, 127, 147, 150, 157-160,
    165, 168, 169, 184-187, 197-199,
    213, 220, 229, 235, 245, 254,
    263, 272, 281, 282, 290, 299,
    329, 359, 374
Union of Soviet Socialist Republics
  Pugwash Group, 282
United Arab Republic. See also
  Egypt
  discussed, 281
  represented, 212, 244, 254, 263,
    298, 317, 328, 358, 359

United Kingdom. See also British
  Pugwash Group
  discussed, 152, 190, 218, 274, 342,
    343, 367
  represented, 1, 4, 11, 18, 37, 39,
    45, 49, 55, 88, 101-103, 107, 111-
    112, 115, 128-129, 134, 147, 149,
    150, 157-159, 165, 168, 169, 184-
    186, 187, 197, 199, 212-214, 220,
    229, 235, 245, 254, 263, 264, 272,
    281, 282, 290, 299, 317, 328, 358,
    374
United Nations. See also Food and
  Agriculture Organization; International Atomic Energy Agency;
  International Bank for Reconstruction and Development; International
  Telecommunications Union; UNESCO;
  World Health Organization; World
  Meteorological Organization
  discussed, 23, 35, 63, 64, 67, 75,
    164, 166, 176, 180, 181, 194, 222,
    225, 229, 232, 237, 238, 251, 259,
    306, 307, 308, 321, 323, 325, 337,
    363
  Eighteen Nation Disarmament Committee, 252, 272, 274, 291, 302,
    304
  Human Rights Council, 308
  represented, 113, 131, 235, 245,
    255, 264, 271, 300, 318, 329,
    359, 375
  Scientific Committee on the Effects
    of Atomic Radiation, 153-154
  Stockholm Conference on the Human
    Environment, 356
  Study Group on the Economic and
    Social Consequences of Disarmament,
    195
United Nations Economic and Social
  Council (ECOSOC), 181, 238
  Advisory Committee on the Application of Science and Technology to
    Development, 249, 265-266, 267, 280
United States of America
  discussed, 143, 152, 174, 175, 188-
    190, 216, 218, 256, 273, 274, 291,
    302, 305, 308, 323, 337, 342, 343,
    361, 364, 368, 369

Subject Index

United States of America (continued)
  represented, 1, 4, 5, 11, 18, 37,
    39, 45, 47, 55, 78, 88, 103-105,
    107, 112-117, 129-130, 134, 147,
    150, 158-159, 160, 165, 168-169,
    171, 184, 186-187, 197-198, 199,
    213, 214, 220, 222, 229, 235,
    245, 254, 255, 263, 264, 272,
    281, 282, 290, 299, 318, 329,
    358-359, 360, 374, 375
United States National Academy of
  Sciences, 45, 49, 54, 71, 79, 85
United States Pugwash Group, 10,
  78, 282
Universities and the Quest for
  Peace (UQP)
  discussed, 280
  represented, 114, 300

Venice Conference. See Pugwash
  Conference, Fourteenth
Vienna Declaration, 5, 8, 41, 86,
  151-158, 166, 185
Vietnam, discussed, 30-34, 64, 67-
  69, 72-74, 75, 78, 118, 242-243,
  251, 256, 259, 262, 269-270, 279,
  286, 293-294, 309-310, 320-321,
  332, 334

War Crimes, 363
Warsaw pact countries, 215, 230,
  257, 305, 306, 367
Water, 67, 172, 250, 258, 326, 361
West Indies, represented, 106, 107,
  130, 254
Western European Union, 134
World Bank, 132, 238
World Centre of Scientific Re-
  search, 193
World Federation of Scientific
  Workers (WFSW), 1
World Health Centre, 233, 281
World Health Organization (WHO)
  discussed, 176-177, 227, 229,
    237, 264, 325, 349, 359
  represented, 114, 132, 221, 235,
    245, 300, 318, 329
World Meteorological Organization
  (WMO), 172, 173
World Science Centre, 118

Yugoslav Academies, Council of, 215
Yugoslav Academies of Science, 56
Yugoslavia, represented, 56, 88, 106,
  107, 113, 130-131, 158, 197, 213,
  220, 229, 235, 245, 254, 264, 290,
  299, 318, 329, 359, 374

Zaire, represented, 131
Zambia, represented, 106, 107, 318